The Rise and Fall of
the Caucasian Race

# The Rise and Fall of the Caucasian Race

*A Political History of Racial Identity*

Bruce Baum

NEW YORK UNIVERSITY PRESS

*New York and London*

NEW YORK UNIVERSITY PRESS
New York and London
www.nyupress.org

Library of Congress Cataloging-in-Publication Data
Baum, Bruce David, 1960–
The rise and fall of the Caucasian race :
a political history of racial identity / Bruce Baum.
p. cm.
Includes bibliographical references and index.
ISBN–13: 978–0–8147–9892–8 (cloth : alk. paper)
ISBN–10: 0–8147–9892–6 (cloth : alk. paper)
1. Caucasian race—History.   2. Race awareness—Political aspects.
3. Whites—Race identity.   I. Title.
HT1575.B385     2006
305.809'073—dc22          2005024718

New York University Press books are printed on acid-free paper,
and their binding materials are chosen for strength and durability.

Manufactured in the United States of America
c 10 9 8 7 6 5 4 3 2 1
p 10 9 8 7 6 5 4 3 2 1

*For Laura*

# Contents

*Preface*                                                                              vii

Introduction: "Caucasians" and the
Political History of Racial Identities                                                   1

1   Before the "Caucasian Race": Antecedents of
    European Racialism, ca. 1000–1684                                                   22

2   Enlightenment Science and the Invention
    of the "Caucasian Race," 1684–1795                                                  58

3   Passage into "Our Ordinary Forms of Expression":
    The "Caucasian Race," ca. 1795–1850                                                 95

4   Racialized Nationalism and the Partial Eclipse
    of the "Caucasian Race," ca. 1840–1935                                             118

5   The Color Line and the "Caucasian Race"
    Revival, 1935–51                                                                   162

6   Not-so-Benign Racialism: The "Caucasian Race"
    after Decolonization, 1952–2005                                                    192

7   "Where Caucasian Means Black": "Race," Nation,
    and the Chechen Wars                                                               219

    Conclusion: Deconstructing "Caucasia,"
    Dismantling Racism                                                                 234

    *Notes*                                                                            255

    *Index*                                                                            327

    *About the Author*                                                                 342

# Preface

One of the better answers I have heard regarding the question of "race" came from my uncle, David Widrow. Several years ago, as I began thinking about this study, I asked him if he thought there were different "human races." He smiled and said, "Sure. There are running races, auto races, boat races." I thought it was a great answer, but at other times my uncle, like most people in the United States, has accepted the current "common sense" view that there are also distinct *human races* in the biological sense.

Part of my argument is that this commonsense view is a historical artifact of the social and political history of the modern world. All ideas about "race," like many other beliefs and theories, need to be understood in relation to their historical contexts, including the view of "race" that I advance here. (Yet, as I will explain, this does not mean that all accounts of "race" are equally valid or invalid.) In the present case, my examination of the "Caucasian race" idea has been motivated by my time and place, as a U.S. citizen, born during the Civil Rights movement. (One of my early memories is of an assembly at my Stamford, Connecticut elementary school in 1968, right after the assassination of Martin Luther King Jr.)

This book joins many related efforts in the post–Civil Rights movement era to understand how much and in what way we—citizens of the United States and members of a would-be global community—need to take account of "race" to move beyond to nefarious legacy of racism. It is largely a history of the Caucasian-race idea written by a scholar of politics. It is also a political theorist's inquiry into the meaning of race, and therefore a few sections are theoretically dense.

I wish to thank several people who helped me complete this book. Sandy Schram read most of the manuscript, provided ongoing encouragement, and pointed me to New York University Press. David Roediger offered important feedback when I began the project. Charles Mills and Joel

Olson provided valuable comments on the introduction and chapter 4, and I'm also indebted to Joel in other ways. My University of British Columbia colleague Alan Jacobs gave pointed comments on a draft of chapter 7. Several former colleagues at Macalester College provided constructive early comments: Duchess Harris, Sal Salerno, Karin Aguilar–San Juan, Andrew Latham, Kiarini Kordela, Michele Edwards, Ruthann Godollei, Leola Johnson, Michal McCall, David Moore, Clay Steinman, Joëlle Vitiello, and Matthew Weinstein. I'm especially thankful to Duchess, Sal, Karin, Andrew, and Kiarini for their encouragement. Patrick Guarasci, a former student, provided early research help. At NYU Press, Stephen Magro, who began this project, and Ilene Kalish, who saw it to completion, were great to work with, and I have also benefited from comments by the reviewers for the press. Taiwo Adetunji Osinubi and Anna Karlen translated some key German texts, and the UBC Political Science Department provided financial support for these translations. Kristin Cavoukian did great work on the index. I owe Sele Nadel-Hayes special thanks for sharing her family history with me. Two friends, David Rafferty and Paul Soper, patiently listened to lots of "Caucasian" talk over the last several years, and my parents, Charles and Rosalyn, and extended family have been continually supportive. Special thanks to my sister, Andrea Stuart, for designing great art for the book's cover, which (sadly) was not used.

Finally, I owe the biggest thanks to Laura Janara. Laura read and commented insightfully on the introduction and chapter 2. More than that, she has been a wonderful, loving partner in the life of the mind and in the joys and trials of daily living.

# Introduction
## *"Caucasians" and the Political History of Racial Identities*

[T]he Light of human minds is Perspicuous Words, but by exact definitions first snuffed, and purged from ambiguity; *Reason* is the *pace*;
Encrease of *Science,* the *way*; and the Benefit of man-kind, the *end*.
And on the contrary, Metaphors, and senselesse and ambiguous
words, are like *ignes fatui*; and reasoning upon them, is wandering
amongst innumerable absurdities.
                            —Thomas Hobbes, *Leviathan* (1651)[1]

The classificatory thinking of each individual is one of the ways by
which [human beings] try to adapt to reality in a way that best meets
their needs. But . . . [t]he world which is given to the individual and
which he [*sic*] must accept and take into account is, in its present
and continuing form, a product of the activity of society as a whole.
. . . The facts which our senses present to us are socially performed in
two ways: through the historical character of the object perceived
and through the historical character of the perceiving organ. Both
are not simply natural; they are shaped by human activity.
                    —Max Horkheimer, "Traditional and Critical Theory" (1937)[2]

How shall we think about the status of our social identities? By social
identity I mean the identities we have as blacks, Caucasians, women,
Latinos, gays, and so on.
                    —Georgia Warnke, "Social Identity as Interpretation" (2002)[3]

One of the many telling artifacts of the modern world is the
fact that there are Caucasians and then there are "Caucasians." That is,
there are the various Caucasian peoples of the Caucasus Mountain region

—for example, Georgians, Dagestanis, Circassians, Chechens, Ossetians, and others—and there are the presumed members of the "Caucasian race." The latter is a curious invention of the modern age; it has been a basic component of numerous influential racial classifications from the late eighteenth century through the dawn of the twenty-first.

This book is primarily concerned with the peculiar career of the idea of a Caucasian race. Yet the histories of the two concepts of Caucasians—peoples of the Caucasus and the Caucasian race—are intertwined. Consider the following:

### Caucasian Slaves in the Middle Ages

Between the thirteenth and fifteenth centuries CE, before there was any notion of a Caucasian race, Caucasian peoples were bought and sold as slaves by Venetian and Genoese merchants. This was part of a long history of enslavement of Christians by Muslims and of Muslims by Christians in the Middle Ages that "prepared the way for the vast Atlantic slave system" in which Europeans subjugated sub-Saharan Africans.[4] David Brion Davis reports that the Venetian and Genoese merchants, also involved in the on-going enslavement of the Moors,[5] "established a booming slave trade from Black Sea ports, purchasing thousands of Georgians, Armenians, Circassians, Mingrelians, and other Caucasian peoples who were classified as infidels even if they were eventually baptized."[6]

This source of slaves was mostly abandoned in the latter half of the fifteenth century. By that time the Portuguese sold increasing numbers of "black" African slaves, especially after the Ottoman Turks' conquest of Constantinople in 1453, which redirected slave traders to sub-Saharan Africa.[7]

### "Goddess with Caucasian Face"

In late May 1989, students of the Central Academy of Fine Arts in China built a statue for the planned pro-democracy demonstration that began May 30 in Tiananmen Square, in the heart of Beijing. The ten-meter-tall statue came to be known as the Goddess of Democracy. Journalists and commentators from the United States quickly concluded that the statue was intentionally modeled after the Statue of Liberty in New York City. In the words of Neil Kottler, a program officer of the Smithsonian Institution in the United States who coedited a book on the "universal" significance of the Statue of Liberty, "The statue symbolized the yearning for freedom among ordinary Chinese people; its resemblance to the Statue of Liberty was intentional, not accidental."[8]

Political theorist Linda Zerilli observes that it was not clear that the Goddess of Democracy was "nothing but a replica of that all-American icon, Lady Liberty."[9] Nonetheless, this perceived similarity was expressed in the *New York Times* by reporter Nicholas Kristoff: "[T]he Goddess closely resembles the Statue of Liberty, to the point of having Caucasian features and a large Western nose." Kristoff added: "A few spectators said they thought it might have been more appropriate for her to have Chinese features, but nobody seemed too concerned about such particulars."[10]

### "Caucasians" by U.S. Law

In U.S. Census counts of 1930 and 1940, "Hindoo" was included as a racial category.[11] This convention followed a series of legal cases between 1878 and 1923 in which U.S. federal courts were called upon to interpret the phrase "free white person" in U.S. naturalization law, which privileged "white persons."[12] The courts adjudicated the claims of a number of prospective U.S. citizens of non-European backgrounds to be counted as "white." Ian Haney López notes that applicants from Hawaii, China, Japan, Burma, and the Philippines and "mixed-race" applicants all failed in their arguments. Meanwhile, the courts declared Mexican and Armenian applicants "white" but "vacillated over the Whiteness of petitioners from Syria, India, and Arabia."[13] In a few cases, judges appealed to English anthropologist A. H. Keane's scholarly analyses of the "Caucasian race" category to determine who was and who was not "white." Then, in *United States v. Bhagat Sigh Thind* (1923), the Supreme Court, while also citing Keane, rejected the claim to "whiteness" of a high-caste Hindu. The Court now declared that the term *Caucasian* "is at best a conventional term, . . . which, under scientific manipulation, has come to include far more than the unscientific suspects."[14]

These U.S. cases did not resolve the "racial" and legal status of South Asians in general or South Asian Hindus in particular vis-à-vis the "Caucasian race." Even recently, a California Superior Court judge ruled that Dale Sandhu, a person of East Indian origin, was ineligible to bring a discrimination claim against his former employer, the Lockheed corporation. Sandhu had claimed that his layoff by Lockheed had been racially motivated. The judge accepted Lockheed's view that Sandhu was "Caucasian" by law and therefore had no legal standing under the California Fair Employment and Housing Act. Subsequently, the Sixth District Court of Appeal reversed the Superior Court's ruling in Sandhu's favor. The appeals court, citing the appearance of the "Asian Indian" category in the 1980 census, ruled that Sandhu was "subject to a discriminatory animus based on his membership in a group perceived as distinct."[15]

### "Kennewick Man"

In July 1996, two college students found a human skull at the edge of the Columbia River in Kennewick, Washington. After they reported their find to the police, the county coroner called on James Chatters, a forensic anthropologist, to look at the skull. Chatters said that the skull and its skeleton were from a male "Caucasoid" individual, approximately forty to fifty-five years old. Yet Chatters also noticed the crowns of teeth worn flat in a manner characteristic of prehistoric Native American skulls, and a large projectile lodged in the right hip that proved to be a stone spear point. The spear point resembled those used by hunters of the region between forty-five hundred and nine thousand years ago. A second anthropologist concurred with Chatters, describing the skeleton was that of a "Caucasian male." Soon thereafter, carbon dating established that "Kennewick Man" was between ninety-two hundred and ninety-five hundred years old. Even so, "Caucasoid" and "Caucasian" designations for Kennewick Man were circulated widely in articles in the *Washington Post* and the *New York Times.*[16]

The Kennewick Man generated considerable speculation about its "racial" character and the origins of the first inhabitants of the Americas. Some scientists asked, "If this Kennewick Man indeed has many Caucasoid traits, how [as was the case] can an Indian tribe claim his remains?"[17] A number of scientists regarded the Kennewick skeleton as "evidence that the earliest inhabitants of the New World may have been a Caucasoid people"; and a headline that introduced the story in *Discover* magazine declared, "Europeans invade America: 20,000 BC."[18] Recent scholarly reassessments suggest that attempts to fit Kennewick Man into modern "racial" categories were dubious and misleading.[19]

### "Dark-skinned" Caucasians

The current war in the Caucasus between Russia and Chechen rebels has sometimes been construed, especially by Russians, in racial terms. This racialization recalls not only a history of Russian imperialism in central Asia and the Caucasus but also one of disputes concerning the "European-ness"—and, implicitly, the "whiteness"—of Russians compared to the supposed "Asiatic" character of Muslim nationalities within Russia and in the Caucasus.[20] One legacy of this history is the recent upsurge of racial epithets that Russians have directed against "dark-skinned" people of the Caucasus, including "Kill the blacks."[21]

These episodes indicate the convoluted history of the "Caucasian race" category. The Chinese Goddess of Democracy and the Kennewick Man have been associated with the idea of the Caucasian race while an actual Caucasian people, the Chechens, have been excluded—at least sometimes—from this designation. Given prevalent ideas about "race," these stories might lead some to wonder whether the Goddess of Democracy or Kennewick Man were really Caucasian, or whether the Chechens really are dark-skinned compared to the "typical" Russian. Yet such questions obscure the more basic one: How have racialized tropes involving the Chechens and the notion of a distinct Caucasian race come to be readily employed by people to describe these events? My immediate objective, therefore, is to explore what the history of the "Caucasian race" category can teach us about the politics of "race" and racism.

To be clear, this study in no way tracks the history of an actually existing *Caucasian race*. Rather, it critically examines the changing fortunes of an intellectual conceit: the rise and fall in the eighteenth and nineteenth centuries, the twentieth-century revival, and the possible final fall in twenty-first century of the notion, manifest in a variety of scientific and popular theories and social practices, that certain people constitute a distinct Caucasian race. Tracing the historical vicissitudes of the "Caucasian race" category demonstrates that race itself is a social and political construction rather than a biologically meaningful concept.

In 1785, German popular philosopher Christoph Meiners posited two great branches of human beings—Caucasian and Mongolian—in his *Outline of the History of Humanity*. Then, in 1795, German physician and anatomist Johann Friedrich Blumenbach, counted among the founders of modern anthropology, adopted the term *Caucasian* in the third edition of his book *On the Natural Variety of Mankind*.[22] Referring to Mount Caucasus, Blumenbach said that he chose Caucasian as a name for what were then called the "white" peoples of Europe and contiguous regions "both because its neighborhood, and especially its southern slope, produces the most beautiful race of men, I mean the Georgian; and because all physiological reasons converge to this, that in that region, if anywhere, it seems we ought with the greatest probability to place the autochthones of mankind."[23] Significantly, as a "racial" designation for the "white" peoples of Europe and contiguous regions, the notion of a Caucasian race was not completely unprecedented.

Blumenbach's innovation is part of a much larger story in which the complex interplay between politics (broadly understood) and science has shaped the development of "race science," the still-prevalent use of "race ideas" to interpret human diversity, and the production and reproduction of racialized social and political inequalities. Within a generation after Blumenbach delineated a "Caucasian variety" of human beings, this "race" idea was widely adopted in Europe and North America. It was partially eclipsed, however, from the second half of the nineteenth century to the start of the twentieth. During this era an upsurge of European nationalism led European race scientists to posit "racial" differences among European peoples who had previously been grouped together as "Caucasians." The fortunes of the "Caucasian race" category shifted again in the 1930s. The Nazi movement in Germany generated a new scrutiny of the "race" concept generally and of existing racial classifications in particular. This gave rise to a more benign—and sometimes explicitly anti-racist—racialism.[24] Anthropologists now reclaimed the notion of a Caucasian race as one of the three great "races of man," alongside "Negroes" and "Mongolians" (sometimes called "Caucasoids," "Negroids," and "Mongoloids").

According to this new view of race, the differences among Europeans were merely "ethnic," while those distinguishing Caucasians, Negroes, and Mongolians were racial. Since 1952, the "Caucasian race" category has retained a prominent place in everyday discourse about race, particularly in the United States, but it has increasingly been called into question by anthropologists and biologists, along with the "race" concept itself, in relation to the changing race politics of this era.

One revealing indicator of the extent to which the career of the "Caucasian race" category is both strange and instructive is how its fate has differed from that of the "Aryan race" idea during the nineteenth and twentieth centuries. Leaving aside the views of certain white supremacists, it now generally goes without saying that there is no such thing as an Aryan race.[25] The "Aryan race" myth was cobbled together from various sources in the mid–nineteenth century—notably, from evidence of an Indo-European language group—and championed by such nineteenth-century racialists as Comte Joseph-Arthur de Gobineau, the German-born English philologist Friedrich Max Müller (for a time), and Houston Stewart Chamberlain, before it became a linchpin of Nazism. Eventually, critical reflection on the horrific legacy of Hitler's Third Reich, ideologically based on the doctrine of Aryan supremacy, thoroughly discredited the Aryan myth—along with related ideas of "Nordic" racial supremacy—among post–World War II raciologists and intellectuals, and then in popular understanding. Not surprisingly, historians of the "race" concept and of European racism have subjected the "Aryan race" myth to much more sustained critical scrutiny than they have given to the "Caucasian race" myth.[26]

By contrast, the notion of a Caucasian race has gone in and out of vogue, and then back into vogue, among raciologists and in popular usage since it was invented in the late eighteenth century.[27] Moreover, as I explain in chapter 4, the decisive refutation of the "Aryan race" idea after World War II coincided with a recovery of the "Caucasian race" category, which had been out of fashion in Europe for most of the previous century. In effect, then, raciologists brought about a dramatic shift in race thinking between the 1930s and 1950s in part by reviving the "Caucasian race" category. Yet the status of Caucasian (or Caucasoid) as a scientifically credible racial category (along with Mongoloid and Negroid) is arguably no better than that of an Aryan race—a point that will become clear through the course of this study.

The contrasting fates of these two race ideas raise several important questions that this study seeks to answer, if only indirectly: Why the difference? Why has the idea of a Caucasian race stubbornly persisted if, ultimately, it has no greater scientific validity that the idea of an Aryan race? Is the difference due solely (or at least largely) to the unique association of "Aryan race" ideas with the Nazis' enormous crime against humanity? If so, how can the difference be squared with the fact that the career of the "Caucasian race" category is also bound up with various crimes against humanity during the past two centuries, even if it has not yet been called into account for its role in these crimes? Or, alternatively, is any comparison with the "Aryan race" myth itself questionable because, quite apart from politics, the revival of the "Caucasian race" category actually marks a scientific advance in our understanding of race?

My thesis is that the changing fortunes of the "Caucasian race" category are the result not of progressive refinements in "race" science but of the subtle and not-so-subtle ways that social and political forces have shaped scientific knowledge of race.[28] Race, in short, is an effect of power. Consequently, this study of the Caucasian race is fundamentally a study of power: how social and political power have produced scientific knowledge of race and what the history of racial knowledge reveals about modern power. It is not that political actors merely exploited the findings of modern race science; instead, the science itself was thoroughly political, with its guiding assumptions and questions informed by prevailing relations of power in society. Thus, the history of the "Caucasian race" idea bears out Stephen Jay Gould's observation that in such matters there is often great value in "treating generalities by particulars."[29]

My broader aim is to contribute to a critical theory of social identities. Social identities, as Georgia Warnke says, are "the identities we have as blacks, Caucasians, women, Latinos, gays, and so on, identities that we grow up as, assert in struggles for recognition, or try to eliminate and avoid."[30] These identities are sources of meaning and affiliation, but they are also bound up with social relations of power and domination. Racial identities in particular have provided people with a way to interpret their place in modern societies; but they have been used to justify oppression and social stratification as well as forms of anti-racist politics. The emergence of race and racism in modern Western societies during the seventeenth and eighteenth centuries coincided with the gradual diffusion of modern egalitarian ideals.[31] Equality has always been difficult for modern nation-states to manage, especially in relation to the dislocations and class-based inequality generated by capitalism. In conjunction with class stratification, race has served as means for nation-states to govern and apportion claims of equality (i.e., who is entitled to equality of what) by providing an ideological justification for selective inequality.[32] For instance, race ideas and categories have been used to limit the workings of competitive labor markets through slavery, colonialism, immigration restriction, and labor market discrimination.

A critical theory of social identity will identify and support a cultural politics of group differentiation—of public recognition for social identities—only insofar as this "can be coherently combined with the social politics of equality."[33] Accordingly, such a theory will illuminate what kinds of public recognition of racial identities, if any, will best support a politics of human equality.

## The Political History of "Race"

It is clear that racial categories and identities have played an enormous and ignominious role in modern politics. The development of a socially and politically influenced scientific racialism buttressed racist social and political practices by insisting on a supposedly natural hierarchy of cognitive capabilities among the so-called races of man (see chapter 2). Meanwhile, there is ongoing debate among scholars over whether or not racism, as distinct from other forms of intergroup prejudice and ethnocentrism, is distinctly modern and Western in its origins.

As George Fredrickson explains, forms of rigid "othering" and ethnocentrism roughly analogous to the racism existed in Western societies in the Middle Ages and in non-Western societies before the modern Western invention of the "race" concept.[34] Some commentators maintain that racism as *race*-ism is a distinctive product of the modern West that subsequently spread—along with "race consciousness"—to other parts of the world as an effect of Europe-centered capitalist development, the rise of the Atlantic slave trade, and European colonialism and imperialism.[35] An alternative view is that the forms of prejudice and ethnocentrism that existed in parts of the premodern West and in non-Western prior to "Western" influence were sufficiently similar to the racism of the modern West (where the term *racism* first came into usage in the 1930s) to be counted as racism as well. Thomas Gossett asserts, with reference to ancient India, China, Egypt, Greece, Rome, and the Jews, "The racism of ancient history, even though it had no science of biology or anthropology behind it, was real, however difficult it may be to judge the extent of its power."[36]

This book will not resolve this controversy, but it will shed light on it. As I explain in chapter 1, there is good reason to conclude that racism, as a specific set of beliefs about human "races" that is used to justify exclusionary practices, institutions, and social structures, is a distinctive product of the development of race thinking in the modern West. From this perspective it is important to recognize that racism in this sense can now be found within many (if not most) societies around the globe; yet it would be misleading to equate other traditions and practices of ethnocentrism, which lack any clear analog to the modern concept of race, with racism per se.

The development of the modern Western scientific project of racially classifying people was shaped by a number of epochal events: the consolidation during the late Middle Ages of the idea of Europe as a geographically distinguishable region within the larger Eurasian land mass; the rise in the early modern period of Europeans' assumptions of their innate physical, intellectual, cultural, religious and moral superiority—assumptions that European elites reinforced and refined in relation to European "discoveries" of the indigenous peoples of the Americas, the development of modern "Negro" slavery, and increasing European colonization of the Americas, Africa, and Asia; and the gradual growth and diffusion of a world capitalist economy, based in Europe and linked to the European "voyages of discovery" and conquest in the fifteenth century.

During the course of the twentieth century a number of insightful social commentators and scientists noted the problematic character of race. In the words of anthropologist Ashley Montagu, an early proponent of the "social constructionist" view of race: "It is a common human failing to believe that if a word exists then there must be something in reality which corresponds to it. Do 'devils' exist, or 'succubi' or 'incubi' or 'dragons' or a thousand and one other figments of our imagination? 'Race' belongs in the same category with these words. It is an invented category, not a discovered one."[37] The claim that race is a political construction and not a biologically meaningful concept is often countered with the claim that there are obvious, observable *racial differences* among people. That is, there are significant phenotypic or morphological differences between groups of people from distinct geographic origins, and the "race" concept denotes precisely these differences.[38]

Yet this seemingly commonsense view begs fundamental questions about race.[39] Given the historical meanings of "race," why should we persist in calling such differences *racial*? What of the fact that there is greater genetic variation among people *within* each of the various groupings of people that are typically classified as distinct races than there is between these so-called races? Moreover, what should we make of the fact that people are now, in our historical moment, likely to assume that *certain* superficial differences—particularly, differences in skin tone, hair texture, and facial features—truly distinguish distinct *human races*, while other comparable differences among people—for example, differences in eye color, the shape of people's skulls (or cranial forms), and blood type—are discounted as indexes of race difference? And what of the fact that the traits taken to be the defining criteria of racial difference have varied widely at different times and places?

The suggestion here is that the "race" concept is best understood in terms of social and political processes of *racialization*, or race-making. To speak of processes of racialization is to call attention to the ideological representational processes whereby "social significance is attached to certain (usually phenotypic) human features, on the basis of which those people possessing those characteristics are designated as a distinct [racial] collectivity."[40] There is no "discovery" of true *racial* differences among groups of people. Rather, racialization emerges from processes by which socially and politically dominant ethnic groups use certain superficial physiognomic differences between themselves and other groups to create a naturalized "sense of group solidarity or peoplehood that can provide the basis for a claim of dominance or privilege over those considered outside the group."[41] One crucial implication of this view is that any talk of "race relations" as a subject for scholarly analysis or public policy making, as if at stake are the relationships among actually existing, biologically distinct *races* of people, is a misnomer; actually, it is racialized relations and racialized identities that are at issue—that is, relationships between various groups of people that have been socially and politically constructed as "racially" distinct.[42] Therefore, to address the distinctive politics of racialized identities (as distinct from ethnic or cultural identities) requires a somewhat different approach from efforts to address problems of cultural diversity or multiculturalism (sometimes addressed under the heading of "cultural pluralism"). Racialized identities have notable cultural dimensions, but they are primarily a manifestation of unequal power between groups and only secondarily about cultural diversity.[43] The injustice produced by systemic racism is not primarily a matter of cultural misunderstanding or disrespect for certain cultures. Instead, racism involves exclusionary practices that establish and perpetuate unequal distributions of social status, opportunity, income, wealth, and power among racialized groups.[44]

The racialization approach to "race" enables us to steer a path between two pitfalls that haunt much popular and scientific thinking about race, historically and still today. The first pitfall is the resort to racial explanations to account for social and political inequalities and cultural differences between groups (e.g., in income, wealth, social status, educational achievement, cultural practices), which mistake the effects of racialization processes for the cause. For instance, since the seventeenth century there have been scholars who have claimed that *racial* (i.e., innate, irremovable) differences between the groups we now call Whites, Asian Americans, Native Americans, African Americans, and Latinos/as are the chief cause of social, political, and economic inequalities between these groups (on average).[45] Yet this view conveniently ignores the theoretical difficulties of race as a biologically meaningful concept and discounts the effects of the different and unequal treatment accorded to the different groups historically, which has been rationalized by dominant groups in racist terms.

The second pitfall is the temptation to move too quickly from the observation that there are no *races* of human beings in the old biological and ethnological sense to the conclusion that we should now renounce any use of racial categories in efforts to overcome racism and its effects. According to social theorist Paul Gilroy, to continue to use "racial" categories, even in efforts to combat racism, is to be complicit "in the reification of racial difference."[46] Gilroy's view, while motivated by commendable goals, fails to address adequately the powerful continuing effects of processes of racialization in shaping the social structures of many modern societies and the lived experience of members of these societies.[47] Understanding race in terms of racialization avoids any reification of racial difference because it emphasizes the historically changing and politically contingent character of processes of racialization; at the same time, it points to the enormous social and political impact of processes of racialization and to the current reality and changeability of *racialized* identities.

## *Power, Knowledge, and "Race": Notes on Method*

To understand race as a political construction poses challenging epistemological and methodological issues for students of race and racism. We are confronted with difficult questions concerning the status *as knowledge* of historically changing scientific discourses about race. My approach to this issue principally involves a historical genealogy of the career of the "Caucasian race" category. Michel Foucault defines genealogy as a "political history of truth": it explores how the production of criteria for what counts as true or false in various fields of knowledge in different historical contexts—what Foucault calls "regimes of truth"—"is thoroughly imbued with relations of power."[48] Taking a genealogical approach to race requires that we go beyond an analysis of how shifting social and political struggles and power relationships (e.g., European colonialism; the Atlantic slave trade; emergent nationalisms; and struggles over immigration, citizenship, and labor market regulation) have shaped the relations between so-called races of people. It simultaneously demands that we explore historically how such power dynamics have shaped the production of scientific and popular knowledge about race.[49]

My point of entry into this vast history is an examination of the changing place of the "Caucasian" category within the "sciences of race" and in prevailing modes of racial classification in the period that stretches from the late eighteenth century to the present. My account focuses on how these shifts are exemplified in the work of key historical figures in the development of the sciences of racial classification, including Carolus Linnaeus (1707–78), Johann Blumenbach (1752–1840), James Cowles Prichard (1786–1848), Samuel George Morton (1799–1851), Anders Retzius (1796–1860), Thomas Henry Huxley (1825–95), Joseph Deniker (1852–1918), Ruth Benedict (1887–1948), and Ashley Montagu (1905–99). Through their varied writings, rooted in botany, zoology, anatomy, ethnology, and anthropology, we can trace the major trends in the dominant modes of scientific racial classifications. These trends include major shifts in the scientific discourses through which the "Caucasian race" category has been authoritatively invented, embraced, displaced, and recovered. It is worth noting that each of these thinkers was a member of the group racialized as dominant in his or her society.[50] Indeed, prior to the twentieth century this was true of almost all the scientists of race whose work introduced significant changes to prevailing racial classifications.[51] I also consider the race ideas of a number of intellectuals from subordinated racialized groups, such as African American physician Martin R. Delany (1812–85), Russian Jewish physical anthropologist Samuel Weissenberg (1867–1928), and African American historian and sociologist W. E. B. Du Bois (1868–1963). These thinkers offer us some insight into how the prevailing modes of race science and racial classification were perceived, reinforced, and resisted by intellectuals who were considered members of "lesser races" in the predominant racial schemes.

As K. Anthony Appiah points out, "throughout the nineteenth century the term 'race' came increasingly to be regarded, even in ordinary usage, as a scientific term." In other words, the concept "race" came to be understood as a way to make true generalizations about the way the world is—specifically, a way to comprehend the true natures of the various peoples who make up the world. As such, scientists and scholars have had a special claim to be considered "experts on how the term worked."[52] Moreover, while it hardly needs to be said that how nonscientists speak about race is influenced by social and political forces that escape their immediate awareness, we might be tempted to think that this has not been the case with scientists. The latter are presumably impelled by the pursuit of knowledge. The history of science is not so pure, however.[53]

This difficulty is strikingly evident in the history of the sciences concerned with race, notably comparative anatomy, ethnology, craniology, anthropology, eugenics, and biology.[54] Gould observes that the scientists of race did not discover and describe an objective reality of naturally occurring human races; instead, their conceptions and perceptions of race and races were deeply shaped by the social, political, and cultural influences of their time.[55] In effect, the anatomists, ethnologists, and anthropologists who developed various schemes of racial classification helped produce our racialized world.

At the same time, despite manifest "impurity" of the scientific study of race over the past two hundred–plus years, it would be a mistake, as Adam Lively warns, "simply to dismiss the anthropology of the late eighteenth and nineteenth centuries as 'bad science.' Its significance goes beyond that, both because of the support it gave to racial[ized] oppression in the real world, and because it was one aspect of a broader 'naturalisation' of European thought that occurred in the eighteenth century. This process of naturalisation was fundamental to the invention of the modern European idea of race."[56] In short, to learn well the myriad lessons that the history of race science can teach us about our present racialized world, we need to develop a historically informed understanding of both how race science was shaped by surrounding social, political, and cultural forces and how it progressed *as science*—that is, as the activity of scientists who typically understood themselves as objectively describing and classifying naturally occurring human races.

For this reason, strict adherence to Foucault's genealogical approach to power and knowledge would be troublesome. If all claims of knowledge are corrupted by relations of power, and if all types of power relationships —from totalitarian regimes to democratic forms of intellectual inquiry— are comparable in how they generate "regimes of truth," then we are left in a distressing predicament: we would have no credible way to adjudicate between the truth claims of racist and anti-racist discourses. In other words, we would have no critical standpoint from which we could "assess the relative adequacy of different accounts of the world, of different regimes of truth."[57] Foucault also leaves us without a way to specify key agents in the development of scientific and popular ideas about race—especially who has done "what to whom, under what circumstances, and why."[58]

Therefore, to move beyond Foucault's important point about the pursuit of truth being enmeshed with relations of power, we need to address the concrete interrelationship of a given society's *cultural system,* its *social structure,* and *human agency* (i.e., people acting to shape their circumstances in relation to inherited ideas and social structures). Within this framework, a society's cultural system consists of the existing stock of ideas and beliefs concerning its practices and institutions at any given time. The social-structural components of a society include relatively enduring (but changeable) social relationships and institutions: the prevailing mode of production and class relations, gender relations, ethnic and racialized hierarchies, government institutions, educational institutions, religious institutions, and prevailing forms of sexual practice.[59] The *agents* of social change in this scheme are primarily collectivities of persons, such as classes, nations, ethnic groups, or people organized around gender or sexual identities or in social movements or political parties; they are not abstract individuals who somehow stand above or outside prevailing social structures and cultures.

The agents bring about social change (or "make history") through social and political interaction with other agents under conditions established by the inherited social structures and cultural systems that define their society at that time. The society's cultural system determines the range of ideas, norms, values, and theories with which different social groups or agents interpret and respond to their world, while the existing social structure determines the allocation of material resources that different groups (e.g., social classes and racialized groups in a racialized capitalist society) bring to their interaction and competition with each other.[60]

This framework yields a fruitful way to make sense of how social and political forces have shaped the changing fortunes of the "Caucasian race" category through its history. This history involves three kinds of conceptual transformation: the genesis of "race" as a scientific concept and a historically novel way for people to describe and interpret human diversity; several distinct shifts in modes of racial classification across time, which determined the changing status of the "Caucasian race" notion; and the recent rise—mostly during the last seventy years—of deep skepticism about the credibility of "race" as a scientific concept. Regarding these conceptual shifts, the existing social structure in a society at any given time, by making certain groups socially and politically dominant, enables some social groups (or agents) to be more influential than others in shaping the prevailing ideas about race and schemes of racial classification. For example, until recently members of dominant ethnic and racialized groups (especially race scientists from these groups) were consistently more influential in the determination of prevailing schemes of racial classification than were the members of subordinate ethnic and racialized groups.

When a change in race ideas is effectively incorporated into a society's scientific, political, and popular discourse, this brings to an end one cycle of social and cultural change and begins another one. Thus, the introduction and diffusion of the "race" concept in a society that previously had *racelike* ideas but no "race" concept per se would constitute the completion of one such cycle. In this way, as I explain later, we can grasp how changing social and political circumstances in the mid–twentieth century helped pave the way for the now prevailing anti-racist science of race (see chapters 5 and 6). In the same breath, because of the complex constellation of factors involved in such conceptual changes—including historical shifts in the place of science in society—a genealogy or conceptual history of this sort cannot hope to be definitive. Sometimes it will only be able to intimate the likely explanations for particular shifts in race thinking.[61]

One crucial factor in the transformations of racial thought has been the history of the human migrations in the modern world—between regions of Europe; from Europe to the Americas, Africa, Asia, New Zealand, and Australia; from Africa to the Americas and to Europe; from Asia to the Americas, Europe, and Africa—along with struggles to regulate immigration in receiving countries. It is not that these migrations have merely spurred "racial conflicts" among actually existing races of people. Rather, migrations, which have been "determined by the interrelation of production, trade and warfare," have been a key factor in shaping and reshaping racial thought in general and racial categories in particular.[62]

In addition, we must not abandon the scientific enterprise entirely if we hope to move constructively beyond Foucault's insight that power relationships shape prevailing forms of knowledge historically. As Tom Nairn observes, a critique of racist pseudo-science that involves a blanket rejection of science undermines "the very foundation of non-racial (and anti-racist) development."[63] In this spirit, critical realist social theory points beyond the relativism implied by Foucault's genealogy—namely, that all discourses of truth are equally contaminated by power relationships—by insisting that there is an external reality, independent of human descriptions of it, against which competing claims of truth can ultimately be assessed. For example, the existence or nonexistence of human races (in the biological sense) is an empirical question about the true *nature* of human beings. Insofar as the idea of biologically distinct human races is illusory, it is crucial to recognize that "this illusoriness can only be demonstrated *within scientific discourse.*"[64] Simultaneously, we need to understand that this claim about the nonexistence of races is distinct from the claim that there *are* still *racialized* identities and inequalities.[65]

Foucault rightly insists that all human access to reality is mediated by existing languages, concepts, and theories. This means that we always struggle to interpret the world in better and worse ways, with fallible conceptual frameworks and theories. Yet different forms of power do not have the same corrupting effect on the pursuit of truth. All other things being equal, forms of power that are relatively inclusive, democratic, and egalitarian are more likely to generate true knowledge about such things as race, gender, and sexuality than are forms of power that are undemocratic, exclusionary, and asymmetrical. This point applies, for example, to modes of intellectual inquiry that are conditioned by relatively democratic social contexts and marked by relatively democratic, nonhierarchical, and inclusive relations of cooperation as opposed to those conditioned and characterized by authoritarian tendencies and social exclusivity.[66] Consequently, democratizing social and political movements such as movements for political democratization, feminist movements, post–World War II decolonization, and the U.S. Civil Rights movement, have often revealed limitations of existing theories about the world and generated advances in human knowledge. Indeed, democratizing movements of the twentieth century arguably helped establish social conditions that fostered a more truthful science of "race."

## *"Race," Political Theory, and Planetary Humanism*

What follows is a work of historical synthesis written by a political theorist and guided by contemporary ethical and political concerns. My genealogy of the "Caucasian race" category relies on the work of many historians and social scientists concerning various dimensions of the histories of race, racism, and related issues. For a political theorist, the histories of race and racism raise a number of fundamental political questions: How have these notions shaped the character and uses of power in various historical contexts? How has power been related to the production of knowledge in the modern world? How has the "race" concept, a notion rooted in natural history and biology, figured in the construction of transformations of modern political communities? And what does this teach us about the various ways in which political communities and citizenship have been established, defined, and regulated?[67] To what extent and in what ways has modern liberal theory and policy melded an avowed commitment to basic human equality with significant qualifications to that commitment?

Other scholars in the field of political studies have recently explored related themes. Rogers Smith examines how lawmakers throughout U.S. history have "pervasively . . . structured U.S. citizenship in terms of illiberal and undemocratic racial, ethnic and gender hierarchies."[68] Michael Goldfield traces how racialized politics in the United States is "the product of a long process of American social and political development," while Anthony Marx compares the historical role of state and nation building in constructing the "boundaries of race" in the United States, Brazil, and South Africa.[69] Closer in spirit to the current work, political theorists Charles Mills, Joel Olson, and Jacqueline Stevens contribute to what Olson calls a "political theory of race."[70] Mills contends that global white supremacy "is *itself* a political system"; Olson, focusing on democratic citizenship in the United States, notes that "white" or "Caucasian" "is not a neutral physical description of certain persons but a political project of securing and protecting privileges"; Stevens looks at how "races are constituted and sustained . . . through explicit and implicit invocations of the state."[71]

The present study approaches the theory and politics of race and racism from a different but complementary angle. By exploring the career of the "Caucasian race" category, it illuminates how various modern forms of power have shaped prevailing scientific and "commonsense" knowledge of race.[72] In doing so, this study offers a unique perspective on how the history of racial domination is bound up with and also reaches beyond the history of racialized "whiteness."[73] The history of the Caucasian race is part of the larger histories of white racialized identity and white supremacism, which emerged in tandem with race theories and racial domination.[74] The idea of a white race preceded the development of the Caucasian race idea by more than a century. Yet during its years of prominence the "Caucasian race" category has represented racial "whiteness ratcheted up to a new epistemological realm of certainty."[75] At the same time, the "Caucasian race" category experienced a partial eclipse among race scientists between 1840 and 1940, when European nationalism surged and ("white") Europeans sought to dominate each other *racially*. Historian Matthew Jacobson has already discussed some of this history with respect to changing immigration policies and transformations of racialized whiteness in the United States. Yet he leaves much of the larger story untold, particularly its European and global aspects, including the history that produced the Caucasian race idea.

To redress this history of racism, this study highlights the vital need for what Paul Gilroy calls a pragmatic, planetary humanism.[76] Against all forms of racialism and racism, planetary humanism insists on the fundamental equality of all human beings *as human beings.* To actualize a planetary humanist ethic requires, among other things, an understanding of the ways in which the "race" concept has been employed historically to establish hierarchies of "humanness" and human rights and to reinforce other forms of inequality, such as class and gender inequalities.

This legacy has led Gilroy to call for the "renunciation of 'race' as a critical concept."[77] Here my approach to planetary humanism departs from his. Gilroy rightly warns us of the risk involved in using racial categories in efforts to overcome racism—that this practice may perpetuate racialist thinking about human diversity despite the most vigilant efforts to deconstruct race. Yet his call to renounce any use of race as a critical concept is problematic in a world of persistent racialized social and political inequalities. If we hope to achieve an egalitarian planetary humanism in a world structured by deep racialized inequalities of opportunities, income, wealth, and power, then we must not forget or evade the ethical, social, and political damage that has been and continues to be done by racialist and racist thought and action.

The consequent ethical and political imperative is, as Richard Lewontin says, to "abolish the conditions that require . . . the illusion of race."[78] Yet to achieve this objective may sometimes require policies that use existing racialized categories and identities in a self-critical and historically contingent way *as a means to dismantle racialized inequalities*—for instance, through affirmative action policies to redress inequities produced by systemic racism. With regard to the "Caucasian race" category in particular, Lewontin's proposition implies a corresponding imperative: that those persons who have, in different ways in different contexts, gained material, psychological, and social status benefits from being racialized as members of dominant races (e.g., as "Caucasian" or "Nordic" or "white") acknowledge and take responsibility for these advantages. People who have been racialized as Caucasians must acknowledge our historically racialized identities as Caucasian—along with the social and material advantages it entails—even as we work with others to end the myth of a "Caucasian race." This is ultimately an ethical and political challenge that must be faced to realize a planetary humanism. It demands concerted collective political action. Among other things, this project demands an understanding of the distinct history and struggles of the actual *Caucasian peoples* in the Caucasus region.

## Outline of a History

With regard to my title, I have been asked if the history of the "Caucasian race" notion is really a "rise and fall" story.[79] My tentative answer is that it is a rise and fall and rise . . . and *possible* fall story. In chapter 1, on the period from roughly 1000 to 1684, I survey beliefs about physical, social, religious, and cultural differences among peoples within and beyond medieval and early modern Europe that prefigured later race thinking and subsequently influenced the contours of modern racial categories. I also examine the rise of the "race" concept and the development of modern racial thought in the seventeenth century.

Chapter 2 examines the social and political forces and scientific developments between the late 1600s and late 1700s that help to explain Johann Blumenbach's fateful use of the "Caucasian race" category in 1795. This time period saw a maturation of natural history along with systematic schemes to classify nature, including human beings. European race scientists in this era were generally inclined to propose racial classifications that scientifically and hierarchically distinguished white people such as themselves from nonwhite peoples.

Chapter 3 examines the period between the end of the eighteenth century and the mid–nineteenth century. During these years Blumenbach's "Caucasian race" notion passed quickly into scientific discourse and ordinary usage in Europe and in the United States. Yet, where Blumenbach used the "Caucasian race" category to refer to one of five principal "varieties" of human beings that *"run into one another by insensible degrees,"*[80] it was now adapted to more explicitly racist modes of racial classification. Raciologists such as Georges Cuvier, William Lawrence, and Samuel George Morton asserted the superiority of the Caucasian race. At the end of this era, English ethnologists James Cowles Prichard and Robert Gordon Latham persuasively pointed out the dubious character of the "Caucasian race" category. Nonetheless, the Caucasian race had already become well established in both scientific and ordinary discourses.

Chapter 4 follows the partial displacement of the "Caucasian race" in race science from about 1840 to about 1940. Between the 1840s and 1870s, a complex set of developments in physical anthropology and European politics and demographics combined to radically alter the prevailing discourse of racial classification, including major migrations of European peoples, the rise of European nationalism, the invention of the "cephalic index" (an index of relative "long-headedness" or "short-headedness"), and the rise of "Aryan race" theory. European raciologists now directed their energies toward identifying the so-called races of Europe—a proliferation of "white races." This trend yielded the racially restrictive Johnson-Reed Act of 1924 in the United States and the German Nazis' doctrine of Aryan supremacy. Meanwhile, the "Caucasian race" category remained useful to those Europeans and Euro-Americans (also Euro-Australians and Euro-New Zealanders) who were preoccupied with uniting their fellow Europeans against what they saw as a "rising tide" of "colored" peoples.

In chapter 5, I turn to the social and political forces behind the recovery of the "Caucasian race" category between roughly 1935 and 1952. The horrors of Nazism along with significant shifts in global geopolitics provoked European and North American anthropologists to rethink prevailing race ideas and racial classifications. This new racial reasoning culminated in two major United Nations Educational, Scientific, and Cultural Organization (UNESCO) Statements on Race in 1950 and 1951.

Chapter 6 explores the gradual decline of the "Caucasian race" category, at least among scientists, from 1952 to the present. Once again, momentous social, political, and cultural shifts around the world spurred changes in race science. Especially notable events were the post–World War II decolonization struggles of people of color in Africa and Asia and the Civil Rights movement in the United States (1954–65).

In chapter 7 I briefly consider the history of Russian expansion into the Caucasus region to make sense of the Russians' racialization of the "dark-skinned" Chechens and other Caucasian peoples, particularly during the ongoing Russian-Chechen wars. The Chechens' struggle highlights the historically contingent and paradoxical relationship between peoples of the Caucasus region and the history of the "Caucasian race" category. It also demonstrates that, as Étienne Balibar says, "the discourses of race and nation are never very far apart."[81]

# 1

# Before the "Caucasian Race"

## *Antecedents of European Racialism, ca. 1000–1684*

Naming occurs in sites, particular places, and at particular times. For a name to do its creative work, it needs authority. One needs usage within institutions. Naming does its work only as a social history works itself out.

         —Ian Hacking[1]

There was no notion of a Caucasian race in the years between 1000 to 1684. In fact, the "race" concept itself was introduced by Europeans elites only near the end of this period, in the seventeenth century, after the rise of the Atlantic slave trade and massive enslavement of "black" Africans. Nevertheless, the ethnic history of Europe during this period, which stretched from the Middle Ages to the Enlightenment, was a prelude to the invention of the "Caucasian race" idea in the late eighteenth century and its subsequent career.

Several medieval and early modern European notions about differences and boundaries between peoples established ideational building blocks for modern race thinking. They sustained ethnic divisions within and beyond Europe that later shaped the shifting boundaries of modern racial categories, including nineteenth-century theories about the "races of Europe" that ruptured the preeminence of "Caucasian race" idea. One significant thread of this history was the development of the idea and actuality of "Europe." After the collapse of the Roman Empire, the region now known as Europe gradually coalesced from great migrations of various peoples who criss-crossed the greater Eurasian landmass during the first millennium, including Angles, Saxons, Celts, Franks, Gauls, and Slavs.

These peoples did not constitute human "races," and they did not understand themselves as such. Moreover, before the establishment of relatively well defined national "homelands" in the later medieval period, they were constantly in motion in the western (now European) part of Eurasia. Norman Davies comments, "It was difficult for tribes to move without coming into contact, and potential conflict, with their predecessors on the trail. . . . There is absolutely no reason to suppose that Celts, Germans, Slavs, and others did not overlap, and sometimes intermingle. The idea of exclusive national homelands is a modern fantasy."[2] This first great migration period in European history did not really end until "the arrival of Turkic peoples in Greece and the Balkans in the thirteenth through the sixteenth centuries."[3] This flux in Europe's formative period informs its subsequent ethnic and racial history.

A few constellations of medieval ideas and concepts were especially significant for the development of the "race" concept and the shifting boundaries of modern racial categories: the ideas of "Christendom" and, later, "Europe," which marked a religiously, culturally, and geographically distinct region; the profound (and often race*like*) alienness or otherness that various peoples in the Middle Ages sometimes ascribed to other peoples, especially those who did not share their religion; and the fact that European Christians adopted the Judaic account of creation and biblical chronology, along with an Old Testament view of the origins of various tribes of human beings. In addition, Cedric Robinson identifies three historical developments that joined this mix to generate modern racial thought:

> the Islamic (i.e., Arab, Persian, Turkish, and African) domination of the Mediterranean civilization and the consequent retarding of European social and cultural life: the Dark Ages; the incorporation of African, Asian, and peoples of the New World into the world system emerging from late feudalism and merchant capitalism [i.e., between the fifteenth and seventeenth centuries CE; and] the dialectic of colonialism, plantocratic slavery, and resistance from the sixteenth century forward, and the formation of industrial labor and labor reserves.[4]

Some of these developments were largely internal to Europe, while the others were indicative of Europe's competition with the Islamic world and its increasing global power and reach.

Medieval Europeans employed certain racelike ideas to comprehend their social order and differentiate between social groups, but these were *ethnic* rather than *racial* designations. Still, a few cases of religious and ethnic conflict in early modern Europe were quite close to modern racism and paved the way for it: Christian anti-Jewish and anti-Muslim ideas and movements that peaked after the fifteenth-century Christian "reconquest" of Spain; associations of "black" Africans with servile status that emerged in the Middle Ages and were compounded when Portuguese sailors acquired West African slaves in the fifteenth century; English Protestant colonial domination of Irish Catholics, particularly between the fifteenth and seventeenth centuries; and conflicts between Franks and Gauls and Normans and Saxons in early modern England and France.

By the latter half of the seventeenth century, race-thinking proper emerged. English settlers in colonial America developed a racial understanding of and justification for the perpetual servitude to which they subjected "black" Africans, and they began to define themselves and other Europeans as "white" people. In relation to the new knowledge of the world and its peoples and the new global politics of the age, European scientists built upon the Scientific Revolution of the sixteenth and seventeenth centuries to develop the new science of "natural history." They sought to explain the world's natural order and the place of human beings within this order. One notable product of natural history was the first recognizably modern racial classification, in 1684, by the French travel writer François Bernier.

## Europe and Its "Others"

Compared to the steady migrations that characterized Latin Christendom and nascent "Europe" in Late Antiquity and the early Middle Ages, the feudal social order that developed in this region during the Middle Ages (ca. 750–1453 CE) was relatively static and marked by a deeply sedimented status hierarchy. "The serf, the slave, the peasant, the artisan, the lord, the king—all were allotted their place in the world by divine sanction. Not just human order but natural order was preordained." All living things were seen as joined in a "Great Chain of Being [that] linked the cosmos from the most miserable mollusc to the Supreme Being."[5] There were also significant distinctions between communities. Ethnocentrism was common between religious and ethnic groups—tribes (*gens*), peoples (*ethne*), and nations (*natios*);[6] Christians, Jews, Muslims, and pagans; the "civilized" and the "barbarian."[7]

Yet these medieval divisions were different from later racialized divisions.[8] This difference, which is important for understanding race and racism, has been obscured in some recent writing about medieval Europe. Robert Bartlett, for instance, examines what he calls the "race relations" of Latin Christendom between 900 and 1250 CE.[9] He says that "while the language of race [in Latin Christendom]—*gens, natio,* 'blood,' 'stock,' etc. —is biological, its medieval reality was almost entirely cultural. . . . When we study race relations in medieval Europe we are analysing the contact between various linguistic and cultural groups, not between breeding stocks."[10] Bartlett cites the canonist Regino of Prüm's four criteria for classifying "ethnic variation" as a classic medieval formulation of medieval "race relations." According to Regino (d. 915), "The various nations differ in descent, customs, language, and law."[11] Bartlett comments that only Regino's first criterion, "descent," is central to modern racism, and he goes on to note that "Regino's other criteria—customs, language, and law— emerge as the primary badges of ethnicity."[12]

Bartlett is correct to speak of ethnicity in this context, but he confuses matters by describing medieval Europeans' notions of ethnic difference in terms of race relations.[13] Medieval Europeans, along with the peoples in other parts of the premodern world, lacked any concept comparable to the modern "race" concept. They emphasized cultural criteria of difference and lacked any clearly developed notion of "fixed natures" of different descent groups.[14] For instance, medieval Christian Europeans used *Arab, Saracen,* and later *Turk* as terms for "Muslim"; Muslims of the Ottoman Empire referred to Europeans as "Franks"; and followers of each religion regarded members of the other faith as "infidels."[15]

The historical development of the idea and territory of Europe was itself one of the most important antecedents of the modern "race" concept. Europe has sometimes been considered a distinct continent, but this is a misnomer (see figure 1). The region we now know as Europe is actually a peninsula of the Eurasian landmass.[16] Europe, as Bartlett says, "is both a region and an idea."[17] The societies and cultures that inhabited the western peninsula of the Eurasian landmass were always diverse. But by the later Middle Ages there was enough commonality among the areas that we now call western and central Europe to constitute a distinct region: "When compared with other culture areas of the globe, such as the Middle East, the Indian subcontinent or China, western or central Europe exhibited (and exhibits) distinctive characteristics. In particular, Latin Europe (that

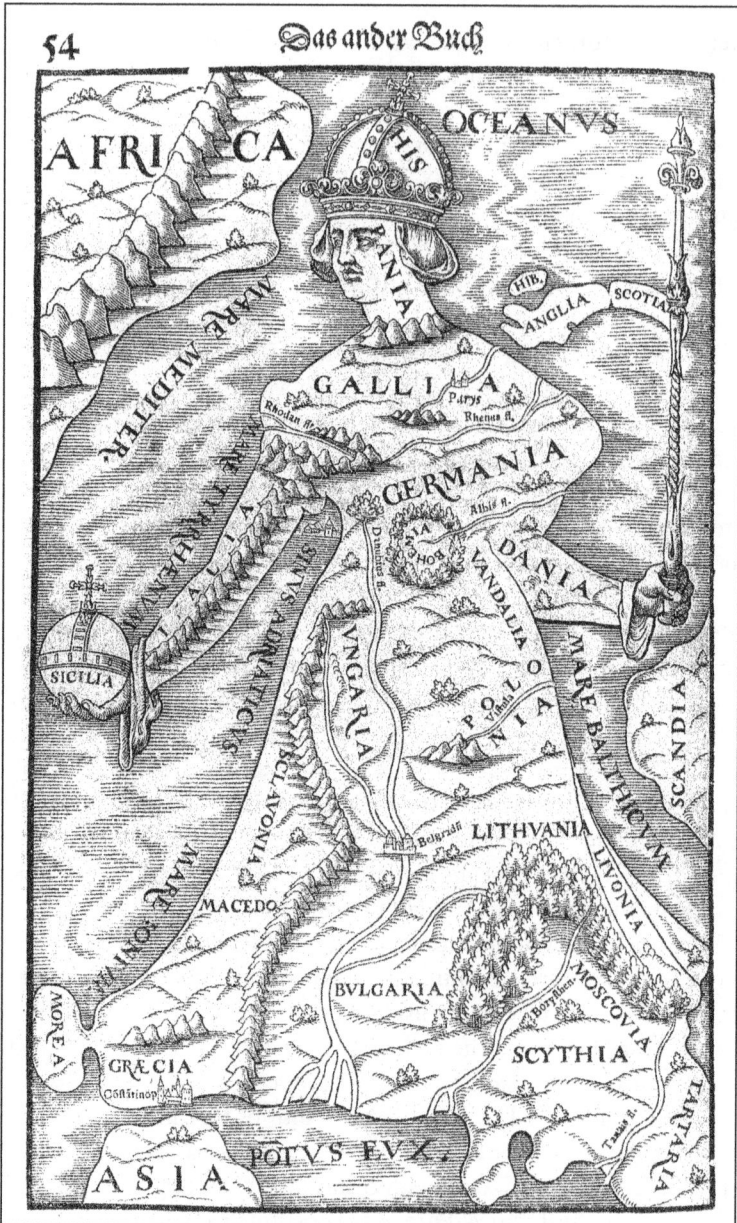

Figure 1: Queen Europe (Regina Europe), from Sebastian Müntzer's *Cosmography* (1588). Reprinted from *Early Modern Europe: An Oxford History* (Oxford: Oxford University Press, 1999), ed. Euan Cameron, p. 20 (British Library, MAPS C21 C13).

is, the part of Europe that was originally Roman Catholic rather than Greek orthodox or non-Christian) formed a zone where strong shared features were as important as geographical or cultural contrasts."[18]

Europe was becoming a kind of "imagined community" in political scientist Benedict Anderson's sense: a loose but geographically and culturally bounded society "conceived as a deep, horizontal comradeship," despite having no obvious or natural boundary to its eastern flank and a somewhat indeterminate southern frontier.[19] Because of its geographical indeterminacy, the idea and boundaries of Europe have been conceived as much in opposition to other cultural and political zones as in relation to what "Europeans" have had in common. For instance, the status of Russia as properly "European" has long been contested, both within the core of Europe and among Russian intellectuals.[20] The "modernizing" regimes of Peter I (Peter the Great, r. 1682–1725) and Catherine II (Empress Catherine, r. 1762–96) "Europeanized" Russia (Catherine declared Russia "a European state" in 1767); yet they did not resolve the issue. Due to this ambiguity, Europe's "official" eastern frontier constantly shifted. "It advanced steadily from the Don, where it had been fixed for a thousand years, to the banks of the Volga at the end of the fifteenth century, to the Ob in the sixteenth, to the Ural river and the Ural mountains in the nineteenth, and finally to the river Emba and the Kerch straits in the twentieth."[21]

To a large extent, the consolidation of Europe was spurred by the rise and expansion of Islam in the seventh and eighth centuries.[22] The expansion of Islamic societies isolated "Christendom" from the rest of the world and defined Europe's boundaries. Muslims also established a major presence at the edges of Europe: first in Iberia (in the seventh century) and later in the Balkans and the Black Sea region (in the fourteenth and fifteenth centuries) and Hungary (capturing Belgrade in 1521), being repelled at Vienna in 1529 and again, decisively, in 1683.[23]

Ongoing contact and conflict between Christians and Muslims had a direct impact on the place of the Caucasus region vis-à-vis Europe and Asia. Several centuries of enslavement of Christians by Muslims and of Muslims by Christians, for instance, continued into the sixteenth and seventeenth centuries. Meanwhile, in the western part of Europe, slavery had largely been done away with between the thirteenth and fifteenth centuries. This achievement followed the consolidation of a sense of "Christian brotherhood" in opposition to perceived Muslim and Jewish "outsiders." This new collective identity was exemplified by the Crusades between the eleventh and thirteenth centuries. This was the context in which thousands of Caucasians, including Georgians, Armenians, Circassians, and Mingrelians, were bought and sold as slaves, along with the Moors, by Venetian and Genoese merchants. These groups "were classified as infidels even if they were eventually baptized." Italian merchants "sold such 'Slavs' . . . , along with Greeks and Turks, in Muslim markets as well as in Christian Crete, Cyprus, Sicily, and such Spanish regions as early-fifteenth-century Valencia."[24]

This source of slaves was mostly abandoned after the Ottoman Turks' conquest of Constantinople in 1453, which redirected slave traders to sub-Saharan Africa.[25] At that time the Portuguese sold increasing numbers of black African slaves. Prior to this Atlantic slave trade, slavery was already a prominent part of the economic and social history of European and Islamic societies in the Middle Ages. Yet *racialized* slavery emerged only with the development of Atlantic slave trade in the sixteenth and seventeenth centuries (see below).

The Caucasus region sits squarely in greater Eurasia, on the isthmus between the Black and Caspian Seas where Europe and Asia meet; but even though it is partly Christian (primarily in Armenia and Georgia), it has never really been considered part of Europe. Christianity was adopted by leaders of Armenia and Georgia in 314 and 330 CE, respectively; Persian (Iranian) influences arrived in the fifth and sixth centuries, and Islam followed in the seventh century.[26] After the Ottoman conquest of Constantinople in 1453, the Ottomans cut Georgia off from western Christendom, and between the sixteenth and eighteenth centuries the region become of a site of Turkish and Persian domination and competition. Russians eventually occupied the northern Caucasus (though without initially controlling it) in the eighteenth century, and Russia annexed Georgia in the nineteenth century.[27] In the sixteenth century, English travelers to Russia, Persia, and central Asia tended to describe the people of this region as "brutish" and as "infidels."[28]

To the south of Europe, northern Africa was somewhat known to Europeans. Although never considered a part of Europe, North Africa "was a frontier region where Berber states and Ottoman client rulers posed a constant threat to the settled places of Christendom until the extinction of Turkish hegemony in the Mediterranean in the late seventeenth century."[29] Africa south of the Atlas Mountains, however, remained largely unknown to Europeans until the nineteenth century, despite Portuguese exploration and settlement on parts its western shores that began in the fifteenth century.[30]

European elites also used a twofold division of the world's peoples between "civilized" and "uncivilized" (sometimes "barbarian") peoples to gauge their place in the world.[31] By the sixteenth and seventeenth centuries, European elites typically judged Europe to be the world's most "advanced" society, but they also tended to include parts of Africa and Asia in the "civilized" world.[32] Meanwhile, before the European feudal monarchies and merchant capitalists turned their energies to colonizing the Americas in the fifteenth century, their main "focus of external interest (and concern) was the Middle East, North Africa and India, collectively known as the Orient." Through their descriptions of the peoples of these areas, European elites created not only "a discourse of an imagined Other at the edge of European civilisation, but . . . [also] a discourse of a real Other represented as a result of conflicting material and political interests with a population which came to mark the boundary of Europe, not only spatially but also in consciousness."[33] This combination of perceived likeness and discrepancy between Europe, on the one hand, and "the Orient," on the other hand, probably influenced the contours of the later "Caucasian race" notion: a Europe-centered notion, invented by Europeans to designate what they took to be the greatest and most beautiful "race," it usually has been conceived so as to encompass peoples from parts of the Middle East, North Africa, and India as well as Europeans.

Another notable factor in the development of European racial thought was the legacy in Christian Europe of the Old Testament Judaic chronology (i.e., the idea of a five-thousand-year history of the earth since its creation), along with the biblical view of the common origins of various tribes of human beings through Adam and Eve, and then through Noah and his sons after the great flood described in Genesis. The biblical account is unclear about the geographic dispersion of Noah's sons, Ham, Shem, and Japhet, and medieval interpreters associated them with the regions of Europe, Asia, and Africa in varying ways.[34] Gradually, the dominant view of the narrative that took hold between the fourth and fourteenth centuries regarded Japhet as the progenitor of the peoples of Europe; Shem, those of Asia; and Ham, those of Africa. "Jerome's rendering of Genesis 9:27, God 'shall enlarge Japhet and he shall dwell in the tents of Shem,' was taken to mean that Japhet would produce more offspring than his brothers and that, one day, his progeny would come to conquer Asia just as they would inherit from the Hebrews the mantle of the true religion."[35] By the early modern period, versions of the biblical view of human dispersion through Shem, Ham, and Japhet after the flood were circulated by writers like Dutch jurist and diplomat Hugo Grotius (1583–1645) and Giambattista Vico (1668–1744), who proposed a "new science" of the human origin that melded "sacred history" with elements of a modern historical consciousness.[36] In addition, the Bible's account of Noah's curse on Ham, which condemned Ham's son Canaan and his descendants to servitude for Ham's transgression against Noah, was eventually elaborated into an explanation and justification for the "blackness" and enslavement of sub-Saharan Africans (see below).[37]

Another set of ethno-cultural divisions in medieval Europe influenced the later contours and career of the "Caucasian race" idea. Discourses of otherness became prevalent that aimed at peoples who are now counted as Europeans. While these intra-European divisions were not originally conceived in racial terms, some of them reemerged as racial distinctions in the nineteenth century. Bartlett explains that

> images of exclusion and otherness available to those who formed and expressed opinions in twelfth-century western Europe included not only the dichotomy Christian/non-Christian, but also that of civilized/barbarian, and the two polarities were often mutually reinforcing. The Welsh were "rude and untamed" and hence "nominally profess Christ but deny him in their life and customs." The Ruthenians, who "confess Christ only in name, but deny him in their deeds," were associated with other "primitive Slavs" and "wild peoples" of "uncivilized barbarism."[38]

Adherence to the Latin Christian liturgy and obedience to the pope were necessary but not sufficient conditions for the full inclusion of a people within the emerging European society of the late Middle Ages. As the peoples of Latin-"Frankish" (i.e., Germanic) Europe "intruded upon societies around and unlike their own, they found both non-Christians (in eastern and Mediterranean lands) and local variants of Christianity (notably in Celtic countries). Their response was to equate the two, if the Christian societies did not have the social and legal characteristics with which they were familiar." That is, they tended to see both kinds of societies as alien or "uncivilized."[39]

Medieval writers such as Geoffrey of Monmouth (in his 1135 *History of the Kings of Britain*) and Gerald of Wales (1146–1223) elaborated notions of ethnic otherness that "became rudiments of later racial discourse."[40] Geoffrey's influential book interpreted antagonisms between English and Norman peoples as an "ancient clash of Britons and Germanic invaders";

Gerald, in books on Wales and Ireland, related biological, political, and territorial categories of kin, tribe, people, and nation to climate, topography, environment, social organization, customs, language, military practice, and national character.[41]

## *The Road to Racialism*

A few ethnic notions that emerged in and around Europe in the Middle Ages and early modern period were especially portentous for the rise of the "race" concept in the seventeenth century and theories about "races of Europe" in the nineteenth. Foremost among these were Latin Christian European elites' ideas about the otherness of Jews, Muslims, Irish, and Slavic peoples within Europe and of black Africans and "Indians" of the Americas. Also significant were ethnic and social status distinctions between Franks and Gauls in France and between Normans and Saxons in England.

### Spain, circa 1492: Jews, Muslims, and "Indians"

There was a significant Jewish population in the Iberian peninsula in the fourteenth century.[42] Anti-Jewish riots in Spain in 1391 marked a period of heightened conflict. Jews were given a choice of conversion or death, and many Jews converted to Christianity. In 1492, at the time of the completion of the Christian reconquest of Spain from Muslims, Jews as such were expelled from Spain. More Jews chose baptism and converted to Christianity to avoid death or expatriation.[43] (Forced conversions in Portugal followed in 1497.) These conversions created a group of hundreds of thousands of formerly Jewish "new Christians," or *conversos,* who did not readily assimilate into Spain's Christian society. Many retained Jewish customs (often secretly) despite their outward change in religion.[44] Muslims who remained in Spain after the reconquest likewise were forced to convert. These formerly Muslim new Christians, the *Moriscos,* were largely peasants and artisans in Spain. They lived in separate communities and resisted even the appearance of cultural assimilation and loss of their "Moorish" culture.[45]

Despite the Christian belief in the regenerative character of baptism, the treatment of the *conversos* and *Moriscos* in Spanish law and theology after the reconquest prefigured later racism. Spanish theologians developed "a doctrine according to which the false beliefs of both the Moors and Jews had soiled their blood, and this stain or 'nota' had been transmitted by heredity to their furthest descendants, who were set apart in the almost untouchable caste of New Christians." Laws were passed to maintain "purity of blood" among people of "genuine" Christian descent.[46]

In Europe more generally, Jews were expelled from a number of countries in the later Middle Ages, and European Christians developed anti-Jewish myths that established a basis for later racialized (and *racist*) anti-Semitism.[47] Due to stiffened Christian prohibitions on "usury" combined with the relatively small amount of capital needed for moneylending, moneylending became one of the more widely practiced activities among Jews. As Jews increasingly worked in the fields of finance and moneylending, "these occupations shaped the stereotypical image of the Jew living in Christendom."[48] Christians also regarded Jews as aliens in Europe in other ways. The strangeness of Jewish religious rites when measured against Christian practices was construed as a sign of a deviant stubbornness that betrayed the devil's influence. In a Lenten sermon in Trent, in 1475, the Italian friar Bernardino of Feltre said that "he had sometimes heard it said that Jews drink the blood of Christians at Eastertide," and that year the Jews of Trent were accused of ritual murder.[49] Similar incidents occurred in Italy and Spain. Myths also circulated about Jews cooking their Passover bread (*matzot*) with Christian blood and "drinking Christian blood to eliminate the smell associated with their diabolical nature."[50]

The reconquest and the expulsion of Jews and Muslims from Spain in 1492 coincided with the voyage of the Genoese sailor Cristoforo Colombo (Christopher Columbus) to "America" while in search of a new route to Asia.[51] The voyages to the Americas by Colombo, Amerigo Vespucci, and the conquistadors Hernán Cortés and Francisco Pizarro became another link between medieval notions of otherness and modern racial thought. The cruelty inflicted on Native Americans by the European conquerors and settlers provoked a great debate among European clergy about the rights of conquerors and the humanity and dignity of the Native Americans. A key episode in this debate was the exchange in Spain, during 1550–51, between Bartolomé de Las Casas, the Dominican bishop of Chiapas, and Juan Ginés de Sepúlveda, a humanist scholar and translator of Aristotle. The gist of the debate concerned whether or not indigenous Americans possessed human reason. Sepúlveda regarded Native Americans as subhuman beings who lacked any elements of civil life and virtue, and he applied Aristotle's notion of "natural slavery" to them. He claimed that hierarchy rather than equality was that natural order of human society.[52] Las Casas countered from the perspective of Christian universalism: "The natural laws and rules and rights of men are common to all nations, Christian and gentile, and whatever their sect, law, state, color and condition, without any difference."[53] He maintained that as people equipped with reason the indigenous Americans, though not Christian, could *become* Christian.[54] Still, while Las Casas opposed indiscriminate exploitation of the Americans, he affirmed the superiority of Christian European "civilization" and thus legitimated Spanish imperial expansion to the Americas.[55]

### Slavic Peoples

In the case of the Slavs, as with the other peoples that I have been discussing, we should avoid any suggestion of some "pure," primordial Slavic people.[56] Yet, by the Middle Ages, Slavic peoples had coalesced in a recognizable way, with a distinct language and culture, in areas that would become eastern Europe. The marginal place of Slavs (including later Czechs, Slovaks, Poles, Ukrainians, Russians, Serbs, and Croats) in the medieval European world is indicated in the following comment, which the English historian Edward Gibbon adapted from the sixth-century Byzantine historian Procopius and from the Emperor Mauritius:

> The Sclavonians used one common language (it was harsh and irregular) and were known by the resemblance of their form which deviated from the swarthy Tartar and approached, without attaining, the lofty stature and fair complexion of the German. Four thousand six hundred villages were scattered over the provinces of Russia and Poland, and their huts were hastily built of rough timber.[57]

This sense of Slavic distinctiveness was reinforced—if not generated—by the somewhat unique association of Slavic peoples with slavery. While slavery was a declining practice *within* most of western Europe, it persisted in Slavic regions. Russia and the Ukraine had the most well developed system of slavery in Europe from the twelfth through the seventeenth centuries, and the Mongol conquest of 1237–1240 resulted in the enslavement of about 10 percent of the eastern Slavs. This made the Slavic areas into one of the world's two great sources of slaves, along with Africa.[58]

One consequence of this strong link between Slavic peoples and slavery is that the word *slave* in many European languages comes from the Latin word *sclavus,* which means a person of Slavic origin.[59]

In Russia, slavery continued into the seventeenth century. It was replaced by serfdom in the seventeenth and early eighteenth centuries. In Poland, there were privately owned slaves in the Middle Ages that eventually blended into serfs in the late Middle Ages. In the Balkans, slavery had been largely eclipsed by serfdom after 1100 under Byzantine rule, which was Orthodox Christian and used Roman law; it was reintroduced in the fifteenth century in the parts of the Balkans that came under the control of the Ottoman Empire, which was Islamic.[60]

The Ottomans' slaves were typically outsiders. Between 1500 and 1700, Crimean Tatars captured and sold as slaves approximately 2.5 million Russians, Ukrainians, Poles, and Hungarians.[61] Most of them went to the Ottoman Empire. Crimeans continued to enslave Poles into the seventeenth and eighteenth centuries, but Russia, under Catherine the Great, ended Crimean slave trading in 1783 when it conquered the Ottomans' Black Sea territories and Crimea, before it extended its reach into Persia, the Caucasus, and central Asia. "After that, slaves in the Ottoman Empire were so-called 'white slaves' kidnapped from the Caucasus (Circassians and Georgians) or black slaves imported through Egypt from Africa."[62] Marginalization of Slavic peoples in Europe was also manifest in other ways. For example, beginning in the early fourteenth century in German-dominated regions of eastern Europe, discriminatory urban legislation was enacted against people of Slavic "stock."[63]

### "Black" Africans

Awareness of differences in the skin color and appearance among the world's peoples can be found in some of the earliest human efforts to record history, geography, and travels. Yet the "color consciousness" that emerged among various peoples before the modern era—including ideas about "white" and "black" peoples in ancient and medieval China—was distinct from modern racialism and "race consciousness."[64] Thus, the ancient Greek historian Herodotus, who wrote his *Histories* in the fifth century BCE based on his travels across the Persian Empire, noted differences in the skin color and appearance among different peoples. In the Middle Ages, Marco Polo (1254–1324), the Venetian traveler, and Ibn Batutah (1304–77), the Muslim geographer from Morocco, recorded the skin color and appearance of the different peoples they encountered, whom they also described with cultural and religious notions such as "infidels." These writers, however, lacked any concept comparable the modern "race" concept with which to interpret these differences.[65]

The ancient Greeks were aware of "black-faced" peoples of Africa ("Ethiopians"), whom they distinguished from Egyptians, but had no sense of any natural inferiority of Africans. Diodorus, the late-first-century BCE Greek historian, regarded some Ethiopians as "primitive" and considered others as "the *first of all men* and as the originators of divine rituals most pleasing to the gods."[66] On the whole, the view of black Africans among the ancient Greeks and Romans was positive. Frank Snowden explains, "Initial, favorable impressions were not altered, in spite of later accounts of wild tribes in the south and even after encounters with blacks had become more frequent. There was a clear cut respect among Mediterranean peoples for Ethiopians and their way of life."[67]

At the same time, the ancient Greeks and Romans as well as medieval Europeans distinguished between black and fair-skinned peoples in ways that conveyed deep symbolic meaning. Stereotypical formulations such as "Can the Ethiop change his skin?" were common in Greco-Roman and Judeo-Christian cultures. The usual implication was that "whiteness" was the positive norm and "blackness" signified a deficiency. By the fourteenth century in Europe, visual and literary images of "black" physiognomies had become familiar markers of territorial distance and cultural exoticism.[68]

By the late Middle Ages, the Old Testament story of the curse of Ham became a stock justification among Europeans for the enslavement of black Africans. According to the book of Genesis, after the flood Ham disrespected his father Noah by looking at his father's naked body as Noah lay drunk. When Noah awoke, he cursed Ham's son Canaan and his descendants for Ham's transgression, declaring that they would be "servants unto servants." Significantly, the narrative is vague about the geographical destinations of Noah's sons and their descendants, and although it concerns servitude it says nothing about skin color.[69] In medieval Europe— where serfs, unlike Jews, Muslims, and lepers, were a numerical majority —the story had been used to explain and justify the subordination of serfs as the descendants of Cain or Ham.[70]

The curse of Ham's son Canaan seems to have been first used to link slavery to "blackness" in the Islamic world during the Middle Ages.[71] Medieval Arabs and Moors used both light-skinned and "black" slaves, but typically relegated "blacks" to the most menial and degrading work.[72]

Muslim expansion into Asia and Africa from the eighth century produced a color consciousness developed in the Islamic world.[73] Muslim thinkers such as the fourteenth-century historian Ibn Khaldun commonly expressed derogatory views of black Africans. Khaldun once wrote that black Africans "are closer to dumb animals than to rational beings." (He held a similar view of Slavs.)[74] These notions were not sufficient to establish a special link between slavery and black Africans, however, because medieval Muslims never developed a distinctly racialized form of slavery. Muslims as well as Christians began to associate sub-Saharan Africans with lifetime servitude when black Africans became conspicuous in southern Iberia as the slaves of light- or tawny-skinned Moors. And this identification of "black skins with servile status" deepened as Europeans ceased to enslave other Europeans and Portuguese sailors acquired slaves during voyages to the Guinea coast in the fifteenth century (see "The 'Race' Concept" section, below).[75]

### England and France: Gauls and Franks, Normans and Saxons

With the Gauls and Franks we return to divisions within Europe. "Francia" or "Frankland" (later France) grew up in the sixth century from Frankish kingdoms established in largely Gallo-Roman territories: Neustria, in the west, comprising primarily Gallo-Romans centered in Paris; Austrasia, east of the Rhine and predominantly Germanic; and Burgundy, which included the old Burgundian kingdom by the Rhône and much of Gaul.[76] (Celtic peoples had settled in the west, forming Brittany.)[77] By the middle of the sixth century in Neustria and Austrasia, most of the elite population, clergy, nobility, and government officials, considered themselves Franks. These Frankish rulers incorporated Burgundy into the larger Frankish kingdom but respected Burgundian social and legal tradition; a sense of Burgundian regional identity was guarded by the area's aristocracy.[78] As of the early seventh century, "regional populations were divided by social strata, not by language, custom, or law; and all of society, . . . with the exception of the Jewish minority, were united in a single faith."[79] By the end of the first millennium the distinction between Gallo-Romans and Franks had disappeared, along with an earlier distinction between Romans and barbarians. This development, however, did not prevent a distinction between Franks and Gallo-Romans (or Gauls) from being recreated in the sixteenth century when the problem of national origins surfaced.[80]

Etymologically, the term *Frank,* referring to a person of Germanic origin, is linked in western languages to the concepts "freedom, integrity and power" as well as to Francia, Frankland, and France. To be called a Frank during the Middle Ages connoted not only a Germanic person but also a "free" person—a status that stood in sharp contrast to that of a serf (*servus*) or slave (*Slav*). Léon Poliakov remarks that a key word in French political history thus "slyly hint[s] at the superiority of the German stock over the Latins and over the Slavs."[81] The Frank/Gaul distinction that was reintroduced in the sixteenth century "made an important contribution to the idea of race."[82] It also exemplified some aspects of the interrelationship between race and class, particularly the way class divisions have sometimes been racialized.[83] In fact, as I will explain, the Frank/Gaul distinction eventually was conceived in an explicitly racialized manner by prominent French writers in the decades after the French Revolution of 1789.

On the Gallic or Gaulish side, the writer François de Belleforest (d. 1583) referred to "our ancestors the Gauls." He suggested that "divine providence" had used the reign of Hugh Capet (r. 987–96) "to restore to the native Gauls authority over their country," which had been usurped by the foreign Franks.[84] For two centuries after Belleforest, the Gauls had few other advocates. The prevailing view asserted a Frankish-aristocratic preeminence in the making of France. During the reign of Louis XIV (r. 1643–1715) the writer Loyseau declared, "The victorious Franks were of noble birth; the vanquished Gauls were of common stock. The conquering Franks claimed for themselves the possession of arms, the administration of public offices, the enjoyment of their fiefs."[85] This theme was reiterated in class-inflected, quasi-racialist terms in the early eighteenth century by champions of the nobility such as Comte Henri de Boulainvilliers, who "claimed a different descent from that of the commonality who were of Gallo-Roman ancestry."[86]

In the era of the French Revolution, writers such as Abbé Sièyes challenged the myth of Germanic-aristocratic Franks with a bourgeois-revolutionary myth about the liberation of the enslaved Gauls. Sièyes, advocate of the rising bourgeoisie, reversed the roles of Franks and Gauls in his 1789 pamphlet *What Is the Third Estate?* He called for the Third Estate, as representatives of a new France descended from Gauls and Romans, to liberate the nation from its Frankish nobility: "Why should [the Third Estate] not relegate to the forests of Franconia all those families which persist in the foolhardy pretense of being descended from the race of conquerors . . . ? The Nation, thus purged, would . . . be able to console itself by the thought that it was constituted of the descendants of the Gauls and the Romans only."[87] Other new proponents of a "Gallic" France, such as La Tour d'Auvergne, wanted to restore the "illustrious race" of Gauls.[88]

Later, pro-aristocratic successors to Boulainvilliers also resorted to racial appeals—now to Germanic-Frankish superiority—and prominent French historians of early-nineteenth-century France embraced racialized ideas about Franks and Gauls.[89] According to historian Augustin Thierry, for instance (writing in 1820), "Recent studies in physiology . . . show that the physical and moral constitution of nations depends far more on their descent from certain primitive ancestors than on the influence of climate." France, he adds, has descended from "two enemy camps," and "whatever may have been the mixture of the two primitive races, their spirit of un-ending contradiction has survived to this day in the two parts of the combined population."[90]

The case of England was similar to that of France. The British Isles were colonized during the first millennium by Iberians, Celts, Romans, Germans, and Scandinavians, capped off by the Norman conquest of 1066. While the terms *British* and *English* have become near synonyms, England's origin myths recall the presence of Celts, Britons, Germans, and Anglo-Saxons (descended from Angles and Germanic Saxons) and also appeal to Hebrew narratives.[91] The most salient myth concerns the conquest of the Norman (French, Frankish, Latin) elite over an established Anglo-Saxon, English-speaking people.[92] In the sixteenth century a Saxonist and anti-French campaign against the "Norman yoke" emerged. Saxonist views became prominent during the seventeenth-century English revolutions, especially when the poorer classes voiced their grievances through popular movements such as the Levelers and the Diggers. These protests foreshadowed the class divide of the French Revolution. The Levelers and Diggers appealed to scriptures and to an idealized, egalitarian Anglo-Saxon past. King James I, in contrast, regarded the English nobility as mostly Norman so that "at the root of the class confrontation was a cultural confrontation which was perceived as a conflict between different bloods."[93] After the Glorious Revolution of 1688, which established a constitutional monarchy and a restricted form of popular sovereignty, these ideas were expanded into a wider tradition of English and Anglophile paeans to the "love of civil liberty" and constitutional government among the Saxons. This tradition of thought reemerged in the 1840s in a racial theory of the Teutonic (Germanic–northern European) roots of English constitutional government.[94]

The Irish

The Irish experience is another thread in Europe's emerging racial discourse. Ireland became part of European Christendom in 461 CE, not long after Gaul (France) in 397, and before England between 597 and 664.[95] Even so, the Irish were subjected to processes of conquest, colonization, and cultural transformation similar to those used eastern Europe and Spain, two other peripheries of Frankish-Latin Europe.[96] By the twelfth century the Irish were seen by elites of England, France, and Italy as alien to Latin Christendom. Bartlett explains, "Although the Irish were of ancient Christian faith and shared the creed of Frankish Europe, they exhibited pronounced differences in culture and social organization." Critics regarded Irish social structures and customs as "barbaric" and "beastlike" and held that even though the Irish were Christian, they could be treated as though they were not.[97]

During the late Middle Ages, England made this view of Irish otherness an effective tool in their colonization of Ireland. At the request of England's King Henry II (1154–89), Pope Adrian IV authorized England to rule over the Irish in order to expand the church's boundaries and "to proclaim the truths of the Christian religion to a rude and ignorant people."[98] The guiding assumption was that the Irish were fellow human beings but lived a less than fully human Christian life.[99] As England's noble families began to reside in Ireland, the English eventually developed policies such as the Statutes of Kilkenny (1366) to differentiate the English and the Irish of Ireland. The statutes acknowledged a "mixed nation" of English families that had intermarried with leading Irish families. To contain this "degeneracy" the statutes banned marriage, "concubinage[,] or amour" between the English and Irish and called for a strict separation between them in language and customs. The English at this time did not regard the Irish as biologically different but rather as "uncivilized."[100] Moreover, until the sixteenth century feudal Ireland remained largely independent from England economically.

England launched a more aggressive colonization under the Tudor Dynasty of Henry VII, Henry VIII, and Elizabeth I. By 1541, Henry VIII had enjoined the Anglo-Irish Parliament to proclaim him the spiritual head of the Church of Ireland, obliged all government officials in Ireland to swear allegiance to the church, and established the king of England as the king of Ireland.[101] This marked the beginning of the Protestant ascendancy in Ireland. Under Elizabeth (r. 1558–1603) and James I (r. 1603–25), English policy became more heavy-handed. This involved the expropriation of Irish-owned land, direct exploitation of Irish labor, and forced resettlement of those whose land had been taken.[102] English policy included attempts to establish plantations in Ireland (mostly unsuccessful). The basic model was for English tenants to supplant Irish tenants and for native Irish to be made the primary laborers, with no rights to own land.[103] With the Protestant Ascendancy and the enactment of the Penal Laws, in the sixteenth and seventeenth centuries, England devised a colonial regime that prefigured expressly racist forms of colonial rule that England adopted elsewhere in its empire. The Penal Laws effectively excluded Catholics, who were three-quarters of the Irish population, from all important positions in their country, ownership of property, and education.[104]

Still, English colonial rule in Ireland from the mid–seventeenth to the late eighteenth century was something distinct from racial oppression.[105] While English domination of the Irish was as harsh as many other cases of colonial subjugation, it was based on claims about cultural and religious differences rather than on race.[106] The English occasionally used the term *race* in loose ways to refer to the "wild Irish," but they lacked a systematic discourse of racial difference.[107] For instance, English Protestants accepted the possibility of Irish Catholics *becoming* Protestant through conversion, something that is precluded by notions of *racial* difference.[108] There is often a fine line between these two forms of oppression, however. Moreover, in nineteenth century, *after* the development of modern racialist thought, the Irish were often explicitly regarded in Europe and the United States as a distinct "Celtic race" by raciologists and in popular racist discourse (see chapters 3 and 4).[109]

## The "Race" Concept

The modern concept of "race" has its roots in these earlier ethnic distinctions. Nonetheless, the invention of the "race" concept by Europeans in the seventeenth and eighteenth centuries constituted a historically novel *naturalizing* of differences between groups of people, a "new epistemology of human difference."[110] The significance of this development becomes evident when we examine the origins of the word *race* and the "race" concept: when they first came into use, how they were first used, and to what effects.[111] As Alan Ryan says, it is important to distinguish between the *word* and the *concept*: "The existence-criteria of concepts may be obscure, but they surely do not come into existence only when what they are concepts of comes into existence; nor do they cease to exist when it does."[112] Concerning race, it is clear that this concept is *not* bound up with the "coming into existence" or ceasing to exist of actual *human races.*[113] This disjunction between the "race" concept and the coming into existence or ceasing to exist of human races is recognized by both racialists and social constructionists. The former maintain that biologically based human races actually exist, but that their "coming into existence" was an effect of ancient processes of "raciation," understood as a fact of *natural history* that preceded by a long time the modern "race" concept.[114] In contrast, social constructionists insist that there are no human races in the biological sense to come into or go out of existence, and that it is only *people's ideas and beliefs about race* that have come into existence and can go out of existence—for example, the *belief* that human beings can be divided meaningfully into distinct races. Social constructionists also maintain that there are integral connections between the rise of the "race" concept and people's various beliefs, theories, and social practices concerning race.[115]

Regarding the distinction between words and concepts, James Farr observes that it often does not need to be explicitly "drawn because our language is so richly developed that most of our concepts—especially our political concepts—express themselves with matching words which name them explicitly and uniquely." He adds, with reference to political concepts, "This is not always so, of course, for someone may possess a concept without (yet) possessing the matching word. . . . However, our ability to identify with any confidence our own much less others' political concepts wholly depends upon the range of (other) words at our or their disposal."[116] With the "race" concept, this means we can conclude with some assurance that people possess (or a society possesses) the *concept* only when they have developed a rich, expressive discourse that makes use of the concept with some consistency. Such a discourse of race would encompass a range of related words and concepts. This view leaves open the possibility that a group or society may possess the concept of race in a rudimentary form without (yet) being in possession of the matching word, *race.* But we need to tread carefully here. It is clear that the origins of the word *race* preceded by a couple of centuries or so the development of systematic ideas and theories of "race." Meanwhile, the development of a systematic discourse of race between the seventeenth and nineteenth centuries had a profound, even revolutionary, effect on the meaning of the word.[117]

The origins of the term *race* in European languages are murky. The word appeared around the late fourteenth century in Italian and Spanish. From there it migrated into other European languages—French and English in the sixteenth century; German (from French) in the eighteenth century.[118] Eric Voegelin notes, "From its first appearance, the meanings of the word revolve around the fact of descent or origin."[119] Through the sixteenth and seventeenth centuries the term had a wide range of connotations, some of which had only loose affinities to the modern "race" concept. Thus, John Foxe, in *The Book of Martyrs* (1570), spoke of "the outward race & stock of Abraham"; Milton, in *Paradise Lost* (1667), wrote, "High proof ye now have giv'n to be the Race Of Satan," and he referred to "That Pigmean Race Beyond the Indian Mount"; Richard Hooker, in *The Laws of the Ecclesiastical Polity* (1594), said, "Such, as either we must acknowledge for our own forefathers or else disdain for the race of Christ."[120] Another relevant early meaning was associated with animal husbandry and aristocratic lineages, denoting a "superior" or "noble" stock, family, or class "to which a person, animal, or plant belongs." In this vein, Shakespeare, in *A Winter's Tale* (1611), spoke of a "bud of a Nobler race."[121] As late as 1790, Edmund Burke still used *race* to refer to an earlier generation of ancestors: "If the last generations of your country appeared without much lustre in your eyes, you might have . . . derived your claims from a more early race of ancestors."[122]

In Europe during the Middle Ages, a concept of "race" in the modern sense was precluded by the prevailing biblical mode of thought. As long as human beings were understood as having a singular and homogeneous origin, they "could not be submitted to zoological divisions, or to the terms used to designate them."[123] Beginning in the fifteenth century, several developments contributed to the modern European invention of the "race" concept: the development of racialized slavery out of more indiscriminate forms of medieval slavery and more limited forms of servitude in the Americas in the sixteenth and seventeenth centuries, along with the growth of the Atlantic slave trade; the gradual replacement of the feudal status order of medieval Europe with the relatively more fluid and ostensibly "meritocratic" class divisions of modern capitalist societies; emerging class conflicts over the availability of wage labor and the conditions of labor; vast new information about the peoples of the world in the age of European exploration and conquest between the fifteenth and seventeenth centuries; and the Scientific Revolution of the sixteenth and seventeenth centuries.[124] Sixteenth-century Spanish writers began to use the term *race* with reference to the new populations that they encountered in their travels. Yet it was left to the English colonizers of North America, who developed a distinctly racialized form of chattel slavery in the late seventeenth century, first to employ the concept of race systematically to differentiate groups of people based on ideas about heritable and fixed physical characteristics.[125]

According to George Fredrickson, "The modern concept of races as basic human types classified by physical characteristics (primarily skin color) was not invented until the eighteenth century."[126] Nevertheless, as I will explain shortly, the basic idea of race differences, whereby human beings were understood to be divisible into discrete physical types, possessed of supposedly unequal moral and intellectual capacities, was fairly well established by the late seventeenth century. By that time the Atlantic slave trade was flourishing, and racialized slavery (of West Africans) had become institutionalized through law and custom in England's American colonies, particularly Virginia and Maryland. These developments were epitomized by the ideological, material, and legal lumping together of diverse West African peoples into the "race" of "Negroes." "This 'Negro,'" Robinson explains,

> was a wholly distinct ideological construct from those images of Africans that had preceded it [e.g., as "African," "Moor," "Ethiop"]. It differed in function and ultimately in kind. Where previously the Blacks were a fearful phenomenon to Europeans because of their historical association with civilizations superior, dominant, and/or antagonistic to Western societies (the most recent being that of Islam), now the ideograph of Blacks came to signify a difference of [race or] species, an exploitable source of energy (labor power) both mindless to the organizational requirements of production and insensitive to the subhuman conditions of work.[127]

By the fifteenth century, Arab slave traders had long plundered African societies for slaves. Slavery existed in the Iberian peninsula prior to Spanish and Portuguese exploration of the Americas.[128] These forms of slavery, however, were not *racially* defined.[129] By contrast, the Atlantic trade in African slaves, initiated by Portugal, eventually produced the racialization of Africans as Negroes, along with the corresponding racialization of most Europeans (and some other peoples) as whites. This divide was arguably the pivot on which racial thought was further elaborated.

After 1500, Portuguese slave traders began to supply Portuguese and Spanish settlements in the Americas with slave labor from enslaved West

Africans. The terms *negro* and *guineu* appeared in Portugal in the fifteenth century. This reflected the fact that "as of that time, in Portugal, the most common kind of slave was . . . African."[130] As I noted earlier, Spanish conquests over the native "Indians" of the Americas had forced them to debate how they should treat these populations. Although the Spanish often treated native Americans brutally, they (like the later English colonists) never made the enslavement of these indigenous peoples a major part of their colonial rule.[131] Meanwhile, the Spanish and Portuguese turned the enslavement of Africans into a vast Atlantic commerce. By around 1550 the English had acquired from the Spanish "the notion that Negroes could be enslaved," even though slavery (as opposed to temporary servitude) went against the grain of English law.[132] At about the same time, the term *negro* was incorporated into the English language despite the fact that the term *black,* with the same basic meaning, already existed in English.[133] By about 1650, the Spanish, Portuguese, English, and Dutch all used African slave labor almost exclusively on sugar plantations.[134]

One reason that European elites of the fifteenth through seventeenth centuries found slavery to be an acceptable institution in their colonies was that they were still influenced by "the heritage of the Middle Ages."[135] "Settlers from Europe," Daniel Segal says, "brought with them hierarchical distinctions which meant that they were many, not one"—that is, they understood European peoples to be different ranks of persons.[136] In the early seventeenth century, peasants constituted the vast majority of Europe's population and servitude was widespread in England's American colonies.[137] The propertied classes in England began to promote sending their poorer countrymen (and fewer women) to the colonies as they grew concerned that a "mass of idle rogues and beggars grew and increasingly threatened the peace of England."[138] The colonies became an outlet for an English population that grew rapidly between 1500 and 1650. Because most of the migrants could not afford passage to the American colonies, many of them came as indentured servants who were bound by contract to serve a master for a fixed number of years to repay their ocean transit.[139]

In seventeenth-century England slavery had been ended, but "indentured" servitude, which did not entail a complete loss of freedom, was still practiced. Early in the century the English were somewhat reluctant to embrace the enslavement of Africans in their colonies. Thus, Richard Jobson said in 1623, in response to a suggestion to buy slaves, "We were a people, who did not deale in any such commodities, neither did we buy or sell one another, or any that had our owne shapes."[140] Moreover, indentured servitude met most of the early needs of the English colonizers of America. Land was available to those who had capital, and labor was relatively scarce.[141] Three primary forms of labor emerged: temporary servitude, based on complex contractual arrangements; "free" wage labor, involving the contractual exchange of labor for a wage; and chattel slavery, which began with captivity, involved no contractual agreements between slaves and masters, and was the last to develop.[142]

This was the context in which a distinctly racialized form of slavery and the "race" concept and were introduced. With reference to the parallel development of slave societies by the English and Dutch in colonial America and at the Cape of Good Hope (South Africa), respectively, Fredrickson notes that these processes

> were conditioned on the crucial assumption that nonwhites were enslavable while Europeans were not. This presumption is sometimes seen as evidence of a conscious racism—a belief that whites were destined by God or nature to rule over peoples whose physical characteristics denoted their innate inferiority. But . . . [t]he evidence strongly suggests that Africans and other non-Europeans were initially enslaved not so much because of their color and physical type as because of their legal and cultural vulnerability. . . . The combination of heathenness and *de facto* captivity was what made people enslavable, not their pigmentation or other physical characteristics.[143]

Therefore, it is "misleading and anachronistic to read the overt physical racism that emerged later back into the thought of this era."[144] The available evidence also supports a more radical conclusion: that the very idea of distinct races, along with systematic racism, emerged largely in the transition from religious and cultural justifications for slavery to distinctly *racial* justifications for it.

The basic dynamics at work in the racialization of Negroes and whites in the seventeenth century were strikingly evident in the social, legal, and ideological shifts in the treatment of Negroes in England's Virginia colony. By the 1630s, poor Englishmen were arriving annually in Virginia "in large numbers, engaged to serve the existing planters for a term of years with the prospect of setting up their own households a few years later."[145] The colony's representative assembly secured certain basic liberties of Englishmen for all European immigrants, who eventually included people (mostly men in the early years) who were French, Spanish, Dutch, Turkish, Portuguese, and African. From the start, the status of the Africans, who were few in number until about 1640, was somewhat distinct from that of English and other European immigrants of the servant and laboring classes. Still, there is little evidence that they were treated much differently from other servants until after 1660. According to Edmund Morgan, "It seems clear that most of the Africans, perhaps all of them, came as slaves, a status that had become obsolete in England, while it was becoming the expected condition of Africans outside Africa and a good many inside. It is equally clear that a substantial number of Virginia's Negroes were free or became free. And all of them, whether servant, slave, or free, enjoyed most of the same rights and duties as other Virginians."[146]

Virginia's planter class began to change this situation after 1660, when perpetual hereditary slavery for Africans was first written into Virginia law. In 1669, African slaves were first designated as chattel rather than as persons whose labor was the property of their masters.[147] Other components of racialized slavery emerged gradually after 1640. After 1640 there emerged "a growing number of freemen who had served their terms but who were unable to afford land of their own except on the frontiers or in the interior." Some of them resigned themselves to working for others for wages, which was understood to be something less than a truly independent existence.[148] This growing class of economically marginal English Virginians worried those "planters who had made it to the top or who had arrived in the colonies already on top, with ample supplies of servants and capital."[149] This threat materialized in Bacon's Rebellion of 1676. The largest popular uprising in the colonies before the American Revolution, it joined poor European Americans and African Americans in a fight to abolish servitude.[150]

This *class*-based alliance of European Americans and African Americans indicates that the notion of a "white race did not yet exist" in the American colonies.[151] The Virginia planter class's response to Bacon's Rebellion, however, was instrumental in consolidating white and black racial identities. The planters recognized that they could not continually respond to discontent among a growing class of poor Englishmen with repression. Therefore, they began to rely much more fully on the labor of enslaved Africans, the cheapest source of labor available to them, which enabled them to avoid actively repressing other English settlers. "In the last years of the seventeenth century they bought [slaves] in such numbers that slaves probably constituted a majority or near majority of the labor force by 1700. . . . The increase in the importation of slaves was matched by a decrease in the importation of indentured servants and consequently a decrease in the dangerous number of new freedmen who annually emerged seeking a place in society that they would be unable to achieve."[152]

Some commentators have questioned whether the planters' increased reliance on slaves was part of a conscious strategy to avoid importing new indentured servants from Europe.[153] A few facts are beyond dispute, however: the planters purchased increasing numbers of slaves from Africa after the 1670s, and by 1700 slaves constituted nearly a majority of the labor force of Virginia; there *was* a corresponding decrease in the importation of indentured servants; and, perhaps most significant, new laws in Virginia (and in other colonies) after 1670 expressly codified racialized (i.e., primarily Negro) slavery.[154] For instance, Virginia's second statutory definition of a slave, in 1682, "awkwardly attempted to rest enslavement on religious difference while excluding from possible enslavement all heathens who were not Indian or Negro." This Virginia law (and others like it) left open the question of whether or not Indians or Negroes who converted to Christianity could be kept as slaves. By around the end of the century new laws in Maryland, New York, Virginia, North and South Carolina, and New Jersey answered this question affirmatively: they held that masters were not required free slaves who had become Christians.[155] A whole series of laws passed in Virginia between 1668 and 1723, including the slave code of 1705, testified to the planter class's aim "not only to impose lifetime hereditary bond-servitude on African-Americans, but to implement it by a system of *racial oppression,* expressed in laws against *free* African-Americans."[156]

In the second half of the seventeenth century the gradual racialization of laws and social relations in American colonies was also expressed in new laws that prohibited sexual relations and marriage between English colonists and Negroes. In 1662, the Virginia assembly doubled the usual fine for "fornication" in the case of "any Christian [who] shall committ Fornication with a negro man or women"; in 1663, Bermuda prohibited "all sexual relations between whites and Negroes"; a 1664 Maryland law banned marriages of "freeborne English women forgetfull of their free Condicion . . . with Negro slaves"; and a 1681 Maryland law described marriages between "white" women and "Negroes" as "always to the Satisfaction of theire Lascivious and Lustful desires, and to the disgrace not only of the English butt allso of many other Christian nations."[157] In 1692, a revised Maryland law against miscegenation dropped the term *Christian* but retained reference to *"white* and *English."*[158]

The racialization of slavery thus involved the de facto invention of a pan-European "white race." In the course of the seventeenth century, English colonizers in North America gradually accepted that the colonies would not remain exclusively English. Virginia enacted legislation in 1671 to support the naturalization of all legal aliens so that they would gain "all such liberties, privileges, immunities whatever, as a naturall borne Englishman is capable of." Maryland adopted similar provisions.[159] Scottish and (especially) Irish servants were sometimes treated harshly, but they were never reduced to a condition of "perpetual slavery," a condition that was reserved for Negroes and, occasionally, Indians.[160] As a result, the institutionalization of racialized slavery in the American colonies in the late seventeenth and early eighteenth centuries joined all the European settlers —regardless of national origins or social class—as members of one white race, at least for the time being (see chapter 4). Segal explains, "the rendering of 'Africans' as a singular race-class [i.e., both Negroes and slaves] meant that settlers from Europe—their class diversity notwithstanding—became a singular race." The rigid European status hierarchy produced by feudalism was exteriorized in the American colonies; that is, "hierarchy was inscribed solely beyond the boundary of what became the collective, racial self—'the white [person].'"[161] The term *white* came into wide use across England's American colonies after about 1680, which marked a further step in the elaboration of racial discourse and race consciousness.[162]

This creation of the white race had a further notable effect, particularly in England's American colonies: it tended to obscure the significance of class differences among those people who were now called "white." Basically, the creation of racialized distinctions produced a kind of "aristocracy of the skin" for those included in the white race.[163] This racialized "ennoblement," however, was different from that characteristic of the earlier Europe feudal hierarchies: "white" racialized identity, like ennoblement within the *ancien regime,* "was a basis for claiming full political rights, for claiming to be subordinate to none." At the same time, unlike the hereditary status hierarchy of feudalism, the new racialized status hierarchy was embedded within an emerging class structure that promised opportunities for equal citizenship, economic and political independence, and social mobility but reserved these prerogatives exclusively for members of the white race (mainly for white *men*).[164] Distinctions between propertied and propertyless whites as well as between large- and small-scale property holders were central to the emerging system of *class* stratifi-cation. Basic to the new *racialized* status hierarchy was a distinction be-tween the poorest member of the dominant racialized group (i.e., the white race) and all members, however propertied, of the oppressed racial-ized groups.[165] Moreover, the new system of racialized domination secured a virtual monopoly of political power and material resources and oppor-tunities for members of the white race.[166] Yet, for lower-class members of the white race, the new racialized order of "white skin privilege" worked to conceal constraints to social mobility that were endemic to the rising class structure.

There were similar patterns of racialization in Portuguese and Dutch colonies. In the fifteenth and sixteenth centuries, Portuguese and Dutch colonial encounters were shaped by their sense of their religious and cul-tural superiority compared to the peoples of Africa, Asia, and the Ameri-cas. By the end of the seventeenth century, Dutch and Portuguese colo-nialists increasingly used racial language, such as Portuguese references to "Asiatic races."[167]

Ultimately, the enslavement of Africans in the Americas by European elites in the sixteenth and seventeenth centuries generated not only a dis-tinctly racialized form of slavery but also modern racism and the concept of race. As David Brion Davis says, "[S]lavery produced racism, in the sense that the negative stereotypes that had been applied to slaves and serfs since antiquity, regardless of ethnicity, were ultimately transferred to black slaves and then to most people of African descent after bondage be-came almost exclusively confined to blacks."[168] The institutionalized en-slavement of Africans also contributed to the development of the concept of race. That is, in the process of codifying and rationalizing racialized slavery, European elites—especially the English colonial planter class—spurred the crystallization of the modern "race" concept. Armed with this concept, European elites created a new system of social stratification based on the idea that human beings are divisible into distinct types (i.e., races) comprising inherited physical characteristics that correspond to different and unequal characters and abilities. All that remained for the full elabo-ration of the concept of race was for intellectuals and scientists working in the fields of "natural history" and biology to use the term to classify sup-posedly distinct types of human beings in a systematic way.

## The Beginnings of Modern Scientific Racialism

Efforts to classify human "races" were a by-product of how new ideas about race in the late seventeenth and early eighteenth centuries were incorporated into the broader project to classify the natural world. The latter was part of the modern Scientific Revolution. The development of the field of natural history in the seventeenth century was an important part of this process. It gave special importance to visible markers of similarity and difference among the myriad parts of nature.[169] In the sixteenth and early seventeenth centuries, books about the natural world bore titles such as *History of the Nature of Birds* (Belon) and *Admirable History of Plants* (Duret); in 1657, Joannes Jonston published his *Natural History of Quadrupeds,* marking the onset of a new way of conceiving of nature historically.[170] Natural history addressed the place of human beings along with plants, animals, and minerals in the natural order of things. It involved a process of naming and classifying living creatures to establish a descriptive order that clarified the various relationships of affinity and difference among them.[171] This new scientific enterprise included work by John Ray and Joseph de Tournefort in the 1680s and 1690s to establish new criteria for classifying plants and animals, and the comparative anatomist Edward Tyson's 1699 argument that the orangutan (his "pygmy") was an "intermediate Link between Ape and Man" in the "Chain of Creation."[172] This classificatory impulse culminated in the Swedish botanist Carolus Linnaeus's *System of Nature* (1735)—a comprehensive classification of the hierarchy of being that encompassed minerals, nonhuman animals, and human beings. With Linnaeus, mature natural history of the eighteenth century also sought to classify distinct "varieties" (or races) of human beings (see chapter 2).

The natural history endeavor to distinguish and classify races of human beings was partially prefigured by a few sixteenth- and seventeenth-century writers on anatomy and nature such as Andreas Vesalius (1514–64) and William Petty (1623–87). Vesalius, a Flemish founder of the modern science of anatomy, advanced claims about the relationship between human skull shapes and national origins that anticipated later racialist craniology. "It seems that certain nations," he wrote,

> have something peculiar in the shape of the head. The heads of the Genoese, and more particularly of Greeks and Turks, almost exhibit a round shape. To this also (which not a few of them think elegant and consider to

be well adapted to the turbans which they use in various ways) the mid-wives sometimes contribute at the urgent request of the mother. The Germans, indeed, have a very flattened occiput and a broad head, because the boys always lie on their backs in their cradles.[173]

Vesalius combined comparative anatomy with an interest in the different customs or ways of life of different nations. Therefore, his approach was distinct from later racialist thought, especially insofar as he regarded the varying head shapes as a consequence of different national customs rather than vice versa (see chapters 2 and 3).

The thought of Petty—English political economist, adventurer, physician, statistician, professor of anatomy and music, and follower of Francis Bacon's "new philosophy"—was closely related to scientific racialism.[174] Petty, a strong advocate for English colonization of Ireland in this era, employed his talent for political economy and statistics in a 1662 proposal that slavery be instituted for "insolent Thieves" in England.[175] He also articulated basic features of the emerging racialist natural history of the late seventeenth century. In 1676–77, he put forward a rudimentary account of distinct human races, which he conceived within a broader theory of "two Scales of animate beings"—that is, "of beings which act by souls."[176] He built upon the notion of a "Great Chain of Being," which held that all beings—from the simplest to the highest creatures, human beings—were linked to each other and to God in a fixed, hierarchical order. Each type of being was categorically distinct from the others, and there was no sense that any higher beings may have developed from any lower order of beings.[177] In the "higher" of his two scales of being, Petty saw a theistic order, with "the maker of the . . . visible world [at] the top and Man at the bottom." In his "lower" scale of earthly beings, he placed human beings, distinguished by capacities for speech and reason, on the top of the scale, with its bottom made up of "the smallest and simplest animall that man can discern."[178]

The "Lower Scale" encompassed "another Scale containing the Severall Stepps and gradations of improuvements which man hath made from the lowest and simplest condition that mankind was ever in, unto the highest."[179] There were several "species" or races of human beings, and the differences in size between the largest and smallest of them—"Gyants and Pigmyes"—corresponded to differences "also in the Memories, Witts, Judgments & withall in their external senses."[180] Along with these differences, there bee others more considerable, that is, between the Guiny Negros & the Middle Europeans; and of the Negros between those of Guiny and those who live about the Cape of Good Hope, which last are the Most beastlike of all the Souls [? Sorts] of Men whom our Travellers are well acquainted. I say that the Europeans do not onely differ from the aforementioned Africans in Collour, which is as much as white differs from black, but also in their Haire which differs as much as a straight line differs from a circle; but they also differ in the shape of their Noses, Lipps and cheek bones, as also in their skulls. They differ also in their Naturall Manners, & in the internall Qualities of their Minds.

Petty added that the peoples who lie in the "Northernmost parts of the Habitable world," including the Laplanders, "are a very mean sort of Men, both in their Statures and understanding."[181]

Seven years after Petty's speculations, the French physician François Bernier (1620–88) was the first writer to use the term *race* in something like the modern sense of "a major division of humanity displaying a distinctive combination of physical traits transmitted through a line of descent."[182] Bernier, who visited Poland, the Near East, and southwest Asia, including Palestine, Syria, Egypt, and India, became famous in France as a travel writer. He served for several years as a physician in the court of the "Grand Mogul" Aurangzeb in Agra (Uttar Pradesh) and traveled to Kashmir and Lahore. He later returned to France by way of Bengal, Surat (on India's west coast), and Persia and wrote about his travels in *Histoire de la dernière révolution des états du Grand Mogol* (1670–71).[183]

Based on his travels, Bernier anonymously proposed his racial classification, "A New Division of the Earth according to the Different Species or Races of Men," in the French *Journal des Scavans* in 1684. He did not use the term *race* precisely or address how his human "races" fit into the broader scheme of nature in the manner of the major eighteenth-century theorists of race, Linnaeus, Buffon, Kant, and Blumenbach.[184] Still, Bernier's scheme marked a break among European writers from "sacred history" of human beings, which relied on the Bible, to natural history (although many raciologists continued to use biblical assumptions implicitly); and his text seems to have had a significant influence on the racial categories that Blumenbach and others later elaborated. Blumenbach himself read and cited Bernier, and the boundaries of Bernier's notion of a European-centered but not exclusively European race largely anticipated the geographical boundaries of Blumenbach's Caucasian race (see chapter 2).

Bernier divided the world's peoples into "four or five species or races of men . . . whose difference is so remarkable that it may be properly made use of as the foundation for a new division of the earth."[185] He used the term *species* (*espèces*) loosely and more or less interchangeably with the term *race*, but he was a *monogenist*—a believer in the basic unity and common origins of all human beings—who did not regard his races as separate biological species.[186] Therefore, where he spoke of different species of human beings his meaning is best understood in terms of the nascent "race" concept. Bernier's first "race" (he did not name his races) included the people of

> France, Spain, England, Denmark, Sweden, Germany, Poland, and gener-
> ally all Europe, except a part of Muscovy. To this may be added a small
> part of Africa, that is from the kingdoms of Fez, Morocco, Algiers, Tunis,
> and Tripoli up to the Nile; and also a good part of Asia, as the empire of
> the Grand Seignior with the three Arabias, the whole of Persia, the states
> of the Grand Mogul, the Kingdom of Golconda, that of Visapore, the
> Maldivias, and a part of the kingdoms of Araucan, Pegu, Siam, Sumatra,
> Bantan and Borneo.[187]

His rationale for including in this first race the northern part of Africa and "a good part of Asia" (mainly western and southern regions) along with most of Europe is telling, especially when we consider more fully his classificatory criteria:

> [A]lthough the Egyptians, for instance, and the Indians are very black, or
> rather copper-coloured, that colour is only an accident in them, and it
> comes because they are constantly exposed to the sun; for those individu-
> als who take care of themselves, and who are not obliged to expose them-
> selves so often as the lower class, are not darker than many Spaniards. It is
> true that most Indians have something very different from us in the shape
> of their face, and in their colour which often comes very near yellow; but
> that does not seem enough to make them a species apart, or else it would
> be necessary to make one of the Spaniards, another of the Germans, and
> so on with the several nations of Europe.[188]

In short, while these various peoples differed somewhat in skin tone and in facial shapes, these differences were only superficial. In particular, those among them with darker skin tones—Egyptians and Indians—were not significantly darker than the other peoples; their evident darkness was merely "accidental."

Significantly, Bernier supported this point with an appeal to *class* differences: his remark that those Egyptians and Indians "who are not obliged to expose themselves [to the sun] so often as the lower class are not darker than many Spaniards" is indicative of the ways in which claims about "racial" affinities or differences between groups frequently have been confused with, or served as tropes for, *real* (but changeable) differences of class, ethnicity, culture, or religion.[189] His remark echoed common symbolism in medieval Europe concerning peasants, who constituted the vast majority of the population. They were often regarded contemptuously by the aristocracy, clergy, and commercial classes, even though these elites relied on their labor. Because of this duality of elite distance from and dependence on the peasants, medieval European images depicted peasants as filthy, stupid, and bestial but also as pious and close to God. As I noted earlier, European elites also appealed to the biblical curse on Ham's son Canaan to explain and justify the subordination of peasants. In Bernier's native France, moreover, serfs and peasants were "often depicted as dark-skinned or 'black,' either by reason of their labor in the sun and their proximity to the earth, or as a sign of their overall hideousness."[190] Such ideas are a likely source for the later theories that *upper-caste* Hindus (but not all Hindus) were members of the Caucasian race.

Bernier's understanding of racial difference becomes clearer when we turn to his typology of four other races. His "second species" encompassed the peoples who inhabited the *rest* of Africa:

> 1. Their thick lips and squab noses, there being very few among them who have aquiline noses or lips of moderate thickness. 2. The blackness which is peculiar to them, and which is not caused by he sun, as many think. . . . The cause must be sought for in the peculiar textures of their bodies, or in the seed, or in the blood—which last are, however, of the same color as everywhere else. 3. Their skin, which is oily smooth, and polished, excepting the places which are burnt with the sun. 4. The three or four hairs of beard. 5. Their hair, which is not properly hair, but rather a species of wool . . . and, finally, their teeth whiter than the finest ivory, their tongue and all the interior of their mouth and their lips as red as coral.[191]

He delineated more succinctly the distinguishing characteristics of his two other races. The third included the peoples in "part of the kingdoms of

Araucan and Siam, the islands of Sumatra and Borneo, the Philippines, Japan, the kingdom of Pegu, Tonkin, Cochin-China, China, Chinese Tartary, Georgia . . . , the Usbek, Turkistan, Zaquetay, and a small part of Muscovy, the little Tartars and Turcomans who live along the Euphrates towards Aleppo." All these people "are truly white; but they have broad shoulders, a flat face, a small squab nose, little pig's eyes long and deep set, and three hairs of beard."[192] The Laplanders ("Lapps") made up his fourth race. They were "thick" and "stunted creatures" with "a face immensely elongated; very ugly and partaking much of the bear," although he admitted to having only limited experience with them.[193] Finally, he considered but rejected the thought that indigenous Americans constituted a fifth "species" or "race." Most of them were "olive-coloured, and their faces modelled in a different way from ours. Still I do not find the difference sufficiently great to make of them a peculiar species different from ours." To support this claim he added that as among Europeans there were great differences among native Americans in "stature, the turn of the face, the color and the hair."[194]

In light of later efforts at racial classification, a few interrelated features of Bernier's typology are especially noteworthy. First, in contrast to some later classifications, his European-centered race included peoples from noncontiguous (and rather widely scattered) areas. He divided peoples from several kingdoms—Araucan, Pegu, Siam, Sumatra, Bantan, and Borneo—into two separate races, and he included Georgians (of the Caucasus) and part of Muscovy (Russia) in his third race rather than his first. The impetus for these moves appears to stem from the two criteria with which he distinguished his first species (or race) from his four others: a Eurocentric aesthetic of "beauty" or "handsomeness" and the presence or absence of the accoutrements of "civilization" as Europeans understood them. Bernier used the aesthetic criteria—chiefly facial features, skin color, and stature—explicitly and the "civilizational" standard only implicitly. Indeed, with a couple of exceptions he refrained from speculating about any intrinsic moral or intellectual traits.[195]

With regard to his aesthetic criteria, while Bernier's first race was not exclusively European, he included other peoples in it (Indians and Egyptians among them; native Americans more provisionally) insofar as they looked like Europeans.[196] Moreover, he not only listed this race first but also made it the standard against which he measured the others.[197] He discussed aesthetic differences mostly with respect to women, saying that "beautiful and ugly ones are found everywhere"; yet he judged beauty by a standard that favored "aquiline noses" and thin lips that were more common to the peoples who make up his first race. Thus, he noted several "very handsome" women among "the blacks of Africa, who had not those thick lips and that squab nose" characteristic of most of black Africans.[198] He spoke of "beautiful brunettes" in the Indies and women of Cashmere who were especially striking, "for besides being as white as those of Europe, they have a soft face, and are a beautiful height."[199] And, foreshadowing another feature of Blumenbach's classification scheme, he mentioned the handsomeness of people from the Caucasus ("handsome slaves who are brought [to Persia] from Georgia and Circassia").[200]

## *"Race" and Racialism, circa 1684*

Bernier's racial classification typified the new way of "knowing" human life that was introduced by natural history and modern racialism. This naturalist view challenged existing sacred and theistic conceptions of human nature and history, notably the biblical viewpoint. In addition, Bernier's specific scheme of four (or five) distinct races of human beings (and others that followed it) represented a big step away from what C. Loring Brace calls "the peasant perspective" on human diversity. From this Old World perspective, "the normal range of human experience was limited to what could be seen in that segment of the world lying within a radius of 25 miles from the place of one's birth"; various human groups were "essentially the same" in appearance, and the perceived differences between groups of people tended to concern "custom and dress and traditions of behavior and speech."[201]

The new discernment of racial differences coincided with the intensification of long-distance oceangoing travel by Europeans. This put Europeans into contact with peoples who visibly differed from them not only culturally and technologically but also in physical appearance. European travelers' reports from distant lands produced a composite picture of human physical differentiation that overshadowed the actual gradation of physiognomic characteristics from one localized human community to the next—something that was evident to such earlier observers as Herodotus, Marco Polo, and Ibn Batutah, who traveled mostly overland.[202] Moreover, the way in which Europeans dominated these new contacts with Africans, Asians, and Americans fueled their religiously and culturally based sense of their own "innate" superiority.

By the end of the seventeenth century, against the backdrop of the At-lantic slave trade, European colonial expansion, and a growing tendency for Europeans to perceive native Americans as fundamentally different from themselves, European naturalists had begun to use "race" and "racial classification" to give these prejudices scientific credence.[203] These preju-dices also informed their science. Racial classifiers such as Bernier and those who followed his initiative during the next century (Linnaeus, Buf-fon, Kant, Blumenbach) were predisposed toward racial classifications that placed "white" peoples such as themselves above "nonwhite" peoples. Thus they began to align science behind new ideas of white supremacy. Simulta-neously, Bernier's emphasis on perceived physical similarities and differ-ences between people led him to refine Eurocentric racialism in an influ-ential way. He included not just nearly "all Europe" but also parts of Africa and Asia in his first ("white") race. (Recall that he also describes his third race as "truly white.") Linnaeus (among others) would later reject this move in favor of a ("white") European "variety" of *homo sapiens*; but Blu-menbach would incorporate it into his "Caucasian race" category (see chapter 2).

Meanwhile, the period of European history from roughly 1000 to 1684 left another formative racial legacy: enduring social, political, ethnic, and religious cleavages *within* Europe that had influenced the development of racial thought. These divisions—including the perceived otherness of Jews, Muslims, Slavs, and the Irish, along with presumed distinctions be-tween Gauls and Franks in France and Normans and Saxons in England—were not initially construed as racial distinctions. These divisions shaped subsequent debates about the racial identity of Europe's Jews, however, and in relation to the rise of nationalism and other social changes in the second half of the nineteenth century, such divisions were routinely given racial meaning by European race scientists (see chapter 4).

# 2

# Enlightenment Science and the Invention of the "Caucasian Race," 1684–1795

Only the Sciences distinguish Wild people, Barbarians and Hottentots, from us; just as a thorny sour Wild apple is distinguished from a
tasty Renette only through cultivation.
>                                    —Carolus Linnaeus, "Tal" (1759)[1]

[A]ll the accounts [of nature] . . . which one adopts, even with the
most critical judgment possible, from others, are in reality, for the
truth-seeking investigators of nature, nothing more and nothing further than a kind of symbolical writing, which he can only so far subscribe to with good conscience, as they actually coincide with the
open book of nature.
>                    —Johann Friedrich Blumenbach, *Contributions to
>                                             Natural History* (1806)[2]

The "Caucasian race" category was a product of the European
Enlightenment and late-eighteenth-century natural history. It was introduced about one hundred years after François Bernier's 1684 "New Division of the Earth," which featured a Europe-centered "white" race. The
boundaries that Bernier surmised for this race, his first, reached beyond
Europe in a way that foreshadowed the boundaries of Johann Friedrich
Blumenbach's "Caucasian" race. Still, Blumenbach's eventual use of the
word *Caucasian,* referring to the Caucasus region between Europe and
Asia (or in central Eurasia), to designate roughly the same peoples is puz-
zling. It went against the grain of then-current European elites' ideas about
Christendom and European civilizational superiority, although the Cau-
casian nations of Georgia and Armenia had long-standing Christian tradi-

tions (see chapter 1). Indeed, during the century separating Bernier and Blumenbach, the leading race scientists—Carolus Linnaeus, George Buffon, and Immanuel Kant—designated these peoples as *Homo europaeus* (Linnaeus), "white Europeans" (Buffon), and "the white race" (Kant).

In all these cases, European race scientists were especially interested in racial classifications that hierarchically distinguished fair-skinned ("white") European people, such as themselves, from the "nonwhite," non-European peoples whom Europeans were increasingly dominating globally. And all the leading racial classifications served this purpose well, while positing somewhat different racial boundaries for "whites" and Europeans. In each case, moreover, racial "whiteness" and "white supremacy" were given scientific credence (with the relatively egalitarian Blumenbach being a partial exception). Furthermore, in an era when European peoples were increasingly rallying behind new liberal and egalitarian ideas concerning "the rights of Man," the new sciences of race—natural history, anthropology, and ethnology—claimed that there were natural (i.e., racial) limits to which peoples were suited for freedom and equality.

The idea of a Caucasian racial branch of humanity was first used, though rather crudely, by the German philosopher Christoph Meiners in 1785. Meiners posited two great "branches" (*Stämme*) of human beings: Caucasian and Mongolian. Soon thereafter Blumenbach, one of the founders of modern anthropology, adopted the term in a narrower and far more influential way to designate one of five principal "varieties" of human beings, in the third edition of his treatise *On the Natural Variety of Mankind* (1795).[3] Blumenbach's enduring racial classification gave the notion of a Caucasian race something like its still-current meaning and boundaries.

This chapter explores the social, political, and cultural factors that paved the way for the emergence of the Caucasian race. To fully appreciate this event, we need to consider the social and political context for the eighteenth-century development of "race" science in the work of Linneaus, Buffon, Kant, and Blumenbach. We also need to consider the ways in which Blumenbach's "Caucasian race" idea built upon and refined the Eurocentric raciology of Linneaus, Buffon, Kant, and others.

## *"Race" in the Eighteenth Century*

The development of modern scientific racialism and popular racism in Europe and North America coincided with the rise of universalistic ideals of human freedom and equality. This simultaneous rise of egalitarian and racial theories was no random coincidence. One sign of this parallelism is that Bernier's 1684 "A New Division of the Earth" (see chapter 1) was published in the same decade as one of the germinal works of liberalism: *Two Treatises of Government* (1689), by the English empiricist philosopher John Locke. While Bernier divided the earth's peoples into a handful of distinct "races or species," Locke famously declared that "all mankind" was by nature free, "equal and independent."[4]

Bernier's and Locke's arguments represented two faces of the Enlightenment's legacy that have always been in tension with each other.[5] Enlightenment thought included, on the one hand, an impulse to differentiate, classify, and systematize the various elements of the natural world. One guiding aim was to gain knowledge that would enable human beings to "rationally regulat[e] their interchange with nature," in Karl Marx's later phrase.[6] On the other hand, the Enlightenment postulated a universalistic and egalitarian ethos that has buttressed struggles for individual freedom, equality, democracy, and universal human rights. Tensions have arisen insofar as the first tendency has generated efforts among human beings not only to dominate nonhuman nature but also systematically to differentiate among groups of people in ways that have rationalized hierarchy, inequality, and domination between groups.[7]

These two faces of the Enlightenment were evident in affinities between Locke and Bernier. Bernier affirmed the idea of a common origin of all human beings (monogenism); yet he also cautioned against theories about "Man in general" and posited some basic "natural" differences of character and capacities among his "races."[8] Locke, who was acquainted with Bernier and some of his writings, combined a defense of human equality and condemnation of slavery ("so vile and miserable an estate of Man")[9] with ethnocentric caveats: he held shares in the Royal Africa Company, the main business of which was the slave trade; he helped draft *The Fundamental Constitutions of Carolina* (1669), which declared, "Every freeman of Carolina shall have absolute power and authority over his negro slaves";[10] and he defended slavery for Africans on the grounds that it saved them from (in Anthony Pagden's words) "the worse fate of eternal damnation and barbarism."[11] Yet Locke's conflicting ideas about slavery were of a distinctly transitional sort: he justified some slavery *without* the concept of race, but his prejudices concerning Africans represented the kind of English (and European) cultural chauvinism that was in the process of becoming racialized.[12]

What Winthrop Jordan says about the development of Anglo-American racialist thought in the late eighteenth century applies to this period's social and political dynamics more broadly: "[T]he prevalence of ordered arrangement and hierarchical imagery was connected with a feeling, which had been strengthening for more than a century, that the arrangement of society was becoming disorderly and rather the opposite of hierarchical."[13] The racial classifiers attempted to give a naturalistic order to the increasingly disorderly human world. Carolus Linnaeus in particular extended the received idea of the "Great Chain of Being" into his influential comprehensive and hierarchical classification scheme, which included human beings along with all other known animals and plants.

Reflecting on why ideas about race and equality emerged in Europe simultaneously in this period, George Fredrickson explains:

> If a culture holds a premise of spiritual and temporal *inequality*, if a hierarchy exists that is unquestioned even by its lower-ranking members, as in the Indian caste system before the modern era, there is no incentive to deny the full humanity of underlings in order to treat them as impure or unworthy. If equality is the norm in the spiritual or temporal realms (or in both at the same time), and there are groups of people within the society who are so despised or disparaged that the upholders of the norms feel compelled to make them exceptions to the promise or realization of equality, they can be denied the prospect of equal status only if they allegedly possess some extraordinary deficiency that makes them less than fully human.[14]

Fredrickson notes that in Western cultures the presumption of human equality can be traced back to before modern revolutionary declarations of equality, to the Christian doctrine of the crucifixion. The latter "offered grace to all willing to receive it and made all Christian believers equal before God."[15] The modern invention of the "race" concept coincided with the secular diffusion of the idea of basic human equality in early modern Europe.

More specifically, the invention of the "race" concept was connected to Europe's transition from feudalism to capitalism. Kenan Malik observes that Enlightenment liberalism and emerging capitalism "established for the first time in history the possibility of human equality but did so in social circumstances that constrained its expression."[16] Enlightenment thinkers and advocates of capitalism appealed to certain egalitarian ideals, such as the liberal-meritocratic notion of careers open to talent, but these ideals had to be reconciled with deeply unequal features of the actual social world.[17] These worldly inequalities encompassed not only racialized slavery in the Americas and Europe's colonial relations in Africa, Asia, and the Americas but also the great social and economic transformations within Europe at this time. As Malik says, "[I]t is not 'race' that gives rise to inequality but inequality that gives rise to 'race.' The nature of modern society has created inequalities between different groups and these have come to be perceived in racial terms."[18]

Europe's new competitive commercial ethos was becoming increasingly prominent in the eighteenth century, as reflected in Anglo-Dutch writer Bernard Mandeville's *The Fable of the Bees* (1714) and Adam Smith's *The Wealth of Nations* (1776). In the emerging commercial capitalist order, social status was becoming less a matter of inherited position in a fixed feudal structure and increasingly the result of people being "winners" or "losers" in competitive market transactions.[19] People entered this competition, however, from sharply unequal positions. For instance, between roughly 1590 and 1720, peasants, who remained the vast majority of Europe's population, found the land that they worked basically expropriated from them. This process varied from region to region, but by 1650 most of Europe was "dominated by large landowners and their economic allies, the large-scale tenant farmers who managed the actual business of farming and marketing. Most peasants had become essentially wage laborers, owning cottages and small amounts of land, but needing to work for others in order to survive."[20]

The concept of race provided a means for eighteenth-century European and Anglo-American elites to reconcile emerging egalitarian ideals with the new and pervasive sources of inequality and social instability. Thus, while Thomas Jefferson declared that "all men are created equal," he insisted, in the same breath, that some were "racially" deficient.[21] Rather than fault changeable social institutions for existing inequalities, the racialist and racist defenders of the emerging commercial order could argue that it provided all persons with equal opportunity to develop their specific talents and abilities. In their view, some people were innately less capable than others of realizing full equality. That is, human "races" could be ranked according to degrees of "humanness."

This inegalitarianism was reinforced by Europeans' colonization of Africa, Asia, the Americas, and the Pacific islands and racialized enslavement of sub-Saharan Africans. As Eric Voegelin observes, the scientific and philosophical problem of the nature of human beings in this period "developed into an ordering of the physical diversity of humanity and thus became connected with the classification of nature due to a particular historical fact, namely, the expansion of the geographic horizon, of the knowledge of [humankind], through the growing wealth of material provided by travelogues ever since the Renaissance."[22]

While these social and political circumstances shaped the race science that culminated in the invention of "Caucasian race" idea, race thinking, once begun, also started to generate its own debates and idiosyncrasies. Two competing theories, monogenism and polygenism, framed the development of racial thought in the eighteenth century. As I will explain shortly, Linnaeus, Buffon, Kant, and Blumenbach brought new scientific rigor to natural history's practice of racially classifying human beings. All monogenists, these thinkers affirmed the biblical view of a single human origin and systematically positioned human beings within the broader animal kingdom. They used "race" to signify natural divisions within a singular human species. "Race" for them indicated something like "varieties" or "subspecies" of the human species.

Others, such as the French provocateur Voltaire, were polygenists. They more radically contested received biblical assumptions about human commonality. Voltaire claimed that "Negroes" and the "Indians" of the Americas were separate *species* from Europeans, with distinct origins: "The negro race is a species of men as different from ours as the breed of spaniels is from that of greyhounds"; the negro intellect was "greatly inferior" to that of the European, and Jews also possessed innate, undesirable traits.[23] Another polygenist, Lord Kames (Henry Home), the Scottish jurist and man of letters, challenged Buffon's claim that "species" are composed of organisms capable of producing fertile offspring, insisting that the animal world includes different species that can interbreed to produce fertile offspring: "There are different species of men as well as of dogs: a mastiff differs not more from a spaniel, than a white man from a negro, or a Laplander from a Dane."[24] Unlike Voltaire, Kames attempted to square his account of race with the story of human creation in Genesis.[25] Both thinkers, however, conceived race to signify deep, intractable differences among unequal species of human beings.[26]

One of the most notorious polygenists, Edward Long, an English judge and defender of slavery, held that orangutans along with black Africans were intermediate species between *Homo sapiens* and the lower primates.[27] Long's *History of Jamaica* (1774) was cited frequently by other anthropological writers, and it was used in the 1830s by white American Southerners to defend slavery, based on its claims about the innate "Negro" inferiority.[28] Starting with "pure white" Europeans as his standard of human perfection, Long regarded the "Aethiopian" as "a separate species of the same genus" and as "void of genius, and . . . almost incapable of making any progress in civility and science."[29] This polygenist view had some earlier precedents, but due to the widespread biblical assumption of a single human creation it remained a minority view among eighteenth-century Europeans.[30]

For the time being, the Enlightenment emphasis on universal human reason and the influence of education and environment on human character and intelligence undercut the influence of polygenism. Most Enlightenment thinkers eschewed ideas of innate racial superiority and inferiority. German philosopher Gottfried Leibniz rejected even Bernier's largely descriptive attempt at racial classification: "[A] certain traveler . . . divided man into certain tribes, races or classes. He made a special race of Lapps or Samoyedes, another of the Chinese and their neighbors, another of the Caffes and Hottentots." Leibniz acknowledged certain differences in appearance and disposition among the world's peoples but argued that there was "no reason why all men who inhabit the earth should not be of the same race, which has been altered by different climates."[31]

## Linnaeus and Human "Races" in the Classification of Nature

Carolus Linnaeus of Sweden (1707–78), a pastor's son and botanist, pioneered the comprehensive classification of the natural world. "The study of natural history," he said in his major work *Systema Naturae* (1735), "is simple, beautiful, and instructive in the collection, arrangement, and exhibition of the various productions of the earth."[32] Linnaeus built upon the Christian idea of the Great Chain of Being to claim the natural world is divided into "three great kingdoms": minerals, vegetables, and animals. He held that all elements of nature have fixed places in the natural order, with human beings having pride of place:[33]

> Man, the last and best created works, formed after the image of his Maker, endowed with a portion of intellectual divinity, the governor and subjugator of all other beings, is, by his wisdom alone, able to form just conclusions from such things as present themselves to the senses, which can only

consist of bodies merely natural. Hence the first step of wisdom is to know these bodies, by the marks imprinted on them by nature and to affix to every object its proper name.[34]

Linnaeus began with the ambition merely to "read nature's Book" and translate it into plain language that reflected the "natural" order.[35] This "self-consciously artificial system" included a "binomial nomenclature, designating each species of flora and fauna by a two-word code consisting of the name of its genus and a species epithet."[36] This artificial taxonomy abstracted from just a few distinguishing characteristics—such as the reproduction parts of flowering plants—to classify each species in relation to others.[37]

Linnaeus continued to revise his taxonomy of the natural world through thirteen editions of his *Systema Naturae* (1735–88, with the last published posthumously) in light of ever-increasing anthropological data and the ongoing discovery of new species. He remained consistent, however, in his basic propositions, and his classification of human beings lent support to the idea that the "highest" of human "varieties" should be "the governor and subjugator of" the "lesser" varieties. Initially, he identified four varieties of *Homo sapiens* within the Order of "Anthropomorpha": *Homo sapiens europaeus albus, Homo sapiens americanus rubescens, Homo sapiens asiaticus fuscus,* and *Homo sapiens africanus niger.*[38] Later, in the influential tenth edition of *Systema naturae,* he replaced the order "Anthropomorpha" with a new order, "Primates," and redivided the genus *Homo* into four major "varieties"—*Americanus, Europaeus, Asiaticus,* and *Afer*—and three "species," *Ferus* (Wild Man), *Monstrosus,* and *Troglodytes*:

MAMMALIA
I. PRIMATES.
Foreteeth, upper 4, parallel
Pectoral mammae, 2
1. HOMO *Know Thyself*
    SAPIENS.   1. Homo Diurnal; varying in culture, place.
    *Ferus*      Four-footed, mute, hairy.
    *American*  Reddish, choleric, erect.
               *Hair*: black, straight, thick.
               *Nostrils*: wide; *Face*: harsh.
               *Beard*: scanty.

|          | *Obstinate,* merry, free. |
|----------|---------------------------|
|          | *Paints* himself with fine red lines. |
|          | *Regulated* by custom. |
| *European* | White, sanguine, muscular. |
|          | *Hair:* flowing, long; *Eyes:* blue. |
|          | *Gentle,* acute, inventive. |
|          | *Covered* with close[-fitting] vestments. |
|          | *Governed* by laws. |
| *Asiatic* | Sallow, melancholy, stiff. |
|          | *Hair:* black; Eyes: dark. |
|          | *Severe,* haughty, avaricious. |
|          | *Covered* with loose garments. |
|          | *Ruled* by opinion. |
| *African* | Black, phlegmatic, indolent. |
|          | *Hair:* black, frizzled; *Skin:* silky; *Nose:* flat; *Lips:* tumid. |
|          | *Women* without shame; *Mammae* lactate profusely. |
|          | *Crafty,* lazy, negligent. |
|          | *Anoints* himself with grease. |
|          | *Governed* by caprice. |
| *Monstrous* | Varies according to region (a) and species (b, c). |
| *Troglodytes* | a. Small, agile, timid mountain-dweller. |
|          | Large, lazy Patagonians. |
|          | 2. Homo nocturnal |
| (Cave-dwelling Man) | Homo sylvestris Orang Outang.[39] |

Linnaeus expressly treated his four varieties of human beings as parts of the larger natural world in the order of primates.[40] While he never clearly articulated the meaning of his "variety" in relation to "race" (a term he did not use) and "species," he did make clear a few key elements of his understanding.[41] Linnaeus and his followers held that the Chain of Being comprised distinct and hierarchically ranked living entities.[42] With his classification of human beings in the order of "Primates" and in positing at least two distinct species in the genus *Homo* (i.e., *Homo sapiens* and *Homo troglodytes*), his framework opened the door to polygenism, despite his avowed monogenism.[43] In *Fauna Suecia* (*Swedish Fauna*, 1746), he famously maintained that he could find no traits that clearly distinguished the human species from apes.[44] The human capacity for speech was only a realized potentiality, "not a characteristic mark."[45] Linnaeus did hold that the capacity to reason distinguished the human species from other species: "[T]here is something in us, which cannot be seen, whence our knowledge of ourselves depends—that is, *reason*, the most noble thing of all, in which man excels to a most surpassing extent all other animals."[46] But, as Phillip Sloan says, "if reason was to be the only mark separating [humankind] from animal, this was, for Linnaeus, a graduated reason, in which one could follow a line of descent within the human species from *Homo sapiens albus* [white European] to *sapiens afer* [black African]."[47] Thus, Linnaeus's undeveloped notion of geographically diversified "varieties" of a singular human species was consistent with later theories that posited fundamental differences between human "races."

Linnaeus's contribution came largely at the level of classification. For him, the production of a rational and usable system of classification exhausted the work of natural history. He offered no cogent theoretical rationale for distinguishing one variety of human beings from another, and his classification of human varieties mixed together physical, characterological, and cultural traits without any clear indication of how these traits were related to each other.[48] Rather, he followed then-conventional geography to allot "four classes of inhabitants to the four quarters of the globe respectively," as Blumenbach later observed.[49] In all this, Linnaeus's scheme was Eurocentric in two respects: he construed his "white Europeans" as the superior variety; and the boundaries of his highest human variety coincided with the boundaries of Europe.

Linnaeus fleshed out the character and boundaries of his *Homo europaeus* and Europe through his commentary on the Laplanders (or Sami people), whom he visited briefly. Lapland had been colonized by the Swedes and Finns by the seventeenth and eighteenth centuries, and the Sami were sometimes forced to labor in Swedish mines.[50] Linnaeus occasionally sympathized with "the poor Lapps," sometimes romanticized them to his fellow Swedes as "our teacher" for their vigorous "natural" ways, and even adopted a faux Sami persona for himself for the frontpiece to his book *Flora Lapponica*—all without gaining any deep knowledge of the Sami.[51] Early on, he distinguished three or four varieties of Swedes according to physical and mental traits—Goths, Finns, Lapps, and a mixture of Goths and Finns (the Goths corresponded to the *Homo europaeus* in his broader classification); and he eventually included the indigenous Lapps within his abnormal category of the "Monstrous" (as the "small, agile, timid mountain-dweller").[52] Linnaeus was also part of a larger tradition of

Swedish speculation about the racial character and identity of Laplanders, Swedes, and Finns, which continued in the nineteenth century. This tradition is indicative of how nationalist (or proto-nationalist) thinking in and beyond Sweden has shaped racial science.[53]


## Buffon and Kant

Linnaeus's great eighteenth-century rival in the field of natural history was the French naturalist George Louis Leclerc, Comte de Buffon (1707–88). Buffon's great work, *Natural History, General and Particular* (*Histoire naturelle, générale et particulière*, 1749–1788), stretched to thirty-six volumes. Enormously popular in France, it was translated into German, English, Spanish, Italian, and Dutch.[54] Where Linnaeus focused on the abstract task of classifying nature, Buffon sought to explain nature's diversity in an avowedly empirical and distinctly anthropocentric manner. Those plants and domestic animals that were most familiar to human beings were the ones most closely *related* to them: "Those which are most necessary and useful will hold the first rank, for example, . . . the horse, the dog, the cow, etc."[55]

Buffon, whose anthropology was deeply indebted to modern European travelogues, followed the lead of Edward Tyson and Linnaeus to treat anthropoid apes as part of a continuum that linked people to nature. Yet, unlike Linnaeus, Buffon unified "the human species in opposition to the ape."[56] "It is evident," he wrote, "that man is of an entirely different nature from that of the animal, that he is in no way similar to it, except externally."[57] Buffon worked from a monogenist perspective not so much to enumerate fundamental divisions among human beings but mainly "to document the variety of biological form and behavior that could be found within the human species."[58] Still, despite his scorn for the Linnaean obsession with classification, he offered his own "racial" classification.

He was perhaps the first naturalist to use the "race" concept in a systemic way in relation to the concept of *species*. His species consisted of "the constant succession and uninterrupted renewal" of the individuals that comprise it.[59] That is, he defined a species in terms of biological reproduction that results in the succession of similar and fertile individuals across time.[60] From here, he theorized racial variation within the human species: "[M]ankind are not composed of species essentially different from each other; . . . on the contrary, there was originally but one species, who, after multiplying and spreading over the whole surface of the earth, have undergone various changes."[61]

Buffon began his account of human racial differences with a description of the "unusual" traits of the Laplanders, who "are small, of olive colour, and have short thick limbs." They "are excellent fishers, and eat their meat and fish raw. . . . They are robust and short lived." The Lapps stood apart from the nearby Finns, who "are white, beautiful, and pretty, large and handsome."[62] Likewise, focusing on skin color, physique, height, and culture, or "what comes naturally to different peoples,"[63] he distinguished five main varieties of the human species: Laplanders (grouped with peoples in the most northern regions of the Americas and Asia), white Europeans, Americans, Africans, and "Oriental Tartars." In contrast to Linnaeus, though, he offered no precise classification scheme, and he found some notable differences among native Americans, between the Chinese and the Tartars, between the "true Negroes" and the Moors of Africa, and among the "different nations" in the "Ancient Continent."[64] Strikingly, Buffon counted the "white" peoples of the most temperate region centered in Europe as the "most beautiful people" with the most "genuine" coloring, and he saw others as having degenerated from this more perfect variety:

> The most temperate climate lies between the 40th and 50th degree of latitude, and it produces the most handsome and beautiful men. It is from this climate that the ideas of the genuine colour of mankind, and of the various degrees of beauty, ought to be derived. The civilized countries situated under this zone, are Georgia, Circassia, the Ukraine, Turkey in Europe, Hungary, the south of Germany, Italy, Switzerland, France, and the northern part of Spain. The natives of these territories are the most handsome and most beautiful people in the world.[65]

Buffon pursued this point in a manner that paralleled his anthropocentric approach to natural history more generally: he conceived racial variation in terms of "degeneration" from a normative "white," European-centered human type.

Buffon's theory of degeneration was his major contribution to racial theory.[66] Climate, Buffon claimed, was the "chief source of the different colours of men," with heat being the main cause of "blackness among the human species." The "very tawny skin" of the "race of Laplanders" indicated that extreme cold "produces effects similar to those of violent heat."

He located the darkest peoples in Senegal and Guinea; whereas "the men are only brown" in the more temperate areas of "Barbary, Mongul, Arabia, &c.," and in the "altogether temperate" regions, such as "Europe and Asia, the men are white."[67] Differences in food also shaped the "form of our bodies"; in particular, "[c]oarse, unwholesome, and ill prepared food, makes the human species degenerate."[68] Different ways of life also caused the human species to degenerate into new "races." The Tartars, he surmised, acquired their difference from the white Europeans by "being always exposed to the air; to their having no cities or fixed habitations; to their sleeping constantly on the ground; and to their rough and savage mode of living." The Europeans, by contrast, lack "nothing to make life easy and comfortable."[69]

Like Linnaeus, Buffon was vague about the precise relationship between the physical and cultural characteristics of different peoples. Still, his approach suggested the prospect of a deterministic scientific racialism that reduced cultural and spiritual differences among different peoples to nothing more than natural expression of their physical (i.e., racial) differences.[70] There are intimations of this in Buffon's reference to "what comes naturally to different peoples" and his de facto classification of human races in terms of their distance from a white European norm. He associated "racial" (i.e., physical) degeneration away from this norm, moreover, with lesser degrees of "civilization." In his chapter "Of Carnivorous Animals," Buffon wrote, "Mankind descends, by imperceptible degrees, from the most enlightened and polished nations, to people of less genius and industry; from the latter, to others more gross, but still subject to kings and to laws; from these, again, to savages."[71]

The Caucasus region played a small but noteworthy role in Buffon's racial theory. He included Georgia and Circassia, in the Caucasus, among the "civilized countries" where the "most handsome" people are found. Furthermore, like many of his contemporaries, he "placed the probable origin of *Homo sapiens* in Asia, which he believed had provided the optimal climatic state for the rise of civilization."[72] At the same time, his speculations about the natural history of the earth radically challenged the biblical chronology. In a published text from 1778, for example, Buffon estimated the earth's age to be seventy-five thousand years.[73]

While Buffon was the first to use the "race" concept coherently in the field of natural history, Immanuel Kant (1724–1804) first gave "a clear and consistent terminological distinction between race and species" and emphasized "the permanence of racial characteristics across generations."[74]

Kant, as an Enlightenment philosopher and "race" theorist, embodied the dual character of Enlightenment thought. His moral and political philosophy expressed such themes as the "categorical imperative" to treat all human beings as "ends in themselves"; the "public use of reason"; and the "Idea for a Universal History from a Cosmopolitan Perspective" (1784).[75] His racism stood in considerable tension with his ethical and political universalism.[76]

Kant wrote speculatively and in a decidedly racist manner about human "races" in his early essay *Observations on the Feeling of the Beautiful and Sublime* (1764). Following David Hume, he claimed, "The Negroes of Africa have by nature no feeling that rises above the trifling." The difference between the "Negroes" and "the whites" was "fundamental" and "appears to be as great in regard to mental capacities as in color." He also demeaningly described Arabs, the Japanese, the Chinese, and the "savages" of North America.[77]

Later, Kant returned more systematically to the topic of race, aiming both to counter polygenist ideas and to show "that the concept of race was a valuable way of organizing the flood of materials about distant peoples that was newly available to European scholars."[78] "Races," Kant said, consist of "deviations that are constantly preserved over many generations," where "interbreeding" between races "always produces half-breed offspring."[79] He contrasted races from mere varieties of human beings within races: "Those deviate forms that always preserve the distinction of their deviation are called variations. Variations resemble each other, but they do not necessarily produce half-breeds when they mix with other [varieties]." He insisted that "Negroes and whites" are one "species of beings . . . but comprise two different races. This is because each of them perpetuate themselves in all regions of the earth and because they both, when they interbreed, necessarily produce half-breed children, or blends (Mullattoes)."[80] In contrast, blondes and brunettes "are not . . . different races of whites, because a blond man who is the child of a brunette woman can also have a distinctly blond child, although each of these deviations is always preserved, even when migration occurs frequently over many generations. For this reason, they are only variations of whites."[81] He further speculated about how, through the course of natural history, different "varieties" of human beings might become distinct "races": insofar as nature "can effect procreation everywhere, she can eventually produce an enduring stock at any time. The people of this stock would always be recognizable and might even be called a race, if their characteristic feature does not seem too insignificant and so difficult to describe that we are unable to use it to establish a special division."[82]

These propositions bear out Voegelin's view that in Kant's work "we are already looking at an advanced stage of the evolution of the race idea."[83] Kant defined "race" in terms of three properties that would remain basic to racial thought for most of the next two centuries: races were distinguished by "characteristic features" or "deviations" that were continually reproduced across succeeding generations; when people of different races reproduced, their progeny would be racial "half-breeds" that combined the distinguishing features of each part of their racial lineage; and to delineate races of human beings rather than mere varieties, the distinguishing "characteristic features" must be sufficiently significant and amenable to clear and consistent description. While Kant rejected polygenism, his understanding of race resembled polygenist thinking insofar as he conceptualized races as, in Peter McLaughlin's words, "irreversible developments of preadopted climatic types."[84] For Kant, "race" connoted natural subdivisions rather than mere "varieties" within the human species. In other words, his conception of race suggested something like several natural subspecies of human beings.[85]

Just as Kant's criteria for racial difference have been typical of racialist thought, his discussion of these criteria exemplified problems with the "race" concept and with the project of racial classification more generally. Kant simply assumed, without offering an explanation, that differences between "Negroes and whites" were sufficiently significant in the relevant way to constitute a *racial* difference. Recall his comment that the difference between Negroes and whites "appears to be as great in regard to mental capacities as in color."[86] Moreover, after he identified four distinct races —"(1) the white race; (2) the Negro race; (3) the Hun race (Mongol or Kalmuck); and (4) the Hindu or Hindustani race"—he commented, "The reason for assuming that the Negroes and whites are the base [i.e., original] races is self-evident."[87] Kant based his contention that blondes and brunettes "are only variations" of the white race and "are not . . . different races of whites" on similarly unargued assumptions. While Kant addressed the heritability of traits before Gregor Mendel and the development of modern genetics, he offered no compelling grounds to conclude that the transmission of traits across generations would be any different when Negroes and whites reproduced than it would be when blondes and brunettes reproduced. His claim that the "characteristic features" that distinguished (white) blondes and (white) brunettes did not constitute a race difference later was directly challenged by nineteenth-century race scientists, though with supporting evidence that was no more or less substantial.

One additional feature of Kant's racial scheme is relevant for understanding the history of the "Caucasian race" idea: the boundaries between his "races." Within his white race, which he located primarily in Europe, he included "the Moors (Mauritanians from Africa), the Arabs . . . , the Turkish-Tatars, and the Persians, including all the other peoples of Asia who are not specifically excepted from them in other divisions."[88] His placement of Hindus in their own category challenged other influential classifications, including Bernier's, which located some Hindus in his first (white) race, and those of Meiners and Blumenbach, which located at least some Hindus in "Caucasian race" categories (see below). While Kant implicitly included the peoples of the Caucasus region in his white race, he attributed no special significance to these peoples.

## *Blumenbach, Meiners, and the "Caucasian race"*

German physician Johann Blumenbach (1752–1840) is generally credited with introducing the term *Caucasian* into racial discourse.[89] This is only half right. The honor (or dishonor, as it were) really belongs to his German contemporary Christoph Meiners, as I will explain shortly. Still, Blumenbach was by far the more important race scientist, and he was the first to give the notion of a Caucasian race scientific credibility. In 1775, the year that Kant published the first version of his essay, "Of the Different Human Races," Blumenbach published *De Generis Humani Varietate Nativa* (*On the Natural Variety of Mankind*), his major anthropological work. Blumenbach's book was reprinted in 1776; he published a revised edition in 1781 and then a more substantially revised, third edition in 1795.[90] As professor of medicine at the University of Göttingen from 1778 to 1840, Blumenbach contributed to the development of natural history, anthropology, physiology, comparative anatomy, and the "theory of generation," which concerned the generative forces in the formation of adult individuals.

While influenced by Linnaeus, he found Linnaeus's classification of the "natural varieties" of human beings crude and confusing.[91] When Blumenbach began his own work in the late 1700s, the scientific project to describe, explain, and classify "varieties" or "races" of human beings was in full swing. In the 1795 edition of *On the Natural Variety of Mankind,* he surveyed twelve competing "divisions of the varieties" of humankind by

European men since Bernier's effort (ONVM, 1795, 266–68). And this was not an exhaustive tally. Polygenist thought, which insisted that several races of human beings were distinct species, was becoming increasingly influential, particularly through the writings of Voltaire and Lord Kames. Moreover, both monogenists such as Kant and polygenists such as Voltaire now generally shared the assumption that there were fundamental, innate differences among the different human "races."

Blumenbach, an ardent monogenist, was for the most part a notable exception to this tendency. He also exhibited considerable insight into the prejudices behind polygenist views. He started the first edition of *On the Natural Variety of Mankind* by saying that among all the species of animals, "man alone ought to be held to possess *speech,* or the voice of reason." He dismissed old travelers' tales of "distant nations . . . endowed with nothing but an inarticulate and . . . brutish voice"; and he attributed the polygenist view that there were several species of human beings to "ill-feeling, negligence, and the love of novelty" (ONVM, 1775, 83, 98, emphasis in the original).[92] Blumenbach explained that after "the first discovery of the Ethiopians, or the beardless inhabitants of America, it was much easier [for Europeans] to pronounce them different species than to inquire into the structure of the human body . . . and investigate the causes of human variety." In contrast, he "endeavored to keep free of all these mistakes; I have written this book quite unprejudiced" in arguing "for the unity of the human species." While there appeared to be a "great difference between widely separate nations, . . . yet when the matter is thoroughly considered, you will see that all do so run into one another, and that one variety of mankind does so sensibly pass into the other, that you cannot mark out the limits between them" (ONVM, 1775, 98–99). He insisted on these points through the three editions of *On the Natural Variety of Mankind,* although he significantly modified his argument along the way.

In the 1775 edition of *On the Natural Variety of Mankind,* Blumenbach followed Linnaeus to distinguish four human "varieties," but defined his varieties "by other boundaries." He said, "The first and most important to us (which is also the primitive one) is that of Europe, Asia this side of the Ganges, and all the country situated to the north of the Amoor," together with the European inhabitants of North America. His second variety encompassed Asia "beyond the Ganges, and below the river Amoor," joined with the "the greater part of the countries that are now called Australia"; his third variety covered Africa; and his fourth variety included "the rest of America, except for so much of the North as was included in the first variety" (ONVM, 1775, 99). Thus, whereas Linnaeus "allotted four classes of inhabitants to the four quarters of the globe respectively," that is, Europe, Asia, Africa, and the Americas, Blumenbach's focus on physical similarities and differences between peoples led him to a division of humanity that blurred the boundary between Europe and Asia. Blumenbach distinguished his varieties of human beings according to observed differences in skull forms, facial structures, skin color, and hair color and texture. He gave special weight to differences in the shapes of skulls, based on the theory that skulls were more permanent than other traits and, therefore, a truer indicator of "racial" distinction (ONVM, 1795, 234–46).[93]

In the 1781 edition, he proposed *five* principal varieties (which he did not yet name) "as more consonant to nature" than his original four varieties, after he had "more accurately investigated the different nations of Eastern Asia and America."[94] He did this primarily by subdividing his initial "fourth variety" into one comprising native Americans and another of the peoples of "the new southern world" of the Pacific, including the Philippine islands, Tahiti, and New Zealand. He also slightly recast his first variety in a way that largely prefigured his later "Caucasian race" category:

> The first of these [five varieties] and the largest, which is the primeval one, embraces the whole of Europe, including the Lapps, whom I cannot in any way separate from the rest of the Europeans, when their appearance and their language bear such testimony to their Finnish origin; and that western part of Asia which lies towards us, this side of the Obi, the Caspian sea, mount Taurus and the Ganges; also northern Africa, and lastly, in America, the Greenlanders and the Esquimaux, for I see in these people a wonderful difference from the other inhabitants of America; and, unless I am altogether deceived, I think they must be derived from the Finns. All these nations regarded as a whole are white in colour, and if compared with the rest, beautiful in form. (ONVM, 1781, 99–100n.4)

In the third edition, Blumenbach reclassified the Lapps and Finns and, more important, he revised some terminology in a subtle but significant way. He had previously spoken mainly of human "varieties," but, while he never completely abandoned this term, by 1788 he adopted the concept of "race" from Kant to denote five principal human races. In the third edition of *On the Natural Variety of Mankind*, as Voegelin notes, he frequently used "the terms *gens* and *gentilitus*, meaning in the scholarly Latin of the time *race* and *racial*."[95] Likewise, he employed the German term *rasse* (race) and spoke of five "principal races" (*hauptrassen*) of humankind in related works published after 1795 (CNH, 303).[96] Simultaneously, though, Blumenbach moved away from a racist racialism in the 1770s to a more avowedly egalitarian racialism after 1786 or 1787.[97]

Blumenbach introduced his now-famous scheme of five principal varieties of human beings—*Caucasian, Mongolian, Ethiopian, American,* and *Malay*—in the third edition of *On the Natural Variety of Mankind,* in 1795. Now a well-established scientist, he based his claims on his large collection of human skulls. In this text, before Blumenbach described his five varieties or races, he emphasized the basic unity of human beings: "*Innumerable varieties of mankind run into one another by insensible degrees. . . .* [And] no variety exists, whether of colour, countenance, or stature, &c., so singular as not to be connected with others of the same kind by such an imperceptible transition, that it is very clear they are all related." He further cautioned "that on account of the multifarious diversity" of characteristics, which vary by degrees, "one or two alone are not sufficient" for classification, and even this "union of characters" varies within each of the varieties (ONVM, 1795, 264–65, Blumenbach's emphasis).[98] He explained his ordering of the five varieties in this way:

> I have allotted the first place to the Caucasian, for reasons given below, which make me esteem it the primeval one. This diverges in both directions into two, most remote and very different from each other; on one side, namely, into the Ethiopian, and on the other into the Mongolian. The remaining two occupy intermediate positions between that primeval one and these two extremes; that is, the American between the Caucasian and Mongolian; the Malay between the same Caucasian and Ethiopian. (ONVM, 1795, 264–65)

He now included in this Caucasian variety "the inhabitants of Europe (except the Lapps and the remaining descendants of the Finns) and those of Eastern Asia, as far as the river Obi, the Caspian Sea and the Ganges; and lastly, those of Northern Africa" (ONVM, 1795, 265).

Historically, the most important feature of Blumenbach's racial classification was his emphasis on strictly physical criteria, which he described and arranged in aesthetic terms. Consistent with his Christian-influenced monogenism, he avoided claims about racial superiority or inferiority.[99] In fact, Blumenbach explicitly rejected claims about supposedly innate intellectual differences among the "races" in a discussion of the "mental capacities" of "Negroes" (CNH, 306–12). He maintained that all varieties of humankind originated in one place and then spread around the globe, acquiring racial variations as they adapted to new regions (ONVM, 1795, 269).[100] Yet, like other European scientists, he relied on European aesthetic criteria, specifically ideas of beauty drawn from Greek and Roman statuary.[101] He appealed to these criteria to claim his Caucasian variety as the "primeval" human variety. While acknowledging the subjectivity of his perspective, he said that in general this variety possessed "that kind of appearance which, according to our opinion of symmetry, we consider most handsome and becoming" (ONVM, 1795, 265). He elaborated: "Colour white, cheeks rosy; hair brown or chestnut-coloured; head subglobular . . . [f]ace oval, straight, the parts moderately marked. The Forehead smooth. Nose narrow, slightly hooked, or at all events somewhat high. The jugal bones in no way prominent. Mouth small, lips . . . gently pronounced. Chin full, round" (ONVM, 1795, 265, 227–28). In contrast, he described the other varieties as aesthetically deficient: in the Mongolian variety the "face [is] broad, at the same time flat and depressed," with a "small, apish" nose; in the Ethiopian, the head is "narrow, compressed at the sides; the forehead knotty, uneven"; and in the American the "forehead [is] short" and the nose is "somewhat apish, but prominent" (ONVM, 1795, 265–66).

Furthermore, Blumenbach based his assessment of the greater beauty of the Caucasian variety partly on "a most beautiful skull of a Georgian female" (ONVM, 1795, 237).[102] Blumenbach's use of the skull of a Georgian female was unusual because, as Londa Schiebinger notes, at this time "the study of racial types was devoted primarily to the study of males," taken as archetypal in comparative anatomy.[103] Blumenbach actually used skulls of females to represent two of his five principal "varieties of mankind": "[a] young Georgian" and "[a]n Ethiopian female of Guinea" (ONVM, 1795, 162). Only the Georgian skull, however, was labeled female in Blumenbach's famous depiction of his five varieties (see figures 2.1–2.5). (He gave an illustration of this skull an even more prominent place his 1810 *Abbildungen naturhistorischer Gegenstände*. See figure 3.)

Blumenbach proposed a particular way to analyze skulls to ascertain their "racial character"—what he called "the vertical scale" (*norma verticalis*). The *norma verticalis* simply entailed viewing skulls from above and behind, with the skulls placed similarly in a row on the same plane. This, he said, was the best angle from which to discern the features that are most indicative of a skull's "racial character," such as "the direction of the jaws, or of the cheekbones, the breadth or narrowness of the skull, [and] the advancing or receding outline of the forehead" (ONVM, 1795, 236–37).

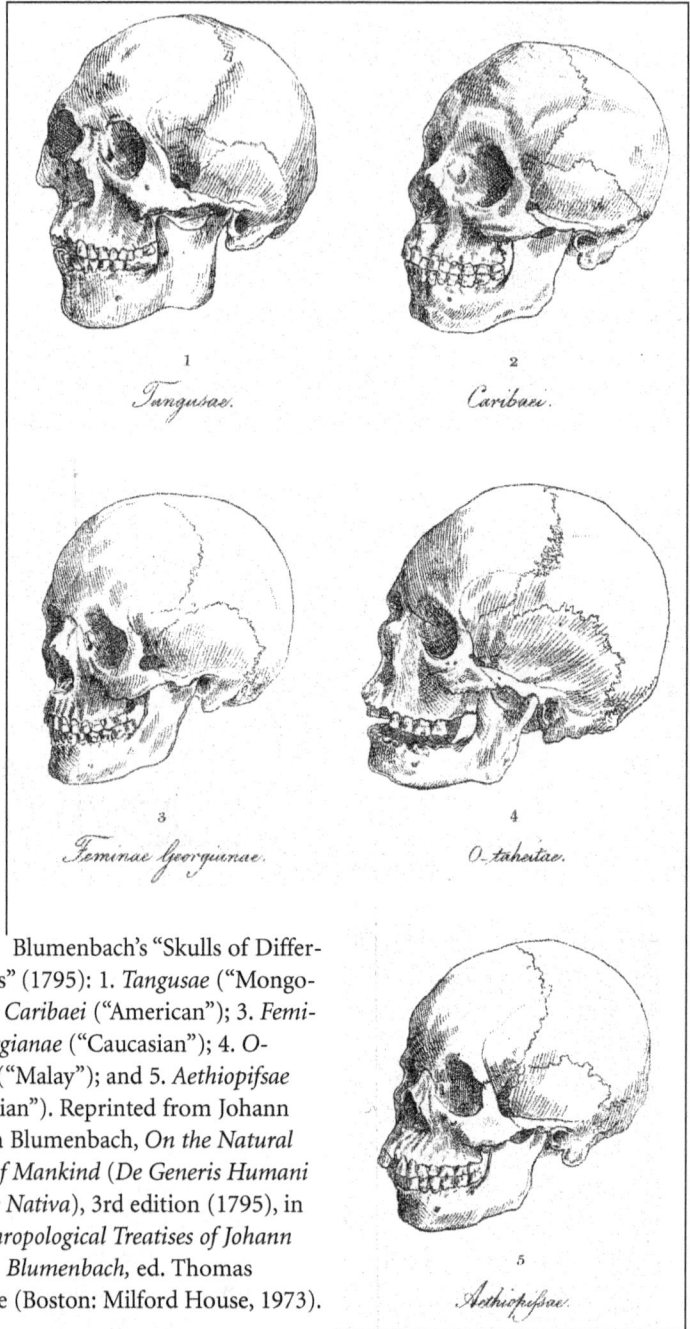

Figure 2: Blumenbach's "Skulls of Different Races" (1795): 1. *Tangusae* ("Mongolian"); 2. *Caribaei* ("American"); 3. *Feminae Georgianae* ("Caucasian"); 4. *O-taheitae* ("Malay"); and 5. *Aethiopifsae* ("Ethiopian"). Reprinted from Johann Friedrich Blumenbach, *On the Natural Variety of Mankind* (*De Generis Humani Varietate Nativa*), 3rd edition (1795), in *The Anthropological Treatises of Johann Friedrich Blumenbach,* ed. Thomas Bendyshe (Boston: Milford House, 1973).

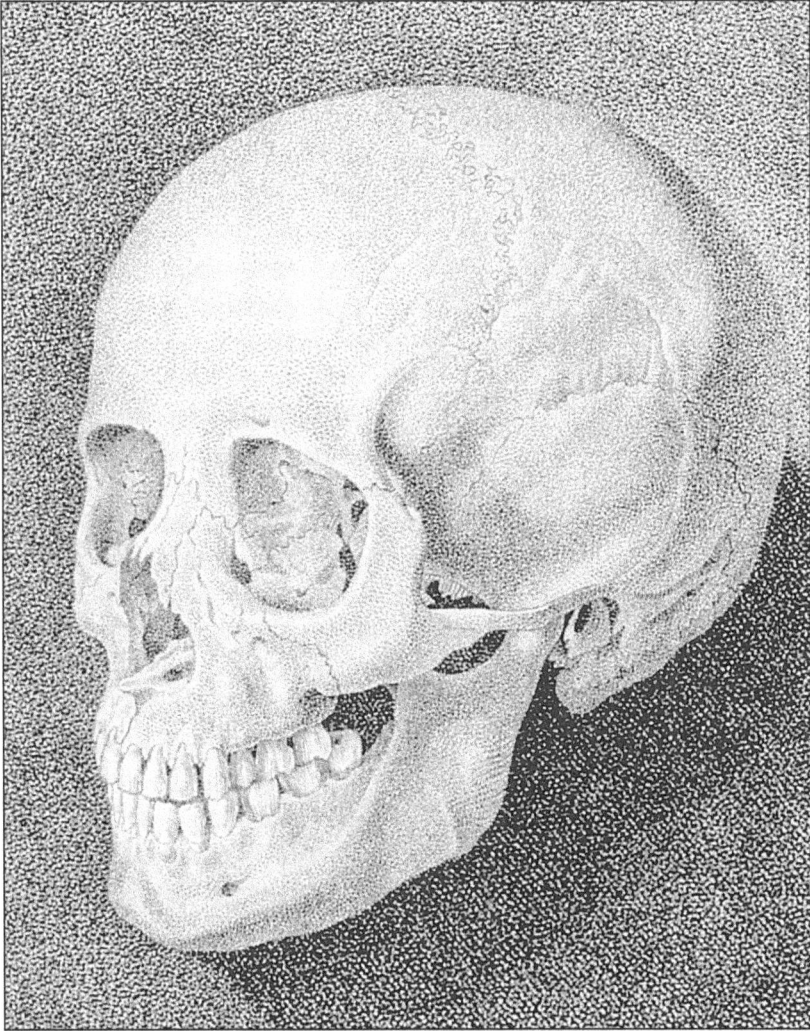

Figure 3: Blumenbach's *Feminae Georgianae* (1810). Reprinted from Johann Friedrich Blumenbach, *Abbildungen naturhistorischer Gegenstände* (Göttingen: Bey Heinrich Dieterich, 1810).

Blumenbach then connected his aesthetic judgments to his conclusions concerning the "primeval" human variety:

> In the first place, that stock displays, as we have seen the most beautiful form of skull, from which, as from a mean and primeval type, the others diverge by most easy gradations on both sides to the two ultimate extremes (that is, on the one side the Mongolian, on the other the Ethiopian). Besides, it is white in colour, which we may fairly assume to have been the primitive colour of mankind, since . . . it is very easy for that to degenerate into brown, but very much more difficult for the dark to become white. (ONVM, 1795, 269)

While this claim about color begs critical scrutiny, the matter of degeneration is more pertinent to present purposes. Like Buffon, Blumenbach maintained that climate was the chief impetus for the degeneration of human varieties away from the primeval (i.e., Caucasian) type, and that diet and "modes of life" also played a role (ONVM, 1795, 197–201).[104] He considered it difficult to measure the impact of climate relative to the other causes of degeneration but speculated that environmental factors have their effects by directing the "formative force" within the human species away from "its determined direction and plan." When this process was "carried on for several series of generations," it resulted in "degeneration into varieties, properly so called" (ONVM, 1795, 195–96).

According to Blumenbach, the Caucasian variety of face "constitutes, as it were, a medium which may fall off by degeneration into two exactly opposite extremes, of which one [the Mongolian] displays a wide and the other [the Ethiopian] an elongated face" (ONVM, 1795, 228). Blumenbach did not use "degeneration" in Buffon's sense of degradation from an ideal, which foreshadowed racist nineteenth- and early-twentieth-century notions of "racial degeneration."[105] He meant it, as Stephen Jay Gould explains, in "the literal sense of departure from an initial form of humanity at creation."[106] That said, since Blumenbach arranged his five varieties according to an aesthetic hierarchy, he encumbered his own notion of degeneration with negative connotations. He conceived degeneration as a diverting of "the formative force from its accustomed path" (ONVM, 1795, 196), and he privileged the Caucasian variety as the archetypal human standard from which other races diverged to varying degrees.

Gould suggests that this "geometry" of racial differentiation, whereby two varieties were seen as "falling off" in opposite directions from the original variety, stood behind Blumenbach's rejection of Linnaeus's geographical four-race model in favor of his own five-race scheme.[107] That is, by dividing his own original Mongolian variety (of 1775) into two varieties, Mongolian and Malay, Blumenbach was able to depict the American variety as transitional between the Caucasian variety and the more "extreme" Mongolian variety, and the Malay variety as transitional between the "medial [i.e., Caucasian] variety [and] the other extreme, namely, the Ethiopian" (ONVM, 1795, 275). Yet, while Blumenbach postulated a geometry of racial degeneration, it is not clear that this is what motivated him to abandon a four-race scheme. In the 1781 edition of his book, after reading Johann Reinhold Forster's *Observations Made during a Voyage Round the World* (1778), Blumenbach added a fifth variety, located in "the new southern world" of the Pacific.[108]

Consistent with his view that "innumerable varieties of mankind run into one another by insensible degrees" (ONVM, 1795, 264), Blumenbach also complicated his scheme of five identifiable varieties or races. "We see nations which are reputed to be colonies of one and the same stock have contracted in different climates different racial faces," he wrote (1795, 231). "Each of [the] five principal varieties contains besides one or more nations which are distinguished by their more or less striking structure from the rest of those in the same division," he explained elsewhere. "Thus the Hindoos might be separated as particular sub-varieties from the rest of the same division," that is, within the Caucasian variety (CNH, 304).[109]

These points clarify the "racial" meaning that Blumenbach gave to his Caucasian, Mongolian, Ethiopian, American, and Malay varieties. Yet they do not answer the riddle of why he chose the term *Caucasian* for his first, European-centered variety. Blumenbach said that he chose *Caucasian* in reference to Mount Caucasus, "both because its neighborhood, and especially its southern slope, produces the most beautiful race of men, I mean the Georgian; and because all physiological reasons converge to this, that in that region, if anywhere, it seems we ought with the greatest probability to place the autochthones of mankind" (ONVM, 1795, 269). Yet this was only part of the story.[110]

Crucially, Blumenbach, like Bernier, included parts of Asia and Africa in his first variety—a move that challenged Linnaeus, Kant, and Buffon, each of whom regarded his "white race" as European. (Buffon, however, included Georgians and Circassians within this racial designation.) This can partly be explained by the fact that both Blumenbach and Bernier emphasized physiognomic affinities and differences between peoples that for them undermined any notion of a strictly European race. Still, other factors were at work. The idea that human beings originated in the Caucasus region was prevalent in Europe at the time, including in Blumenbach's intellectual circle at the University of Göttingen. The ancient Greeks, who called the region "Kaukasos" (Latinized into "Caucasus"), saw the Caucasus range as the site of the suffering of Prometheus. According to the myth, Prometheus was chained to Mount Caucasus for stealing fire to save humankind. In another Greek tale, Jason and the Argonauts sought to recover the Golden Fleece in the land of Colchis (the modern Kolkhida Lowland, in Georgia along the shore of the Black Sea).[111]

In Christian Europe, the most important source for beliefs about humanity's origins in the Caucasus was the then-prevailing account of where Noah's ark landed after the flood. Martin Bernal notes that this view was based on the Judaic and Christian

> religious belief—given publicity by Vico in the eighteenth century—that man could usefully be seen as coming after the flood and, as everyone knows, that Noah's Ark had landed on Mount Ararat in the Southern Caucasus. There was also the increasingly important German Romantic tendency to place the origins of mankind—and therefore of the Europeans—in the Eastern mountains, not in the river valleys of the Nile and Euphrates, as the ancients had believed. As [Johann Gottfried] Herder put it: "Let us scale the mountains laboriously to the summits of Asia."[112]

Blumenbach himself quoted the seventeenth-century French John Chardin account of the great beauty of the Georgians, in *Travels of Sir John Chardin into Persia and the East Indies* (1686), to which I will return shortly. But he did not cite Chardin's report that Georgians, Persians, and Armenians all claimed that Noah had dwelt in their lands. After saying that Georgia is "as fertile a Country as any that can be imagined," Chardin added, "The People of this Country boast, That *Noah* dwelt in this country after he came out of the *Ark,* and that his sons built 'em every one a castle."[113] Later, while discussing Persian and Armenian claims about the landing place of Noah's ark, Chardin noted that "the Holy Scripture gives no particular Name, it only says, That *the Ark rested upon the Mountain of Ararat,* which is *Armenia.*"[114]

By Blumenbach's time, the Noachian story of the origin of humans and other animals after the flood had been, in Janet Browne's words, "thoroughly adapted to the demands of the temporal scientific world."[115] For instance, noted German geographer E. A. W. Zimmermann (1743–1815), cited by both Blumenbach and Meiners, adopted Kant's racial classification scheme and located the origins of humankind in central Asia near the Caucasus. Zimmermann argued that the original human beings were white-skinned and brunette and originated, in Blumenbach's words, in the "elevated Scythico-Asiatic plain, near the source of the Indus, Ganges, and Obi rivers" (ONVM, 1795, 268). Zimmermann thought that a first group of people migrated from there to "the region between the Ural and the Caucasus"; subsequent groups scattered more widely.[116]

In addition, raciologists of the time often used widely circulating travelers' reports about the beauty of certain peoples beyond Europe to link them to Europeans racially, and even to ascertain Europe's boundaries. As David Bindman says, "If Europe became increasingly stable as a concept in the eighteenth century, it remained far from stable as a geographical entity. The only agreed border was the Mediterranean; beyond that the limits were vague. There was a sense also that the peoples beyond the eastern border of the Holy Roman Empire—the Circassians and others—were of exceptional beauty, as were those in parts of India; the presumption of their aesthetic superiority played a part in their incorporation into what was in the nineteenth century to become the 'Aryan' race."[117] Thus, Buffon considered the renowned beauty of Georgians and Circassians as grounds for locating them within his "European" race.

This approach to the peoples of the Caucasus also figured in two works of the 1770s with which Blumenbach was familiar. Like Buffon, the English writer and polygenist Oliver Goldsmith included Caucasian peoples in his delineation of a superior European-centered variety of human beings among six distinct human varieties:

> The sixth and last variety of the human species, is that of the Europeans and the nations bordering on them. In this class we may reckon the Georgians, Circassians, and Mingrelians, the inhabitants of Asia Minor, and the northern parts of Africa, together with a part of those countries which lie northwest of the Caspian sea. The inhabitants of these countries differ a good deal from each other; but they generally agree in the colour of their bodies, the beauty of their complexions, the largeness of their limbs, and the vigour of their understandings. Those arts which might have had their invention among the other races of mankind, have come to perfection there.[118]

Edinburgh physician John Hunter also remarked upon the beauty of the peoples while proposing a classification scheme of seven "races." Like Blumenbach, Hunter defended monogenism; but for present purposes his argument is most notable for how he defended it: he noted the resemblances between parents and progeny that would result from procreation by "a man and a woman most widely different from each other; let the one be the most beautiful Circassian woman and the other an African born in Guinea, as black and ugly as possible."[119]

Blumenbach treated reports about the beauty of the Georgians in a similar way. To buttress his own assertion about their beauty, he quoted Chardin as a "classical . . . eyewitness": "The blood of Georgian is the best of the East, and perhaps in the world. I have not observed a single ugly face in that country, in either sex; but I have seen angelical ones. Nature has there lavished upon the women beauties which are not to be seen elsewhere. . . . It would be impossible to paint more charming visages, or better figures, than those of the Georgians" (Chardin, quoted in ONVM, 1795, 269n.1).[120] Chardin added a few other notable remarks about the Georgians that Blumenbach did not quote, but which probably informed Blumenbach's image of the Georgians: "The Georgians also are Naturally very Witty," Chardin wrote. "Nor would there be more Learned Men, or more ingenious Masters in the World, were they but improv'd by the Knowledge of Arts and Sciences: but their Education . . . mean and paltry." Georgian women "have an Extraordinary Addiction to the Male Sex" and bear significant responsibility for the "Torrent of Uncleanness which overflows all the Country." At the same time, "the Georgians are Civil and Courteous, and more then [*sic*] that, they are Grave and Moderate."[121]

Finally, Christoph Meiners (1747–1810), the University of Göttingen "popular philosopher" and historian, first gave the term *Caucasian* racial meaning in his *Grundriss der Geschichte der Menschheit* (*Outline of the History of Humanity,* 1785). "Popular philosophy," a branch of German Enlightenment thought that was closely linked to a new German interest in anthropology around the 1760s, was intended as a "philosophy *for* the people." This philosophy rejected metaphysical speculation and emphasized empirical inquiry into human existence.[122] Meiners's notion of popular philosophy led him to ambitious work on the natural history of humanity. "History of mankind," he wrote, "has filled the gap which lay between the general doctrines of philosophy and the particular facts of history."[123] Meiners pursued this "Göttingen program" of inquiry in extensive historical-anthropological writings, which included two editions of his *Outline of the History of Humanity* and numerous articles in *Göttingisches Historisches Magazin.*

The 1785 edition of *Outline of the History of Humanity* became the urtext of "Caucasian race" theory. Meiners divided humanity into two main branches, Caucasian (or Tartar) and Mongolian:

> Of all the foundations and observations I have made, no other seems to be based on so many testimonies and facts, and none so rich in scientific deductions as this: the present human race exists of two main branches (*Stamm*), the Tartar or Caucasian and the Mongolian. The latter is not only much weaker in body and spirit, but much worse in its ways and devoid of virtue compared to the Caucasian. The Caucasian branch divided into two races, the Celtic and the Slavic, among which the former is richer in spiritual gifts and virtue than the latter. From this observation, one can explain how the human race spread itself over the surface of the earth and how the different nations originated and related to each other. Further, one can also explain why great lawmakers, the wise, and heroes, and the arts and sciences only developed under certain nations and were made worse under others, . . . why certain nations were always rulers and others servants, why the goddess of freedom lives in such tight boundaries and why the terrible despotism sits on an unshakable throne among the nations of the world, why the European nations separate themselves so much from the wildness and barbarity of others in their greater virtue, their openness towards discovery, their constitutions, laws, art of war, and their behavior towards their wives, slaves, and enemies.[124]

For Meiners, in contrast to Blumenbach, character and cultural differences between Europeans and the other peoples of the world (whom he crudely stereotyped) were *due to* innate "race" differences between them. Concerning his use of *Caucasian,* Meiners said, "Almost all of the Sagas and tales of ancient nations indicate that the human race originated on the Caucasus [mountain range] and the plains to the south of it. From here, the humans spread to all ends of the world."[125] Meanwhile, he located the origins of his Mongolian branch in a way that indicated a nascent polygenism: "In the valleys of the Altai [Mongolia] settled one human branch in particular, which was so different in terms of body-structure and mental capacity from the race originating in the Caucasus, that one could perceive it as originating from a different genesis entirely."[126] Meiners nonetheless cast his racial theory in monogenist terms, whereby human beings comprised a singular species divided into the two main branches, with "several races" in each branch.

He maintained that the "Caucasian or Tartar" branch of humanity "was created and sustained in the Caucasus" but added:

> The Caucasians are no longer very pure and unmixed in the Caucasus. The Caucasians, however, especially their women, are the most beautiful people in the entire world. These nations and their offspring differ from the Mongolian nations through their height and the structure of their bodies, through a more beautiful facial formation and other body parts, through stronger hair growth and through nobility of spirit and heart.[127]

Consistent with his views about the relative beauty and nobility of the two branches, he contended that "the Tibetans and the lower castes in Hindustan, Ceylon, and the Maldives" were descended from the Mongolian branch, but that the "higher castes in these countries are undeniably of Caucasian or Tartar origin." He further conjectured:

> Out of the lowest caste or from many of the oldest inhabitants of Hindustan originated the blacks or the Negroes in Tunkin; in most of the East-Indian and in many of the South-Sea islands originated the Negroes of New Guinea and New Holland. . . . The more beautiful and whiter inhabitants of several East-Indian and South-Sea Islands originated from the higher Hindu castes and also from the Arabs.[128]

These last speculations, which echoed Bernier's from a century earlier, reflected a tendency evident among many Europeans at the time and later to posit a racial affinity between Europeans and upper-caste Hindus in the Indian subcontinent, and racially to distinguish both these groups from lower-caste Hindus. For instance, the distinguished British Orientalist and philologist William Jones soon discovered that Sanskrit belonged to an Indo-European linguistic group, "along with Persian, Greek, Latin, as well as the Germanic and Celtic languages."[129] Based on this evidence, Jones posited, among other things, a racial affinity between Europeans and Indians:

> [T]he first race of Persians and Indians, to whom we may add the Romans and Greeks, the Goths, and the old Egyptians, or Ethiops, originally spoke the same language . . . [while] the Jews and Arabs, the Assyrians, or second Persian race, the people who spoke Syriak, and a numerous tribe of

Abyssinians used one primitive dialect. . . . [Additionally,] that the settlers of China and Japan had a common origin with the Hindus is no more than highly probable and that the Tartars . . . were primarily of a third and separate branch, totally different from the two others in language, manner, and features. . . . [Thus, it appeared] that the whole earth was peopled by a variety of shoots from the Indian, Arabian, and Tartarian branches, or by mixtures of them, . . . in the course of ages.[130]

Jones's influential research was spurred by British colonial rule in India. Bengal Brahmans had been ordered to translate ancient laws and sacred writings of India into English, and Jones had decided to learn Sanskrit.[131] His findings informed Blumenbach's later work, the research of the important nineteenth-century English anthropologists James Cowles Prichard and Robert Gordon Latham, and the development of "Aryan race" theory in the nineteenth century.

Meiners, meanwhile, substantially revised his terminology in the 1793 edition of his *Outline,* independent of Jones's ideas. While he had previously named the two "branches" of humanity the Caucasians and the Mongolians, he now asserted (although occasionally he still used these names) that it was an error to name peoples after their assumed place of origin. Physical attributes were the best way to identify the different branches of humanity.[132] He now referred to his former Mongolians as the "dark-colored and ugly" people and to his former Caucasians as the "white-skinned and beautiful."[133] Only the whites possessed "true bravery [and] love of freedom," while the "dark and ugly peoples" had "despicable attributes," lacked virtues, and were "untamable" and inclined toward "unnatural desires."[134] In addition, he now divided the "white and beautiful" people into three races—Celts, Sarmatians (or Slavs), and eastern peoples (such as the Persians); and he identified the Celtic nations as all of the originally non-Finnish and non-Sarmatian (i.e., non-Slavic) peoples of Europe. He added, "I reserve this name [Celtic] for the noble branch of mankind—unless someone comes up with a better name."[135] The Slavs and eastern peoples were much more similar to each other than they were to the Germanic and Celtic peoples, and the Europeans (or Celts) were the most intelligent and virtuous.[136] In the second edition of his book, then, Meiners replaced the term *Caucasian* as a racial name with the designation "white and beautiful" and the term *Celtic.* He indirectly suggested a further rationale for this change when he located some tendencies for "degeneration" of character among the whites:

White and beautiful peoples [*Völker*] can become primitive and die out [*verwildern und ausarten*] due to physical and moral factors. Such a possibility is illustrated not only by the history of the Greeks and the Romans, but also by that of the *present inhabitants of the Caucasus* as well as the history of almost all European settlements in the warm parts of the world. Only nations of a superior stock [*Stamm*] retain even in the most primitive and degenerate conditions their defining qualities and distinctiveness from others.[137]

In addition, Meiners expressed ideas that later found favor with Nazi "race" theorists. In 1790, he identified Germans as the superior peoples among the (European) Celts, with "a dazzling white skin, blond curly hair, and blue eyes; courage and love of freedom, that never finds itself submissive to other nations, inexhaustible invention, and an unbounded talent for the arts and sciences."[138] His classification scheme also regarded Europe's Jews as an "Asian" people.[139] This thesis was also supported by William Jones's new racialized linguistic ideas; and even Blumenbach provided some support for it when he discussed whether "different nations" can be identified by their physiognomies. He said that the Jewish people presented "the most notorious and least deceptive [example], which can easily be recognized everywhere by their eyes alone, which breathe of the East" (ONVM, 1775, 122).[140]

The connection between Meiners's ideas about a Caucasian branch of humanity and Blumenbach's later conception of a Caucasian variety (eventually, a Caucasian race) is not completely clear. What *is* clear is that the two editions of Meiners's *Outline* were published between the second edition of Blumenbach's *On the Natural Variety of Mankind* and the third edition, where Blumenbach first used the term *Caucasian*. Blumenbach cited Meiners once in 1795, but only to include Meiners's 1793 division of humanity into "handsome and white" and "ugly and dark" peoples among several alternative "divisions of the varieties of mankind."[141] Yet Blumenbach must have been aware of Meiners's earlier designation of Caucasian and Mongolian branches of humanity, as the two men knew each other as colleagues at the University of Göttingen.[142] The way that Blumenbach embraced the term *Caucasian* suggests that he worked to distance his own anthropological thinking from that of Meiners while recovering the term *Caucasian* for his own more refined racial classification: he made no mention of Meiners's 1785 usage and gave the term a new meaning. Even so, *Caucasian* was first introduced into scientific racialism in Meiners's crude racist taxonomy of the "white-skinned and beautiful" ("Caucasians") and the "dark-skinned and ugly" ("Mongolians"), and Blumenbach relied on related aesthetic-evaluative reasoning to delineate his "Caucasian," "Mongolian," "Ethiopian," "American," and "Malay" varieties (or races) of humankind.[143]

All in all, Blumenbach left a paradoxical racial legacy. He was one of the least racist of Enlightenment thinkers but nonetheless reinforced racist ideas by establishing a "hierarchical ordering of human diversity."[144] The egalitarian and universalistic side of his thinking is vividly evident in the noble-looking illustrations he chose for "Characteristic heads of representatives of the five principal races of humankind": 1. *Mongolian,* the Calmuck Feodor Iwanowitsch; 2. *American,* the Mohawk tribal leader Taydaneega (known as Captain Joseph Brant); 3. *Caucasian,* the Persian Mohammed Jumla; 4. *Malay,* the Tahitian O-Mai; 5. *Ethiopian,* the Negro Pastor Jac. Jo. Eliza Capitein (see figures 4.1–4.5). These images depict cultural differences along with the equal humanity of all the human "races." It is also notable that Blumenbach chose a Persian, whose home was near the Caucasus, to represent the Europe-centered "Caucasian race."[145] Still, his theory of degeneration and his aesthetic ordering of races convey a contrary vision. While Blumenbach conceived degeneration simply as a departure from the original human form, he nevertheless constructed an aesthetic hierarchy among his five races in terms of their distance (and falling away) from the Caucasian ideal.[146] Because of this, later racist raciologists such as French naturalist Isidore Geoffroy Saint-Hilaire could appropriate Blumenbach's work to support expressly hierarchical modes of racial classification. According to Saint-Hilaire, "Blumenbach was more or less aware of three truths whose importance no one can dispute in anthropological taxonomy, that is to say, The plurality of races of man; the importance of the characteristics deduced from the conformation of the head; and the necessity of not placing in the same rank all the divisions of mankind, which bear the common title of races."[147] Furthermore, while Blumenbach held that "no other very definite boundaries can be drawn between" the varieties of humankind (CNH, 303), his scheme of five varieties or races of humankind implicitly suggested that any such racial boundaries were arbitrarily drawn but real.

Figure 4: Blumenbach's "Characteristic Racial Heads" (1810): 1. Feodor Iwanowitsch ("Mongolian"); 2. Taydaneega ("American"); 3. Mohammed Jumla ("Caucasian"); 4. O-Mai ("Malay"); 5. Jac. Jo. Eliza Capitein ("Ethiopian"). Reprinted from Johann Friedrich Blumenbach, *Abbildungen naturhistorischer Gegenstände* (Göttingen: Bey Heinrich Dieterich, 1810).

*Omai.*

*Jac. Jo. Eliza Capitein.*

## Conclusion

In 1806, taking stock of his own scientific efforts, Blumenbach reflected on the "symbolic" character of any reading of nature. He spoke of his desire for a thorough knowledge of natural history "so as to provide myself always more and more supports in this behalf out of nature itself." Then he added, "For all the accounts on that point which one adopts, even with the most critical judgment possible, from others, are in reality, for the truth-seeking investigators of nature, nothing more and nothing further than a kind of symbolical writing, which he can only so far subscribe to with good conscience, as they actually coincide with the open book of nature" (CNH, 298). This remark serves as a commentary on how the "race" concept was *read into nature* in the seventeenth and eighteenth centuries.

One vivid case of this in Blumenbach's time was the influential "facial angle" conceived by Dutch anatomist Petrus Camper (1722–89). Camper used drawings of representative skulls to compare the profile lines (facial angles) of "Negro," "Calmuck," and "European" races of the human species to those of a tailed ape, an orangutan, and a Greek god, representing the Grecian ideal. He charted the skulls in a series, with the tailed ape, with a facial angle of forty-two degrees, at the low end, followed by the orang-utan at fifty-eight degrees, the "Negro" and then the Calmuck at seventy degrees, the European at eighty degrees, and the Grecian head, with a facial angle of one hundred degrees, at the high end. Camper himself resisted categorical racial distinctions and maintained that the difference between the European and non-European was small and that the far more significant divide was between all human beings and the animals. Nonetheless, his "scientific" typology placed Africans near the apes and Europeans near the Greek god.[148]

More broadly, preeminent eighteenth-century racial readings of the "book of nature" were informed by existing social and geographical divisions and cultural representations of difference, as these were perceived by elite European men.[149] Blumenbach gave the notion of a Caucasian race a privileged place in scientific and popular discourses about race, but alternative theories about humankind were available. For instance, Benjamin Franklin, the great eighteenth-century American statesman and scientist, perceived significant "race" differences among European peoples. "The number of purely white people in the world is proportionately very small," Franklin declared in his *Observations Concerning the Increase of Mankind* (1751):

> All Africa is black or tawney. Asia chiefly tawney. America (exclusive of the new Comers) wholly so. And in Europe, the Spaniards, Italians, French, Russians and Swedes, are generally of what we call a swarthy Complexion; as are the Germans also, the Saxons excepted, who with the English, make the principal Body of the White People on the Face of the Earth. I could wish their numbers were increased.[150]

Insofar as select physiognomic traits were used to establish racial differences among different groups of people, Franklin's remarks highlight the arbitrariness of privileging any one trait or set of traits (such as skin color or skull shapes) over others as *racially* significant. Franklin's perception of significant differences between "purely white" and "swarthy" European peoples was no less (and no more) a plausible basis for a "racial" distinction than Blumenbach's emphasis on different skull types. Reflecting such arbitrariness, the idea that racial differences could be discerned *among* Europeans gained new proponents in Europe and North America in the latter half of the nineteenth century, under different social and political circumstances.

Yet racialist schemes were not the only available option for understanding human diversity. German philosopher Johann Gottfried Herder, Kant's great rival, offered a compelling alternative to any form of racialism in *Ideas on the Philosophy of the History of Humankind* (1784). To comprehend the basic unity of humankind "with the innumerable diversity on earth," Herder called for a return "to the simplest statement: only *One and the same species of humankind on earth.*"[151] This monogenist declaration was consistent with Blumenbach's ideas, but Herder went further. He was one of the few anthropological theorists in the eighteenth century to reject (almost) entirely the idea of racial classification. Others with a "zeal for a comprehensive science," Herder wrote, have

> ventured to call four or five divisions among humans, which were originally constructed according to regions or even according to colors, *races*; I see no reason for this name. Race derives from a difference in ancestry that either does not occur here or that includes the most diverse races within each of these regions in each of these colors. For each people is a people: it has its national culture and its language; the zone in which each of them is placed has sometimes put its stamp, sometimes only a thin veil, on each of them, but it has not destroyed the original ancestral core of the construction of the nation. . . . In short, there are neither four nor five races, nor are there exclusive varieties on earth. The colors run into one another; the cultures serve the genetic character; and . . . everything is only a shade of one and the same great portrait that extends across all the spaces and times of the earth.

Human diversity, then, "belongs less to the systematic history of nature than to the physical-geographical history of humanity."[152] Rather than speculate rashly that human physical or racial differences can explain moral, cultural, and intellectual differences among people, the real issue for anthropology was how different peoples—all *"One and the same species of humankind"*—have adapted culturally to different environments in different ways.

Herder was not completely free of racialist assumptions, and his belief that each nation possessed a unique *Volksgeist* (folk spirit) lent support for subsequent forms of racism.[153] Nevertheless, from Herder's perspective the whole idea of a Caucasian race was a nonstarter. It would make sense to speak of Caucasian peoples or nations, such as Georgians, Armenians, Circassians, and Chechens (as long as we do not naturalize these nationalities); but there is no basis for speaking of a biologically defined Caucasian race, however we might define its boundaries. Herder's emphasis on *nations* has a further advantage: it enables us to address cogently the recent and continuing national-political struggles in the Caucasus, particularly the recent achievement of independence by Georgians from the old Soviet Union and the continuing struggle of Chechens for independence from the Russian Federation.

Unfortunately for the history of human relations, the relevant scientific and scholarly community—primarily male European scientists and philosophers—was guided by what Blumenbach called the "European conception of beauty" and also by ideas about European technological and civilizational superiority. These ideas were fueled by European travelogues, European colonial expansion, and the enslavement of black Africans by white Europeans and European Americans. In this context, most eighteenth-century scientists and philosophers of race were predisposed toward race thinking and racial classifications that hierarchically distinguished recognizably "white" peoples such as themselves from recognizably "nonwhite" peoples. At the end of the century, Blumenbach's "Caucasian race" category served this purpose in an authoritative way.

# 3

# Passage into "Our Ordinary Forms of Expression"

*The "Caucasian Race," ca. 1795–1850*

> [Blumenbach's racial] divisions and their designations having been adopted by Cuvier, and having passed into our ordinary forms of expression, require a brief notice; although they are no longer scientifically appropriate.
>
> —William Carpenter, "Ethnology, or the Science of Races" (1848)[1]

In the first half of the nineteenth century, Johann Blumenbach's notion of a "Caucasian race" passed quickly into both scientific and ordinary usage in Europe and in the United States. In this period, European elites sought to shore up social hierarchies in the wake of the French Revolution and its Napoleonic aftermath, and "Negro" slavery intensified in the United States. Consequently, scientific racialism steadily hardened into a scientific racism that was far removed from Blumenbach's thinking. Whereas Blumenbach used the notion of a Caucasian race to designate one of five principal "varieties" of human beings that *run into one another by insensible degrees,*[2] the "Caucasian race" category was now widely adapted to more explicitly racist—specifically, "white" supremacist—modes of racial classification.

Between 1817 and 1839 in particular, several influential race scientists in Europe and the United States adopted the "Caucasian race" category but redefined it in ways that were sharply at odds with Blumenbach's egalitarian view of human varieties; notable among these scientists were French naturalist Georges Cuvier, English naturalist William Lawrence, and U.S. physician and naturalist Samuel George Morton. These writers exemplified a increasing tendency to use "race" to signify irreducible, innate differences between peoples that were purportedly discernible through scientific investigation. Within this broad framework, race scientists such as Cuvier, Lawrence, and Morton asserted the innate superiority of the "Caucasian race," and Morton, among others, advanced polygenist race theories.

Between 1845 and 1853, two influential English anthropologists, James Cowles Prichard and Robert Gordon Latham, persuasively critiqued dubious aspects of the "Caucasian race" category. They did so, however, not to reject racialism but to place ethnology, "the science of races," on firmer intellectual foundations. Despite this challenge, the "Caucasian race" had become firmly established—for the time being at least—in both scientific and ordinary language discourses about race.

## "Race" Science and Society, ca. 1795–1850

There were some European thinkers in the first half of the nineteenth century who reiterated Herder's critique of the "race" concept. In turn-of-the-century France, Joseph Marie de Gérando (1772–1842), or Citizen Degérando, emphasized cultural variation among peoples and avoided the concept of race in his *Considerations on the Diverse Methods to Follow in the Observation of Savage Peoples.* He was certain about the superiority of European civilization; but in the tradition of egalitarian humanism, he considered the civilizational backwardness of "savage" peoples the result of environment rather than heredity.[3] In 1845 the German scientist and traveler Alexander von Humboldt (1769–1859) wrote: "Whilst we maintain the unity of the human species, we at the same time repel the depressing assumption of superior and inferior races of men."[4] For the most part, however, racialism—the conviction that were physiologically distinct human "races"—had become the prevailing view among European and North American scientists and, more and more, among nonscientists. Anthropologists and biologists sought not only ever more precise measures of racial difference but also "proof" of the hereditary "racial" basis for the presumed cultural and intellectual inequalities between different peoples.[5] The idea of civilization, as it emerged in the eighteenth century, "was seen as the destined goal of all mankind, and was in fact often used to account for apparent racial differences. But in the nineteenth century more and more men saw civilization as the peculiar achievement of certain 'races.'"[6]

The emergence of a resolute and deterministic scientific racism was conditioned by broader social and political forces, including the French Revolution of 1789 and Napoleon's effort to unify Europe. The revolution suggested to many people the changeability of inherited hierarchies and the possibility of a society based on universal freedom and equality. For its opponents, such as the English conservative Edmund Burke, it threatened time-honored traditions and "was synonymous with the dark forces of mob rule and terror."[7] Napoleon's fall ushered in a period of reaction in Europe, inaugurated by the Congress of Vienna (1815). Napoleon also indirectly encouraged the development of German anti-Semitism by forcing Jewish emancipation on German principalities.[8]

European intellectuals moved away from Enlightenment egalitarian and environmentalist notions to "theories of inequality and organicism," sometimes adopting a naturalistic fatalism about human affairs.[9] Writers such as the distinguished English physician and polygenist Charles White emphasized deep "race" differences among people as part of a conservative call for order and stability.[10] In *An Account of the Regular Gradation in Man* (1799), White advanced a detailed scientific case for polygenism, the plural origins of human "races." Although he opposed slavery and attempted to reconcile his polygenism with the Bible, he drew upon Petrus Camper's "facial angle" theory (see chapter 2) to rest his case on "the hard facts of anatomical structure."[11] Appealing to the "Great Chain of Being," White claimed that "Negroes" and "Whites" were physically distinct and occupied unequal "stations" in the chain:[12] "In whatever respect the African differs from the European the particularity brings him nearer to the ape."[13] White also put forth one of the most eroticized and gendered visions of white European racial supremacy:

> Ascending the line of gradation, we come at last to the white European, who, being the most removed from the brute creation, may . . . be considered as the most beautiful of the human race. . . . Where shall we find, unless in the European, that nobly arched head, containing such a quantity of brain. . . . Where that erect posture of body and noble gait? In what other quarter of the globe shall we find the blush that overspreads the soft features of the beautiful women of Europe . . . ? Where that nice expression of the amiable and softer passions in the countenance; and that general elegance of features and complexion? Where, except on the bosom of the European woman two such plump and snowy hemispheres, tipt with vermilion?[14]

In revolutionary France, similar ideas were put forth by Jean-Joseph Virey (1774–1847), a follower of Christoph Meiners. Like Meiners, Virey claimed that the "human races ... may be divided ... into those who are fair and white and those which are ugly and dark or black." He asked rhetorically, "What would our world be without Europeans? Powerful nations, a proud and indomitable race, immortal geniuses in the arts and sciences."[15] In postrevolutionary France, prominent French historians Augustin Thierry, Jules Michelet, and François Guizot embraced class-inflected, racialist ideas about "enemy camps" of Franks and Gauls (see chapter 1). A more startling case is the French "utopian socialist" Claude Henri, Comte de Saint-Simon (1760–1825). Saint-Simon's ideal was a stratified, technologically advanced, industrialized society that would be a harmonious association of people "fundamentally dissimilar in their most essential natures, organized in three natural classes."[16] In 1803, a year after Napoleon reinstituted slavery in the colonies, he argued that the French revolutionaries had erred in applying "the principle of equality" to "Negroes." The physiologists had established that "the Negro is organically incapable . . . of being educated to the same level of intelligence as the Europeans."[17]

In the wake of Napoleon's victory at Jena in 1806, which presaged his defeat of Prussia, Johann Gottlieb Fichte (1762–1814) rallied young Germans with his *Address to the German Nation* (1808). Fichte held that all Europeans, except the Slavs, were of Germanic stock. At the same time, he distinguished between the "original people" (*Urvolk*), the Germans proper, and deficient, de-Germanized "neo-Latin peoples." Humankind's "hope of recuperation" lay with the Germans, according to Fichte, who also questioned whether Jesus was of Jewish stock.[18] Concurrent with Fichte's *Address,* German philologist Friedrich Schlegel (1772–1829) laid the groundwork for the later "Aryan race" myth (see chapter 4). In 1808, Schlegel supplemented William Jones's conclusions about the affinity between Sanskrit and European languages with the anthropological claim that all the "famous nations sprang from one stock, and that their colonies were all one people directly or indirectly, of Indian origin."[19] Schlegel did not use the terms *Aryan, Indo-German,* or *Indo-European* in this work. He did adopt the term *Aryan* in 1819, however; and between 1816 and 1833, the comparative philologist Franz Bopp confirmed structural affinities between what he eventually called the Indo-European languages. (Many German authors preferred "Indo-German," while other Europeans preferred "Indo-European," which was coined by an English writer in 1816.)[20]

There were several national liberation movements in Europe in this period, notably in Belgium, Poland, Italy, and Greece, that encouraged nationalist divisions among Europeans. These movements were different from the strident nationalisms that mushroomed in Europe after 1848, however (see chapter 4). While members of these movements tended to focus on their own nations, they typically saw themselves as part of a broader European revolutionary movement and "saw no contradiction between their own demands and those of other nations."[21]

The growth of racialized slavery in the Americas was another major influence on new racial thought. Eli Whitney's invention of the cotton gin in 1793 gave slavery in the United States a new impetus. After the 1790s the cotton plantations of the southern United States supplied a soaring demand for cotton in English mills. The international slave trade was officially abolished in 1815, and slavery itself was ended in British colonies in 1834; but, spurred by commerce, slavery continued to expand in Brazil and the United States. In the latter, the number of slaves grew from about seven hundred thousand in 1790 to 2.5 million in 1840 and 3.2 million in 1850.[22] By 1820, about 8 million enslaved Africans had been forcibly transported to the Americas—primarily to the Caribbean, Brazil, and English colonial North America and the United States.[23] In the 1830s, a vigorous abolitionist movement in the United States provoked "proslavery southerners and their northern sympathizers to develop and promulgate a racist theory" to justify slavery.[24] U.S. policy toward native Americans took a related turn in 1830 with the passage of the Indian Removal Act. The act resulted in the forced resettlement of thousands of members of the Cherokee, Choctaw, and Creek nations to the Oklahoma territory.[25]

Among the European states, Britain forced Ireland into the United Kingdom with the second Act of Union (1801) but postponed Catholic emancipation until 1829, and it deepened its colonial rule over India. In 1833, Thomas Macaulay summarized the rationale for British colonial policy in India and the "civilizing mission" proclaimed by many European colonialists during the next century: "[B]y good government we may educate our subjects into a capacity for better government; that having become instructed in European knowledge they may, in some future age, demand European institutions." France conquered Algeria between 1830 and 1847; the Dutch maintained colonial rule over Indonesia; and, while Latin Americans liberated themselves from Spanish and Portuguese colonial rule, Spain retained control over Cuba and the Philippines.[26]

In the sciences, the expansive field of natural history gave rise to the specialized sciences of biology, anatomy, anthropology, psychology, and philology (historical linguistics). Biology as advanced by the Alsatian comparative anatomist Georges Cuvier, to whom I will return shortly, yielded a new approach to "racial" classification. Cuvier's biology involved "establishing indicative relations between superficial, and therefore visible elements, and others that are concealed in the depths of the body."[27] For the study of human "races," this entailed a turn away from environmental explanations for racial variation to an emphasis on internal, physiological causes that led some races to stagnate and others to flourish. This biological view supported polygenic tendencies in race science.[28]

In 1795, a new science of phrenology was initiated when the Austrian anatomist Johann Franz Gall claimed that there was a correlation "between people's mental abilities and the shape of their heads."[29] Phrenology was eventually discredited, but it was a burgeoning science in the beginning of the nineteenth century. Phrenologists sought to study the brain and its functions by close analysis of the skull. This research reinforced trends toward "racial" determinism in science by regarding culture as a outgrowth of biology and by "offering the scientist new techniques for the measurement of national and racial types."[30]

The "race" concept itself became a defining feature of the modern disciplines of anthropology and ethnology (the science of races) in the first half of the nineteenth century. The work of James Cowles Prichard (1786–1848), the leading English anthropologist of the era, exemplified one of the two major approaches to these new fields of inquiry; the other was a heightened emphasis on biology, craniology, and comparative anatomy, particularly in France and the United States.[31] Prichard drew on anatomy, physiology, zoology, geography, history, archeology, and philology to explain the "ethnological problem" of the unity of the human species. He countered the rise of comparative anatomy, which tended "toward a radically diversified" and polygenist view of the humankind.[32] The Société d'Ethnologique de Paris was formed in 1839, and in England the Ethnological Society was started in 1842, having adopted its name from the French association.[33] In 1848, the year of Prichard's death, an article on his work in the *Edinburgh Review*, titled "Ethnology, or the Science of Races," confirmed the impact of these developments.[34] By the next decade, Prichard's approach to anthropology was widely challenged by a new physical anthropology. James Hunt's Anthropological Society of London devoted itself to "the anatomical aspects of ethnology," and Paul Broca championed a similar approach in the Société d'Anthropologie de Paris.[35]

These "sciences of race" remained integrally connected to Europeans' assumptions about their own physical, intellectual, cultural, religious, and moral superiority.[36] Yet beyond this common assumption were divergent conceptions of race. For monogenists like Prichard, the "ethnological problem" was to explain how the fundamental unity of human beings could be squared with their evident physical and cultural diversity. The "race" concept filled an analytical gap between positing distinct "species" of beings and merely identifying minor variations (or "varieties") within the human species. After the 1820s monogenism was increasingly contested by a polygenist school of thought, which was decisively refuted only after Darwin proposed his evolutionary view of the common "descent of man." Polygenists insisted that the differences between the races were too great to reflect a common origin. They regarded different human races as different *species*, with distinct geographical origins and substantially different moral and intellectual capacities. Not surprisingly, polygenist thought became especially influential in the United States, where European settlers enslaved Africans and decimated the indigenous peoples.[37]

## The "Caucasian Race" in the New "Racial" Anthropology

Against this backdrop, European and North American raciologists widely adopted Blumenbach's "Caucasian race" category by the early 1800s. For example, the French naturalist Jean Baptiste Lamarck (1744–1829), who is best known for his theory of evolution through the inheritance of acquired characteristics, adopted it in *Zoological Philosophy* (1809). Lamarck identified Caucasian, Hyperborean, Mongolian, American, Malay, and Ethiopian varieties of human beings.[38] More significant to the history of race science was Cuvier (1769–1832), who also adopted the "Caucasian race" category and whose thinking about race differences changed during his lifetime in a way that matched the broader shift toward scientific racism. Early in his life, in 1790, Cuvier criticized a friend for accepting ideas about innate "Negro" inferiority and for trying to explain differences in "intellectual faculties" in terms of differences in brain structure. He maintained that the apparent "stupidity" of "Negroes" was a consequence of their "lack of civilization."[39] By the time he published his influential

1817 book, *The Animal Kingdom* (*Le régne animal distribuè d'aprés son organisation*), he had adopted more strident racialism.

In the intervening years, following the French Revolution, Cuvier became a professor of anatomy (1795) and inspector general in the Department of Education (1802) and attained political prominence during the Napoleonic era (1804–15). After the restoration of the Bourbon monarchy, in 1815, he retained his stature and was made a baron.[40] In *The Animal Kingdom*, Cuvier defined *race* in terms of certain observable "hereditary peculiarities of conformation" and identified three primary human "races": "the *Caucasian* or white, the *Mongolian* or yellow, and *Ethiopian* or negro."[41] Three features of his classification scheme are especially noteworthy. First, his tripartite division was rooted in the then widely accepted biblical scheme that divided the world's people's into the descendants of Shem, Ham, and Japheth, the three sons of Noah.[42] Second, Cuvier's division of three "primary races" has had a long-lasting influence, as I explain in chapter 5.[43] Third, although Cuvier was a monogenist, his racialism had a quasi-polygenist dimension and crossed into scientific racism. Consequently, he effectively gave the notion of a Caucasian race a new meaning.

This last feature of Cuvier's thought was part of a wider trend. He echoed Blumenbach's aesthetic claims about the Caucasian race (he said it "is distinguished by the beauty of the oval formed by its head"); but he added further claims about intellectual and characterological traits of the Caucasians: "To this variety, the most civilized nations, and those which have generally held all others in subjection, are indebted for their origin." Conversely, the Mongolian and Negro races fell short on both aesthetic and civilizational scales: the former had a "flat visage," and although it had established "great empires" in China and Japan, it "always remained stationary . . . [in] civilization"; the latter was "confined to the south of mount Atlas," resembled "the monkey tribe" in facial appearance, and "the hordes of which it consists have always remained in the . . . state of utter barbarism."[44] The peoples of Europe and contiguous regions are rightly called "*Caucasian,* because tradition and the filiation of nations seem to refer its origin to that group of mountains situated between the Caspian and Black seas, whence, as from a centre, it has extended like the radii of a circle." He followed Blumenbach, moreover, in claiming that the people of the Caucasus, particularly "the Georgians and Circassians, are . . . the handsomest on earth."[45]

Cuvier also developed a geological theory of eight epochs of natural history that informed his view of race. He speculated that the earth had experienced a series of natural catastrophes that had killed numerous species. He affirmed the monogenist view that all humans were descended from Adam but held that the three major human "races"—Caucasian, Mongolian, and Ethiopian—had "escaped in different directions after the last catastrophe, some five thousand years before, and had developed in geographical isolation from each other." His argument, which influenced writers in France, the United States, and Great Britain, reconciled assumptions about significant racial differentiation among human beings with the generally accepted biblical chronology.[46]

In addition, Cuvier divided the Caucasian race into three principal branches. The first was the Armenian or Syrian branch, which stretched to the south of Europe and produced the Assyrians, Chaldeans, Arabs, Phoenicians, Jews, Abyssinians, "and most probably the Egyptians." This branch had produced great achievements in religion, the arts, and literature.[47] His second branch—Indians, Germans, and Pelasgics—was more widespread and diverse, though joined by important linguistic affinities. "It is by this great and venerable branch of the Caucasian stock that philosophy, the arts, and the sciences have been carried to the greatest perfection." Cuvier included the present-day descendants of the ancient Persians in this branch of Caucasians but claimed that the Celts and the Cantabrians (from northern and northwestern Spain) were distinct peoples who preceded the Indian-German-Pelasgic branch of the Caucasian race into Europe.[48] Finally, Cuvier classed the "predatory tribes" to the north and northwest of Europe in a Scythian and Tartar branch of the Caucasian race. He distinguished this branch, which included Scythians, Parthians, Turks, Finlanders, and Hungarians, from "their more civilized brethren," and he located the Mongolian race to the east of the Tartar branch of the Caucasian.[49] Cuvier's subdivisions of the Caucasian race, with three branches ranked according to cultural achievements, foreshadowed later tendencies to subdivide the Caucasian race into several distinct "races."

This last tendency was more evident in the thinking of the British physiologist William Lawrence (1783–1867), who adopted the "Caucasian" category around the same time as Cuvier. In his controversial *Lectures on Physiology, Zoology, and the Natural History of Man* (1819), Lawrence followed Blumenbach to divide the human species into Caucasian, Mongolian, Ethiopian, American, and Malay varieties.[50] He was a monogenist like Cuvier, but he took the scientific practice of "racial" classification in a more starkly racist direction. According to Lawrence, there were moral and intellectual differences not only between the "dark" and "white" races but also among the "white races" that comprised the "Caucasian variety" of human beings: "[T]he races of mankind are no less characterized by diversity of mental endowments, than by . . . differences of [physical] organisation. . . . The distinction of colour between the white and black races is not more striking, than the pre-eminence of the former in moral feelings and in mental endowments."[51] The latter difference was even more apparent in "the intellectual faculties . . . than in moral feelings and dispositions," and the "same general character, with some . . . modifications, is applicable to most of the native Americans, of the Africans, and of the Mongolian nations of Asia," as well as to the Malays and other Pacific islanders.[52] Only in the "white races" that the Caucasian variety comprised do "we meet, in full perfection, with true bravery, love of liberty, and other passions and virtues of great souls."[53]

Lawrence's thinking, even more than Cuvier's, prefigured the eclipse of the pan-European "Caucasian" category later in the nineteenth century. He was one of the first anthropological theorists to extend the idea of superior and inferior races to European nations. The Caucasian variety, he claimed, encompassed "numerous races":

> all ancient and modern Europeans, except the Laplanders and the rest of the Finnish race; the former and present inhabitants of Western Asia, as far as the river Ob, the Caspian Sea, and the Ganges; that is, the Assyrians, Medes, and Chaldeans; the Sarmatians, Scythians, and Parthians; the Philistines, Phoenicians, Jews, and the inhabitants of Syria generally; the Tartars . . . ; the several tribes actually occupying the chain of Caucasus; the Georgians, Circassians, Mingrelians, Armenians; the Turks, Persians, Arabians, Afghauns, and Hindoos of high caste; the northern Africans, including . . . even some tribes in more southern regions; the Egyptians, Abyssinians, and Guanches.[54]

Assigning all these "races" to "one variety" of the human species should not be understood to mean that "they are all alike in physical and moral traits." Indeed, he claimed that strongly marked variations of these sorts "are more numerous in the Caucasian than in the other varieties."[55] Lawrence acknowledged that it was difficult to know how much of the "distinctions of moral and intellectual endowments" was due to environmental factors—for example, education, religion, and government—and how much to "original difference." Nevertheless, he asserted that the more noble "virtues and talents" were found "in a higher degree among the

Celtic and German, than among the Slavonic and Oriental people."[56] (His pairing of Celtic and German peoples is noteworthy in relation to how late-nineteenth-century raciologists regarded Celts and Germans as distinct races.)[57]

Lawrence also heralded a new style of anthropology, although he himself did not pursue it.[58] He noted differences in the crania (or skulls) of people from different nations—French, Germans, Italians—and suggested that these were probably connected to differences in "intellectual powers." He cautioned, however, that any such conclusions must "await the result of more numerous and accurate comparisons."[59] The project to attain such comparisons soon defined the anthropological subdiscipline of physical anthropology, which focused on measuring various parts of the human body, but principally the skull (see chapter 4).[60]

By the 1820s, the "Caucasian race" category was also adopted French physiologist Louis-Antoine Desmoulins, a staunch polygenist. In 1825, Desmoulins proposed a classification of eleven human *species*. He raised the number to sixteen in 1826. In the later scheme he included a distinct Caucasian species that included Georgians, Mingrelians, and Armenians of the Caucasus region.[61] His scheme had little lasting prestige but exemplified a couple of significant trends: a tendency toward the proliferation of "races" in racial classifications throughout the nineteenth century, which indicated the arbitrariness of the whole practice, and occasional efforts to place the peoples of the Caucasus in their own separate racial category.

Polygenism found a more effective advocate in Desmoulins's contemporary Samuel George Morton (1799–1851), a physician and professor of anatomy. Morton led an "American school" of polygenist thought that was influential in the United States between the 1830s and 1850s, against the backdrop of the increasingly violent debate over slavery. Along with Blumenbach and Lawrence, Morton thought that human cranial forms had special importance for the study of race differences, and he attributed great importance to the estimated "cranial capacity" of the skulls of Blumenbach's five races. While he accepted the framework of biblical chronology, he maintained that the characteristic features of the various human races could be traced back to the earliest recorded history.[62] Each race "was adapted from the beginning to its peculiar local destination. In other words, it is assumed, that the physical characteristics which distinguish the different Races, are independent of external causes."[63]

Morton basically imposed two major alterations on Blumenbach's five "great divisions" of human beings. First, in his classification scheme "the word *race* is substituted for the word *varieties*."[64] In effect, Morton (and his followers) regarded *Homo sapiens* as a *genus* that was divided into several distinct *species*; and, in contrast to Blumenbach, he used "race" to signify innate, irreducible differences.[65] Second, he subdivided each of his races into "families" to arrive at a total of twenty-two families, which were not themselves races; they were "groups of nations possessing, to a greater or less extent, similarity of physical and moral character, and language." While some of these families possessed traits characteristic of the "aboriginal races," others were of mixed and relatively recent origin. The primary races had distinct moral and intellectual characters, with some variation across the families in each of them.[66]

Members of the Caucasian race had "large and oval" skulls, and the race was "distinguished for the facility with which it attains the highest intellectual endowments."[67] The Mongolian, Malay, American, and Ethiopian races, respectively, were progressively less "ingenious" and "susceptible of cultivation." The Mongolians were "ingenious, imitative, and highly susceptible of cultivation"; the Malay were "active and ingenious" but also "migratory" and "predacious"; the American race (i.e., native Americans) was "averse to cultivation, and slow in acquiring knowledge"; and the nations that comprised the Ethiopian race "present a singular diversity of intellectual character, of which the far extreme is the lowest grade of humanity."[68]

Within his "Caucasian race," Morton included seven "families": Caucasian, Germanic, Celtic, Arabian, Lybian, Nilotic, and Indostanic.[69] Like Cuvier, he subdivided his Caucasian family further into three branches—the Caucasian proper, the Persian, and the Pelasgic—and in describing his Caucasian family, he reiterated the long-standing mythology about the Caucasus region. It was "a spot to which history and tradition refer the primeval family of man" and the origin of many nations that "have peopled the finest portions of the earth, and given birth to its fairest inhabitants," especially the beautiful Circassians and Georgians.[70]

Morton's discussion of the Caucasian race also prefigured later nineteenth-century racialized nationalism. He said that the Caucasian, Germanic, Celtic, and Hindu families "constitute the great chain of what are called the *Indo-European nations*."[71] While he regarded the Celts in a generally favorable light, he described those from the southwest of Ireland as "the most unsophisticated Celts, . . . whose wild look and manner, mud cabins and funereal howlings, recall the memory of a barbarous age." In contrast, the Teutonic (i.e., Germanic) stock that make up the "hybrid" people that "we call the English or Anglo-Saxons . . . [is] inferior to no one of the Caucasian families in intellectual endowments, and possessed of indomitable courage" and enterprise—traits manifest in its colonial endeavors.[72]

Morton's chief contribution to ethnology was his elaborate method to estimate the average "cranial capacity" of different races by measuring the volume of skulls. While such an emphasis on cranial forms could be traced back to Blumenbach, it marked a decisive shift from the old-style anthropology represented by Prichard, which emphasized history and philology, to a physical anthropology that focused on quantitative measurement of human bodies.[73] Initially, Morton did not explicitly equate cranial capacity with intelligence. Not surprisingly, though, his measures of the cranial capacity of the different races—which have since been shown to be dubious—corresponded to his assessments of their relative "ingenuity."[74] He maintained that the Caucasian race had the largest cranial capacity, followed in descending order by the Mongolian, Malay, American, and Ethiopian races (see table 3.1).[75] Morton's followers were less hesitant to assert a close relationship between "cranial capacity" and intelligence, and in an 1840 lecture Morton himself implied that such a connection existed—even as he acknowledged the "comparatively limited scale" of his observations. While some differences in brain size may be due to differences in climate, the principal cause is "those primeval attributes of mind, which . . . have given our [i.e., Caucasian] race a decided and unquestionable superiority over all other nations of the earth."[76]

Given the fierce struggles over slavery, Morton's claims about the racial identity of the ancient Egyptians are also instructive. In *Crania America* (1839) he classified the ancient Egyptians in the Caucasian race. The

TABLE 3.1
*Morton's "Cranial Capacity" Measurements*

| Races | No. of Skulls | Mean Internal Capacity in Cubic Inches | Largest in the Series | Smallest in the Series |
|---|---|---|---|---|
| 1. Caucasian | 52 | 87 | 109 | 75 |
| 2. Mongolian | 10 | 83 | 93 | 69 |
| 3. Malay | 18 | 81 | 89 | 64 |
| 4. Aboriginal American | 147 | 80 | 100 | 60 |
| 5. Ethiopian | 29 | 78 | 94 | 65 |

From *Chambers's Information for the People*, new edition, vol. 2 (London and Edinburgh: W. & R. Chambers, 1850), p. 9.

Copts, members of the "Nilotic family" of the Caucasian race, were descendants of the ancient Egyptians, but subsequent oppression by Persians, Greeks, Romans, Arabians, and Turks had left them as "the degenerate remains, both physically and intellectually, of that mighty people." He called the "present Egyptians" a "mixed race of Copts and Egyptians."[77] In a separate note, he countered the "vulgar error . . . which classes the ancient Egyptians with the Negro race."[78] Yet to do this he merely quoted Cuvier's claim that whatever the skin color of the ancient Egyptians, "they belonged to the same race as ourselves [i.e., Caucasian]."[79]

Morton subsequently returned to this issue at the urging of his follower Josiah Nott. Nott, who along with George Glidden later published the influential book *Types of Mankind* (1854), wanted to prove "that the Caucasian or white, and the Negro races were distinct at a very remote date, and *that the Egyptians were Caucasians*."[80] Morton took up this task in *Crania Aegyptica* (1844).[81] Based on his comparison of 137 human skulls with the various cranial forms depicted on ancient Egyptian monuments, Morton concluded that all the crania "may be referred to two great races of men, the Caucasian and the Negro."[82] He grouped the "Caucasian" heads further into three groups: the Pelasgic type (which represented "the perfect type of cranio-facial outline"); the Semitic type (marked by "long, arched, and very prominent nose . . . and strong, and often harsh, development of the whole facial structure"); and the Egyptian type (which "differs from the Pelasgic in having a narrower and more receding forehead, while in the face being more prominent"). The "true *Negro* conformation requires no comment," he said, although some of the heads show "mixed characters, in which those of the Negro predominate."[83] The Nile Valley "was originally peopled by a branch of the Caucasian race," and "Negroes were numerous in Egypt, but their social position in ancient times was the same that it now is [in the United States], that of servants and slaves."[84]

Nott and Glidden, among others, actively appealed to Morton's ideas to justify slavery.[85] In Morton's discussion of ancient Egypt they found "an ancient historical precedent for a white society with black slaves." For Nott and Glidden, racial division was permanent, and the differences between the "Negro" and "Caucasian" races in the United States in the 1840s paralleled the differences between them in ancient Egypt.[86]

## The Passage into "Our Ordinary Forms of Expression"

In the mid–nineteenth century the validity of Blumenbach's "Caucasian race" category faced its first major, though largely ineffective, challenge: critiques by Prichard and Robert Gordon Latham. Both ethnologists carried forward the project of racial classification but rejected the "Caucasian" category. Prichard approached the issue of race differences in light of his (Christian) religiously informed monogenism, which he defended for more than thirty years. At the start of the first edition of his *Researches into the Physical History of Man* (1813), he strikingly conveyed how human diversity appeared to many European thinkers in the early nineteenth century:

> If an illiterate person, bred in some remote corner of England, who had never seen or heard of any human creatures different from the natives of his own vacinity, were suddenly transported into the western continent, and introduced to a horde of the naked and dusty barbarians who wander the shores of Mississippi, or if he were presented to a tribe of yellow or bald-headed Mongoles, or carried into the midst of the black population of a negro hamlet, he would certainly experience strong emotions of wonder and surprise. He would indeed recognise the beings whom he saw as men, for the expression of rational intellect; the likeness of the Creator which was imprinted on the first of the human kind, is every where instantly striking and conspicuous. But a spectator in such circumstances would be exceedingly perplexed in contemplating appearances so new to him, and in comparing with himself persons who differed from him in so extraordinary manner, and yet resembled him.[87]

He noted differences "of voice and gesture and manners of life" along with "peculiarities of natural structure." Philosophers tended to attribute differences of the former kind to "accident and education," but "there still remains a great variety in the physical constitution of the several races of men" that required explanation.[88]

In this edition of his *Researches*, Prichard argued that the civilizing process was chiefly responsible for human racial variation, similar to how variation in plants and animals has been produced through "domestication."[89] Based on this theory, which inverted the degeneration theories of Buffon and Blumenbach, he suggested the original color of the human species was "black" rather than "white." In short, racial variation occurred through "the transmutation of the characteristics of the Negro into those of the European, or the evolution of white varieties in black races of men."[90] Prichard backed away from this view somewhat in subsequent editions of his *Researches,* but he retained elements of it in his later writings.[91] In line with the broader trends in anthropology, he considered craniological evidence to determine racial affinities among nations but relied more on philological, historical, and geographical evidence of linguistic kinships and migrations. By the 1840s, he was influenced somewhat by the gathering strength of polygenist thought and often contrasted different nations and "races" in strongly evaluative terms.[92] He now said that "same inward and mental nature is to be recognized in all races of men . . . , though not always in the same degree of forwardness or ripeness of improvement."[93]

In his critique of the "Caucasian race" category, Prichard examined the theory popularized by Cuvier that linked three primary human races to three great mountain chains: Mount Caucasus being the original home of the "race of white men" of Europe and western Asia; Mount Altai, in eastern Asia, the original location of the Mongolians; and Mount Atlas, in northwestern Africa, the original home of African Negroes.[94] This theory was based on a "mixture of somewhat vague notions, partly connected with physical theories, and in part derived from . . . mythology," which assumed that "the mountains of high Asia must have been the part of the world first inhabited by men."[95] Prichard added that various religious traditions—Hindu, Zoroastrian, Confucian—have regarded the high mountains as "scenes of the first mythical adventures of gods and men."[96] Because of these traditions, the Caucasus region "came in for a share of the reverence paid to high places of the earth. Caucasus, however, was not the cradle of the human race, but the dwelling place of Prometheus, the maker of men, and the teacher of astronomy." Prichard himself maintained that it was more likely that the "cradles or nurseries of the first nations . . . appear to have been extensive plains or valleys traversed by navigable channels."[97]

He suggested that the three earliest human civilizations were those of the *Semitic* or *Syro-Arabian* (or *Shemite*) nations, the *Indo-European* or *Japhetic people,* and the people of "the land of Ham."[98] Thus, he partially reaffirmed the Noachian story of the common origin of three distinct peoples *cum* "races." Yet he regarded these three ancient groups as the "groundwork of an ethnological system" that included seven principal varieties of human beings: Syro-Arabian or Semitic; Egyptian; Indo-Euro-

pean or "Arian"; Africans (including "Hottentots" or "Bushmen" and nations of West Africa); nations of High Asia; native American tribes; and
the tribes of the Austral and South Seas.[99] He said that there were numerous races and nations within each of these principal varieties, but he offered no precise distinction between "nations" and "races."[100]

Meanwhile, Prichard considered the Caucasus region itself to be also
ethnologically distinctive. The Caucasian peoples were largely unrelated to
the movement of Indo-European peoples into Europe, "since we know
that chain of mountains to have been occupied from remote times by
tribes of a race quite distinct from the Indo-Europeans."[101] They were
known from their distinct history and languages "to consist of four distinct races, in each of which are several tribes unintelligible to each
other."[102] The Ossetians were an exception to this rule insofar as they were
a branch of the "Arian race in Asia . . . who dwell on a small part of the
Caucasian chain."[103] At the same time, he rejected Morton's account of the
Caucasian racial identity of the ancient Egyptians. He maintained that
they "were a dark-colored people, and . . . that great varieties existed
among them." The typical shape of their skulls was the oval form "common to highly developed nations"; yet in other respects their "physical
type" was similar to that of the other people of Africa.[104]

After Prichard died in 1849, his anthropological orientation was carried
forward in the 1850s by British ethnologist and philologist Robert Gordon
Latham (1812–1888).[105] By this time, polygenist thought was ascendant
along with the new anatomical (or physical) anthropology. The latter approach usually combined an emphasis on observable physical differences
among races with explicit assumptions of white supremacy.[106] In England
this trend was exemplified in Charles Hamilton Smith's 1848 book, *The
Natural History of the Human Species*. A disciple of Cuvier who had
worked in the West Indies, Smith used the "Caucasian" category to refer to
basically the same peoples so designated by Blumenbach; but he did so
from an implicitly polygenist perspective.[107] Intriguingly, Latham responded to this trend in his 1850 book, *The Natural History of the Varieties
of Man,* by avoiding the term *race* in his effort to correct previous attempts
at ethnological classification. He understood *race* to denote "a class of individuals concerning which there are doubts as to whether they constitute
a separate species, or a variety of a recognised one. Hence the term is *subjective*; i.e., it applies to the *opinion of the investigator rather than to the object of investigation*."[108] That is, the term *race* had an indeterminate meaning among anthropological writers such that its use obscured the task of

comprehending human diversity. Since Latham believed that there was "no tribe or family" of people that could reasonably be counted as a "new species," he chose to not use "the word *race* at all," except inadvertently. "Its proper place is in *investigation* not in exposition." Instead of "races," he returned to the eighteenth-century concept of "varieties," defining a *variety* as "a class of individuals, each belonging to the same species, but each differing from other individuals of the species in points wherein they agree amongst themselves."[109]

Latham considered a combination of cranial forms, skin colors, hair types, and especially linguistic evidence to arrive at three primary varieties of human beings: "Mongolidae," "Atlantidae," and "Japetidae," or Mongolians (encompassing Asia, Polynesia, and America), Africans, and Europeans.[110] He vehemently rejected Blumenbach's "Caucasian" category as unscientific and misleading. The term is "*mis*-applied for the sake of denoting the so-called Caucasian race, consisting, or said to consist, of Jews, Greeks, Circassians, Scotchmen, ancient Romans, and other heterogeneous elements . . . in more than one celebrated work of fiction."[111] Latham acknowledged that due to the widespread use of Blumenbach's terminology his own alternative left him on "debatable ground": "So long has the term Caucasian been used to denote a type of physical conformation closely akin to the Japetidae (*i.e.,* preeminently European), that to place the Georgians and Circassians in the midst of the Mongolidae, is a paradox."[112] Nevertheless, he insisted that the languages of the various Caucasian or "Dioscurian" nations and tribes are most closely related to the "Aptotic" languages of the Mongolians.[113] Latham also dismissed the notion that the Caucasian nations should be classified with "Europeans" based on the alleged "symmetry of shape and delicacy of complexion . . . of the Georgians and Circassians." He had a different sense of the relevant facts: "It is only among the chiefs where the personal beauty of the male portion of the population is at all remarkable. The tillers of the soil are, comparatively speaking, coarse and unshapely."[114] Blumenbach had erred:

> Blumenbach had a solitary Georgian skull; and that skull was the finest in his collection—that of a Greek being the next. Hence it was taken as the type of skull of the more organised divisions of our species. More than this; it gave its name to the type, and introduced the name *Caucasian.* Never has a single head done as much harm to science than was done in the way of posthumous mischief by the head of this well-shaped female from Georgia.[115]

Latham classified the Caucasian peoples as a Dioscurian division of his Mongolidae variety. His scheme was also notable in a few other respects. He placed Jews, Syrians, Assyrians, Babylonians, Arabs, and Ethiopians, among others, in a "Semitic Atlantidae" division of the Atlantidae variety.[116] He located the "true Negro"—or "Negro Atlantidae," whom he described in condescending terms—mainly in western Africa, which happened to have been the primary source of African slaves. "No fact is more necessary to be remembered than the difference between the Negro and the African." He divided his Japetidae variety into two divisions: the "Celts," who broke away "from the mother stock" at an early stage in the development of their common language, and the "Indo-Germanic," which included a European subdivision and an "Iranian Indo-European" one.[117] Finally, Latham's reference to a Japetidae variety and to Semitic peoples revealed a continuing influence of the Noachian origins narrative.

His overall classification scheme had some influence for a time. He presented a slightly revised version of it in his article on "Ethnology" in the *Encyclopaedia Britannica* (8th ed., 1853), and his classification scheme was also recommended in articles on "Ethnology" and "Anthropology" in the 1850 and 1875 editions of *Chambers's Information for the People.*[118] Tellingly, though, the *Chambers's* articles used Blumenbach's categories to visually represent the races of humankind, and the 1875 article stated flatly of Blumenbach's "Caucasian variety," "This is the highest race of all as regards moral feeling and intellect" (see figures 5.1–5.5).[119]

The *Chambers's* articles also conveyed a significant irony concerning the criticisms by Prichard and Latham of the "Caucasian race" category: these anthropologists effectively highlighted peculiarities of Blumenbach's Caucasian race, yet by this time the notion of a Caucasian race had become part of common usage. Another critic, William Carpenter, noted this in 1848. Blumenbach's categories, after having been adopted by Cuvier, had "passed into our ordinary forms of expression, . . . although they are no longer scientifically appropriate."[120]

A few examples will reveal just how far the "Caucasian race" had passed into ordinary usage by this time, particularly in Europe and the United States. In 1843, U.S. politician Daniel Webster, in a speech to commemorate the landing of the pilgrims, celebrated the achievements of the "Anglo-American" branch of the "English race" that "issued from the great Caucasian fountain."[121] In England, Benjamin Disraeli pointedly used the "Caucasian race" category in his 1844 novel, *Coningsby.* He had his character Sidonia, a Jewish banker, use it to explain to Coningsby his peculiar

Figure 5: Blumenbach's Five Races, as depicted from *Chambers's Information for the People* (1850): 1. Caucasian Variety; 2. Mongolian Variety; 3. Ethiopic (African); Variety; 4. American Variety; 5. Malay Variety. Reprinted from the new edition, vol. 2 (London and Edinburgh: W. & R. Chambers, 1850), p. 2.

position as a Jew in England and to insist that a relatively minor humilia-tion cannot keep down the Caucasian "Jewish race": "Do you think that the quiet humdrum persecution of a decorous representative of an English university can crush those who have successively baffled the Pharaohs, Nebuchadnezzar, Rome, and the Feudal ages? The fact is, you cannot de-stroy a pure race of the Caucasian organization. It is a physiological fact; a simple law of nature."[122] Also in England, John Stuart Mill, in the 1848 edition of his *Principles of Political Economy,* acknowledged social progress in the United States along with problems of slavery and inequalities be-tween the sexes. He remarked that the "northern and middle states of America" had reached an agreeable "stage of civilization" with respect to "all social injustices and inequalities that affect persons of Caucasian race and of the male sex."[123] From a different tradition, the German anarchist Max Stirner (1806–56) propounded a dialectical theory of the Caucasian race's special destiny in *The Ego and His Own*:

> The history of the world, whose shaping properly belongs altogether to the Caucasian race, seems till now to have run through two Caucasian ages, in the first of which we had to work off our innate *Negroidity*; this was followed in the second by *Mongoloidity* (Chineseness), which must likewise be terribly made an end of.[124]

## Conclusion

As I noted earlier, Robert Gordon Latham challenged the efficacy of the "race" concept along with the notion of a Caucasian race. Classifying "varieties of mankind," he said, "is very like that of the species of a genus. The practical proof of a clear consciousness on the part of a writer that he is classifying *varieties* rather than *species,* is the care he takes to guard his reader against mistaking one for the other, and the attention he bestows on the transition from one type to another." Rather than rigorously adhering to this principle, however, ethnologists "have introduced a new and lax term—*race.* This means something which is neither a variety nor yet a species—a *tertium quid.*"[125] Still, his own proposal to speak of human varieties mostly reinforced racialism. (What he really disputed was the polygenist view of multiple species of *Homo sapiens.*) Furthermore, on another occasion Latham himself used *race* to denote "certain original differences of organization, faculties, and capacities stamped upon different divisions of the human species from the beginning; innate qualities, as distinguished from mere developments."[126]

At the time, Latham's questioning of the "race" concept was no more successful than his criticism of the "Caucasian race" category. Both proposals ran counter to dominant trends. In both anthropology and popular discourse in Europe and the United States, "race" was now widely used to indicate fundamental "differences of organization, faculties, and capacities stamped upon different divisions of the human species." For instance, alluding to race differences, William Smellie claimed in an 1835 book, "Independent of all political institutions, nature herself has formed the human species into castes and ranks."[127] For Europeans and European Americans, the "race" concept had become (along with gender) a means for dominant groups to assert the *naturalness* of certain social and political hierarchies, particularly with respect to Europe's colonies and European Americans' claims of a "manifest destiny" for the United States.

From about 1800 to the early 1850s, the Caucasian race was typically given first rank among the supposed human races by scientists and in popular discourse in both Europe and North America. Blumenbach's "Caucasian race" category retained some currency among race scientists for the next twenty years or so (even longer in the United States). In 1860, for example, the French naturalist Isidore Geoffroy Saint-Hilaire, a polygenist, distinguished four principal races—Caucasian, Mongolian, Ethiopian, and Hottentot—along with thirteen secondary races among them.[128] In 1855, Paul Broca, the leading French physical anthropologist of the time, supported his own polygenist view that the different human races constituted distinct species in part by insisting that "certain peoples" differed greatly from "the Caucasians" in "intellectual and moral capacities" as well as in their physical traits.[129] Later, in opposition to polygenist ideas, Charles Darwin, in *The Descent of Man,* spoke of "Caucasian features" among some "negro" tribes to indicate that "even the most distinct races of man are much more like each other in form than would at first be supposed."[130]

Ultimately, the criticisms of the "Caucasian race" idea by Prichard and Latham had little worldly impact. For the most part, these two English ethnologists shared Blumenbach's basic anthropological orientation: they were all monogenists; each of them sometimes spoke of human "varieties" rather than human "races"; and they all saw most Europeans (excepting Laplanders and Finns) as "racially" united.[131] Prichard and Latham simply disputed Blumenbach's racial designations. Meanwhile, as the notion of a Caucasian race had, for the time being, "passed into . . . ordinary forms of expression," the dominant racial discourse was actually on the verge of changing momentously. Several historical and scientific developments in Europe and the United States that began in the 1840s worked emphatically to displace Blumenbach's "Caucasian race" category, especially in Europe, ushering in nearly a century of new theories about the "races of Europe."

# 4

# Racialized Nationalism and the Partial Eclipse of the "Caucasian Race," ca. 1840–1935

Every industrial and commercial centre in England now possesses a working class *divided* into two *hostile* camps. English proletarians and Irish proletarians. The ordinary English worker hates the Irish worker who lowers his standard of life. In relation to the Irish worker he feels himself a member of the *ruling nation* and so turns himself into a tool of the aristocrats and capitalists of his country against Ireland thus strengthening their domination *over himself.* He cherishes religious, social, and national prejudices against the Irish worker. His attitude towards him is much the same as that of the "poor whites" to the "niggers" in the former slave states of the U.S.A. The Irishman pays him back with interest in his own money. He sees in the English worker at once the accomplice and the stupid tool of English rule in Ireland.

—Karl Marx to Sigfrid Meyer and August Vogt, 9 April 1870[1]

The conflict of races is now about to start openly within nations and between nations, and one can only ask oneself if the ideas of the fraternity and equality of man were not against nature. . . . *I am convinced that in the next century people will slaughter each other by the million because of a difference of a degree or two in the cephalic index. It is by this sign . . . that men will be identified . . . and the last sentimentalists will be able to witness the most massive exterminations of peoples.*

—Georges Vacher de Lapouge, *L'Aryen, son rôle social* (1899)[2]

French writer Georges Vacher de Lapouge's remarks eerily foreshadowed the most brutal consequence of the latest race science in Europe and North America between roughly 1840 and 1935: the Nazis' murder of nearly 6 million European Jews, among others, during 1942–

45. Marx's comments highlighted one of the key social dynamics that re-configured racial thought in this period: mass migrations and intense labor market competition among workers of different European national-ities and ethnicities in the context of uneven capitalist development across European states. As in Marx's English example, such competition was often between European peoples who only recently had been classified to-gether racially as "Caucasians."

Ambiguities intrinsic to the "race" concept facilitated this proliferation of new races. In German philosopher Immanuel Kant's influential formu-lation, human races were distinguished by "characteristic features" that were amenable to clear description and reproduced continually across succeeding generations (see chapter 2). Yet neither Kant nor subsequent theorists gave any compelling account of why some traits but not others (for instance, skin color but not eye color) distinguished human races.

Initially, drawing on Eurocentric preconceptions, European race scien-tists distinguished a Europe-centered "white" or "Caucasian" race from a few other primary races, reinforcing white supremacism; but by the mid–nineteenth century the legacy of Kant's vague notion of "characteristic fea-tures" was redirected. Nineteenth-century raciologists posited "racial" characteristics that were different from the ones identified earlier by the likes of Kant and Blumenbach. Craniology, the study of skull forms initi-ated by Blumenbach and Camper, proved especially malleable. Whereas Blumenbach and Camper, like Kant, validated then-prevailing European and Anglo-American assumptions about a superior "white race" (incar-nated by Blumenbach's "Caucasian race"), European ethnologists in the second half of the nineteenth century used craniology to discern racial differences between European peoples.

This new belief in European races was not completely unprecedented. Recall that medieval Europeans possessed related ideas about ethnic dif-ferences between Franks, Gauls, Saxons, Celts, Slavs, Jews, and Muslims. The sixteenth-century anatomist Andreas Vesalius said that "certain na-tions have something peculiar in the shape of the head"; in 1751, Ben-jamin Franklin contrasted "swarthy" Spaniards, Italians, French, Russians, Swedes, and Germans ("Saxons excepted") with "purely white" English and German Saxons; and Blumenbach spoke of different "national skulls" within each of his five races. These ideas were overshadowed, however, by more dominant suppositions about "white," pan-European (and beyond) racial affinity, as exemplified by Blumenbach's Caucasian race.

Between 1840 and 1935 new theories about "the races of Europe" flourished. They largely displaced Blumenbach's Caucasian race, especially in Europe. Despite the earlier cleavages within European "Christendom," it was not that nineteenth-century European race scientists finally developed methods necessary to identify actually existing European races. Instead, these scientists were spurred by emerging social and political forces to adapt existing race ideas in novel ways: the legacy of the failed European revolutions of 1848; the articulation by U.S. elites of an Anglo-American "manifest destiny"; uneven capitalist development across Europe and North America, along with the extension of commodity production, competitive wage labor markets, and class conflicts; vastly expanding European migrations, especially international labor migrations, with immigrants frequently perceived as "outsiders"; and rising European nationalism, which saw humankind divided into discrete "nations" and was often used by states "to regulate migration by policing the boundary of the nation."[3] The new nationalism was especially consequential. As John Higham says, "Under the pressure of a growing national consciousness, a number of European naturalists began to subdivide the European white man into biological types, often using linguistic similarity as evidence of hereditary connection. For their part, the nationalists slowly absorbed biological assumptions about the nature of race, until every national trait seemed wholly dependent on hereditary transmission."[4]

Race and racism figured increasingly in the struggles of nation-states, national bourgeoisie, and national working classes to navigate the dislocations wrought by capitalist development.[5] European and Anglo-American race scientists responded to these developments by revising inherited race ideas to produce new theories about the races of Europe. These theories contributed to the racialization of social and political relations *among* Europeans. Moreover, within this new European race science the peoples of the Caucasus region (Georgians, Circassians, and Mingrelians among them) were generally regarded either as only marginally European or as "Asiatic." Given the broader trend, the German Nazis' version of the "Aryan race" myth, which originated in this period, was aberrant only in its extremism and its role as an official state ideology.

Yet the "Caucasian race" category did not disappear completely. It continued to resonate with European (and eventually Anglo-American) global dominance and imperialism. It also served those Europeans and Euro-Americans (also Euro-Australians and New Zealanders) who were preoccupied with getting their fellow Europeans to stand "shoulder to shoulder against the colored hordes of black, red, and yellow men."[6] Thus, the "Caucasian race" idea persisted alongside the new ideas in the United States where the history of Negro slavery and subsequent "Jim Crow" segregation in the South highlighted a black/white "color line." That said, where the "Caucasian race" category had been used to distinguish racially so-called whites from nonwhites, the new "races of Europe" theories established racial hierarchies among the white peoples who had previously been grouped together as Caucasians.[7]

## *"Race" Science and Society, 1840–1935*

Two poems epitomized the two main threads of racial thought during this time period. In 1899, during the high tide of European and U.S. imperialism, Rudyard Kipling (1865–1936) famously summed the imperialist ethos in his ode to the U.S. conquest of the Philippines, "The White Man's Burden."[8] His poem read in part:

> Take up the White Man's Burden—
> Send forth the best ye breed—
> Go, blind your sons to exile
> To serve your captives' need;
> To wait, in heavy harness,
> On fluttered folk and wild—
> Your new-caught sullen peoples,
> Half devil and half child.[9]

Kipling's "White Man's Burden" was continuous with earlier notions of white and Caucasian supremacy and spoke to several racialized divisions of global politics in these years: British colonial rule in India; French colonialism in Algeria; the wars of the United States against the native Americans of the western plains, and the U.S. 1898 annexation of Hawaii and its seizure that same year (after its war on Spain) of Puerto Rico, Guam, the Mariana Islands, and the Philippines; Negro slavery in the United States and Brazil and subsequent Jim Crow segregation in the United States; the "scramble for Africa" among European states in the late nineteenth century; and Japan's victory over Russia in Russo-Japanese War of 1904–5.[10]

These episodes were only one aspect of the racism of the time, however. The second major trend was an obsessive quest among European raciologists in the latter half of the nineteenth century to describe and classify races of Europeans. Near the end of the era, the British writer Hilaire Belloc (1870–1953), in "The Three Races," satirized one of the products of this trend—a division between so-called Nordic, Alpine, and Mediterranean races:

> Behold, my child, the Nordic Man,
> And be as like him as you can.
> His legs are long; his mind is slow.
> His hair is lank and made of tow.
> And here we have the Alpine Race.
> Oh! What a broad and foolish face!
> His skin is of a dirty yellow.
> He is a most unpleasant fellow.
> The most degraded of them all
> Mediterranean we call.
> His hair is crisp, even the curls.
> And he is saucy with the girls.[11]

As I mentioned earlier, several developments within Europe impelled this transformation in European and North American race thinking. First, there was a major economic and demographic transition in Europe between 1800 and 1850. Cathy Frierson notes, "Europe shifted from a world in which roughly 80 percent of the population continued to live and labor in the countryside to one in which the push of agricultural reform and the pull of industrial development and urbanization was displacing, rearranging, and in some cases, destroying the parts making up the preindustrial village." Land and labor increasingly became commodities.[12] By the 1830s capitalist development had generated widespread urban discontent and the working class was becoming a force in European politics. This was evident in revolutionary uprisings of 1830 in France, Germany, Italy, and Poland, and in the more "proletarian" though short-lived European revolutions of 1848. Growing European nationalism, especially after 1848 and 1870, coincided with the incorporation of increasing numbers of poor Europeans into fluctuating capitalist wage labor markets and uneven capitalist development across European states. The reaction of cotton-factory workers in northern France to Belgian immigrants who flooded into the region during the European depression of the mid-1840s was emblematic. French "cotton operatives . . . took out their desperation on the equally desperate Belgian immigrants . . . rather than on the government or even on their employers."[13] In the revolutionary struggles of 1848, workers did direct their desperation at governments and the employing capitalist class. But after the failure of revolution in 1848, workers increasingly subordinated possible working-class unity to national allegiances.

Second, social unrest in Europe following the failed revolutions of 1848 fueled new "us" versus "them" thinking. This was evident in growing nationalism and in a tendency among European thinkers to interpret class struggles racially.[14] Some of the old ethnic divisions within Europe in the Middle Ages—concerning Franks, Gauls, Angles, Saxons, Teutons, Celts, Slavs, and Jews, among others—were reconceptualized in *racial* terms. Third, economic and political changes in Europe uprooted millions of Europeans. This uprooting, Eric Hobsbawm says, was "perhaps the most important single phenomenon of the nineteenth century. . . . Migration and emigration, of which migration to the USA is the most convenient index, increased notably from the 1820s, though it did not reach anything like major proportions until the 1840s, when one and three-quarter millions crossed the North Atlantic."[15]

The first great wave of Irish emigration, set off by the famine in Ireland between 1845 and 1849, was one of the first direct antecedents of the new European and North American race thinking. Between 1841 and 1861 about half a million Irish settled in Britain. In England, where there had been no large-scale immigration since the Norman conquest (1066), the arrival of Irish immigrants to the cities was experienced as an "urban invasion." Between 1846 and 1850, about nine hundred thousand Irish immigrated to North America, and by 1860 the Irish population in the United States had risen to 1.5 million.[16] This Irish migration was no isolated event. "The European working classes and surplus rural populations moved from peripheries [of Europe] sharing underdevelopment . . . to segmented internationalized labor markets in the industrialized core of the Atlantic economies. . . . Migrants faced complex stratified and segmented labor markets." More desirable and better-paying jobs were mostly "held by native-born workers"; unskilled migrants were generally routed into jobs in the "secondary stagnating, exploitative, and competitive sector [of the labor market], . . . characterized by irregular employment, low pay, and hazardous or unpleasant working conditions."[17]

North America and (to a lesser degree) South America were the major destinations of the more than 50 million people who left Europe between 1815 and 1939. Within Europe, "England, the Netherlands and Belgium,

France, the western and central areas of Germany, Lower Austria, Bohemia, and Switzerland became labor-importing industrialized core countries."[18] The peripheral labor-supplying regions included Ireland, Portugal and Spain, Italy and southeastern Europe, the Polish and eastern European Jewish territories, and the Scandinavian countries. People from England and German-speaking lands actually constituted the largest streams of European emigrants overseas for most of the nineteenth century; but British imperial power turned British emigrants into "founding peoples," and both British and German emigrants sometimes maintained "attitudes of superiority."[19] The migrants from "peripheral" regions of Europe included a second major wave of Irish after 1871 (going mostly to the United States but also to England, Wales, and Scotland); several million Poles between 1860 and 1914; about 2.5 million Jews from Russia between 1880 to 1914 (more than 2 million went to the United States, about two hundred thousand to England, and sixty thousand to Palestine); and nearly 14 million Italians from 1876 to 1914, and another 4 million between 1915 and 1930.[20] These migrations were important because of how "the status of the outsider—the one that does not belong to the extant community—marks the immigrant."[21] This mark of difference played a major role in the new modes of racialization.

This new racialization was exemplified by similar responses in the United States, England, and Scotland to Irish immigrants of the 1840s and 1850s. Social commentators from the dominant ethnic groups in the receiving countries—"native" Scots and "Anglo-Saxons" of England and the United States—increasingly described the immigrant Irish as racially deficient "Celts." In the United States during the 1820s to 1830s, commentary about the Irish focused on negative effects of their poverty on their habits and conduct. Writers described the Irish poor as "dirty," "ragged," "unkempt," and sometimes "dark" and "carrot headed," but most held that their bad traits would be ameliorated by their new surroundings.[22] The sharp upturn in Irish immigration in the 1840s coincided with a new association of "American" nationality with Anglo-American, Gothic, or Anglo-Saxon ethnicity, a linkage forged by Anglo-American elites.[23] This new nationalism celebrated a special capacity of "Anglo-Saxons" for self-government and was expressed in the assertion of Anglo-Saxon "manifest destiny" to conquer the continent.[24]

The confluence of U.S. Anglo-Saxonism with burgeoning Irish immigration led Anglo-Saxon elites to produce a new racial discourse about the Irish. In the mid-1840s, negative traits that were thought to be common among them increasingly were considered products of nature rather than nurture. By the 1850s "references to the Anglo-Saxon (or Anglo-American) and Celtic 'races' in America and descriptions of the innate and ineradicable characteristics of each permeated the columns of newspapers, political monthlies, and literary magazines and were even filtering into schoolbooks and ... government publications."[25] In 1860, the U.S. Bureau of the Census divided the country's "white" population into categories of "native," "foreign," and "Irish" and included a discussion of "Teutonic" and "Celtic" elements of the populace.[26] Similar processes occurred in England and Scotland. Irish immigrants "tended to be employed in jobs which, because of the physical effort required or because of limited prospects, were not attractive to a large proportion of 'native' labour."[27] By the 1840s and 1850s the Irish were frequently described "as a 'race,' as a separate physical type ... with [an associated] range of negative social and cultural characteristics."[28]

This racialization was not a calculated effort by united national ruling classes to divide and subdue working classes but more a disjointed process. Racialization was advanced by both "native" elites (state officials, industrialists, journalists, ethnologists) and working-class people from dominant ethnic groups who mobilized around racial ideas. Even some working people from subordinated groups, such as the Irish, reinforced racialization processes. For example, in the late-nineteenth-century United States, Irish immigrants actively distanced themselves from Negroes to reposition themselves as racially white or Caucasian.[29]

Similar dynamics were evident in Europe's growing anti-Semitism. While Europe's Jewish population grew from around 2 million in 1800 to about 9 million in 1900, anti-Semitism "was fanned by the migrations which brought many Europeans into contact with Jews for the first time, by adverse social conditions, especially burgeoning cities, and by the rising tide of nationalism."[30] Anti-Semitism erupted in Russian pogroms against Jews in the 1880s, the 1894 Dreyfus Affair in France (in which a Jewish officer was wrongly convicted of espionage for Germany), and the infamous forgery of the *Protocols of the Elders of Zion* in the 1890s. The *Protocols,* with its tale of "learned elders of Zion" plotting to achieve world domination, synthesized widespread anti-Jewish conspiracy theories.[31]

Anti-Semitism was manifest in "national socialist" movements in France, Austria, and Germany in the late nineteenth and early twentieth centuries. Against the backdrop of economic crisis at the end of the nineteenth century and the well-known role of the powerful House of Rothschild in European finance, anti-capitalist and anti-Semitic national socialists such as Édouard Drumont (1844–1917) of France called for a more equal distribution of wealth and directed their reproaches at finance capital.[32] They drew on long-standing stereotypes of "the Jew" as usurer to make the image of "the Jew as finance capitalist . . . symbolic of the power of unproductive wealth confronting the producers who unjustly lived in misery."[33] For Drumont, putting an end to "[t]he expropriation of society through finance capital" would require rallying the lower classes to eliminate Jews from national life.[34] In Austria, pan-German leader Georg von Schönerer spoke of "the Jews versus the people" while reaching out to industrial workers of Bohemia, who felt that their livelihood was threatened by Czech immigration.[35] Tensions in this region between Germans and Czechs fostered widespread and long-lasting racism.[36] In Germany proper, national socialist ideas were promoted in the 1880s by writers such Karl Dühring, who considered the "Jewish question" a matter of race.[37]

Social and political divisions in Italy generated related race ideas. Southern Italy was characterized by poor, "backward" agricultural provinces with a history of colonial subjugation. These provinces were the chief source of the peasants and manual laborers who emigrated en masse to the United States.[38] While southern Italians mostly emigrated overseas, northern Italians mainly went to other European countries. Both groups found themselves unwelcomed by "native" workers.[39] In this context, Italian anthropologists such as Giuseppe Sergi and Cesare Lambroso argued that southern Italy, a meeting ground of Africa, Europe, and Asia, had produced a dark people, the "Mediterranean race," who were racially inferior to the lighter northern Italian ("Nordic") ruling classes.[40]

European racial thinking was given further impetus by the Crimean War (1853–56) and the Franco-Prussian War (1870–71). The Crimean War resulted from the conjunction of Russian imperial expansionism and the decline of the Ottoman Empire. It pitted Russia against England, France, Ottoman Turkey, and Sardinia. The Ottoman Empire's collapse gave rise to the "Eastern Question," which sparked independence struggles of the Balkan nations (Bosnia, Herzegovina, Bulgaria, Serbia, Montenegro, and Romania) and the excessive nationalism that culminated in World War I.[41] The Franco-Prussian War, which was won by Prussia and resulted in German and Italian unification, gave rise to racial theories that contrasted "Germanic" (or "Teutonic" or "Aryan") versus "Celtic" (or "Gaulic" or "Latin") nations.[42] In 1871, French anthropologist Jean-Louis Armand de Quatrefages argued in *La race prussienne* that Prussians were distinct from the "Teutonic race"—the "true" Germanic people. Prussians, he said, were actually Finns or "Slavo-Finns," and the "true German" was a mixture of Celtic, Gallic, and German blood.[43] Liberal Berlin anthropologist Rudolf Virchow disputed Quatrefages's claim about the Prussians. In the 1870s, Virchow and the German Anthropological Society persuaded the German government to authorize a census of 6 million schoolchildren in the German empire. They sought to "determine the fate of the fair-skinned, blond, blue-eyed 'classic Teutons' . . . and the origins of the brown-skinned, brown-haired, brown-eyed individuals who had become so predominant in Germany."[44]

In the United States, the "white man's burden" motif remained more prominent as Negro slavery was practiced until the Civil War (1861–65), and racial thought and politics remained partly defined by an overriding white/black divide. In 1870 and 1875, Congress amended the 1790 Naturalization Act (which had restricted naturalization and citizenship rights to "free white persons") to "apply to aliens being free white persons, and to aliens of African nativity and to persons of African descent."[45] The Thirteenth Amendment to the U.S. Constitution outlawed slavery, but in *Plessy v. Ferguson* (1896) the Supreme Court upheld the new southern Jim Crow system of legal segregation of whites and Negroes with the doctrine of "separate but equal." Justice Henry Brown noted the petitioner Homer Plessy's claim that he "was seven eighths Caucasian and one eighth African blood; [and] that the mixture of colored blood was not discernible in him."[46]

U.S. "whites" also carried out racialized domination of other "non-white" races (native American Indians, "Mexicans," and Asian "Mongolians"), and there was racialized conflict *among* "white races" as well. As Chinese immigration increased, a U.S. Circuit Court in California was petitioned to decide whether a Chinese man counted as a white person for naturalization purposes. In *In re Ah Yup* (1878), Judge Sawyer acknowledged that "white person" referred to "a very indefinite description of a class of persons, where none can be said to be literally white." He added: "As ordinarily used everywhere in the United States, one would scarcely fail to understand that the party employing the words 'white person' would intend a person of the Caucasian race." The judge cited Blumenbach's racial scheme as summarized in *Webster's Dictionary*.[47] The 1882 Chinese Exclusion Act, which was backed by white workers and the American Federation of Labor, suspended all Chinese immigration for ten years and forbade the naturalization of Chinese persons already in the country.[48]

Further racially restrictive national immigration laws followed in the early twentieth century, capped by the 1924 Johnson-Reed Immigration Act. This law sharply restricted immigration by members of "lesser European races," including Jews, Italians, Poles, and Greeks, and extended "Asiatic" exclusion.[49] Adolf Hitler admired the Johnson-Reed Act. He wrote in 1928, "It is not by chance that the American union is in a state in which by far the greatest number of bold, sometimes unbelievably so, inventions are currently taking place." Hitler added, "The achievements of a thousand racially questionable Europeans cannot equate with the capabilities of a thousand first-rate Americans."[50]

Race scientists responded to these developments in two phases: the first phase followed the 1840s Irish emigration and the European revolutions of 1848; the second followed the Franco-Prussian War of 1870–71. In an 1849 obituary for anthropologist James Cowles Prichard, Thomas Hodgkin summarized the racialized nationalism of the first stage. Recalling the recent European revolutions, Hodgkin said that 1848 was "disgraced" by "the war of races."[51] In the same year, English historian John Mitchell Kemble cited England's "Anglo-Saxon" stock to explain why his country had escaped the continent's upheavals. Kemble typified a range of writers who praised Germanic or Saxon nations while criticizing Celts as impulsive, violent, and childish.[52]

Such ideas became commonplace by mid-century. John Knox declared in *The Races of Man* (1850) that in "human history race is everything."[53] Knox warned of cultural "decay" in the United States due to race mixing among Anglo-Saxons, Celts, and Teutons. While the Anglo-Saxons had a genius for representative government, the Celtic race "never could . . . comprehend the meaning of the word liberty."[54] A few years later, Arthur de Gobineau, in *The Inequality of the Human Races,* declared an "irreconcilable antagonism between races and cultures."[55] Gobineau distinguished three primary races, "the white, the black, and the yellow." He insisted on the superiority of the whites, including "those races which are called Caucasian, Semitic, or Japhetic."[56] Europe was inhabited mostly by "white" peoples but with "the non-Aryan elements . . . the most numerous." "There is no civilization among European peoples where the Aryan branch is not predominant." Thus, there were innate inequalities among the "different groups within the white race."[57]

"Aryan race" theories proliferated in this period. Swiss scholar Adolphe Pictet claimed in *Indo-European Origins, or the Primitive Aryas* (1859) that all Europeans were from a common "Aryan" stock that had migrated from

Persia.[58] The "Aryan race" myth was popularized in the 1850s and 1860s by the French scholar Ernest Renan and the German-born English philologist Friedrich Max Müller. Renan, an admirer of Gobineau, wrote of the common origins of the two "great and noble races, the Aryan and the Semitic"; but he saw the Aryan race as ascendant and the Semitic race as decadent and declining.[59] Leading European anthropologists—Paul Broca and Paul Topinard of France, England's Edward Tylor, and the German Theodore Waitz—disputed "Aryan race" theory on the ground that language was not an accurate indicator of race. The "Indian Mutiny" of 1857 against British colonial rule in India led many Britons to reject ideas about an Aryan affinity between themselves and dark-skinned Hindus.[60] In 1872, in the wake of the Franco-Prussian War, even Max Müller accepted this point.[61] Nonetheless, with the aid of newspapers, the "Aryan race" idea circulated widely in scholarly and popular racial discourse.[62] In Europe, Houston Stewart Chamberlain used "Aryan," "Indo-European," and "Teutonic races" interchangeably and pitted this group against "the Jews" in his influential *Foundations of the Nineteenth Century* (1899).[63] "To this day these two powers—Jews and Teutonic peoples—stand . . . always as alien forces face to face." Chamberlain included Celts, Germans, and Slavs among the "North-European races" but held that "the Teuton" or German "has proved himself . . . intellectually, morally, and physically pre-eminent among his kinsmen."[64]

A few broader scientific developments in this era were linked to trends in race science. The most important of these were the invention of the "cephalic index" (a measure of relative "long-headedness" and "short-headedness") by the Swedish comparative anatomist Anders Retzius, which I will discuss shortly, and Charles Darwin's formulation of evolutionary theory in *The Origin of Species* (1859). Although Darwin devoted little attention to racial classification, his work had a profound impact on race science. His theory of the "descent of man" from higher primates eventually discredited polygenist claims that human beings comprised several distinct "species" with separate origins. Accordingly, it reshaped the range of meanings that could plausibly be given to "race." In other respects, Darwinian theory gave scientific racism new theoretical tools. This was evident in polygenist tendencies that, as George Stocking says, persisted in physical anthropology into the twentieth century: "the assumption that the cultural differences of [human beings] were the direct products of their differences in physical structure; the idea that the . . . physical differences between human races were virtually primordial; the idea that the most important of these differences were those involving the human skull and brain; and the assumption that out of the heterogeneity of modern populations there could be reconstructed 'types' which were representative of 'pure races' from which these populations derived."[65] Some post-Darwinian writers adopted the "neo-polygenist" view that the common human ancestry was sufficiently far in the past that different races had acquired through natural selection the intellectual capacities that marked them all as human in unequal ways.[66]

In 1866, the British physician J. Landon Down identified the genetic condition now known as Down syndrome and called it "mongolism" "because it produced children with almond-shaped eyes reminiscent, to at least one nineteenth-century British mind, of Central Asian faces."[67] Francis Galton, a cousin of Darwin, published *Hereditary Genius* (1869), which marked the beginning of eugenics. Eugenicists sought to improve society through selective breeding practices that favored superior races and classes.[68] Closely related to eugenics was the development of intelligence testing, pioneered in the early twentieth century by French psychologist Alfred Binet and Stanford University's Lewis Terman (who conceived of the "intelligence quotient").[69] Intelligence testing was used at various times to "prove" cognitive deficiencies of Negroes, Jews, Italians, Russians, and Slavs.[70] These new sciences reflected widespread anxiety among European elites about the degeneration of European society and the dangers of emerging democratic politics.[71] In contrast to the narrow biological meaning of *degeneration* used by Buffon and Blumenbach, the term now "expressed, at one and the same time, the physical and moral depravity of the lower orders, the decadence of the governing classes and the racial impoverishment of society as a whole."[72]

## The Cephalic Index

By the 1840s, with Anders Retzius's (1796–1860) invention of the cephalic index, these social, political, and scientific developments began to reshape the practice of racial classification. Retzius's initial focus was his homeland, Sweden. He first used the cephalic index to compare the Finns, who he believed were an indigenous race, with the Swedes, who he believed had migrated from central Asia. Retzius arrived at the cephalic (or length-breadth) index by dividing the breadth of a skull by its length and then multiplying the result by one hundred. He termed long, narrow skulls (with an index of eighty or less) *dolichocephalic* and broad skulls (with an index of more than eighty) *brachycephalic*. He concluded that the broad-headed or brachycephalic Finns were distinct from the long-headed or dolichocephalic Swedes.[73] Retzius also drew on the methods of Dutch anatomist Petrus Camper to subdivide brachycephalics and dolicho-cephalics according to the extent that the frontal conformation of the skull jutted forward, or was protrusive. He termed less protrusive skulls *orthog-nathic* and less protrusive skulls *prognathic*.

Retzius's initial findings resonated among European scientists and gave craniology new scientific credibility.[74] Widespread adoption of the cephalic index by European raciologists in the late nineteenth century needs to be understood, however, as a consequence of the growing Euro-pean nationalism. Given the pervasive belief in race differences, and faced with rising nationalism and expanding European migrations, European raciologists were now primed to look for racial differences among Euro-peans. Retzius's focus on differences in cranial forms did the trick. It also marked a decisive shift toward a self-consciously scientific anthropology that prioritized purely physical and measurable characteristics to classify human races.[75]

The historical context of Retzius's effort to distinguish racially Swedes and Finns is instructive here. Retzius followed a long-standing tendency in anthropology to regard Finns (along with Laplanders) as a race apart from the "white European" or "Caucasian race." Swedes such as Harald Vallerius and Linnaeus participated in this debate along with other important fig-ures in race science, such as Blumenbach (see chapter 2). Two influential figures in Swedish anthropology established a direct precedent for Retz-ius's work: Avrid Henrik Florman published the first measurements of the skulls of Laplanders in 1823; and during the 1830s and 1840s, Sven Nils-son cataloged the proportions of the skulls found among Sweden's various ethnic groups and speculated that the Lapps were Sweden's first inhabi-tants.[76]

Moreover, this Swedish anthropology emerged in the context of Swedish colonialism in Finland and Lapland. During the eleventh and twelfth centuries, Swedes converted to Christianity, and Swedish rulers conquered Finland in the thirteenth century. They conceived their con-quests of the pagan Finns as crusades. By the time of the Peace of Note-borg (1323), Sweden controlled most of Finland. While Finns held on to their own language, Swedes increasingly dominated Finland's economic and civic life.[77] Swedish rule ended after a series of wars in Finland between Sweden and Russia in 1741–43, 1788–90, and 1808–9, the last of which established Russian control of Finland. Russian czar Alexander I recognized the legal system that had developed during the centuries of Swedish control and the Protestantism that Finns had acquired through the Swedish Reformation. Other legacies of Swedish rule also survived, notably class and status divisions that largely coincided with divisions between Swedes and Finns. "The practical conduct of public affairs was in the hands of Swedes, who formed almost the whole landowning class and most of the prosperous townsmen. Swedish was the official language of the country, though about 85 percent of the population were Finnish-speaking."[78] In the decades preceding Retzius's research of the 1840s, a small, educated elite among the Finnish majority initiated the Finnish nationalist movement. This Finnish elite had prospered within the Swedish culture "but began to demand on behalf of its uneducated compatriots an education in Finnish, and the use of Finnish side by side with Swedish in public life."[79] The nationalist movement aimed chiefly at the Swedish-speaking privileged classes rather the Russian government.[80]

## The "Races of Europe"

In the 1850s, amid growing European nationalism, Retzius extended his analysis of skull forms to classify racially virtually all the peoples of Europe according to two sets of traits: dolichocephaly or brachycephaly (i.e., long-headedness or broad-headedness) and prognathism or orthognathism (having a more or less "protrusive" skull). Significantly, his racial division of Europe paralleled the political-economic division between its western and northern industrialized, labor-importing "core" countries and its less-industrialized, labor-supplying eastern and southern regions: most western Europeans were dolichocephalic and most eastern Europeans brachycephalic, although both groups tended to be orthognathic. Retzius's European dolichocephalic peoples included the "Germans" (encompassing Norwegians and Normans in France and England, Swedes, Danes, the Dutch, Flemings, Burgundians, Germans of the Germanic stock, Franks, Anglo-Saxons, and Goths of Italy and Spain) along with the "Celts" (the Celtic Scots, Irish, and English; the Welsh; Gauls in France, Switzerland, and Germany; the "Proper Romans"; and the descendants of the ancient Greeks). European brachycephalic peoples included Ugrians, Turks, Slavonians, Lithuanians, Albanians, Etruscans, Tuscans, Rhetians, Tyrolese, and

Basques.[81] He classified several peoples who had often previously been counted as Caucasians in categories of "Asiatic dolichocephali" ("orthognathic" Hindus, Aryan Persians, Arabs, and Jews; "prognathic" Tungusians and Chinese) and "Asiatic brachycephali" ("prognathic" Ugrians, Turks, most of the tribes of the Caucasus, Turkomans, Afghans, Lascars, Tartars, Mongolians in Russia and Mongolia, and Malays).[82]

Retzius's work influenced two lines of subsequent racial classification that resulted in the partial eclipse of Blumenbach's "Caucasian race" in European ethnology between the 1860s and 1930s. The first line of new racial classification ran through the work of English anthropologists Thomas Henry Huxley and Edward Burnett Tylor and Irish anthropologist A. H. Keane; the second, through the writings of English anthropologist John Beddoe, U.S. economist and ethnologist William Ripley, and Russian-born French anthropologist Joseph Deniker. Huxley, Tylor, and Keane placed greater emphasis on distinguishing between "white" and "nonwhite" races; Beddoe, Ripley, and Deniker were somewhat more concerned to distinguish *among* "white races."

In 1865, Thomas Henry Huxley (1825–95) reflected both Retzius's influence and the shift toward "scientific" ethnology in "On the Methods and Results of Ethnology." An influential follower of Darwin, Huxley drew on Darwin's evolutionary theory to argue that all human beings originated in "one locality."[83] Huxley classified human races according to three sets of physical characteristics: straight or wavy hair (*Leiotrichi*) versus "crisp, woolly, or tufted hair" (*Ulotrichi*), which distinguished aboriginal Australians (dark skins and wavy hair) from Negroes and South African "Bushmen" (dark skins and woolly hair); long-headedness or broad-headedness; and the darkness or lightness of people's skin and hair.

For present purposes, Huxley's most significant innovation was his division of Blumenbach's "Caucasian race" into two groups: "Xanthochroi," those "'yellow' haired and 'pale' in complexion" (also usually blue-eyed and sometimes red-haired); and "Melanochroi," those with "black or dark" hair and eyes.[84] Where Retzius's emphasis on cranial forms yielded a mostly east/west racial division of Europeans, Huxley's focus on hair and skin color generated a different division. His Xanthochroi category included "the Scandinavians, wholly, the Germans, to a great extent, the Slavonian and the Finnish tribes, some of the inhabitants of Greece, many Turks, some Kirghis, and some Mantchous, the Ossetes in the Caucasus, the Siahposh, and the Rohillas."[85] The Melanochroi were from the British Isles; western and southern Gaul (France); Spain; Italy (south of the Po);

parts of Greece, Syria, Arabia, Persia; much of the Caucasus; Africa north of the Sahara; and the Canary Islands. "They are known as Kelts, Iberians, Etruscans, Romans, Pelasgians, Berbers, Semites."[86] (In 1870, Huxley supplemented his five principal races—Negroid, Australoid, Mongoloid, Xanthochroid, and Melanochroid—with subdivisions that yielded fourteen "secondary" races.)[87]

While subdividing Blumenbach's Caucasians, Huxley also explicitly rebuked Blumenbach's "Caucasian race" category:

> Of all the odd myths that have arisen in the scientific world, the "Caucasian mystery," invented quite innocently by Blumenbach, is the oddest. A Georgian woman's skull was the handsomest in his collection. Hence it became his model exemplar of human skulls . . . ; and out of this, by some strange intellectual hocus-pocus, grew up the notion that the Caucasian man is the prototypic "Adamic" man, and his country the primitive centre of our kind. Perhaps the most curious thing of all is, the said Georgian skull, after all, is not a skull of average form, but distinctly belongs to the brachycephalic group.[88]

It is important to note that Huxley could conclude that the Georgian skull diverged from the "average" skull form only insofar as he assumed that Retzius's cephalic index improved upon Blumenbach's "vertical scale" (see chapter 2). Furthermore, just as Blumenbach set up his Caucasian race as the model of perfection, Huxley implicitly regarded the dolichocephalic cranial form as "normal" and the brachycephalic form as subpar.

Yet even as he challenged the idea of a unitary Caucasian race, Huxley simultaneously reaffirmed white racial supremacy. He asserted elsewhere that the U.S. Civil War had settled the question of whether or not "negroes" were "brothers" to white people but conceived of this "kinship" in a way that upheld white superiority. And in *this* context he retained the term *Caucasian*:

> It may be quite true that some negroes are better than some white men; but no rational man, cognisant of the facts, believes that the average negro is the equal . . . of the average white man. And, if this be true, it is simply incredible that, when all his inabilities are removed, . . . he will be able to compete successfully with his bigger-brained and smaller-jawed rival. . . . But whatever the position of stable equilibrium may bring the negro, all responsibility for the result will henceforward lie between Nature and

him. The white man may wash his hands of it, and the Caucasian conscience be void of reproach for evermore.[89]

In addition, in a challenge to those writers who venerated a common "Teutonic" heritage of Germans and "Anglo-Saxons," Huxley racially distinguished most Scandinavians and Germans from the peoples of the British Isles, as well as those of France, Spain, and Italy. Along with Beddoe, he held that the people of Britain were not "unmixed Teutons." He said in 1871 that they were divided between dark whites and fair whites, "two separate races in the biological sense of the word."[90] Huxley also dismissed claims arguments about "Celtic" virtues and "Celtic blood," maintaining that Celtic (or Gaelic) was a language but not a racial category.[91]

Huxley's replacement of the Caucasian race with Xanthochroid and Melanochroid directly influenced the work of Tylor and Keane. Edward Tylor (1832–1917) was a leading figure in the development of modern cultural anthropology.[92] His surveys of late-nineteenth-century anthropology indicate the extent to which racial determinism—the belief that race determined people's characters and cognitive capacities—had become commonplace in race science. In the ninth edition of the *Encyclopaedia Britannica* (1875), Tylor strongly defended the division of human beings into different "varieties or races, on grounds which are within limits not only obvious but definite." A Negro, a Chinese, an Australian, and a European were "plainly distinguishable from each other." This "division takes for granted the idea, which is involved in the word race, that each of these varieties is due to specific ancestry, . . . however these breeds or stocks may have had their origin." He added that the characteristics on which racial classification rely "are in great measure physical, though intellectual and traditional peculiarities . . . furnish important aid."[93]

Regarding racial classification, Tyler dismissed Blumenbach's "Caucasian race" and recommended Huxley's scheme. "The ill-chosen name of Caucasian, used by Blumenbach to denote what may be called white men, is still current; it brings into one race peoples such as Arabs and Swedes, although these are scarcely less different than Americans and Malays, who are set down as two distinct races."[94] By contrast, Huxley's 1870 scheme was probably the best "from a zoological point of view, though anthropologists may be disposed to erect into separate races several of his widely differing sub-races." Tyler endorsed Huxley's division between "fair whites" and "dark whites," stating that the latter have darker complexions, hair, and eyes and smaller stature.[95]

He returned to the topic of racial classification in *Anthropology* (1881). Here he ended his chapter on "Races of Mankind" with a discussion of "the white men, whose nations have all through history been growing more and more dominant intellectually, morally and politically on the earth."[96] They were "not a single uniform race, but a varied and mixed population," and it was a positive "step toward classing them to separate them into . . . the dark-whites and fair-whites (melanochroi, xanthochroi)."[97] Tylor included illustrations of a group of Georgians (a Caucasian people) to represent "dark-whites" and of a group of Swedes to represent "fair-whites" (see figures 6.1–6.2). Following Huxley, he surmised that the fair-whites were the original stock and that their intermixing with "the brown races of the far south may have given rise to the various kinds of dark-whites."[98]

Irish anthropologist A. H. Keane (1833–1912) partly bucked the "races of Europe" trend. Keane continued to speak of a "Caucasian race" but in a way that affirmed racial distinctions among "white" people generally and Europeans in particular. Keane also had a more direct political influence than most ethnologists: between 1909 and 1923, U.S. federal courts cited his work to grasp the meaning of the phrase "free white person" in U.S. naturalization law. The courts frequently appealed to scholarly accounts of the "Caucasian race" category to interpret "white person," including Keane's writings, which were well suited to the Jim Crow United States.[99] Eventually, in *United States v. Bhagat Sigh Thind* (1923), the U.S. Supreme Court, in opposition to Keane's view, rejected the claim to "whiteness" of a high-caste Hindu from Punjab, India. This Court held that as a racial designation the "word 'Caucasian' is in scarcely better repute" than the term *Aryan*:

> It is at best a conventional term, with an altogether fortuitous origin, which, under scientific manipulation, has come to include far more than the unscientific suspects. According to Keane, for example, it includes not only the Hindu, but some of the Polynesians, (that is the Maori, Tahitians, Samoans, Hawaiians and others), the Hamites of Africa, upon the ground of the Caucasic cast of their features, though in color they range from brown to black. We venture to think that the average white American would learn with some degree of astonishment that the race to which he belongs is made up of such heterogeneous elements.[100]

Keane summarized his case for the "Caucasian race" category in *Ethnology* (1895), the first comprehensive survey of ethnology in the wake of

Darwin.[101] For Keane, races had a zoological position among the *Hominidae*, or "human family," that was just a step removed from marking distinct species. "It may be concluded with Darwin that, at the initial stage of their evolution, races having a common origin are varieties of a species, which tend themselves to become species" but "have not yet reached this stage."[102] In a racial determinist vein, he said that insofar as ethnology aimed to determine the "relative position" of different groups it needed to consider "mental as well as physical" traits as "criteria of racial affinities."[103] Keane claimed that relative brain size correlated directly with mental capacity such that "cranial capacity serves as a connecting link between the physical and mental criteria."[104]

Turning to racial classification, he observed that most recent classifications returned to "the broad groupings of Linné and Blumenbach."[105] Accordingly, he identified four branches of Hominidae: *Homo Aethiopicus*, *Homo Mongolicus*, *Homo Americanus*, and *Homo Caucasicus*.[106] Consistent with Huxley's and Tylor's views of white superiority, Keane placed the "Caucasic type" on the highest branch of his Hominidae "Family Tree": "Such is the dominant position of this highest of the Hominidae, which seems alone destined to a great future, as it is heir to a great past."[107] He advanced this view in a neo-polygenist manner. Regarding his four primary groups—*Homo Aethiopicus, Homo Mongolicus, Homo Americanus*, and *Homo Caucasicus*—he said, "These groups are to be regarded as so many main varieties of a single species, and not as so many distinct species of genus Homo."[108] He added, "As the Negro stands somewhat apart, and admittedly at a lower grade than the other three branches, it might be conceived as diverging first in the process of an upward development from the main stem, from which others ramified later."[109] Evidence from comparative craniological studies indicated that the differences between the four groups were "already established in neolithic times." Therefore, the existing "disparities" could be explained only by the development of each variety "simultaneously in separate areas."[110] That is, the different groups branched off from the common family tree at different times, yielding different levels of cognitive development (see figure 7).[111]

Keane acknowledged the objections to Blumenbach's "Caucasian race" but called them "needless": "the word, like so many others in scientific nomenclature, is purely conventional and not restricted to the inhabitants of the Caucasus, who are merely taken as somewhat typical members of a whole family."[112] It was more important not to confuse "Caucasian" with "Aryan" or "Indo-European," since the latter were "linguistic rather than

Figure 6: Tylor's "Dark-whites" (Georgians) and "Fair-whites" (Swedes) (1881). Reprinted from Edward B. Tylor, *Anthropology: An Introduction to the Study of Man and Civilization* (New York: Appleton and Co., 1898), pp. 110–11.

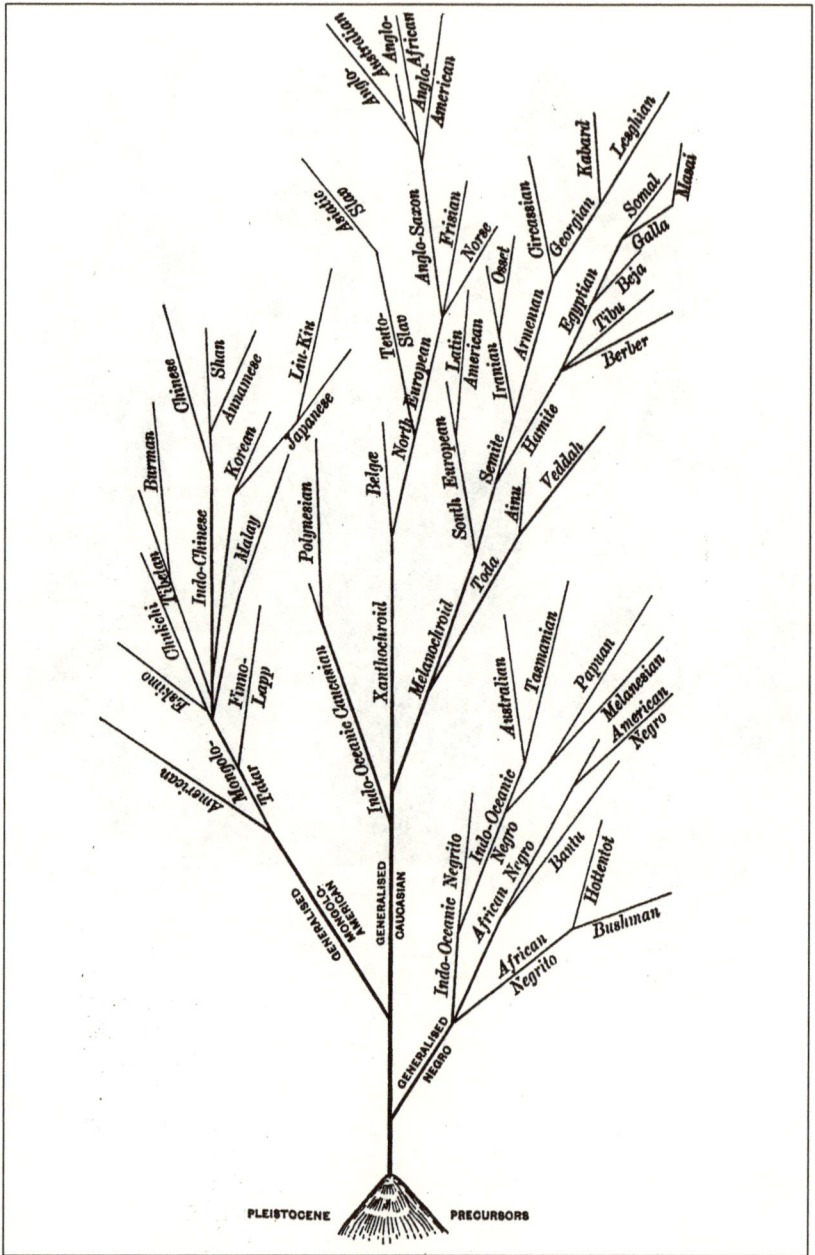

Figure 7: A. H. Keane's "Family Tree of Hominidae" (1895). Reprinted from A. H. Keane, *Ethnology* (Cambridge: Cambridge University Press, 1901), p. 224.

ethnical designations." Moreover, if an Aryan race was admitted it "would only form one of the many branches of the Caucasic division, which . . . also comprises Semites, Hamites, Iranians, besides some aberrant groups."[113]

Even so, Keane subdivided his Caucasians in a way that resembled "races of Europe" theories. He located the probable origins of the Caucasic peoples in North Africa and suggested that they had migrated "eastwards into the Nile valley and West Asia, northwards to Iberia, and thence to West and Central Europe."[114] This migration was lengthy and "several varieties of Homo Caucasicus were already developed in neolithic times in Western Europe."[115] He went beyond Huxley's division of Caucasians into "fair and dark types" to place several North and Northeast African peoples in his *Homo Caucasicus,* including Berbers, Egyptians, Somalis, and "many people who are darker than the average Negro."[116] And based on aesthetic considerations, he concluded that the "'black Caucasians' . . . cannot be separated anthropologically" from the generally "light-coloured Caucasic division." Indeed, some of them were "amongst the very finest representatives of the Caucasian types."[117] Overall, Keane divided *Homo Caucasicus* into three main branches: Indonesians; Xanthochroi (including Teutons, North Europeans, and Slavs); and Melanochroi (encompassing Celts, southern Europeans, Semites, Caucasian tribes, Iranians, Hindus, and "Hamites"— including Egyptians and other North Africans). Not surprisingly, he placed the Xanthochroi on the highest branch of his Caucasian family tree.[118]

A posthumously published 1920 edition of Keane's 1899 book, *Man: Past and Present,* which was significantly revised by A. Hingston Quiggin and A. C. Haddon after Keane's death in 1912, affirmed more fully the "races of Europe" trend.[119] It included a substantial alteration of Keane's earlier classification of "Caucasic peoples" and reflected several recent scientific and political developments. First, it responded to emerging concerns among white commentators that the white race (or races) might get "swamped" by the world's "colored" peoples.[120] The book regarded "gloomy forebodings regarding the ultimate fate of the Caucasic races" as unfounded in the face of expanding "Caucasic" dominion.[121] Second, the authors now tentatively located the center of "evolution and dispersion for all the main branches of the Caucasic family" in southern Asia rather than North Africa.[122] Third, based on recent work by Ripley, De Lapouge, and Sergi, the book divided the "Caucasic family" into three major races: "The tall fair blue-eyed dolichocephals (Northern Race) and the short dark dolichocephals (Mediterranean Race) may be regarded as two varieties of a common stock"; "the third type" was a "non-Mongolian brachycephalic

... Alpine race," centered to the west of the central Asian plateaus.[123] The authors also identified additional races within each of the three main Caucasic types.[124]

The book's survey of Caucasic peoples began with a "Conspectus" that included the following remarks on "temperament":

> [Mediterranean and Alpine]. Brilliant, quick-witted, excitable, and impulsive; sociable and courteous, but fickle, untrustworthy, and even treacherous (Iberian, South Italian); often atrociously cruel (many Slavs, Persians, Semites, Indonesians and even South Europeans); aesthetic sense highly, ethic slightly developed. All brave, imaginative, musical, and richly endowed intellectually. [Nordic]. Earnest, energetic, and enterprising; steadfast, solid, and stolid; outwardly reserved, thoughtful, and deeply religious; humane, firm, but not normally cruel.[125]

This discussion began with the following caveat: "It is a remarkable fact that the Caucasic division of the human family, of which nearly all students of the subject are members, with which we are in any case, so to say, on the most intimate terms, and with the constituent elements of which we might consequently be supposed to be best acquainted, is the most debatable field in the whole range of anthropological studies."[126] "Undoubtedly," the authors admitted, "the term 'Caucasic' cannot be defended on ethnical grounds." Nonetheless, "no really satisfactory substitute for 'Caucasic' has yet been suggested, and it is doubtful if any name could be found sufficiently comprehensive to include all the races, long-headed and short-headed, fair and dark, tall and short, that we are at present content to group under this non-committal heading."[127] After dismissing the term *Aryan* ("of an Aryan race there can be no further question"), the authors said that the really important question was

> by what right are so many and such diverse peoples grouped together and ticketed 'Caucasians'? Are they to be really taken as objectively one, or are they merely artificial groupings, arbitrarily arranged abstractions? ... It seems to require a strong mental effort to sweep into a single category, however elastic, so many different peoples—Europeans, North Africans, West Asiatics, Iranians and others.[128]

A wide range of complexions was found among these peoples, "from white to the deepest brown or even black." Nonetheless, certain "common characteristics" indicated a "common racial stamp."[129] Following Keane's earlier claims, the authors appealed to "regular features" to include several "black or very dark races" in the "Caucasian family."[130] The 1920 edition *Man: Past and Present,* then, combined Eurocentric assumptions of "white" or "Caucasian race" supremacy with the recent ethnological theories about racial differences among "Caucasic" peoples.

When we turn to Beddoe, Ripley, and Deniker, we find a starker delineation of the races of Europe—an idea that remained influential at least as late as Carleton Coon's encyclopedic 1939 book, *The Races of Europe.*[131] Physician John Beddoe (1826–1911) was a founding member of the British Ethnological Society (1857) and a president of the Anthropological Society (1869–70) and the Royal Anthropological Society (1889–91). His writings were influenced by the nationalistic reaction to the revolutions of 1848 and later British elite concerns about Britain's "racial fitness." In 1848, for example, he reflected in his diaries about how the "treacherous Italians" could "withstand the steadfast Teuton and the impetuous Slave [i.e., Slav]."[132]

In *The Anthropological History of Europe* (1891–93), Beddoe divided Europe into "three craniological, if not racial, areas." He said that if the Lapps and Finns were counted as a "second brachykephalic mass" there would be "four such areas."[133] The three main groups were the "broadheads," occupying mountain regions of Europe and some adjacent territories; the "northern or blond longheads" of northern regions (with the exception of the "brachykephalic" Lapps, Quaens, and Finns); and "the Southern or Mediterranean longheads." The latter ranged over the Pyrenees and south of them, as well as part of western France, the coast of Liguria, Corsica, Sardinia, Sicily, southern Italy, and parts of Greece and Bulgaria.[134] Beddoe was particularly concerned with the question "To what races or types . . . [does] the future belong?"[135] He contended that the northern "dolichos" were multiplying "freely" and extending their domain through colonization of North America and Australia.[136] Yet he saw disconcerting advances by the less capable broad-headed types, including the growing European Jewish population. There were two "curiously discriminated Jewish types": the Sephardim, with the "small oval true Semitic type of head," and the mostly "broad-headed" Ashkenazim. The Ashkenazim appeared to be "gaining" on the Sephardim, even though it was the latter who had "distinguished themselves from the common herd of their fellow-believers, and that in ways more noble than money-making."[137]

This bigoted remark was characteristic of Beddoe's assessment of the relative capabilities of the "two great races of northern and central Europe." He endorsed De Lapouge's view that most men of genius "have been among the long-headed blonds" but insisted that it was incorrect to call them the Aryans.[138] He cautioned against "extreme" generalizations, since "no people is homogeneous." "Still," he said, "certain qualities do adhere to races."[139]

U.S. economist William Ripley (1867–1941) elaborated more fully the idea of distinct European races in *The Races of Europe* (1899). Aside from the brief flowering of Anglo-Saxonist and anti-Celtic racial theories in the mid–nineteenth century, Ripley's work represented a new departure in U.S. race science. Prior to Ripley, U.S. scientists in the late nineteenth century made no contributions to raciology comparable to those of European theorists. Most anthropologists "immersed themselves in narrowly empirical studies of primitive folk, chiefly Indians."[140] Despite earlier ideas about Celts and Anglo-Saxons, theories about European races had relatively little impact on U.S. racial thought until the beginning of the twentieth century.[141] As I noted earlier, the "Caucasian race" notion retained considerable salience in the United States. The new receptiveness to "races of Europe" theories was due to the conjunction of a massive influx of southern and eastern European immigrants after 1880 with domestic class conflict. The latter was exemplified in 1886 by nationwide "eight-hour" strikes and the Haymarket Square bombing in Chicago. "Anglo-Saxon"-identified intellectuals reacted to the social unrest by adopting a "racial nativist" stance toward the new immigrants, whom they saw as a threat to the country's stability. Gradually these concerns became focused on "the cultural remoteness of southern and eastern European 'races.'"[142] While anthropologists were somewhat resistant to racism, other U.S. racial theorists increasingly drew on European anthropological theories to distinguish racially the new eastern and southern European immigrants from the earlier "Anglo-Teutonic" Americans. The European theories provided a means "to arrange these races in a hierarchy of merit and thereby prove the irremediable inferiority of the newcomers."[143]

Ripley was instrumental in importing into North America "races of Europe" theories and residual polygenist ideas of European physical anthropology. He also popularized the notion of three European races. His book *The Races of Europe* summarized and synthesized vast data from physical anthropological researches in Europe from 1865 to 1895—data collected by others from "some twenty-five million or more individuals," mostly public-school children along with some conscripts from European armies.[144] Ripley noted that the sample population represented all classes, "but more especially the peasantry in all the nooks and corners of Europe."[145] The adults were almost all men but the upper classes, who often went to private schools and avoided military service, were less fully represented than peasants. Ripley claimed that this fact simplified matters, "since it is the proletariat which alone clearly reflects the influence of race or of environment."[146] (He confounded "race" and class insofar as class difference by definition *entails* environmental differences.) He cautioned that many writers mistakenly used race to explain "mental attributes" that were due to cultural factors.[147] Still, he insisted that race was a significant factor in history. "It is . . . the raw material from which each of these patterns is made up. . . . Race denotes what man *is*; all these other details of social life represent what man *does.*"[148]

Ripley's central thesis was that "there is no single European or white race of men."[149] He challenged "the misnomer 'white race'" along with "the current mouthings about Aryans and pre-Aryans; and . . . such appellations as the 'Caucasian' or the 'Indo-Germanic' race."[150] Only the hereditary character of physical "types . . . justifies the term *races.*"[151] The task of identifying the European races was complicated by the "amalgamation of various peoples" in Europe such that there were no European races that had retained their "purity."[152] Nonetheless, "three ideal racial types in Europe [could] be distinguished from one another," even though their most characteristic physical expressions "have often dissolved in the common population."[153]

Ripley's three European races corresponded to Beddoe's. Ripley called the first and "most characteristic" European race the "Teutonic" race. "Restricted to northwestern Europe, with a centre of dispersion in Scandinavia," it tended toward blondness, with blue or light gray eyes, "flaxen, tawny, reddish or sandy hair," and "prominent and narrow" noses.[154] The second, the "Alpine race," was characterized by a short, broad head shape and round face, with "the chin full, and the nose rather heavy," grayish eyes and brown hair, medium height, and stocky build.[155] It was centered in the "elevated portions of western Europe," including parts of France, Spain, Italy, Germany, and Albania.[156] The third, Giuseppe Sergi's "Mediterranean race," had the same long type of head as the Teutonic.[157] It differed from the Teutonic primarily in its darker hair and eyes and "less amply proportioned" physique. The Mediterranean racial type contained two varieties—a shorter group to the north and larger African Berbers to the south—and had an "affinity . . . with the negro" (see figure 8).[158]

19.   *Teutonic types*. NORWAY. Pure blond.   20.

21. *Alpine type*. AUSTRIAN. Blue eyes, brown hair. Index 88. 22.

23. *Mediterranean type*. PALERMO, Sicily. Pure brunet. Index 77. 24.

THE THREE EUROPEAN RACIAL TYPES.

146

Consistent with his view that "[r]ace denotes what man *is*," Ripley considered "intellectual differences between these three races" because upon these differences "the future social complexion of Europe is dependent."[159] He attributed differences between the races in suicide and divorce rates, political leanings, and the distribution of literary awards partly to environmental factors.[160] Simultaneously, he upheld an "urban selection" version of racial determinism to assert the superiority of the Teutonic race in "the new phases of nineteenth-century competition": "All through history this type has been characteristic of the dominant classes. . . . The contrast of this type, whose energy has carried it all over Europe, with the persistently sedentary Alpine race is very marked."[161] He added with reference to the Mediterranean type, which also showed urban propensities, that there may be "in brunetness, in the dark hair and eye, some indication of vital superiority" that enabled brunettes to break their rural ties and succeed in cities.[162]

Ripley also added his voice to criticisms of Blumenbach's "Caucasian race" category (and Keane's use of it) while discussing western Asia. Here he appealed to "Indo-European" or "Aryan" linguistic affinities among Europeans to dismiss "[t]he utter absurdity of the misnomer Caucasian, as applied to the blue-eyed and fair-haired 'Aryan' (?) race of Western Europe." There were "two indisputable facts. In the first place, this ideal blond type does not occur within many hundreds of miles of Caucasia; and, secondly, nowhere along the Caucasian chain is there a single native tribe making use of a purely inflectional or Aryan language."[163] Concerning Keane's *Homo Caucasicus* he said, "Not even the charm of mystery remains in support of a Caucasian race theory to-day. In our present state of knowledge, it is therefore difficult to excuse . . . a recent authority, who still persists in the title *Homo Caucasicus* as applied to the peoples of Europe."[164] Ripley noted the heterogeneity of peoples, languages, and religions in the Caucasus. Like Huxley, he maintained that the Caucasian peoples were "strongly inclined to be broad-headed," with the partial exception of the Ossetes, who were "immigrants."[165] Ultimately, the Caucasians, along with the Armenians, were probably the "connecting link between the [broad-headed] Alpine racial type of western Europe and its prototype . . . in the highlands of western Asia" (see figures 9.1–9.2).[166]

---

Figure 8: Ripley's "The Three European Racial Types," original captions: 19. & 20. *Teutonic types*. NORWAY. Pure blond.; 21. & 22. *Alpine type*. AUSTRIAN. Blue eyes, brown hair. Index 88.; 23. & 24. *Mediterranean type*. PALERMO, Sicily. Pure brunet. Index 77. Reprinted from William Z. Ripley, *The Races of Europe* (New York: D. Appleton & Co., 1899), p. 120.

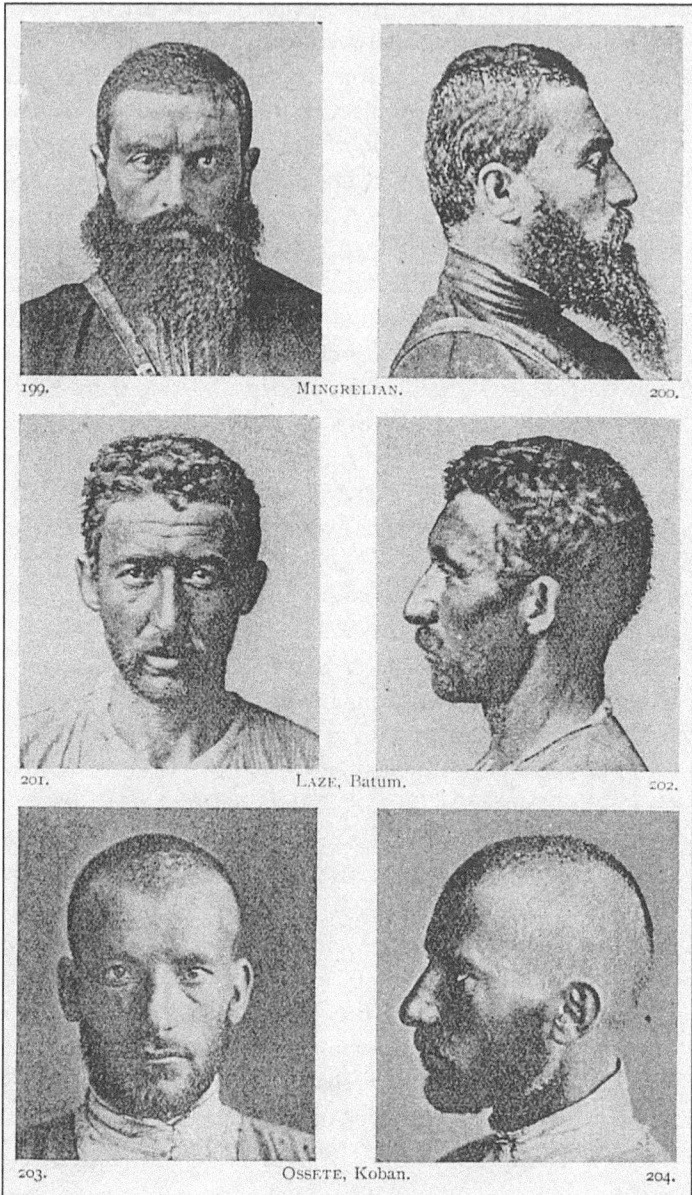

Figure 9:  Ripley's "Caucasia" and "Caucasus Mountains," original captions: 199. & 200. MINGRELIAN.; 201. & 202. LAZE, Batum.; 203. & 204. OSSETE, Koban.; 205. & 206. TSCHETSCHEN. Cephalic Index 82.3.; 207. & 208. INGOUCHE (Tschetschen group). Cephalic Index 84.4.; 209. & 210. LESGHIAN from Gounib. Reprinted from William Z. Ripley, *The Races of Europe* (New York: D. Appleton & Co., 1899), p. 120.

205.         Tschetschen,    Cephalic Index 82.3.       206.

207.       Ingouche (Tschetschen group).   Cephalic Index 84.4.    208.

209.           Lesghian from Gounib.        210.

Ripley went on to discuss European Jews in a way that reflected the era's rising anti-Semitism. The Jews were "not a race, but a people."[167] Yet, pointing ominously to the "four or five million" Jews in Russia alone who were poised to flood into Germany and Austria, he said that anti-Semitism "is not to-day . . . to any great extent an uprising against an existing evil; rather does it appear to be a protest against a future possibility."[168] "Germany shudders at the dark and threatening cloud of population of the most ignorant and wretched description which overhangs her eastern frontier. . . . That is also our American problem. This great Polish swamp of miserable human beings, terrific in its proportions, threatens to drain itself off into our country as well, unless we restrict its ingress."[169] Jews possessed "an inherent dislike . . . [for] exertion in any form"; they "live by brain, not brawn," and thus tended toward "physical degeneracy."[170]

In 1908, Ripley expressed a more unabashed Teutonic-Anglo-Saxon supremacism in the *Atlantic Monthly,* joining those who warned about the recent "swarm" of immigrants from lesser (white) European races: "Whereas, until about twenty years ago our immigrants were drawn from the Anglo-Saxon or Teutonic populations of northwestern Europe, they have swarmed over here in rapidly growing proportions since that time from Mediterranean, Slavic, and Oriental sources." Now fewer than "one-sixth" of U.S. immigrants were "truly Teutonic or Anglo-Saxon."[171] To illustrate this "problem," he included a table that reclassified the immigration of 1907 "in conformity with the racial groupings of the *Races of Europe*" as follows: "330,000 Mediterranean Race . . . ; 194,000 Alpine Race . . . ; 330,000 Slavic Race . . . ; 146,000 Jewish (mainly Russian)."[172] (He now set apart Slavs and Jews from his three European races.)[173] "We have even tapped the political sinks of Europe and are now drawing large numbers of Greeks, Armenians, and Syrians. No people is too mean or lowly to seek an asylum on our shores."[174] Because of their high birthrates compared to the older Anglo-Saxon stock, this "flood of continental peoples" threatened to "submerge" the Anglo-Saxons.[175] Jewish immigrants were particularly worrisome, with many becoming agnostics, freethinkers, or socialists.[176] Yet, since the races differed "only in their degree of physical and mental evolution," all was not lost: "the torch of [the Anglo-Saxon stock's] civilization . . . may still continue to illuminate the way."[177]

Ripley's *Atlantic* article bridged mainstream "race science" and popular white supremacist polemics in the United States that claimed scientific authority. Madison Grant's *The Passing of the Great Race* (1916), which went through several editions, and Lothrop Stoddard's *The Rising Tide of Color against White World Supremacy* (1920) rallied "Nordic"-identified elites behind the movement to restrict immigration.[178] As I noted earlier, this movement culminated in the 1924 Johnson Act, which restricted immigration by "undesirable" European "racial" elements. Grant presented a Ripley-influenced division between "three European *sub-species*": "Nordic," "Alpine," and "Mediterranean" races.[179] His "great race" was the Nordic race, and he rejected the "Caucasian race" category, "except where it is used in the United States, to contrast white populations with Negroes or Indians or in the Old World with Mongols." He explained, "The name 'Caucasian' arose a century ago from a false assumption that the cradle of the blond Europeans was in the Caucasus."[180]

Back in the mainstream of European raciology, Russian-born French anthropologist Joseph Deniker (1852–1918), like Ripley, included "races of Europe" in his grand synthesis of humanity's racial and "ethnical" diversity, *The Races of Man* (1900).[181] Deniker acknowledged concerns about the scientific status of the race concept, but he multiplied European races in particular and human races in general. Despite the impact of Darwin's theory, Deniker called the debate over monogenesis and polygenesis "sterile and futile."[182] Whether the genus *Homo* comprised one species or a plurality of species, "we shall always be obliged to recognise the positive fact of the existence in mankind of several somatological units having each a character of its own, the combinations and intermingling of which constitute the different ethnic groups."[183]

He called for a combination of cultural anthropology, or "ethnography," and physical anthropology, or "ethnology," to comprehend human diversity. The "somatological units" were the human races where the "differences between 'races' are shown in the somatological characteristics" manifest in "man considered as an *individual* of a zoological group." Ethnic groups, by contrast, were "manifest . . . in ethnical, linguistic, or social characteristics . . . [of] the grouping of individuals in *societies*."[184] A sound racial classification, therefore, must not "confuse ethnic groups and races."[185] While ethnic groups were distinguished by linguistic differences and "ethnic characters," racial classification required strict attention to "physical" or "race-characters": hair, skin, and eye color; hair form; stature; cranial forms ("mesocephalic," dolichocephalic," and "brachycephalic"); and facial features. The number of human races was relatively small, but various combinations of these had yielded a "multitude of ethnic groups."[186]

Deniker distinguished twenty-nine human races, which he combined into seventeen broader "affinity" groups.[187] He identified six European races, four of which comprised the "Melanochroid" group of "dark-complexioned races of Europe": "Littoral-European," "Ibero-insular," "Western European," and "Ariatic." The two others—"Northern-" and "Eastern-European"—were the "two fair races of Europe." He associated most of the peoples of the Caucasus with the "Arab or Semitic race" of his "North African" group, while placing "some Armenians and Jews" (among others) in "the Assyroid race."[188] (He also appears to have been the first to call northern Europeans "Nordics.")[189]

Deniker went on to distinguish the Caucasian peoples *ethnically* from other Europeans. Europe comprised "two linguistic groups: Aryan and Anaryan, and a geographic group, . . . the Caucasians." The Aryans were comprised of Latins or Romans (such as Spaniards and the French), Germans, Slavs, Helleno-Illyrians (Greeks and Albanians), Celts, and Letto-Lithuanians (Letts and Lithuanians). Anaryans included Basques and "peoples of Finno-Ugrian languages" (Lapps, Finns, and Hungarians), while the "native peoples of the Caucasus" were the "Lesgian, Georgian or Kartvel, Cherkess [Circassians], and Ossets."[190] While the "fifty various tribes" in the Caucasus differed in cranial forms—from "sub-brachycephalic" to "mesocephalics"—only the Georgians possessed "a special mode of writing, and a literature."[191]

## Subaltern Ethnology

Such racial thinking was so pervasive in this era that it was largely accepted by many subaltern ethnologists—thinkers from subordinated groups, such as "Negroes" and Jews—even as they challenged it. Writers like African Americans Martin Delany and W. E. B. Du Bois and Jewish-Ukrainian Samuel Weissenberg generally rejected racist aspects of existing race science but accepted the idea of race differences.[192] The Black Nationalist Martin Delany (1812–85) wrote extensively on the prospects of the "colored race." In 1852, Delany maintained that Blacks were actually "physically superior to either the European or American [Indian] races."[193] He published *Principia of Ethnology: The Origin of Races and Color* in 1879, in the wake of the Reconstruction era of 1865–77. African Americans had recently gained citizenship status but remained at the bottom of a castelike system of racial domination, and "races of Europe" theories had not yet become influential in the United States. Delany's primary aim was to explain the differences in color between the world's major "pure races" and highlight the contributions of African people to world history. He appealed to the Bible's narrative of the migration of Noah's sons, Shem, Ham, and Japheth, to Asia, Africa, and Europe to explain the fundamental "unity of races" and origin of race distinctions.[194] Noah's sons were the forerunners of the "three original races: Mongolian, African, and Caucasian, or Yellow, Black, and White."[195] Delany basically reaffirmed Georges Cuvier's earlier biblically informed three-race classification (see chapter 3); but where Cuvier asserted Caucasian race supremacy, Delany emphasized the cultural achievements of ancient Egyptians and Ethiopians.[196] Given the hardships of Africans in the Americas, Delany cautioned that "the African race should not be adjudged by those portions of that race out of Africa. . . . Untrammeled in its native purity, the race is a noble one, and worthy to emulate the noble Caucasian and Anglo-Saxon."[197]

Du Bois (1868–1963), the great social scientist and political activist, challenged prevailing racial thought from the late nineteenth through the mid–twentieth century.[198] He published "The Conservation of Races" in 1897, just a year after the U.S. Supreme Court upheld the constitutionality of Jim Crow segregation in *Plessy v. Ferguson* and at a time when "races of Europe" ideas were gaining ground in the country. In this early essay Du Bois walked a fine line between understanding race as a social and political construct and admitting some significant "physical differences" between peoples. He emphasized the contributions of all races, including Negroes, to the human history and conceived race as a hybrid of biology, history, and culture. "What, then, is a race? It is a vast family of human beings, generally of common blood and language, always of common history, traditions, and impulses, who are both voluntarily and involuntarily striving together for . . . certain more or less vividly conceived ideals of life."[199] While science had delineated "two, perhaps three, great families of human beings," eight great races had resulted from the historical "intermingling" of primary races:

> We find . . . today eight distinctly differentiated races, in the sense in which History tells us the word must be used. They are, the Slavs of eastern Europe, the Teutons of middle Europe, the English of Great Britain and America, the Romance nations of Southern and Western Europe, the Negroes of Africa and America, the Semitic people of Western Asia and Northern Africa, the Hindoos of Central Asia and the Mongolians of Eastern Asia.[200]

Du Bois accepted that, generally speaking, "these eight great races of to-day follow the cleavage of physical race distinctions; the English and Teuton represent the white variety of mankind; the Mongolian, the yellow; the Negroes, the black." Yet he insisted that "no mere physical distinctions would really define or explain the deeper differences—the cohesiveness and continuity of these groups." These differences were "spiritual, psychical—undoubtedly based on the physical, but infinitely transcending them."[201]

Jewish-Ukrainian physical anthropologist Samuel Weissenberg (1867–1928), considered "the world's foremost authority on the Jews as a race," engaged the "races of Europe" theories directly.[202] He joined a continuing debate in European ethnology about the racial identity of Jews. Recall that Blumenbach included Jews in his Caucasian race but said they had a distinctive "national face." Robert Gordon Latham derided the "so-called Caucasian race" partly because it encompassed such "heterogeneous elements" as "Jews, Greeks, Circassians, Scotchmen, [and] ancient Romans."[203] Beddoe told the Ethnological Society of London in 1861 that Ashkenazic and Sephardic Jews comprised two distinct Jewish racial types but that both were part of "the Caucasian family."[204] As anti-Semitism deepened, speculation about the racial identity of Jews intensified. The massive German ethnological survey spearheaded by Virchow in the 1870s lent scholarly support for the view that Jews were racially distinct from the "blond German type." Even though Virchow opposed anti-Semitism, the study rested on an assumed racial difference between Jewish and non-Jewish Germans. Therefore, while researchers cataloged "racial characteristics" of Jewish as well as non-Jewish German children—principally eye, hair, and skin color—Jews were set apart in both the survey process and the tabulation of data.[205]

Anti-Jewish writings proliferated in the late nineteenth century. In Germany, journalist Wilhelm Marr warned in *Jewry's Victory over Teutonism* (1879) that Jews were a threat to Germans in the battle for racial survival, and Hermann Ahlwardt, a former member of the German diet, published *The Desperate Struggle between Aryan and Jew* (1890).[206] Meanwhile, Richard Andree, the non-Jewish German pioneer of Jewish ethnography, argued in 1881 that Jews represented a distinct racial type, but Jews and Aryans were both Caucasians.[207] And Jewish writers such as Elias Auerbach contributed to the German *Journal for Racial and Social Biology*, a eugenicist journal, and affirmed the idea of a "Jewish race."[208]

Weissenberg, trained as a physician in Germany, used physical anthropology to refute anti-Semitic claims about Jewish inferiority.[209] He also endorsed the idea of several white races. In 1910, in the face of an ascendant Aryan racial discourse in Germany, he wrote that the non-Jew "seeks today to exclude the Jew out of state and society because the Jew is a bearer of specific, and to him peculiar, physical and mental traits which prevent him from living peacefully with Aryans. This is the dogma of modern antisemitism."[210] Earlier, he contended that Jews were composed of seven distinct racial types: "coarse," "fine," "Slavic," "southern European," "northern European," "general Caucasian," and "Mongoloid."[211] He attributed physical differences between the two main groups of Jews—Sephardic and Ashkenazic—largely to their "intermixture with their neighbors."[212] At the same time, he maintained that the "typically Jewish" appearance was mostly a product of culture rather than of physiology, "not of bodily form but of bodily deportment."[213]

From his standpoint, Weissenberg offered a distinctive perspective on the ethnological significance of the Caucasus region. "Anthropology and history must go hand in hand to solve the dark question of the origin of the Russian Jews," he said. There was historical evidence of a Jewish presence in the Caucasus before the destruction of the second temple, and much of the variation in Jewish racial types was due to Jewish migration across the Caucasus into southern Russia before the Christian era.[214] For Weissenberg, this meant that "European Jews were intimately linked to Europeans by having been racially transformed by the intermixture that had taken place in the Caucasus."[215]

## From Scientific Racism to Nazism

The First World War and the revolutions that followed it intensified racist thought and increased the visibility and vulnerability of Europe's Jews. Nationalism and anti-liberal and anti-Semitic forces deepened along with "a certain brutalization of the European conscience."[216] A radical right emerged in central and eastern Europe. Germany, which had been defeated in the war, faced foreign occupation during 1919–1920, the threat of revolution between 1918 and 1920, and then a decade of economic hardship. It became especially receptive to anti-Semitism, along with Austria and eastern Europe.[217]

Scientific racism flourished, but without producing new innovations in racial classification. In Germany, many scientists promoted the "racial hygiene" movement (Germany's eugenics) to "improve the race" through selective reproduction.[218] Racial hygienists such as Hans Günther established connections with the growing Nordic movement in Germany and popularized virulent strains of "races of Europe" thinking. Günther, a "Nordic race" supremacist, was a prolific writer whose fifteen racial tracts reached a circulation of half a million volumes by 1940. He became a professor of anthropology at the University of Jena in 1932, and his writings linked mainstream scientific racism to Nazism.[219] (Hitler attended his inaugural lecture at Jena.) In *The Racial Elements of European History* (1927), Günther, following Deniker, Ripley, and others, spoke of "the Nordic race" where the Nazis referred to "the Aryan race." He said that ethnology provided few examples of unmixed races. Yet, "from the anthropological standpoint," Europeans could be divided into five "European races"—Nordic, Mediterranean, Dinaric, Alpine, and East Baltic—based on racial traits (height, cephalic index, facial index, hair color, and eye color).[220] He heralded the Nordic race as the basis for a "New Nobility":

> the Nordic race is . . . not given as a gift but as a task; and in this sense it was that, in speaking of "the Nordic ideal among the Germans," we necessarily spoke of the Nordic man as the model for the working selection in the German people, and showed that no less a task is laid on the Nordic movement than the revival of a whole culture.
>
> The question is not so much whether we men now living are more or less Nordic; but the question put to us is whether we have courage enough to make ready for future generations a world cleansing itself racially and eugenically. . . . Race theory and investigations on heredity call forth and give strength to a New Nobility.[221]

Günther also synthesized current ideas about Europe's "Jewish problem." The Jews were "a nation" rather than a race. Still, the racial composition of the Jews was "quite other" than that of most Europeans, with Asian, African, Mediterranean, and east Baltic roots. Moreover, due to "seclusion and interbreeding" the Jewish nation was "on the way to become a race, a 'secondary race.'"[222] Europe's "Jewish problem" concerned the "influence of the Jewish spirit, and influence won through economic predominance, [which] brings with it the very greatest danger for the life of the European peoples and of the North American people alike." A solution "lies in that separation of the Jews and the Gentiles, that withdrawing of the Jews from the Gentiles which Zionism seeks to bring about."[223] The transition from Günther's Nordic supremacism to Nazi Aryan race supremacism required only minor alterations: replacement of Günther's "Nordic race" with the "Aryan race" myth and a more unequivocal appeal to the "Jewish race" idea.[224] While Günther rejected the "Aryan race" idea (along with that of a "white or Caucasian race"),[225] Adolf Hitler adopted the "Aryan race" myth in *Mein Kampf* (1925–26) from various sources, including Richard Wagner and Houston Stewart Chamberlain.[226]

## Conclusion

Even before the Nazis rose to power in 1933, the broader scientific project of racial classification became marked by disarray, evident in the eleventh edition of the *Encyclopaedia Britannica* in 1911. Edward Tylor, in his article on "Anthropology," reiterated his preference for Huxley's 1870 scheme of racial classification.[227] An unsigned article on "Ethnology and Ethnography" presented a tripartite division of "Ethiopic, Mongolic, and Caucasic races."[228] John Bealby, in an article on "Caucasia," declared that ethnologically "the population belongs to a great variety of races." Bealby presented a chart based on demographic data from the Russian Census Committee of 1897 that classified the population by language into several racial groups; the four primary groups were "Aryans," "Semites," "Ural-Altraians," and "Caucasians."[229] The 1922 *Encyclopaedia Britannica* contained a new article on "Anthropology" by physical anthropologist Grafton Elliot Smith, who divided Europeans into the "Brown or Mediterranean race," the "Alpine or Armenoid race," and the "Nordic race."[230]

Classification of European races, variously construed, was a central feature of race science from 1840 to 1935. Not all European and U.S. race scientists accepted this racial division of Europe, however. Two notable dissenters were Virchow, who led the German ethnological survey of the 1870s, and Jewish German-born U.S. anthropologist Franz Boas (1858–1942). "Once mankind has been broken into races," Virchow wrote in 1896, "there is no reference point from which to determine the number of the original races." Given this uncertainty, he settled on "those races over whose acceptance there is common agreement. In the Old World these are the white, the black, and the yellow races."[231] Retzius's effort "to select a few categories of skull type as the basic principle for classifying man . . . has had no thoroughgoing success," and skull form was an unreliable marker of racial identity.[232] Virchow added that both "short heads" and brunetness "appear as legitimate appurtenances of white men."[233]

Boas published a related critique of Ripley's European racial types in 1899. Ripley's European races were not really distinct races, and *race* could be employed meaningfully only to distinguish major "divisions of mankind": "I do not think the term 'Races of Europe' a fortunate one, [and] . . . I am inclined to reserve the term [*race*] for the largest divisions of mankind. The differences between the three European types are certainly not equal in value to the differences between Europeans, Africans and Mongols; but they are subordinate to these. The term 'type' appears most appropriate for the subdivisions of each race."[234] Boas, who soon became a vigorous critic of scientific racism, did not reject the project of racial classification. Instead, he concluded that the "cephalic index and pigmentation alone [are not] a sufficiently broad basis for the characterization of racial types."[235] He later challenged "races of Europe" theories through anthropometric research on the crania of European immigrants to the United States and their descendants, which he published in 1911. Using the cephalic index, Boas found that descendants of immigrants born in the United States differed in cranial "type from their foreign-born parents." Cranial form, on which European race theories depended, was not stable; it was affected by environment.[236]

Significantly, while Virchow and Boas strongly criticized "races of Europe" theories, they accepted without question the belief that there were, in fact, racial differences between "Europeans, Africans and Mongols," or "the white, the black, and the yellow races." As I explain in chapters 5 and 6, the latter belief was just as tenuous as the former. At the time, there was indeed "common agreement" among raciologists about white, black, and yellow races. But what Virchow and Boas could not apprehend was that this belief was based on long-standing prejudices rather than solid evidence.

There were other critics of the "races of Europe" as well. In 1922, Théophile Simar of Belgium, in *Étude critique sur la formation de la doctrine des races au XVIIIe siècle et son expansion au XIXe siècle*, rejected "the doctrine of Germanic or Teutonic superiority over other Europeans."[237] Yet he evaded the atrocities that Belgians committed against Africans in the Congo and criticized Houston Chamberlain's Teutonic supremacism without addressing Chamberlain's anti-Semitism.[238] U.S. sociologist Frank Hankin, in *The Racial Basis of Civilization* (1926), challenged "the extravagant claims of the Nordicists," along with doctrines of Teutonism and Aryanism; but he simultaneously dismissed "the equally perverse and doctrinaire claim of the race egalitarians" and believed in "Negro" racial inferiority.[239]

Meanwhile, Deniker's discussion of *ethnic groups* in *The Races of Man* (1900) offered an alternative to racial accounts of human diversity, even though he himself affirmed the belief in human race differences. Deniker wrote that there were "groups of mankind, dispersed over the whole habitable surface of the globe, to which are commonly given the names of peoples, nations, clans, tribes, etc.," such as Arabs, Swiss, Australians, Sioux Indians, and Negroes:

> Do these real and palpable groups represent unions of individuals which . . . are capable of forming what zoologists call "species," "sub-species," "varieties," in the case of wild animals, or "races" in the case of domestic animals? They are *ethnic groups* formed by virtue of community of language, religion, social institutions, etc., which have the power of uniting human beings of one or several species, races, or varieties, and are by no means zoological species.[240]

The pitfalls of the "race" concept might have led Deniker to conclude that *ethnic* groups, with their "ethnical, linguistic, or social characteristics," were "real and palpable" in a way that races were not.[241] He was too invested in racialist assumptions to draw this conclusion, however, and he insisted that race differences were just as "real and palpable" as ethnic ones.[242] Moreover, while acknowledging exceptions, he counted as *racial* certain "psychology characters—that is to say, of temperament and different manifestations of mind, feeling, and affections."[243]

Given Deniker's context, his racialism was hardly surprising. Even critics of racism in this period, such as Du Bois and Boas, tended to accept that there were distinct human races. Du Bois and Boas became part of a nascent movement of scientists who began actively to challenge scientific racism. This movement coalesced in the 1911 Universal Races Congress in London. The Congress discussed, "in the light of science and modern conscience, the general relations subsisting between the peoples of the West and those of the East, between so-called white and so-called coloured peoples, with a view to encouraging between them a fuller understanding . . . and a heartier co-operation."[244] Du Bois, who attended, commented that "its most important work" was to "make clear the present state of scientific knowledge concerning the meaning of the term 'race.'"[245] The participants drew conclusions about "race" that foreshadowed the anti-racist racialism that would emerge between 1935 and 1951 as the new consensus view among scientists: they mostly accepted the scientific validity of "race" but rejected the idea that race differences corresponded to differences of character or intellect. Gustav Spiller, the conference secretary, summarized their conclusions as follows:

1. It is not legitimate to argue from differences in physical characteristics to differences in mental characteristics.
2. Physical and mental characteristic of races are not permanent. . . . [T]hey are capable of being profoundly modified in a few generations by changes in education, public sentiment and environment generally.
3. The status of a race at any particular time offers no index as to its innate or inherited capacities.[246]

Jean Finot of France went even further: "The word race will doubtless long survive, even tho it may have lost all meaning. . . . [Men] will be certain to preserve this most scientific term which incites to hatred and unjustifiable contempt for our fellow men, instead of replacing it by some word implying the brotherhood of man."[247]

Boas and Du Bois were among those who elaborated these ideas over the next two decades. In 1912, shortly before the First World War, Boas criticized "[t]he modern enthusiasm for the superiority of the so-called 'Aryan race,' of the 'Teutonic Race,' the Pan-German and 'Pan-Slavic ideals.'" Such sentiments were merely "the old feelings of specific differences between social groups in a new disguise."[248] While Boas continued to accept the reality of human races during the 1920s and 1930s, he said that whatever differences in "mental characteristics" among people may be attributable to anatomical "differences between the races . . . are altogether irrelevant as compared with the powerful influence of cultural environment."[249] Du Bois increasingly examined "race" in light of history, sociology, and political economy. In 1917, he identified racism as a distinctively modern phenomenon rooted in "modern world commerce, modern imperialism, the modern factory system and the modern labor problem [which] began with the African slave trade."[250] By 1933 he looked forward to the "day of Inter-nation, of Humanity, and the disappearance of 'race' from our vocabulary." Yet, faced with ongoing racist oppression of Negroes, he called for concerted "group action" by Negroes to achieve this humanistic end, including "deliberate propaganda for race pride."[251]

Before the late 1930s, few people, including few scientists, were ready to affirm these insights. Du Bois observed in 1911, "It would be wrong to say that all anthropologists today would subscribe to the main conclusions of those who attended the Races Congress or that the doctrine of inevitable race superiority is dead."[252] Although the "Caucasian race" category was in partial eclipse, scientific racialism and racism were going strong under other designations.

# 5

## The Color Line and the "Caucasian Race" Revival, 1935–51

Racialism is a myth, and a dangerous myth at that.
—Julian Huxley and A. C. Haddon, *We Europeans* (1935)[1]

[A]t the present time most anthropologists agree on classifying the greater part of present-day humanity into three major divisions, as follows: the Mongoloid Division, the Negroid Division, the Caucasoid Division. The biological processes which the classifier has here embalmed, as it were, are dynamic, not static. These divisions were not the same in the past as they are at present, and there is every reason to believe that they will change in the future.
—UNESCO, "Statement on Race" (1950)[2]

Between 1933 and 1945, from Hitler's rise to power to Germany's defeat in World War II, Europe realized De Lapouge's 1899 prediction that a "conflict of races is now about to start" in which "people will slaughter each other by the million because of a difference of a degree or two in the cephalic index" (see chapter 4). Violent conflict between "races" had characterized modern politics since the seventeenth century. Now, however, it came home to Europe with a vengeance. The Nazis enacted an aggressive eugenics program through the Sterilization Law of 1933. They denied German Jews citizenship and expropriated Jewish businesses with the 1935 Nuremberg Laws, which were followed by *Kristallnacht* (Night of Broken Glass) in 1938, forced "resettlement" of Jews, and eventually "the Final Solution"—mass murder of Jews that began in 1941–42. All told, the Nazis systematically murdered nearly 6 million European Jews, tens of thousands of Roma, about two hundred thousand mentally and physically disabled persons, not to mention the millions of war fatalities.[3]

Largely in response to the Holocaust, anthropologists and biologists who specialized in the study of race retreated from scientific racism between 1935 and 1951.[4] This period also featured the revival of the "Caucasian race" category. The dominant trend in scientific race thinking in these years yielded an avowedly anti-racist and largely egalitarian racialism that was expressed in a revised version of French biologist Georges Cuvier's 1817 classification of Mongolian, Negro, and Caucasian races. This scheme gradually was recovered during this era and then authoritatively endorsed in an influential 1950 UNESCO "Statement on Race." One major feature of the new view was that while *racial* differences existed between certain geographically defined groups, the differences between European peoples were merely *ethnic* rather than *racial.*

These developments left the "race" concept in place but profoundly altered its meaning. While previous scholars have examined the reasons for this transformation of race science, they have paid much less attention to why this change resulted in the rehabilitation of Cuvier's old three-race classification scheme and the revival of the "Caucasian race" category.[5] This turn of events, like the scientists' turn against racism, was no simple triumph of scientific objectivity. Rather, it was largely impelled by changing social and political circumstances, including the consolidation of a new global "color line" and a global repositioning of Europe. The ultimate impact of these new circumstances on prevailing race science was a reversal of how the rising global dominance of European states in the seventeenth and eighteenth centuries had shaped the invention of the "race" concept and the lineaments of early racial classifications.

## "The Problem of the Colour Line," ca. 1900–1951

The rise of Hitler and the Nazis in Germany in 1933 and, later, widespread revulsion at the Holocaust provided the most immediate impetus to the sea change in race science that crystallized in Britain and the United States during 1935–1951. Yet neither the scientific community's reaction to Nazism nor developments internal to science explain the specific contours of the new science, which abandoned "races of Europe" theories, embraced egalitarian racialism, and renewed an old distinction between "white" and "nonwhite" races.

Several other circumstances produced these changes, which were expressed in part through the recovery of the pan-European "Caucasian race" category. European imperialism in Asia and Africa in the last quarter of the nineteenth century gave new force to old European ideas about "white" versus "colored" peoples of the world. European imperialism was "attended by a conscious cultural mission to 'europeanize' the colonies in the image of the mother countries."[6] European elites envisioned the spread of European peoples "far and wide, settling the new colonial territories, providing the bulk of the population, in others at least a strong administrative cadre, but in any event maintaining an indissoluble link with the imperial nexus." This global development involved a striking "disparity of treatment between the 'white' dominions and the 'coloured' colonies."[7]

Between 1875 and 1935, ideas about a global racial divide between "white" and "colored" peoples coexisted in the minds of European and U.S. raciologists with theories about European races. Even so, a shift away from the "races of Europe" paradigm to a simplified racialized division of the world into "white" and "dark" or "colored" races was underway by the start of the twentieth century. W. E. B. Du Bois vividly summed up this development in his famous declaration about the "colour line" in the *Report on the Pan-African Conference* of 1900: "The problem of the twentieth century is the problem of the colour line, the question as to how far differences of race . . . are going to be made, hereafter, the basis of denying to over half the world the right of sharing to their utmost ability the opportunities and privileges of modern civilisation." Du Bois and fellow conferees were chiefly concerned with the "present situation and outlook of the darker races of mankind . . . the millions of black men in Africa, America, and the Islands of the Sea, not to speak of the brown and yellow myriads elsewhere."[8] For those on the dominating side of the color line, imperialism seemed to provide material confirmation of "the thesis of white, Western superiority."[9] "Imperialist expansion," Frank Füredi says, "helped to establish a world where power, privilege and race coincided . . . where the balance of power was readily conceptualised in racial terms."[10] Anglo-American political elites saw the world in large part in terms of a racialized global divide between white and dark peoples, or "white versus the rest."[11]

This vision was partially realized in the British "white" settler colonies of Canada, Australia, New Zealand, and South Africa. As they acquired self-governing dominion status—in 1867, 1901, 1907, and 1910, respectively—they extended the global reach of white racial dominance.[12] In 1896, Australian colonial governments enacted Colored Races Restriction and Regulation Acts, which excluded from Australia native inhabitants of

Asia, Africa, and the Pacific islands, and in 1901 the new Commonwealth of Australia formally adopted a "White Australia" policy. Canadians enacted a "white Canada" policy with the 1910 Immigration Act, which prohibited "immigrants belonging to any race deemed unsuitable to the climate or requirements of Canada."[13] "White" South Africans established the foundations for apartheid. The "Land Acts of 1913 and 1936 allocated to blacks thirteen percent of the most arid and impoverished land, reserving for whites (sixteen percent of the population) eighty-seven percent of fertile and productive South Africa."[14]

At the same time, leaders of the pan-European "white" world of Europe, the United States, Canada, Australia, New Zealand, and South Africa experienced increasing racial anxieties about maintaining their global dominance.[15] In 1931, for example, Polish émigré anthropologist Bronislaw Malinowski, a leading figure in British cultural anthropology who researched in the Trobriand Islands during World War I, defended a "color bar" between white and nonwhite races as necessary and justified. Races, Malinowski contended, were naturally averse to each other, so the color bar was needed to prevent racial conflict: "I believe that a great many of members of other non-European races feel as strongly as we do, and would welcome an effective colour bar protecting them from the European."[16] In the same year, the editor of the British periodical *The Spectator* denounced racial supremacism while upholding the belief in race difference:

> We will avoid talking or thinking of superiority and inferiority, but we need not fly in the face of common sense and ignore differences which are no fault of either side. Coloured people must accept these differences, for they will never annihilate them. Let them take a nobler path than aiming at any merging with the white races as though the differences could be ignored. Let them cultivate a nobler pride in their own races side by side with the white races.[17]

Fascist Italy's brutal invasion of Ethiopia in 1935, which killed tens of thousands of Ethiopians and preceded Italy's domestic racial laws of 1938, exemplified the color line's stark inhumanity.[18]

In the interwar years, the color line generated widespread concern among Anglo-American elites about rising anti-colonial "race consciousness" among colonized peoples. "Race consciousness," Füredi explains, was understood to inspire "the so-called subject races against white domination . . . [and] there was little doubt that the international conflict of colour provided the underpinning for the discussion of race consciousness."[19] For instance, Ellsworth Huntington warned in *The Character of Races* (1924) that "whether or not the present conception of racial differences is right or wrong, it seems destined to play a great part in the history of the next few generations."[20] British foreign secretary Sir John Simon warned in 1933 that the "colour question" should be analyzed "in advance, before the time comes when some of the peoples of Africa and elsewhere whom we are accustomed to call the backward races claim more fully than they do now their full status as men and equals."[21]

Likewise, U.S. and British commentators in the interwar years increasingly grew concerned about pan-African and pan-Asian movements and unity among the "colored races." A 1922 study of the 1919 Paris Peace Settlement asked, "[I]f the white races do not recognize the equality of the Asiatic races, will these Eastern races, which number half of the human race, be forced to a new kind of racial alliance?"[22] U.S. sociologist W. O. Brown warned in 1931, "[T]he modern world of oppressed races have a common foe, the white peoples of Western Europe and their cousins in the United States."[23] Brown added, "The Negro in the United States . . . sympathizes with the struggles of the African natives, protests against the imperialism of the United States in the Caribbean, appreciates the nationalism of the Indians and the Chinese and is in sympathy generally with struggling minorities."[24] In England, Malinowski and others expressed similar views of global politics.[25]

Simultaneously, global demographic shifts diminished Europe's relative global power and standing. By 1900, Europe was losing ground demographically due to a major shift in the world's population.[26] European population growth leveled off between 1890 and 1930, with England's population beginning to level off around 1890 and that of the United States and the white settler colonies, particularly Australia and New Zealand, around 1930. Meanwhile, the populations of Asia and Africa were growing.[27] India's population grew by 83 million during 1920–40, following years of fluctuations, and Japan's population doubled between 1872 and 1930 after about a century of population stasis. By 1953, China's population reached 583 million, which "implied . . . a growth rate of over 16 million a year."[28] These trends indicated a global shift in the balance of power "between 'white' and 'coloured' races" and the emergence, "far away from Europe, of new centres of population, production, and power."[29] Between 1890 and 1914, Japan began to industrialize, and the rate of industrialization in Russia and the United States outpaced that of Europe's leading industrial states.[30] By the 1920s, white elites in Europe, North America, Australia, and South Africa became concerned "that the white race was under pressure from more fertile others."[31] Sociologists Robert Park and Ernest Burgess concluded in 1926 that demographic trends were a major source of white racial anxieties: "The factor of numbers embraces, indeed, the very crux of the problems arising from contact between races."[32]

Japan's emergence as a global power further fueled a defensive white racial consciousness and white racism. After Japan's military victory over Russia in 1905, commentators in the United States and Europe spoke of "the Yellow Peril."[33] In the United States, in response to growing concerns about Japanese power and a modest increase in Japanese immigration between 1901 and 1924 (mostly to California), white labor groups and elites spearheaded an anti-Japanese movement that resulted in Japanese exclusion provisions in the 1924 Immigration Act.[34] A 1912 statement on this issue by soon-to-be president Woodrow Wilson typified the prevailing white racist sentiment: "In the matter of Chinese and Japanese coolie immigration I stand for the national policy of exclusion. We cannot make a homogeneous population out of a people who do not blend with the Caucasian race. . . . Oriental coolieism will give us another race problem to solve and surely we have had our lesson."[35]

Japan's growing power, along with the Russian revolution of 1905, which reverberated throughout Asia, presaged several events that signaled fissures in European imperialism in Asia and Africa.[36] There was unrest in Vietnam; the Indian National Congress movement, founded in 1885, was revitalized in 1907, becoming a mass movement in 1920 when Gandhi initiated a national civil disobedience campaign; and revolutions erupted in Persia (1906), Turkey (1908), and China (1911).[37] By 1914 there were radical and revolutionary movements throughout Asia and the Arab world, although not yet in Africa. These movements were largely in reaction to European colonialism. European capital investment in Asia during World War I and in Africa during World War II transformed local economies and produced industrial development and urbanization. A new commercial and industrial middle class emerged in each region, along with an educated anti-colonial and nationalist elite and a "factory working class that could be mobilized for political action."[38]

The reaction of pan-European leaders to a Japanese anti-racism initiative at the 1919 Paris Peace Conference was telling. Japan proposed to extend the provision on religious equality in the League of Nations Covenant to encompass racial equality.[39] The amendment called upon the League member states to accord "to all alien nationals . . . equal and just treatment in every respect, making no distinction . . . on account of their race or nationality."[40] Britain, the United States, and Australia rejected this provision, which challenged British colonial policies as well as the domestic policies of Australia, Canada, and the United States.[41] Colonel House, adviser to U.S. president Wilson, worried, "It will surely raise the race issue throughout the world."[42] Retrospectively, Harold Nicholson of the British delegation called the proposal a "painful amendment" that "implied the equality of the yellow man with the white man" and might even "imply the terrific theory of the equality of the white man with the black."[43] Meanwhile, Japan's push for racial equality gained considerable support in the Afro-Asian world. Even China, which clashed with Japan on other matters, supported the proposal, and Japan emerged as a leader of the anti-imperialist movement.[44] Du Bois remarked in 1935: "Japan is regarded by all coloured peoples as their logical leader, as the one non-white nation which has escaped for ever the dominance and exploitation of the white world."[45]

The second Pan-African Congress also met in Paris in 1919. Although it had limited practical effect, other congresses followed in 1921 and 1927, indicating the spread globally of ideals of self-government and self-determination. The Bolsheviks tapped into the discontent in Asia by organizing the Congress of the Peoples of Asia in Baku in 1920, and pan-Islamic movements emerged that linked nationalist groups in the Dutch East Indies, French North Africa, and India.[46] These various events marked the relative decline of Europe's global political standing between the end of the nineteenth century and 1945. At the start of the First World War, Norman Davies notes, "Europe's power and prestige were unrivaled. . . . Through their colonial empires and trading companies, European powers dominated the globe." By the end of World War II, "European political power was greatly diminished; Europe's military and economic power was overtaken; European colonial power was no longer sustainable."[47]

This relative decline of Europe led some European leaders to propose cooperation among European states in the 1920s, although this movement was interrupted by nationalist reactions to the Great Depression and Nazism. British Labour Party leader Ramsay MacDonald spoke in 1925 of the need for a European "federation of Free Trade nations," and in 1926 the British monthly the *Round Table* envisioned a consolidated Europe as an economic counterweight to rising U.S. global dominance.[48] The 1925 Locarno treaties, which heralded French-German cooperation, were seen as "the draft of the constitution of a European family within the orbit of the League of Nations . . . the beginning of a magnificent work, the renewal of Europe."[49] Likewise, the chairman of the 1927 International Economic Conference in Geneva envisioned "an economic league of Nations whose long-term goal . . . is the creation of a United States of Europe."[50] These initiatives emerged, however, in the context of a fragile European economic and political recovery from the First World War, when European leaders were mostly embracing economic protectionism. Economic nationalism became more pronounced after the onset of the Great Depression in 1929. The most extreme manifestations of this new nationalist capitalism were Mussolini's fascism and Hitler's Nazi regime.[51]

These economic pressures encouraged many commentators to divide the world along Du Bois's color line. In the United States, while pro-Nordic writer Madison Grant dismissed the "Caucasian" category as a misnomer, he suggested it was "a convenient term" with which to denote "the three European subspecies when considered as divisions of one of the primary branches or species of mankind."[52] His fellow U.S. polemicist Lothrop Stoddard more fully reasserted a "pan-white-supremacist logic."[53] Like Grant, Stoddard worried that the superior "Nordic" stock that had settled the United States was being "crowded out" by the "prolific" invading "hordes of immigrant Alpines and Mediterraneans, not to mention Asiatic elements like Levantines and Jews." At the same time, he envisioned racial solidarity among the world's "white races." The "white world," weakened by World War I and "facing internal Bolshevik disaffection," was now vulnerable to "the rising tide" of "colored" peoples.[54] After the 1924 Johnson Act was passed, Stoddard sought to "reforge" a distinctly white United States. The recent European immigrants, he said, "are racially not too remote for ultimate assimilation"; but the same cannot be said of "non-white immigrants, like the Chinese, Japanese, or Mexicans; neither does it apply to the large resident negro element" of the population.[55] These writings marked a transition in the United States from a racialized pattern of "Anglo-Saxonist exclusivity," which prevailed between about 1840 and the 1920s, to a "pattern of Caucasian unity [that] gradually took its place in the 1920s and after."[56]

This shift toward "Caucasian unity" in the United States was also evident in the proliferation of residential "restrictive covenants" in the North between the 1910s and 1940s—the era of the "great migration" of millions of African Americans from the rural South to northern cities.[57] White property owners' associations established thousands of restrictive covenants that aimed to prohibit the purchase or occupancy of property by "any person other than of the Caucasian race."[58] These restrictive covenants were sanctioned by the U.S. Supreme Court from 1926 to 1948, when the Court finally ruled them "unenforceable as law."[59]

Europeans as well turned to a white versus nonwhite racial polarity. In 1932 the German philosophical historian Oswald Spengler linked in racial terms the emergence of the nonwestern "exploited world" with the decline of Europe: "Today more or less everywhere—in the Far East, India, South America, South Africa—industrial regions are in being, or coming into being which, owing to the low scale of wages, will face us with deadly competition. The unassailable privileges of the white races have been thrown away, squandered, betrayed. . . . The exploited world is beginning to take its revenge on its lords."[60] This sense of white racial unity was also fostered across the pan-European world by the gradual admittance of the white working class into full citizenship in national political systems.[61] Parliamentary democracy was briefly established across much of Europe after World War I and the collapse of the empires of Russia, Austria-Hungary, Hohenzollern Germany, and Ottoman Turkey.[62] This democratizing trend was short-lived, and it coexisted with elite anxieties—on both the Right and the Left—about the competence of "the masses" for democratic self-government.[63] The eugenics movement, vigorous in the United States and Europe until about 1940, was a striking manifestation of these concerns.[64]

The Second World War crystallized the return to color-coded racial thought and politics. The Allies' anti-Nazi campaign called attention to the inconsistency of denouncing Nazism without renouncing racial discrimination more generally.[65] In early 1941, U.S. president Franklin Roosevelt declared before Congress, "Freedom means the supremacy of human rights everywhere."[66] By the year's end Roosevelt and British prime minister Winston Churchill reiterated this idea in the Atlantic Charter (signed by twenty-six countries in January 1942), which became the basis for the Declaration of the United Nations.[67] The question remained, however, whether these principles would be applied to the colonies of Britain, France, the United States, the Netherlands, Portugal, or Spain, or to oppressed racialized groups within the United States, Canada, Europe, Australia, New Zealand, or South Africa.[68] Swedish economist Gunnar Myrdal wrote in 1944 that in "this War the principle of democracy had to be applied more explicitly to race."[69] Political elites in Britain and the United States, while increasingly wary about proclaiming white racial supremacy, tended to characterize the war against Japan in racial terms and resisted claims of racial equality.[70]

The racial dimensions of the war fostered increasing opposition among nonwhites to European colonialism and calls for a more equitable global order in the colonies—issues that were widely construed in racial terms.[71] Black activists in the United States promoted a "Double V" campaign for "victory over the Axis abroad and victory over racial discrimination at home."[72] In 1942 the Congress of Racial Equality (CORE) organized its first campaign for civil rights. CORE's leader, Walter White, wrote to President Roosevelt that if the war ended "with the continuation of white overlordship over brown, yellow, and black peoples of the world, there will inevitably be another war and continued misery for the colored peoples of the United States, the West Indies, South America, Africa, and the Pacific."[73]

The war also inspired nationalist movements in Asia and Africa. Political leaders in the Far East, India, and the Pacific debated the global "white-versus-colored" conflict and called for the end of colonialism in Asia. Black activists around the globe, such as Du Bois, George Padmore (Trinidad and Britain), Kwame Nkrumah (Ghana), and Harold Moody (Britain), revitalized the pan-African movement. Moody's League of Colored Peoples drew up the "Charter for Colored Peoples," which demanded racial equality and a transition to African self-government.[74] These themes were elaborated at the fifth Pan-African Congress in Manchester in October 1945, which included strong representation from labor unions and organizations from Africa.[75]

By the end of the war, Anglo-American elites recognized the need to affirm racial equality as a principle of international relations. The immediate impetus for this shift was less Nazism than the challenge that Japanese power posed to Western global dominance.[76] In this context the United Nations became an important forum for international struggles to eliminate racial discrimination. At the UN's founding conference in spring 1945, political alignments among participating governments on the contentious issue of the UN's role in fostering universal human rights and racial equality largely matched the color line dividing colonizers from colonized. Representatives from Egypt, India, Panama, Uruguay, Brazil, Mexico, the Dominican Republic, Cuba, Venezuela, the Philippines, and China called for the United Nations to affirm racial equality and prohibit racial discrimination.[77] Britain and the United States supported general proclamations against formal discrimination but worked (with Australia and New Zealand) "to prevent the United Nations from having any jurisdiction over the domestic practices of member states and . . . sought to undermine any United Nations action directed against South Africa."[78]

After the war the pan-European countries "sought to emphasize their internal virtues as integrative nations untroubled by racist oppression." The practical effects of this posture included widespread support in the pan-European world for the state of Israel, founded in 1948, and a new ecumenism within Western Christianity, along with appeals to a common "Judeo-Christian tradition."[79] In this spirit, English bishop George Bell aimed to reconsolidate the idea of "Christian Europe." In a postwar broadcast to Germany in 1945, Bell said, "Today, one of the principal goals . . . should be the recovery of Christendom. We want to see Europe as Christendom. . . . No nation, no church, no individual is guiltless."[80] Gradually, North American and European political and economic cooperation and a "European community" emerged. Through the Marshall Plan, the United States gave and loaned $12 billion to sixteen European countries for economic reconstruction between 1948 and 1952. For security purposes the United States, Canada, and Western Europe established the North Atlantic Treaty Organization (NATO) in 1949. (The USSR responded by creating the Warsaw Pact with Eastern Europe in 1955.) The beginnings of the "Europeanization" of national economies was apparent in the establishment of the European Coal and Steel Community (ECSC) in 1952, which joined West Germany and France and was the precursor of the European Economic Community.[81] These developments took place at the start of the postwar economic boom in the pan-European world.[82]

At the same time, pan-European elites carried ideas about a global color line into the postwar world. Philip Noel Baker, British secretary for the commonwealth, expressed a typical sentiment when he warned Parliament in 1949 that the "most probable and dangerous conflict" in coming years would be "between the peoples of Asia and Africa on the one hand

and the peoples of European origin and culture on the other."[83] The end of the 1940s witnessed the beginnings of decolonization, and Baker's forecast seemed a safe bet. In 1947, India achieved independence from Britain, and in 1948, Britain granted independence to Burma and Ceylon (now Sri Lanka) and withdrew from Palestine. In 1949 the People's Republic of China was established and the Dutch granted independence to Indonesia.[84] South Africa was an outlier. The Afrikaner-dominated Nationalist Party was elected in 1948 on a platform of apartheid (separate development). It completed the program of racial segregation and dominance that earlier white regimes had begun.[85]

## *The Decline of Scientific Racism*

One significant development in the scholarly study of race emerged in the United States in the 1920s. Park and Burgess pioneered the sociological "race relations" paradigm in *An Introduction to the Science of Sociology* (1921).[86] Park later defined race relations as "the relations existing between peoples distinguished by marks of racial descent, particularly when these racial differences enter into the consciousness of the individuals and groups so distinguished, and by doing so determine in each case the individual's conception of himself as well as his status in the community."[87] "Race relations" research, including Gunnar Myrdal's analysis of U.S. racism in *An American Dilemma,* challenged received notions about the innate character of "race prejudice." Yet it also accepted the prevailing notion of race differences—that is, that human groups were "distinguished by marks of racial descent" even before social practices constituted certain physical traits as racial.[88] Nonetheless, race relations theory partly shifted the scholarly study of race from the terrain of biology to that of social and political relations.[89] In the wake of Hitler's rise to power in 1933, various writers advanced critiques of racism. German Jewish social scientist and champion of homosexual rights Magnus Hirschfeld introduced the term *racism* in "Rassismus," published in English as *Racism* in 1938.[90] In 1937, the French-born U.S. cultural historian Jacques Barzun published *Race: A Study in Modern Superstition.*

By this time physical anthropology was losing its hold over the scientific study of race. Physical anthropologists, Elazar Barkan explains, had "accumulated data which had no epistemological justification," and their focus on visible physical differences had produced no consistent racial typologies. The study of race differences was addressed increasingly by the new sciences of genetics, social and cultural anthropology, sociology, and psychology.[91] In 1931, English biologist Lancelot Hogben summarized the growing confusion among scientists: "Geneticists believe that anthropologists have decided what race is. Ethnologists assume that their classifications embody principles which genetic science has proved correct. Politicians believe that their prejudices have the sanction of genetic laws and the findings of physical anthropology to sustain them."[92] More and more, scientists in this period challenged the notion of racial inequality, but without rejecting the concept of race. Since the notion of race difference was ultimately biological, the controversial ideal of basic human equality, as Barkan says, "had to be established on biological grounds."[93]

Developments in the science of race between 1935 and 1951 bear directly on the question of the relationship between science and politics, or truth and power. From a contemporary perspective, we might be tempted to see the refutation of scientific racism within science as straightforward evidence of the self-correcting character of the scientific method. On this view, once a sufficient number of scientists in the 1930s and 1940s distanced themselves from a priori racist assumptions, they were able to produce objective research that refuted scientific racism. But politics and science remained strongly intertwined in the study of race.[94] In Nancy Stepan's words, while science, "as always, depended for its character on empirical tests of its ideas, . . . politics, as always, influenced science by providing new motives for making scientific inquiries, and by shaping the theories put forward."[95]

The key to the transformation of race science was a profound shift in basic assumptions that guided scientific inquiry. From its beginnings until the 1930s, excepting rare scholars (such as Blumenbach, Virchow, and Boas), the scientific study of race typically started with a priori assumptions of race difference and inequality. In the 1930s, however, a critical mass of biologists and anthropologists began to approach race in light of more egalitarian assumptions *that had their sources outside their scientific disciplines.*[96] How these scientists reacted to major social and political trends during the 1920s and 1930s was especially significant. Barkan explains:

> Prosperity and immigration restriction in the United States erased Yankee xenophobia. The Great Depression furthered the belief in biological equality. Massive new poverty made it painfully real that destitution was

not caused by a biological flaw. The Depression undermined the confidence of the middle classes, and unsettled belief in heredity. The lesson was shared in Britain, and in both countries was accentuated during the 1930s by the rise of Nazism.[97]

In light of these social and political circumstances, a significant number of scientists began to question the validity of "biological explanations of social events."[98]

Race science was also affected by the "social diversification of the scientific community" in the interwar period. Members of subordinate "groups were coming to play a growing role in the scientific community, and to assert their political interests. Immigrants, women and Jews, created new spaces and provided necessary data to refute claims of their own 'inferior' qualities."[99] In addition, several of the pioneers of the new science of race, such as Boas and Ashley Montagu in the United States and Hogben and Julian Huxley in Britain, were political liberals or radicals. These scientists emphasized the role of environmental factors in shaping inherited human capacities.[100] Hogben, a prominent biologist and popular author who worked for a time in South Africa, was a critic of imperialism and war and had connections with Quakers and the socialist Fabians. He pioneered the genetic critique of the race concept.[101] By 1931, noting the difficulties of classifying humankind racially by skin color, head form, hair texture, "nasal index," or blood type, Hogben questioned the plausibility of racial classification based on genetics: "We have very little justification for assuming a close approximation to genetic purity when we define a group of human beings by a large and heterogeneous assemblage of physical traits."[102] Advocating "experimental skepticism," Hogben went on to say, "Experiment and experiment alone can decide the limits of development imposed by whatever genetic differences distinguish one racial group considered as a fictitious whole from another group considered as a fictitious whole."[103]

The case of the liberal Huxley, grandson of T. H. Huxley, is especially instructive for understanding the changes in race science. Huxley shifted from expressing conventional racism in the 1920s, especially with regard to "Negroes," to avowed but limited anti-racism in the 1930s, while continuing to support elements of racialism and even backhanded racism. He supported a social-scientific form of eugenics into the 1930s, and his speculations about race reflected prevalent pan-European prejudices about the global color line.[104]

Reporting on his travels to Africa, which led him to question the concept of race, he wrote in 1932, "White and black [peoples] overlap largely in regard to intelligence, energy, ability, and character."[105] He also challenged race egalitarians, suggesting that "there is not the least reason why races should not differ in the average of their inborn mental capacities as they do in their physical traits."[106] Huxley criticized the self-serving character of European imperialism but added, in the manner of "color line" racism, "There is also certain evidence that the negro is an earlier product of evolution than the Mongolian or the European, and as such might be expected to have advanced less, both in body and mind."[107] At the same time, he qualified his racial determinism with environmentalism. In a 1936 lecture on "Eugenics and Society," Huxley supported equality for blacks on moral grounds, emphasized the role of environmental factors on the differential achievements of different peoples, and said that no "eugenically significant point of racial differences has yet to be established."[108] Yet he reiterated that "the existence of marked genetic differences in physical characters (as between yellow, black, white and brown) make it *prima facie* likely that differences in intelligence and temperament also exist."[109] In the 1940s, Huxley still defended British colonial rule in Africa, as Africans remained "for the most part . . . in an early stage of barbarism."[110]

Huxley's major contribution to the critique of scientific racism, *We Europeans* (1935), coauthored with anthropologist A. C. Haddon, was part of a larger transnational and interdisciplinary response to Nazism among scientists from 1933 through the 1940s.[111] In the United States, Boas began in 1933 to rally anthropologists behind an anti-racism campaign but was stymied by divisions within the profession.[112] In Britain, the Royal Anthropological Institute, with the Institute of Sociology, formed the Race and Culture Committee to study the "racial factor in cultural development."[113] The committee, which included biologists and anthropologists, racists as well as anti-racists, published an interim report in 1936. But, as with Boas's initiatives, its internal disagreements prevented it from making any unequivocal anti-racist statement.[114] In *We Europeans,* Huxley and Haddon argued that "[a] vast pseudo-science of 'racial biology' has been erected which serves to justify political ambitions, economic ends, social grudges, class prejudices."[115] As their title indicates, they focused on refuting the idea that Europeans could be divided meaningfully into distinct races. They said that when we examine "more strictly" the differences that are commonly used to posit discrete "'racial stocks' and nationalities" among Europeans, "it will usually be found that there is very little in them that has any close relation to the physical characters by which 'race' in the biological sense can be distinguished. It is more probable that, so far as European populations are concerned, nothing in the nature of 'pure race' in the biological sense has any real existence."[116]

Huxley and Haddon extended this line of argument to a broader critique of the race concept, but in a way that effectively reinforced racialism. They pointed out that in the era of European voyages to Africa, Asia, and the Americas, "it was the *differences* between human types which impressed themselves upon general [European] thought."[117] More recent anthropological research, however, has yielded a "different picture":

> The different main types exist, but they are vague and less well-defined than was at first thought. . . . [A]lmost every gradation exists between the negro and the European along several lines, via Hamite, Semite and Mediterranean; every gradation exists between the white man and the yellow, through East Central Europe, across Russia, to Mongolia and China; every gradation exists between the yellow man and the already mixed dark brown Asiatic.[118]

This understanding parallels Blumenbach's 1795 view that "[i]nnumerable varieties of mankind run into one another by insensible degrees."

For Huxley and Haddon, "[t]he word 'race,' as applied scientifically to human groupings, has lost any sharpness of meaning. Today it is hardly definable in scientific terms, except as an abstract concept which *may*, under certain circumstances, . . . have been realized in the past, and *might*, under certain other but equally different conditions, be realized in the distant future."[119] They concluded that "the term *race* as applied to human groups should be dropped from the vocabulary of science."[120] Like Hogben, they noted that in efforts to map the frequency with which different physical characteristics (head form, stature, nose form, eye color, and hair form) occur in different geographic regions, it had become evident "that the various distributions by no means coincide." For instance, the geographical distribution of blood groups does not correspond to that of the other traits.[121]

Accordingly, they recommended the use of *ethnic group* in place of *race* when referring to "the existing populations," but their usage was confusing in notable ways.[122] They used *ethnic group* to refer to the same kinds of *physical* differences between groups that were (and still are) usually called *racial* differences. Thus, they offered their "ethnic classification" of peoples with respect to characteristics that were "obvious and easily accessible, if possible measurable, with a predominantly genetic basis, and little susceptible to environmental modification."[123] To further muddle matters, they suggested that the term *race* had some meaning, if only abstractly, with reference to the main subdivisions of humanity, the "well-marked 'geographical races' or sub-species, whose distinctions are largely adaptive in reference to the area of their evolution."[124] They said that these subdivisions, but only in their presumed "original state," "might legitimately be called 'primary races,' though both for the sake of conformity with general biological usage, and to avoid the unfortunate connotations of the word *race,* the term sub-species is preferable."[125]

Their use of *subspecies* solved nothing, though, since "the unfortunate connotations of the word *race*" were (and are) due in part to how this term suggests the kind of irreducible difference between peoples connoted by the notion of subspecies. Moreover, Huxley and Haddon reinforced racialism (if not racism) in other ways. For instance, in discussing the importance of environmental factors in shaping human psychological traits, they said, "Do not let us be misunderstood. It is clear that there must exist innate genetic differences between human groups in regard to intelligence, temperament, and other psychological traits." Yet they qualified this remark as follows: "[T]his need not mean that the mental differences are highly correlated with the physical—that a black skin, for instance, automatically connotes a tendency towards low intelligence or irresponsible temperament."[126]

In sum, Huxley and Haddon pointed the way to a thoroughgoing scientific critique of scientific racism, but they remained ambivalent with respect to the "race" concept and the possibility of racial differences. This position typified advanced scientific views of the time. After 1938, as the political situation in Germany grew more dire, scientists outside Germany shifted increasingly toward anti-racist positions. Several scientific organizations, including the American Anthropological Association, the executive council for the Psychological Study of Social Issues, and leading geneticists at the International Congress of Genetics in Edinburgh (in the Geneticists' Manifesto), issued anti-racist declarations. These organizations all opposed Nazi racism, but they did not define *race* in egalitarian terms.[127]

Some individual scholars continued the critique of scientific racism begun by Huxley and Haddon. In the United States, Ruth Benedict, a student of Boas, published *Race: Science and Politics* (1940).[128] She popularized her argument in a 1943 educational pamphlet, "The Races of Man," coauthored with fellow anthropologist Gene Weltfish. The pamphlet ran into political controversy—the House Military Affairs Sub-Committee charged that it exhibited "all the techniques of Communist propaganda" —but it was soon translated into several languages and widely circulated.[129] Benedict and Weltfish asserted that all human beings are essentially the same physiologically, "and all the racial differences among them are in nonessentials such as texture of head hair, amount of body hair, shape of nose or head, or color of the eyes and the skin."[130] Yet, while they rejected the idea that race differences were linked to differences in character, intelligence, culture, and civilization, they did not discount the possibility of race differences.[131]

U.S. anthropologist Ashley Montagu (1905–99), another of Boas's students, more boldly critiqued racial thought in *Man's Most Dangerous Myth: The Fallacy of Race* (1942): "The idea of 'race' represents one of the greatest, if not the greatest, of the errors of our times, and the most tragic."[132] What people typically understood as racial differences were merely the phenotypic (i.e., external) expressions of varying gene frequencies across populations:

> The common definition of 'race' is based upon an arbitrary and superficial selection of external characters. At its very best it may, in genetic terms, be re-defined as a group of individuals of whom an appreciable majority, taken at a particular time level, are characterized by the possession of a certain number of genes phenotypically . . . selected as marking 'racial' boundaries between them and other groups of individuals of the same species population not characterized by so high a degree of frequency of these particular genes.[133]

In short, the "race" concept denotes clear boundaries between groups in relation to discrete "complexes of characters" where there are no such discrete complexes of characters between so-called races. There are only varying frequencies of genes that differ in a graduated way between such groups.[134] "And upon what grounds," Montagu asked, "are such characters to be considered as significantly defining a 'race'?"[135]

Yet even Montagu, one of the most thoroughly egalitarian writers about race in this period, was ambivalent about the "race" concept. At one point he accepted a narrow version of it (which he rejected more roundly in later editions):

> In biology a race is defined as a sub-division of a species which inherits physical characteristics distinguishing it from other populations of the species. . . . In the biological sense there do, of course, exist races of mankind. That is to say, mankind is comprised of many groups which are physically sufficiently distinguishable from one another to justify their being classified as separate races. But not all groups of mankind can be so classified.[136]

In the end, he followed Huxley and Haddon in proposing to replace *race* with *ethnic group*: "An ethnic group represents one of a number of populations . . . which individually maintain their differences, physical and cultural, by means of isolating mechanisms such as geographic and social barriers."[137]

Despite these mounting critiques of scientific racism, no clear consensus had emerged among scientists to redefine race in egalitarian cultural terms. Even in 1950, when UNESCO issued its first "Statement on Race," there remained no unqualified egalitarian consensus.[138] According to the 1950 statement,

> the term "race" designates a group or population characterized by some concentrations, relative as to the frequency and distribution, of hereditary particles (genes) or physical characters, which appear, fluctuate, and often disappear in the course of time by reason of geographic and/or cultural isolation. The varying manifestations of these traits in different populations are perceived in different ways by each group. . . . The biological fact of race and the myth of "race" should be distinguished. For all practical purposes "race" is not so much a biological phenomenon as a social myth.[139]

As Barkan summarizes, "The Statement presented four premises, three of which were generally accepted: that mental capacities of all races are similar; that no evidence for biological deterioration as a result of hybridization [i.e., race crossing] existed; that there was no correlation between national or religious groups and any race." The fourth major claim, however, that race was more a "social myth" than a biological phenomenon, provoked significant criticism, along with the assertion that "biological studies lend support to the ethic of universal brotherhood."[140]

This led UNESCO to publish a second, more circumspect "Statement on the Nature of Race and Race Differences," by physical anthropologists and geneticists, in 1951.[141] According to the second UN-ESCO statement, "the word 'race' should be reserved for groups of mankind possessing well-developed and primarily heritable physical differences from other groups. Many populations can be so classified but . . . there are also many populations which cannot easily be fitted into a racial classification."[142] The 1951 statement avoided any suggestion that race was a social myth but noted that there was no evidence for racial "superiority" or "inferiority."[143] By the end of the era, then, scientists produced a substantially revised understanding of race but did not yet repudiate the "race" concept.

## Egalitarian Racialism and the "Caucasian Race" Revival

The second key feature of the transformation of scientific racial thought in this period was the rehabilitation of Cuvier's old three-race classification scheme. This involved the revival of the pan-European "Caucasian race" category alongside "Negro" and "Mongolian" races as the three major racial divisions of humankind. This turn of thought was foreshadowed by Virchow's and Boas's 1890s critiques of "races of Europe" theories. Virchow referred to those races whose existence was commonly accepted, "the white, the black, and the yellow races." Boas recommended that the term *race* be reserved for the major "divisions of mankind," the "Europeans, Africans and Mongols." It is noteworthy that Virchow and Boas advanced their color-coded view of the major "divisions of mankind" during the era of late-nineteenth-century European imperialism and within a few years of Du Bois's declaration about "the problem of the color line." It is also important to remember that while the "Caucasian race" category was largely eclipsed in Europe between 1848 and 1935 by the "races of Europe," it persisted in the United States. In contrast to Europe, a white/nonwhite color line was central to U.S. domestic politics in these years. There was no parallel European view until *after* World War II. During the 1920s and 1930s, the "Caucasian race" category began its comeback in a raciological rendering of the "color line"—a renewed emphasis on so-called white, black, and yellow races.[144]

The prolific U.S. anthropologist A. L. Kroeber's 1923 defense of a tripartite division of humankind heralded the new view. Kroeber's discussion of racial classification also exemplified basic problems with the practice, and his own classification incorporated a version of the "races of Europe." "It is true that a Negro and a north European cannot be confused," he stated, because "they happen to be extreme types. Yet as soon as we operate with less divergent races we find that variations between individuals of the same race are often greater than differences between the races."[145] Generally speaking, "demarcations between races" were uncertain.[146] It would be relatively easy to "arrive at a clear-cut classification by grouping all the peoples of the earth according to a single trait, such as the shape of the nose, or color. But any such classification must be artificial and largely unsound, just because it disregards the majority of traits." A classification would rest on "a true and natural basis" only insofar as it took account of "as many traits possible, and weight[ed] the important more heavily than the unimportant features."[147]

Kroeber maintained that the cephalic index—used to distinguish broad- from long-headed peoples—had "certain definite advantages," such as being "little affected by the environment."[148] It was useful for "distinguishing subtypes, nation from nation," but not the "primary races" from each other, since they were "not uniform" in this respect. "There are narrow headed, medium headed and broad headed Caucasians."[149] The "nasal index," which distinguished broad versus narrow noses, was useful because it ran "relatively constant in the great races." "Cranial capacity" was not useful because it was "considerably dependent on bodily size." Hair texture was "now universally regarded as one of the most valuable criteria for classifying races, possibly the most valuable of all." Hairiness of the body merited some consideration: "Caucasians are definitely a hairy race, Mongoloids and most Negroids glabrous or smooth-skinned." And color, including skin, hair, and eye color, was "the most conspicuous trait of any race" but presented some difficulties for the anthropologist due to so many "transition shades."[150]

Kroeber offered no cogent rationale for distinguishing "important" from "unimportant" features. Yet his comment that "a Negro and a north European cannot be confused" presumed, without any supporting argument, that the physical traits used to distinguish these groups—skin color, hair texture, and (sometimes) hair and eye color—*were* racially significant. Likewise, his judgments about the relative racial importance of the cephalic index, the nasal index, and "hairiness" appear to have stemmed from his preconceptions about which peoples were racially distinct. Thus, the significance of the nasal index and hairiness were confirmed because they effectively differentiated "Caucasian," "Mongoloid," and "Negroid" races.[151] Conversely, while he thought that the cephalic index had "advantages," he judged it to be of limited value because "the primary races are not uniform" in this respect; that is, its results actually cut across those groupings that he already believed to be the "primary races."

Kroeber reconciled these disparate conclusions as follows. There were "three grand divisions" of humanity: the "Caucasian, Negroid, and Mongoloid . . . of which the European, the Negro, and the Chinaman may be taken as representative."[152] (He noted the color terms, "White, Black, and Yellow," but said they had "no descriptive value.") These three divisions encompassed perhaps 99 percent of humankind. There also were "some aberrant forms" that were "best kept separate," notably the Ainu (of Japan), Australians, and Polynesians. Moreover, he maintained that each of the three "primary stocks" included "several natural subdivisions" or "races" (see figures 10 and 11).[153]

Kroeber was indebted to both Keane and William Ripley for his subdivisions of "the Caucasian races."[154] "Three of the four Caucasian races live, in whole or part, in Europe," he said, "the fourth consists of the Hindus. The three European races are the Nordic, the Alpine, and the Mediterranean."[155] The Mediterranean race extended beyond Europe to "the shores of the Mediterranean Sea, in Asia and Africa as well as in Europe," and the Hindu was largely "a narrow headed dark skinned Caucasian," similar to the Mediterranean.[156] Kroeber went on to claim that a general acceptance of a division of "mankind . . . into Caucasian, Negroid, and Mongoloid" was evident even in the works of anthropologists such as Joseph Deniker, who proposed classifications that were, at least on the surface, quite different from this view. He maintained, for instance, that Deniker's "6 grand divisions, 17 minor divisions, and 29 separate races" actually "coincid[ed] quite closely" with his own classification of three "primary stocks" and various subdivisions.[157]

By the 1930s, other influential scientists affirmed versions of the three primary stocks or "three-race" view. Aleš Hrdlička, curator at the Smithsonian Institution and the leading U.S. physical anthropologist in the first half of the twentieth century, affirmed a classification scheme similar to Kroeber's.[158] Hrdlička relied primarily on physical traits along with "careful consideration of the views of others" and "extensive personal knowledge of peoples, and that of both the living and the skeletal remains," to classify human races as follows: "There are three primary *Stems* or *Races of Man*. They are the White, the Yellow-brown, and the Black; or the Caucasoid, the Mongoloid, and the Negroid." He said that these terms are "all more or less unsatisfactory, but they are the best we have and the most

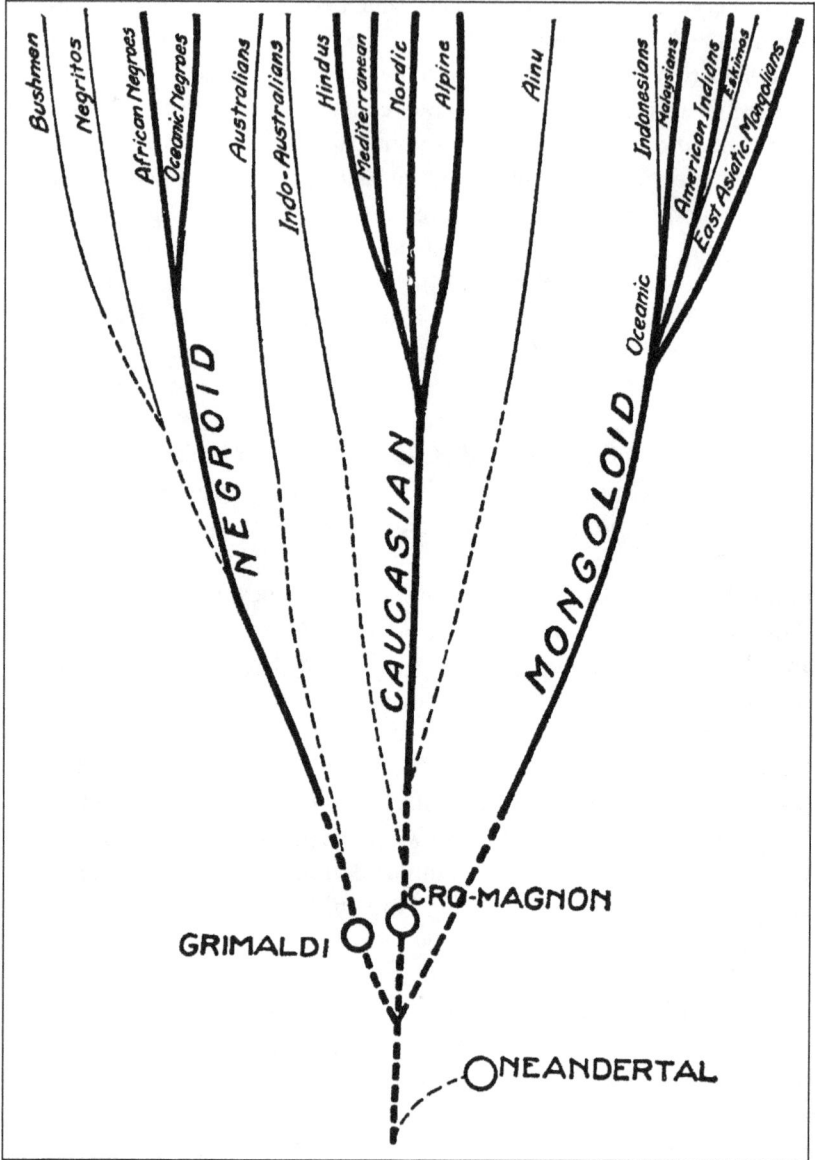

Figure 10: Kroeber's "Fig. 9: Tentative Family Tree of the Human Races" (1923).
Reprinted from A. L. Kroeber, *Anthropology* (New York: Harcourt, Brace, and
Company, 1923), p. 48.

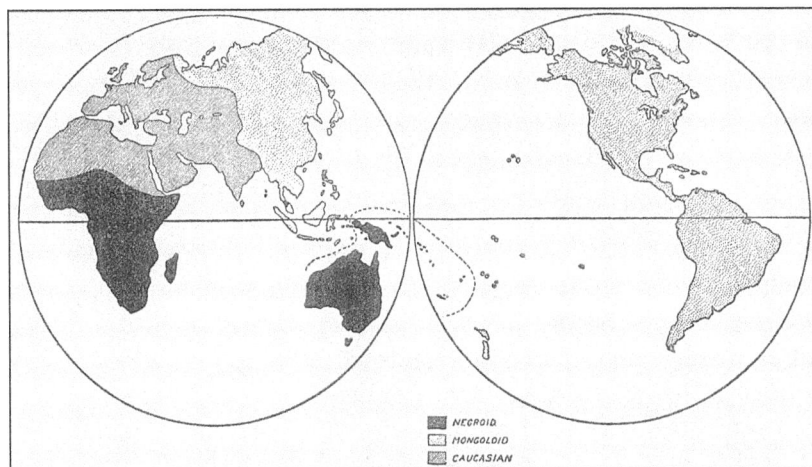

Figure 11: Kroeber's "Fig. 10: Outline distribution of the primary racial stocks of mankind according to the three-fold classification, Australians, Ainu, Vedda, Polynesians, etc., being included in the stock with which they appear to affiliate most closely. A larger map with more shadings would be required to do even approximate justice to the intricacies of a complete race classification." (1923). Reprinted from A. L. Kroeber, *Anthropology* (New York: Harcourt, Brace, and Company, 1923), p. 50.

generally understood."[159] These three stems differed in several ways, but no characteristic was "the exclusive property of any one. The whites and the negroes stand in general the furthest apart. The yellow-browns are more or less intermediate, but mostly nearer to the white man than the negro."[160]

Like Kroeber, Hrdlička did not abandon the "races of Europe" approach. He identified several "secondary racial groups," including Polynesians and Australians, and several "well-established . . . daughter races" in each of the "three human stems or main races." In the "white stem" these races were the Hamitic, Semitic, Mediterranean, Alpine, and Nordic.[161] In addition, Hrdlička was no race egalitarian. Although there was little "thorough scientific investigation" of comparative cognitive capacities of the major races, he concluded that geographical locales and circumstances favored the "development of intellectual differences": "In broad lines it is legitimate . . . to speak of 'advanced' and 'belated' human groups or races," principally "the whites and the blacks," respectively.[162]

This mode of racial classification became common in U.S. anthropology in the 1930s. For instance, Ralph Linton, in 1936, listed three main "stocks," "the Caucasic, or white, the Negroid, or black, and the Mongoloid, or yellow." Within the "Caucasic stock" alone there were "at least five races": "Nordic," "Alpine," "Mediterranean," "Armenoid," and "Hindi."[163] Boas, writing on "Race" in the collection *General Anthropology* (1938), recommended a related scheme. Race, he said, should be understood "as a group of common origin and stable type." Accordingly, "extreme forms like Australians, Negroes, Mongolians, and Europeans may be described as races, because each has certain characteristics which set them off from other groups, and which are strictly hereditary."[164] Boas also reiterated his view that different European populations could not meaningfully be divided into "fundamental racial types" because it had not been established that "long-headedness" and "round-headedness" were "stable features."[165]

The leading critics of the "race" concept in England and the United States also retrieved Cuvier's three-race scheme. In England, Hogben, who cited Kroeber, said in 1931 that the "bulk of mankind can be classified on the basis of two discrete structural characteristics which serve to differentiate three major assemblages concentrated in fairly well-defined geographical regions."[166] The physical characteristics were hair texture and "the shape of the nose," and the three groups were "the Negroids, the Mongoloids, and the Caucasians." Hogben pointed out, however, that "great variety of skin colour exists, and both long- and broad-headed skull types" within each of the groups, and that the Australian Aborigines stood outside this scheme.[167] He also noted that this classification did not coincide with the geographical distribution of blood types, the one human difference that had been subject to genetic analysis at that point.[168]

Huxley and Haddon affirmed the three-race view more explicitly in *We Europeans*. While they proposed to replace *race* with *ethnic group*, they said that the term *race* had some value with respect the "well-marked 'geographical races,'" represented by "the typical Negro, typical Mongol, and typical Leucoderm," or "white skinned (Caucasian) peoples."[169] They referred to the so-called Nordic, Eurasiatic, and Mediterranean "types" within Europe as constituting the "'white' sub-species"; these types could be considered "minor sub-species as opposed to the major sub-species."[170] In effect, Huxley and Haddon implied that the differences between the "primary geographical groups" were racial after all, but the differences among European populations were merely "ethnic."

Back in the United States, Montagu, despite his vigorous criticism of "race" thinking, supported a similar racial classification scheme—though closer to Blumenbach's than to Cuvier's. "Truth will not be advanced," he said, "by denying the existence of large groups of mankind characterized, more or less, by distinctive inherited traits." Although none of the "great divisions" was "pure" or unmixed, we "may recognize five or six great 'races' or divisions of mankind, Mongolian, Caucasian, Negro, Australo-Melanesian and Polynesian. Within these five or six races there exist many local types, but most of these local types are very much mixed."[171]

Benedict affirmed the three-race view. She was largely concerned to clarify what race was—merely "a classification based on traits which are hereditary"—and what it is not—"socially acquired" traits, or culture.[172] Regarding "racial characteristics" she wrote, "Chinese have yellowish skin and slanting eyes. Negroes have a dark skin and wide flat noses. Caucasians have a lighter skin and high thin noses. The color and texture of the hair of these peoples differ as much as their skin and noses."[173] Benedict and Weltfish identified "three primary races"—"Caucasian," Mongoloid," and "Negroid." They added that "Aryans, Jews, Italians are *not* races" and that the "Caucasian race" was subdivided into "Nordics," "Alpines," and "Mediterraneans."[174]

Later, the 1950 UNESCO "Statement on Race" conferred broad scientific and political authority on the "Caucasian race" revival with a relatively egalitarian version of Cuvier's three-race scheme. It asserted that "most anthropologists agree in classifying the greater part of present-day mankind into three major divisions, . . . the Mongoloid Division; the Negroid Division; the Caucasoid Division."[175] By the 1960s, this "authoritative" view of three "principal races of man" was popularized in *World Book Encyclopedia* and elsewhere and had become commonplace in North America (see figure 12).[176]

In the United States, this reorientation of racial thinking became established in popular racial discourse during the 1930s and 1940s. A 1939 handbook for high school teachers by the Council Against Intolerance in America declared that scientists "apply the term 'race' only to the broadest subdivisions of mankind, Negro, Caucasian, Mongolian, Malayan, and Australian."[177] Laura Hobson, in her 1947 novel *Gentlemen's Agreement* (which became a movie starring Gregory Peck), had one of her characters refer to "the Jewish race" before correcting herself: "She knew perfectly well that the three great divisions of mankind were the Caucasian race, the Mongoloid, the Negroid. She remembered [her fiancé Philip Green's] fin-

# MAIN CHARACTERISTICS
## OF THE THREE GREAT STOCKS OF MAN

**Three Primary Stocks** make up the peoples of the earth. Each stock shows important differences in appearance. Each single trait is not always much different in one race from the same trait in another race. But the combination of these traits adds up to an important total. These differences are only general.

| NEGROID | CAUCASOID | MONGOLOID |
|---|---|---|
| **Hair** is coarse and is wavy or even curly. It often coils in spirals. | **Hair** texture is fine and may be straight, or wavy or curly. | **Hair** texture of Mongoloids is coarse and entirely straight. |
| **Heads** of most Negroid peoples are long and fairly narrow, although pygmies are usually round-headed. | **Head** shapes range from long in Northwest Europe to broad in Central Europe and short in Southeast Europe. | **Head** shape is typically round, although long-headed people are frequently found in North China. |
| **Skin** colors of Negroes range from light to dark brown and black. | **Skin** colors range from pinkish-white and olive to dark brown. | **Skin** color ranges from saffron-yellow to light shades of brown. |
| **Nose** is broad and flat with flaring wings. Nasal root is low and wide. | **Nose** and nasal root are high and narrow with pressed-in wings. | **Nose** tends to be intermediate but closer to Caucasoid in shape. |
| **Lips** are thick and turned out. Mouth is fairly wide in most Negroid peoples. | **Lips** are thin and are not turned out. Mouth is small to fairly wide. | **Lips** are fairly thin and not turned out. Mouth is wide to very wide. |
| **Eyes** have no folds at the corners, although there may be a fold in the middle of the eyelid. Color is brown. | **Eyes** of Caucasoid peoples have no corner or lid folds. Color of eyes ranges from light blue to dark brown. | **Eyes** have lid folds in inner corners which make eyes look slanted or almond-shaped. Color is dark brown. |

Figure 12: "Main Characteristics of the Three Great Stocks of Man" (1965). Reprinted from *The World Book Encyclopedia* (Chicago: Field Enterprises Educational Corporation, 1965), p. 58. By permission of World Book, Inc. www .worldbook.com.

ger pointing out a phrase in a pamphlet written by leading anthropologists. 'There is no Jewish race.'"[178] The premise of Hobson's book, however, was that Jews were not yet unequivocally counted as white.[179] By the 1950s and 1960s, the Alpine and Mediterranean races of the late nineteenth and early twentieth centuries—for example, Slavs, Celts, Jews, and Italians (sometimes called "dark whites")—had been reclassified as "Caucasian" (i.e., simply "white"). As Matthew Frye Jacobson explains, "[A]s race moved to the center of political discussion nationally, 'difference' among the former white races diminished, race itself was recast as color, and race-as-difference was reified along the lines of . . . the 'three great divisions of mankind.'"[180]

## Reflections on the "Caucasian Race" Revival

The years between 1935 and 1951 witnessed a radical transformation in the science of race. After some two hundred years of scientific racism since Linnaeus's work, a critical mass of scientists signed on to a new, basically egalitarian racialism.[181] The new race science, however, left unresolved questions about the epistemic status of the "race" concept in general and the "Caucasian race" (along with the associated "Mongolian" and "Negro" race categories) in particular.

Two difficulties stand out. First, none of the racial classifications offered in this period, including Montagu's 1942 scheme and UNESCO's influential 1950 division of humankind "into three major divisions," persuasively answered crucial questions that Montagu raised about racial classification in light of genetics:

> The common definition of "race" is based upon an arbitrary and superficial selection of external characters. At its very best it may, in genetic terms, be re-defined as a group of individuals of whom an appreciable majority, taken at a particular time level, are characterized by the possession of a certain number of genes phenotypically (that is on the basis of external characters) selected as marking "racial" boundaries between them and other groups of individuals of the same species population not characterized by so high a degree of these particular genes.[182]

Then he asked: "What . . . does 'an appreciable majority' refer to? What are the characters which are exhibited by this 'appreciable majority'? And upon what ground are such characters to be considered as significantly defining a 'race'?"[183]

Such questions had bedeviled efforts at "racial" classification from the very start: the task depended on the assumption that certain visible or measurable characteristics—skin color, hair texture, nose shape, cranial form, and so forth—were sufficiently "significant," as Kant said in 1777 and Kroeber reiterated in 1923, to *racially* differentiate groups of *Homo sapiens*. At the same time, scientists increasingly recognized that with respect to many such traits (e.g., skin color or cranial form), the range of variation *within* the so-called great divisions was larger than the range of variation *between* them. Yet they continued to evade Montagu's basic question: "[U]pon what ground are such characters to be considered as significantly defining a 'race'?" The recommendation by Huxley and Haddon and Montagu to replace the term *race* with *ethnic group* failed to resolve the problem because these thinkers used *ethnic group* in a quasi-racial sense, as an alternative label for the same kinds of physical distinctions. Moreover, this use of *ethnic group* precluded the more promising cultural usage suggested by Deniker in *The Races of Man* (1900): that an "ethnic group" was marked by distinctive "linguistic or social characteristics." Meanwhile, others like Boas, Benedict, and the UNESCO scientists retained the "race" concept but gave it a new, supposedly benign meaning. They sought to detach it from its associations with ideas about innate superiority and inferiority, and to use it merely as, in Benedict's words, "a classification based on [physical] traits which are hereditary."[184] All these efforts begged Montagu's question.

Second, the rejection of racism within science and the apparent consensus supporting the three-race scheme were no abstract triumphs of disengaged scientific objectivity. The former certainly signaled scientific progress, and widespread support among scientists for the revised three-race scheme, as expressed in the UNESCO statements, was historically unprecedented. Nevertheless, both developments were encouraged by changing social and political circumstances. The rise of Nazism and the Great Depression provided the most immediate impetus for the "retreat of scientific racism," and changing circumstances also informed the specific racial judgments embodied in the recovery of Cuvier's three-race scheme and the "Caucasian race" revival. In effect, as I explain in the concluding chapter, increasingly egalitarian social conditions fostered greater scientific objectivity.

Ultimately, few of the scientists involved in the rejection of scientific racism were prepared to reject the "race" concept outright. Apparently, after centuries of dubious speculations about the "races of man," the scientific community wanted to recommend *some* racial classification as part of their efforts to redefine race. Meanwhile, to understand why pan-European scientists coalesced around the three-race view and drew the race boundaries they did between 1935 and 1951 (as in the UNESCO's statements), we need to remember Du Bois's comment about "the problem of the color line," which concerned the "present situation and outlook of the darker races of mankind." That is, we need to appreciate the shift in the dominant racialized divisions of global politics between roughly 1875 and 1935—as least as these were perceived in Europe and the (white) European settler societies (particularly the United States, Canada, Australia, New Zealand, and South Africa). In the previous global racial order, which persisted in some ways through the current period, a division between "white" and "colored" peoples—which went back to the start of race thinking and racism—coexisted with theories about "European races." The new global racial order was increasingly characterized by a global color line that was widely conceived by European and U.S. elites in terms of the so-called white, black, and yellow races. The obvious raciological rendering of this color line was an updated version of Cuvier's old Caucasian, Mongolian, and Negro races.

# 6

## Not-so-Benign Racialism

*The "Caucasian Race" after*
*Decolonization, 1952–2005*

I was staring at a news item that baffled me. . . . *Twenty-nine free and*
*independent nations of Asia and Africa are meeting in Bandung, In-*
*donesia, to discuss "racialism and colonialism."* . . . I scanned the list of
nations involved: China, India, Indonesia, Japan, Burma, Egypt,
Turkey, the Philippines, Ethiopia, Gold Coast, etc. My God! I began a
rapid calculation of the populations of the nations listed and, when
my total topped the billion mark, I stopped, pulled off my glasses,
and tried to think. A stream of realizations claimed my mind: these
people were ex-colonial subjects, people whom the white West called
"colored" peoples. Almost all of the nations mentioned had been, in
some form or other, under the domination of Western Europe. . . .
This was a meeting of almost all of the human race living in the
main geopolitical center of gravity of the earth.

—Richard Wright, *The Color Curtain* (1956)[1]

Race has become a trope of ultimate, irreducible difference between
cultures, linguistic groups, or adherents of specific belief systems
which—more often than not—also have fundamentally opposed
economic interests.

—Henry Louis Gates Jr., "Writing 'Race' and the
Difference It Makes" (1985)[2]

Between 1952 and 2005 the career of the "Caucasian race" idea
has taken another major turn. Scholars in biology, social sciences, and humanities have increasingly recognized the difficulty—if not impossibility
—of answering the basic question about race that Ashley Montagu asked
in *Man's Most Dangerous Myth* (1942): On what grounds can the various

physical characteristics that have been selected historically as markers of *race* difference "be considered as significantly defining a 'race'?" (see chapter 5). More and more scholars have concluded that the zoological concept of race cannot meaningfully be applied to the physiological differences among human beings. That is, there are no human races in the old biological sense, which means that there is no actually existing "Caucasian" (or "Caucasoid") race, and no "Negro" or "Mongolian" race.

In addition to heightened skepticism about biological race among biologists and anthropologists, there has been a wider proliferation of scholarship on race and racism since the 1960s and 1970s. Recently, as John Solomos and Les Back note, a number of new critical questions have come to the fore, shifting attention beyond "race relations" to questions about racism and processes of racialization: "What kinds of meaning can be given to the category 'race'? How should racism be identified as a political force within European societies, the USA and other parts of the globe? Have we seen a growth of new forms of racist expression in contemporary societies?"[3] While these questions do not exhaust the range of critical analysis, they are indicative of its main directions. At the same time, some scholars have continued to defend the notion of biological human races; and a few have continued to use "race" (along with "Caucasian" and associated racial categories) in ways that recapitulate now-discredited scientific racism. Meanwhile, new forms of racism around the globe have increasingly attenuated links to prevailing scientific views of race.

To some extent, the new tendency to reject biological race can be traced to prior developments in biology, particularly the new genetics. Geneticists such as Hogben began to develop this "new science of human diversity" between the 1920s and 1940s. Yet anthropologists like Montagu began only in the 1940s to utilize the new genetics to rethink "the old racial science," which had been preoccupied with racial classification;[4] and the full impact of the new genetics has become evident only recently.

As I explained in chapter 5, however, a major factor in the emergence of the anti-racist science of race during 1935–51 had its source outside science: for the first time a critical mass of biologists and anthropologists began to approach race in light of egalitarian assumptions. After 1951, a series of momentous social and political events deepened this egalitarian turn and fostered widespread critical scrutiny of the "race" concept: the decolonization movement in Asia and Africa, the U.S. Civil Rights movement, UN initiatives against racism and for "humanity" and human rights, the movement toward European unity, and the ending of South African apartheid. Howard Winant aptly calls this profound historical transformation the "postwar break": the "global rupture . . . in the continuity of worldwide white supremacy."[5] Before this period "the existence of *race* was a given; the only items debated were the origins and equality of races."[6] The break coincided with an emerging scientific consensus around an avowedly egalitarian racialism—well represented by the 1950/51 UN-ESCO-sponsored view that there were three major "races" but they were all equal. The anti-racist political movements of the 1950s and 1960s spurred many scholars of race to adopt the bolder view that "race" was and is a social construction.[7]

Developments in the science and politics of race over the past fifty-three years thus shed new light on the interrelationship between the science and politics of race. The evidence might be taken to indicate that the new science of race has become autonomous from politics, or social and political power dynamics. Yet, while mainstream science of race has largely distanced itself from racist politics, it would be a mistake to conclude that the science of race now proceeds independently of politics.[8] Instead, the development of an anti-racist (and increasingly anti-*racial*) science of race and human diversity has been part of the broader social and political shift concerning race over the last fifty to seventy years: the profound (although incomplete) rethinking and restructuring of the world's global racial order. As scientists have pursued the new genetics without old racial assumptions, they have increasingly developed more sound, nonracial accounts of human biological diversity.

## "Race" in the Postcolonial World, 1952–2005

The postwar break represented by the great movements for decolonization, civil rights, and global human rights has reshaped the place of "race" in the world since 1952, but the break remains incomplete. Descendants of former slaves and colonized peoples achieved a partial dismantling of the most visible and official forms of racial domination by European peoples who had learned to call themselves "white." The last stage of this process was the end of South Africa's apartheid system and the election of a new government between 1990 and 1994.[9] Yet these changes did not create a postracial world; instead, "the global racial order entered a new period of instability and tension in the last decades of the twentieth century."[10]

Racialized inequalities are still widespread, and new forms of racism have emerged.

Regarding the "break," global political realignments produced by World War II paved the way for decolonization in Asia and Africa and the U.S. Civil Rights movement of 1954–65. The war and its aftermath undermined the colonial empires of Italy and the Netherlands and eventually those of Great Britain, France, Belgium, and Portugal.[11] The United States, which emerged as the world's major power, was left to address the conflict between its claim to lead the "free world" and its internal racism. The general trend was heralded in UNESCO's constitution of 1945, which declared its support for the "democratic principles of the dignity, equality and mutual respect of men [*sic*]," and its opposition to "the doctrine of the inequality of men [*sic*] and races."[12]

Decolonization quickly followed the war's end. Between 1945 and 1952 "no less than 40 countries with a population of eight hundred million— more than a quarter of the world's inhabitants—revolted against colonialism and won their independence." Asian and African peoples "reacted against European domination, against what they regarded as exploitation for the benefit of European interests."[13] Pivotal events included North Vietnam's defeat of the French at Dien Bien Phu in 1953; the inauguration of Kwame Nkruma in 1957 as the first president of Ghana; the Congo's independence from Belgium in 1960, with the brief rise of Patrice Lumumba; and Algeria's independence from France in 1962. Decolonization reconfigured the existing global racial order, as white colonizers retreated and formerly colonized peoples gained sovereign states. At the 1955 Bandung (Indonesia) Conference of new Asian and African states, leaders of the "colored races" of the world expressly challenged continuing global white supremacy.[14] Participants at the 1956 Congress of Negro-African Writers and Artists in Paris (Le Congrès des Escrivans et Artistes Noir) joined similar criticisms of white racism with calls for a "renaissance of black people."[15]

In the United States, the 1954 Supreme Court decision in *Brown v. Board of Education* declared unconstitutional state laws that required or permitted racial segregation in primary and secondary schools, although the Court refrained from demanding an effective transition to "nonracial" schooling.[16] The Civil Rights movement continued the work begun by *Brown*. It overturned the legal edifice of racialized segregation of and discrimination against African Americans, culminating with the Civil Rights

Act of 1964 and Voting Rights Act of 1965. In 1967 the Supreme Court finally declared existing anti-miscegenation laws to be unconstitutional. Additionally, the postwar economic boom of the 1950s produced a favorable context for renewed immigration. The Walter-McCarran Act of 1952 finally removed racial requirements for U.S. citizenship, and immigration was substantially expanded by the 1965 immigration reform, which ended national-origin quotas that were adopted in 1924.[17] In 1977 the federal government standardized its use of racial and ethnic categories. It recognized four "racial" groups—American Indian or Alaskan Native, Asian or Pacific Islander, Black, and White—while designating "Hispanics and/or Latinos . . . as an ethnic group, not a *race*, because of their Spanish origin and culture."[18] This has also been an era of "ethnic revival" and the emergence of "white ethnics" in U.S. politics.[19]

It soon became evident, however, that formal equality before the law was insufficient to overcome generations of racial oppression in the United States. In 1968 the Kerner Commission, appointed by President Lyndon Johnson in 1967 to report on civil disorders and racialized inequality, declared, "Our nation is moving toward two societies, one black, one white—separate and unequal."[20] While the commission's stark assessment has not been borne out entirely, the United States remains to this day marked by deep racialized inequalities of income, wealth, poverty, education, employment, imprisonment, and health—particularly but not exclusively between Whites and Blacks.[21]

In the midst of these events, and reflecting on the modern history of "Negro" enslavement and European colonialism, black activist intellectuals such as Frantz Fanon and James Baldwin apprehended "race" as a political construct that had rationalized pan-European "white" domination of "colored" peoples. Martinique-born, French-educated Fanon emphasized the relational character of racial identities in *Black Skins, White Masks* (1952). "Ontology," he wrote, "does not permit us to understand the being of the black man. For not only must the black man be black; he must be black in relation to the white man."[22] That is, some people become "black" (or "Negro") only when, and for as long as, others define themselves as "white." These "racial" identities did not signify actual *racial* differences; rather, Europeans forged them to rationalize their domination of the African peoples whom they called "Negro" or "black." Baldwin, the African American writer, offered a related insight in *The Fire Next Time* (1963): "[C]olor [i.e., race] is not a human or personal reality; it is a political reality. But this distinction is so extremely hard to make that the West has not been able to make it yet. . . . [O]ne must be careful not to take refuge in any delusion—and the value placed on the color of the skin is always and everywhere and forever a delusion."[23] The West, in short, continued to regard "color" or "race" as a fundamental reality because it was so deeply invested—psychically, socially, and politically—in this delusion.

Several other events and circumstances have shaped the science (and broader scholarly study) of race since 1952. The development of the European Community confirmed Europe's changing global position. The European Coal and Steel Community (ECSC) of 1952 established the basis for the more ambitious European Economic Community (EEC), formed in 1957. The EEC, known as the European Community (EC) after 1967, brought together France, West Germany, Italy, Belgium, the Netherlands, and Luxembourg and became "the focal point of Europe's economic development." The EC was refined through the Single European Act (1987), which heralded a European common market, and the Maastricht revisions of 1993, which wrought the European Union (EU).[24] The EU gradually expanded to create an economic bloc of 450 million people.[25] Europe, reconfigured as the EU, has expanded, developed "supranational institutions of economic and political integration," and diminished internal barriers to the flow of capital, goods, and persons.[26] This process has taken place in the context of major economic and demographic shifts and has generated new, sometimes racially conceived debates concerning Europe's boundaries. The boundary question has been particularly prominent with respect to struggles over which nations and immigrants are included in, or excluded from, the European Union and European citizenship.[27]

The "racial" significance of European unification has been amplified by broader social and economic trends in the postwar pan-European world. From roughly 1950 to 1972, Europe and the rest of the pan-European world, particularly the United States, experienced sustained economic expansion and generalized prosperity. Across Europe, state spending on social welfare programs increased simultaneously, so that welfare provisions for citizens "have been matched by spreading democratization, secularization, greater personal freedoms, a breakdown of restrictive class structures, and increasing educational opportunities."[28] To varying degrees across the pan-European world this new prosperity has been monopolized by those nationals racially defined as white.[29]

Concurrently, the postwar economic boom facilitated another major demographic shift in Europe and in the rest of the pan-European world: pan-European states experienced labor shortages, and Europe became major destination for immigrants. Europe "increasingly sought foreigners for unskilled jobs in agriculture, production, and services. . . . States sought them out, recruited them, and attempted to control their movements." Northwestern Europe in particular became "a core attraction for Asians and Africans, as well as for Europeans from the south and east."[30] In some ways the new immigration mirrored the great nineteenth-century migrations, when people moved from poorer to richer regions within Europe and from poor regions of Europe to North and South America (see chapter 4). The new immigrants came from much poorer regions of the world, and they "complemented . . . the native-born in the labor force by taking the difficult, low-status jobs that Europeans avoided."[31] Many of these immigrants were from countries formerly colonized by European states, including Indians, Pakistanis, and Algerians. Britain, which experienced substantial immigration from former colonies in the Caribbean, the Indian subcontinent, and Africa, restricted the influx of Commonwealth citizens with the racially motivated Commonwealth Immigrants Act of 1962.[32] In the 1970s, West Germany, France, Switzerland, Belgium, and the Netherlands "hosted nearly 8 million nationals from Italy, Spain, Portugal, Greece, Yugoslavia, Turkey, Tunisia, Algeria, and Morocco."[33]

By this time it was becoming evident that many new "foreign" residents were not just temporary migrant workers; they were establishing immigrant communities. Meanwhile, the economic downturn of the 1970s generated hostility to immigrant workers and gave rise to several anti-immigrant movements.[34] Host countries acted to restrict immigration, often with "racial" biases and usually with limited success. In 1973, for instance, West Germany banned foreign workers from countries outside the European Community, and other governments quickly followed suit.[35] Furthermore, the steps to European unification realized in the 1992 Maastricht Treaty "shifted the definition of 'foreigner' from neighbors, such as Italians in Germany or Spaniards in Switzerland, to those outside the European community."[36]

By the 1980s, European social scientists discerned a "new racism" that appealed more to ethnic and cultural differences than to biological markers of difference. This "neo-racism" has tended to essentialize and reify cultural differences in ways that "make culture do the work of race."[37] With reference to France, Étienne Balibar explains that neo-racism is

> a racism of the era of "decolonization," of the reversal of population movements between the old colonies and the old metropolises, and the

division of humanity within a single space. Ideologically, current racism, which in France centres upon the immigration complex, fits into a framework of "racism without races" which is already widely developed in other countries. . . . It is a racism whose dominant theme is not biological heredity but the insurmountability of cultural differences, a racism which, at first sight, does not postulate the superiority of certain groups or peoples in relation to others but "only" the harmfulness of abolishing frontiers, the incompatibility of life-styles and traditions.[38]

Finally, as I discussed in chapter 5, soon after World War II the United Nations and UNESCO initiated an international response to issues of race and racism. In addition to UNESCO's 1950 and 1951 statements on race, UNESCO sponsored a series of short books on "The Race Question in Modern Science" in 1952.[39] In 1964, UNESCO published "Proposals on the Biological Aspects of Race," and a fourth UNESCO "Statement on Race and Racial Prejudice" (1967) made a provisional (though limited) effort to address *racism.*[40] In 1965 new member states of Africa, with an eye to racist regimes of southern Africa, pushed the United Nations to adopt the International Convention on the Elimination of All Forms of Racial Discrimination (ICERD); and in 1978, UNESCO's General Conference adopted a Declaration on Race and Racial Prejudice that focused special attention on South Africa's apartheid system. The United Nations also sponsored three world conferences to combat racism and racial discrimination in 1968, 1983, and 2001, the last being the World Conference Against Racism, Racial Discrimination, Xenophobia and Related Forms of Intolerance, in Durban, South Africa.[41]

The Durban conference's emphasis on "xenophobia and related forms of intolerance" along with racism indicates a broadening of global anti-racist activism since the 1955 Bandung Conference. Racism, Makani Thmba-Nixon notes, has increasingly been conceptualized in terms of *racisms,* as anti-racism activists have "tried to make sense of its varied and complex transmutations." At Durban this shift was expressed in "the de-emphasis of white supremacy and 'North-South' tensions and the emphasis on other issues emerging from a broad range of 'oppression' of which race is a part."[42] Old notions about "Caucasoids," "Negroids," and "Mongoloids," or "white," "black," "brown," and "yellow" races, have continued to influence some forms of contemporary racism—for instance, in discourses about "whiteness" and "blackness" in Brazil, "black" Caribbean and South Asian immigrants in England, and "black" Chechens in Russia (see chapter 7)—but the current era is marked by an array of historically diversified racisms.[43]

## Salvage Operations

In the past half century, race science has moved in step with the changing politics of "race." Nancy Stepan has summarized the major shifts in the science of race before and after the Second World War as follows:

> [T]he methods of studying human [biological] variation, and the questions asked about the human species, have changed drastically from the methods and questions of before [World War II]. Subsidiary now are the detailed cranial measurements, the tables of racial comparisons, and the construction of racial histories. In their place we find discussions of populations, gene frequencies, selection and adaptation. The biological study of human diversity has been permeated with the language of genetics and evolution. In fact it is probably right to say that a new science has come into existence which has directed inquiry away from race and towards new issues.[44]

In both biology and the "new genetical anthropology," the new emphasis on populations and gene frequencies constituted a major shift in "the perception of the biological significance of human races."[45] By the early 1960s, several biologists and genetic anthropologists, including Ashley Montagu, spoke of "the nonexistence of human races."[46] Some biologists have resisted this "no race" view, along with a few old-line anthropologists who persisted in the project of racial classification.[47]

Among those who pursued racial classification, U.S. physical anthropologists Carleton Coon and Stanley Garn have been especially prominent. Writing together in 1955, they advanced their notion of "geographic races." This notion, they claimed, resolved a disagreement concerning two competing accounts of the "number of races of mankind" that were proposed in 1950: their own earlier claim that there were thirty human races, and William Boyd's claim that there were six. They ignored the UNESCO scientists' scheme of three "major races" and said that the disagreement between themselves and Boyd was due to "a lack of agreement on just what taxonomic unit is properly designated as a race." Boyd called "a race a geographical unit," while they counted as *races* populations that "merit[ed] no special label in Boyd's system."[48]

They said that while early race classifiers such as Linnaeus and Blumenbach "distinguished a small number of geographically delimited races," more recent usage, particularly in population genetics, "favors restricting the term 'race' to the breeding or Mendelian population."[49] It was best, they said, "to retain both meanings while moving in the direction of simplicity and clarity." There were "collections of human populations having an obvious similarity and contained within particular geographical limits," or "geographical races." And there were also populations within each of the geographical races that constituted "local races."[50] A "geographical race" was "a collection of (race) populations having common features, such as a high frequency for blood group B, and extending over a geographically definable area." Geography was important because "seas, oceans, and major mountain chains" once constituted major "barriers to migration and 'gene-flow.'" In contrast, the "local races" were identifiable in terms of "their nearly complete isolation" from other local populations.[51]

As I will explain shortly, their conception of race was neither rigorous nor compelling.[52] Nevertheless, they claimed that there were "approximately six or seven . . . geographical races," corresponding to the "limited number of continents and islandic chains," and more than thirty "local and microgeographical races."[53] Their geographical races included a "European and Western Asiatic geographical race conforming to Blumenbach's category 'Caucasian,'" along with "a Northern and Eastern Asiatic geographic race" and African, Indian, Micronesian-Melanesian, Polynesian, and (native) American geographic races.[54]

William Boyd offered an alternative, genetically based classification in 1963. "Racial differentiation," he said, "is the end result of the action of natural selection on the raw material provided by random mutations in a population sufficiently isolated genetically."[55] Based on the assumption that genes are the basis for hereditary traits, Boyd emphasized the advantages of genetics for racial classification. He based his classification on blood-type groups, which were already subject to genetic analysis and enabled scientists "to separate the peoples of the world into clear-cut races which make sense geographically."[56] Although he had once identified six human races, he now distinguished "13 races, which fall into seven main groups," including a "European group" that encompassed four separate races (partly reprising "races of Europe" notions), along with African groups, an American group, and a Pacific group.[57] Yet Boyd's view of racial differences involved the circular reasoning that typified race science. He defined races in terms of "characteristic ranges of gene frequencies" that correlated with discrete geographical domains; but he offered no compelling grounds to regard such correlations as *racially* meaningful.[58]

Garn and Coon, meanwhile, refined their notion of "geographical races" in subsequent decades, but without rectifying their guiding view of "race." Garn wrote in the 1974 edition of the *World Book Encyclopedia*, "Human races . . . are based on heredity. . . . All hereditary characteristics are determined by tiny particles called *genes*. Members of the same race have more genes in common than do members of different races."[59] He now expressly rejected the "three-race theory" as a remnant of an earlier age when Europeans had a limited view of the world's "large geographically isolated groups," and he identified nine geographical races: African, American Indian, Asian, Australian, European, Indian, Melanesian, Micronesian, and Polynesian.[60] Elsewhere, Garn maintained that the so-called Caucasoid race should be called "the 'European geographical race.' In this way, the original geographical centre is defined, and the inclusion of purely local races is more clearly understood."[61] The 1989 edition of the *New Encyclopaedia Britannica* reprinted a contribution from Coon (who had died in 1981) on "Races of Homo Sapiens." Coon asserted, "Races . . . differ physiologically and anatomically from one another. These differences involve the blood (and blood vessels), the endocrine hormones, the nervous system, and, to a certain extent, behavior."[62] He went on to identify six broad geographical races, including "Caucasoids," with local racial groupings within each.[63] Garn, in the 1998 *New Encyclopaedia Britannica*, reiterated his (and Coon's) notion of geographic and local races.[64] He claimed that there was "broad consensus" among scientists affirming the nine "historical geographic races" that he identified in 1974.[65]

At the end of their 1955 article, Garn and Coon acknowledged the arbitrariness in their racial classification—"that geographical races are to a large extent collections of convenience, useful more for pedagogic purposes than as units for empirical investigation."[66] Yet, since they simply assumed that "race" was a meaningful way to comprehend human biological diversity, they never addressed the basic question of just what "pedagogic purposes" are served by any such "convenient" delineations of races. For Coon, although perhaps not for Garn, the chief pedagogic purpose was likely rooted in his long-standing commitment to a discredited neo-polygenist theory of fundamental differences, including "racial differences in temperament" between at least five distinct subspecies or geographic races.[67]

## *"No Races, . . . Only Clines"*

By the early 1960s, the post–World War II challenge to global white supremacism represented by decolonization and the U.S. Civil Rights movement inspired major changes in the scholarly study of race. In the sociological study of race relations, scholars increasingly explored issues of racism and colonialism and "sought modes of analysis which would assist the oppressed by exposing the sources within the white power structure of the attitudes and practices which maintained inequality."[68] A related shift was evident among anthropologists and biologists. While some scholars, such as Coon and Garn, continued to assume that the scientific task was to explain the origins of races, many more began to question the "race" concept itself. They began to see race as a dangerous myth that misrepresented the actual character of human physical diversity. In 1964, Ashley Montagu summarized this emerging view while placing the "race" concept in a historical perspective:

> The history of science is littered with relics of over-simplified theories and outmoded methodological devices. It is also, in large part, the history of fruitful errors. . . . [W]hen the history of the concept of race comes to be written, it is unlikely that it will figure prominently, if at all, among the fruitful errors. The probabilities are high that the concept will be afforded a similar status to that now occupied by the nonexistent substance known as "phlogiston." Phlogiston was the substance [wrongly] supposed to be present in all materials and given off by burning. . . .
> Race is the phlogiston of our time.[69]

The "race" concept was a scientific error, like phlogiston, but a more harmful error. Its history, bound up with the "age of nationalist and imperialist expansion," has helped to perpetuate three hundred years of misunderstandings concerning human biological similarity and diversity:

> [N]ationalist pride played no small part in [the taxonomists'] naming and classification of fossil as well as of living forms of men [*sic*]. If the concept

of race had not existed it would have had to be invented during this period. There were reasons for recognizing differences of a biological nature
between human groups. Hence, the concentration on differences and
their description became the principal occupation of the classifier of the
races he was only too convinced were awaiting recognition and discrimination.[70]

Recall that the concept of race was invented by Europeans in their seventeenth-century age of "discovery" from a word that loosely connoted descent or origin (see chapter 1). English settlers employed the concept in
colonial America to distinguish between "black" (western African) people,
as a "race" that could be rightfully subjected to perpetual slavery, and
"white" (European) people, as a "race" that could not rightfully be kept in
perpetual servitude. By the eighteenth and nineteenth centuries, European
colonial expansion, emerging capitalism, and nascent struggles for democracy presented European elites and subordinates with the challenge of
sorting out questions of basic human equality and inequality. By then the
"race" concept was available (along with notions of sex difference) as a
way to assert, scientifically, fundamental biological differences between
human groups.

The new genetics, however, now illuminated how the "race" concept
muddled our understanding of the biological differences between human
populations that actually exist. "For what the investigator calls 'the problem of human races,'" Montagu explained, "is immediately circumscribed
and delimited the moment he uses the word 'races.'"[71] He noted that Garn
and Coon did just this when they defined a geographical race: "The term
'geographical race' immediately delimits the group of populations embraced by it from others, as if the so-called 'geographical race' were a biological entity 'racially' distinct from others. Such a group of populations is
not 'racially' distinct, but differs from others in the frequencies of certain
of its genes."[72] To call such a difference "racial" does not make it so.

In the same volume, French anthropologist Jean Hiernaux and U.S. anthropologist Frank Livingstone also pressed the case against the "race"
concept. In Hiernaux's words, "[T]o dismember mankind into races as a
convenient approximation requires such a distortion of facts that any usefulness disappears."[73] For a concept of race "to be useful, [it] must be genetical"; it cannot be based solely on observable characteristics, or phenotypes, but must be based on heredity. This concerns genotypes and "the
tendency, at least, [for traits] to remain stable from one generation to the

next."[74] With respect to genetic affinities and differences, the only useful way to group together individuals is in terms of breeding populations—populations that participate "within the same circle of mating" and therefore have a tendency "toward stability from generation to generation."[75]

Breeding populations, however, should not be equated with "races." "One word is enough for one thing, and a taxonomic class may not be equated with the units to be classified," Hiernaux stated. *Race* would be more useful to designate "a grouping of populations," but this usage would involve further problems.[76] Human populations are *polymorphic* with respect to virtually every genetic characteristic. That is, humankind "cannot be subdivided [into] one group with zero per cent and one group with 100 per cent frequencies for any one [heritable] character. The properties used for classification will therefore be expressed as frequencies or means. Cluster analysis will be the basic taxonomic procedure." In short, rather than finding some gene or genes present in all members of one population and completely absent in all members of another, we typically find different gene frequencies in different populations. These differences can sometimes be grouped into clusters, marked by different average frequencies for different genes; but these gene frequencies vary more or less continuously (rather than discontinuously) from one population to the next. Consequently, taxonomies that subdivide populations "into discrete units," or "races," must be arbitrary.[77]

Hiernaux maintained that for cluster analysis to establish a credible basis for racial classification, we would need to find that human populations form gene frequency "clusters within which the distances are less than the inter-cluster distances."[78] In other words, we would need to find that the genetic variation *within* different populations is less than the genetic variation *between* populations. (Even then, such a finding would not be sufficient for racial classification: it would still have to be demonstrated that those differences were *racially* significant.) While the data necessary to draw broad conclusions was not yet available, Hiernaux presciently predicted that following this procedure would not support "the classical subdivision of mankind into three main groups: Whites, Blacks, and Yellows." Moreover, adding "more 'oids' [as in Caucasoids, Negroids, Mongoloids] to this three-fold division would not improve it."[79]

Livingstone also maintained that the evidence of population genetics was clear: "There are no races, there are only clines."[80] This was not to deny biological or genetic variability within the human species; the point was "simply that this variability does not conform to the discrete packages labeled races or subspecies."[81] The concept of *clines* refers to gradients in the measurable genetic character within groups or populations of a species, which usually can be correlated with gradients "in the climate, geography or ecology of the groups."[82] Rather than finding biologically discrete groups that can be readily correlated with discrete (current or historical) geographic locales, as implied in the "race" concept, what one actually finds are populations with graduated gene frequencies (clines) for hereditary traits that effectively blend into each other from one population to the next. Moreover, while racial analysis focuses arbitrarily on select traits that are presumed to possess "racial" meaning, "clinal analysis . . . can describe all gene frequency differences."[83]

In response to an earlier version of Livingstone's argument, noted geneticist Theodosius Dobzhansky defended the race concept. Dobzhansky acknowledged "that if races have to be 'discrete units,' then there are no races, and if 'race' is used as an 'explanation' of the human variability, rather than vice versa, then the explanation is invalid." Nonetheless, "race differences are objectively ascertainable phenomena," and the difficulties arise because "race is also a category of biological classification."[84] Human populations are "racially distinct" insofar as they "differ in the frequencies of one or more, usually several to many, genetic variables." But for the purposes of racial classification, "it does not follow that any racially distinct populations must be given racial (or subspecific) labels. Discovery of races is a biological problem, naming races is a nomenclatorial problem."[85]

Livingstone pointed out that Dobzhansky's proposed definition of *race* actually constituted a major *redefinition* of the term. Moreover, it obscured the extent to which population genetics undermined racial accounts of to human biological diversity: "In applying the theory of population genetics to humanity, the species is divided up into breeding populations although for any area or group of people this concept may be difficult to apply. It is likely that each group will prove to be genetically unique, so that all will be racially distinct in Dobzhansky's terms."[86] A breeding population is a contiguous grouping within a species, whose members interbreed with each other to a greater degree than they interbreed with individuals outside the group. Due to this interbreeding, along with genetic drift and natural selection, each breeding population (and there may be hundreds or thousands of them) is likely to be *somewhat* genetically distinctive. Therefore, each breeding population would constitute a "race" in Dobzhansky's sense. Yet this is "not the general use of the concept of race in biology, and the concept in the past has not been associated with this theory of human diversity. Race has instead been considered as a concept of the Linnaean system of classification within which it is applied to populations within a species."[87] Dobzhansky's redefinition of "race" is problematic, then, because it makes *race* synonymous with *population*. This would mean using the word *race* to describe differences between groups that are radically different from the kinds of differences that historically have been counted as *racial* differences in biology, anthropology, and popular discourse.

We could, of course, accept Dobzhansky's redefinition of "race," but this would create more problems that it would solve. The purpose of scientific concepts of science is not just "to divide up or label reality, but to explain it."[88] Yet Dobzhansky's redefinition of "race" would obscure more than it clarifies, because he provided no cogent rationale for regarding the differing gene frequencies that distinguish populations from each other as *racially* significant. Furthermore, as Montagu said, given the range of false meanings popularly given the term *race,* it would be misleading and confusing

> to distinguish as a "race" a population which happens to differ from other populations in the frequency of one or more genes. Why call such populations "races" when the operational definition of what they are is sharply and clearly stated in the words used to convey what we mean, namely, populations which differ from one another in particular frequencies of certain specified genes?[89]

Therefore, continuing use of the "race" concept would reinforce popular misconceptions. "The deep implicit meanings this term possesses for the majority of its users are such that they require immediate challenge whenever and by whomsoever the term 'race' is used."[90]

## The Newest Genetics

In the 1970s and 1980s, scholars further transformed the study of race. Social scientists were beginning to advance basic criticisms of the "race relations" approach to racism and "racial" conflict, including the tendency of this approach to take for granted the existence of human races.[91] Meanwhile, new research methods enabled biologists to find further evidence in favor of a nonracial approach to human diversity. "In the last five years," Richard Lewontin reported in 1972, "there has been a revolution in our assessment of inherited variation, as a result of the application of molecular biological techniques to population problems."[92] He added:

> It has always been obvious that organisms vary. . . . It has been equally apparent, even to those post-Darwinians for whom variation between individuals is the central fact of evolutionary dynamics . . . that individuals fall in clusters in the space of phenotypic description, and that those clusters, which we call demes, or races, or species, are the outcome of an evolutionary process acting on the individual variation. *What has changed during the evolution of scientific thought, and is still changing, is our perception of the relative importance and extent of intragroup as opposed to intergroup variation.*[93]

The new molecular biology has clarified the relative extent of intragroup and intergroup genetic variation. Various molecular biologists, anthropologists, and philosophers have differed, however, about the significance of this new information for the existence or nonexistence of human races.

This disagreement was evident in the two important 1972 studies of what Lewontin called "the apportionment of human diversity": Lewontin's own and a study by Masatoshi Nei and Arun Roychoudhury. Nei and Roychoudhury assumed the validity of the three-race theory as their starting point and sought to discover the degree of genetic difference "between the three major ethnic groups, Caucasoids, Negroids, and Mongoloids."[94] They estimated the genetic differences between these populations based on gene frequency data for protein loci. Their results indicated "that the gene differences between individuals from different ethnic groups are only slightly greater than those between individuals from the same group." In addition, "the genes in the three major ethnic groups of man [*sic*] are remarkably similar, although the phenotypic differences in such characteristics as pigmentation and facial structure are conspicuous."[95]

Nei and Roychoudhury followed the admonitions of commentators such as Huxley and Haddon and Montagu to speak of *ethnic groups* rather than *races.* Nevertheless, they failed to consider how their finding that the greater part of all the genetic variation was accounted for by genetic differences *within* the populations rather than *between* the populations challenged their guiding assumption that there were three discrete populations, "Caucasoids, Negroids, and Mongoloids." Because these broad categories encompassed numerous breeding populations, and because the largest part of all genetic diversity was found within these categories rather than between them, some populations within each category must be closer genetically to some populations of the other categories than to some populations of their own presumed category. For instance, some "Caucasoids" must be genetically closer to some "Negroids" and to some "Mongoloids" than they are to some other "Caucasoids." This finding challenged Nei and Roychoudhury's use of the three-group racial classification.

Moreover, they compounded this error in a 1982 article, where they called these groups "the three major races of man." There, in opposition to Carleton Coon's view that there were "five subspecies" of humanity, they noted that the genetic differences for protein loci between these three main "races" were "of the same order of magnitude as those for local populations in other organisms and considerably smaller than those for subspecies." They noted that "interracial genic variation (genetic distance) relative to intraracial genic variation . . . is quite small. . . . Namely, the proportion of genic variation attributable to racial differences is only about 9–11%," which means that the largest proportion of genetic variation, by far, was attributable to differences *within* each race.[96] Once again, though, they did not consider that this finding called into question the very existence of *races*. Instead, they simply assumed that the different population groupings constituted distinct races (e.g., in their reference to "interracial" and "intraracial" genic variation), and they provided no rationale for regarding such interpopulation differences as *racial*.

Lewontin, in contrast, offered an anti-racial interpretation of similar evidence. He compared differences in gene frequencies for seventeen genes in seven "races," as conventionally understood: Caucasian, African, Mongoloid, South Asian aborigines, Amerinds, Oceanians (i.e., Pacific islanders), and Australian Aborigines.[97] He found that the "mean proportion of total species diversity [for all the genes] that is contained within populations is 85.4%," which means that less "than 15% of all human genetic diversity is accounted for by differences between human groups! Moreover, the difference between populations within a race [i.e., as conventionally understood] accounts for an additional 8.3%, so that only 6.3% is accounted for by racial classification."[98] These results called into question the whole practice of racial classification:

It is clear that our perception of relatively large differences between human races and subgroups, as compared to the variation within these groups, is indeed a biased perception and that, based on randomly chosen genetic differences, human races and populations are remarkably similar to each other, with the largest part by far of human variation being accounted for by the differences between individuals.[99]

Like Montagu, Lewontin concluded that the "race" concept was scientifically erroneous and ethically noxious: "Human racial classification is of no social value and is positively destructive of social and human relations. Since such racial classification is now seen to be of virtually no genetic or taxonomic significance either, no justification can be offered for its continuance."[100]

Significantly, Lewontin's approach to race embodied the kind of "experimental skepticism" that Lancelot Hogben recommended in the 1930s. Rather than assuming a priori the existence of races, he merely used "the classical racial groupings with a few switches based on obvious genetic differences" to examine genetic diversity within and between population groups that were widely assumed to constitute races.[101] He found that the "race" concept misrepresented the character of human genetic variation.

The basic findings of Nei and Roychoudhury and Lewontin were confirmed and extended in a major study by published in *Science* in 2002.[102] Several researchers studied 1,056 individuals from fifty-two populations.[103] They found that the "average proportion of genetic differences between individuals from different populations only slightly exceeds that between unrelated individuals from a single population. That is, the within-population component of genetic variation, estimated here as 93 to 95%, accounts for most of the genetic diversity."[104] The basic similarity of all human populations was "also evident in the widespread nature of most alleles"—that is, the various forms of genes. Almost half of the 4,199 alleles they studied were found "in all major regions," and only 7.4 percent "were exclusive to one region."[105] Since most of the alleles were widespread, the genetic differences between populations were due mainly to "gradations in allele frequencies rather than" to genotypes that were unique to particular regions.[106]

The researchers also used a technique that enabled them to identify five different regionally localized population clusters, "subgroups" with "distinctive allele frequencies."[107] Five of these clusters corresponded to major geographic regions—Africa, Europe, Asia, America, and Oceania —but there were also subclusters within regions, and the isolated Kalish of northwestern Pakistan formed a cluster. Individuals from several populations "had partial membership in several clusters," and the "Adygei

[Circassians], from the Caucasus, shared membership in Europe and Central/South Asia."[108] In addition, the authors noted that because their "sampling was population based, the sample likely produced clusters that were more distinct than would have been found with random worldwide representation." That is, the sampling somewhat understated the degree of continuity of allele (or gene) frequencies from one population to the next.[109]

## The Race Concept Revisited

Despite such findings, there is continuing confusion about the existence or nonexistence of biological human races and the meaning of the "race" concept. A *New York Times* story on the *Science* article by Nicholas Wade exemplified this confusion. Wade highlighted the researchers' *secondary* finding "that people belong to five principal groups corresponding to the major geographical regions of the world: Africa, Europe, Asia, Melanesia and the Americas."[110] Additionally, he went far beyond anything that the *Science* authors said to claim that this finding provided support for popular ideas about race: "These regions broadly correspond with popular notions of race, the researchers said in interviews." After noting that several scientific journal editors have begun to eschew references to "race," Wade cited Stanford University population geneticist Neil Risch's view that it is valid to speak of race here because (in Wade's words) "it reflects the genetic differences that arose on each continent after the ancestral human population dispersed from its African homeland."[111] While Wade noted that the authors of the *Science* article avoided using the word *race* (they referred to "populations," not "races"), he said that the senior author of the study, Marcus Feldman of Stanford, "said that the finding essentially confirmed the popular conception of race."[112]

Wade's report was highly misleading, however. In contrast, the *Los Angeles Times* reported more accurately that the research team "separated people by the major migrations of ancient humankind, from Africa into Eurasia, East Asia, Oceania and the Americas, *in a way that overturns conventional notions of race.*"[113] Recently, Noah Rosenberg, the lead author of the *Science* article, confirmed this interpretation. Rosenberg said that he, for one, does "not believe that as *The New York Times* says 'the finding essentially confirmed the popular conception of race.'" He also doubted that there was "any significant disagreement about this among

[his] co-authors," and that Wade had paraphrased Feldman rather than quoting him.[114]

Feldman, moreover, recently challenged the usefulness of the "race" concept in an article in *Nature* that he coauthored with Lewontin and Mary-Claire King. They state:

> The classical definition of race, as applied to our species, is based on phenotypes such as skin colour, facial features and hair form that clearly differ between native inhabitants of different regions of the world. An underlying assumption is that all of these defining features . . . are characteristic of the genome in general. In other words, just as there are large differences between races in genes for skin colour, so there should be large genetic differences between races in general. In the previous absence of data to confirm or deny this assumption, it was not an unreasonable one to make.
>
> But recent studies of genetic variability indicate that the genes underlying the phenotypic differences used [historically] to assign race categories are atypical, in that they vary much more than genes do in general. Together, the iconic features of race correlate well with continent of origin but do not reflect genome-wide differences between groups.[115]

These considerations have important implications for answering Montagu's question about whether any of the physical characteristics that are posited as markers of *race* difference can "be considered as significantly defining a 'race.'" Although the authors do not draw this conclusion, their analysis suggests that what they call "the iconic features of race" should not be considered as *racially* significant at all. Genetically speaking, the phenotypic differences are superficial. They are related to genes that, concerning their geographic distribution, "are not typical of the human genome in general," and they obscure the fact that "most genetic diversity occurs within groups, and that very little is found between them."[116]

The great Italian population geneticist Luigi Luca Cavalli-Sforza offers further grounds to doubt that phenotypic differences between populations are racially significant; yet he also represents a continuing ambivalence toward racial classifications and indirectly perpetuates the myth of the Caucasian race. Cavalli-Sforza notes that the phenotypic characteristics people have often used as markers of race difference—skin color, eye shape, hair type, body and facial form—are "at least partly genetically determined."[117] At the same time, they are "surface characteristics" of the body that were probably biological adaptations to different climates for which "[m]ost likely only a small bunch of genes are responsible."[118]

Some of Cavalli-Sforza's conclusions are speculative, but his main point is well established: "Visible differences lead us to believe in the existence of 'pure' races, but . . . these are very narrow, essentially incorrect criteria." While the idea was that classification "based on continental origin could furnish a first approximation of racial division," all racial classification systems "lack clear and satisfying criteria for classifying. . . . [A]bove all it is true that one encounters near total genetic continuity between all regions while attempting to select even the most homogeneous races." Given the extent of genetic variation within human populations relative to that between populations, we should "abandon any attempt at racial classification along traditional lines."[119] Even so, he suggests a "practical" justification for "some sort of classification on the basis of genetic differences": humans live in social groups, and most people "like to identify with their social group and give a name to it."[120]

This is undoubtedly true, but it does not entail that *racial* groups are real or that people need racial groups with which to identify themselves. Indeed, Cavalli-Sforza's analysis indicates both that biological races do not exist and that such entities are not a necessary source for social group identifications. He says, for instance, that the "number of languages existing today is 5,000–6,000, and the number of social groups that may exist today in the world must be greater than 10,000, or even 100,000," and that there could be as many as 1 million distinct social groups "from a genetic point of view."[121] Yet while, as he notes, it would be absurd to speak of so many different *races,* we can speak meaningfully of so many different *ethnic groups,* defining them not by biology but by language, culture, and self-identification. I return to this point in the final chapter.

In addition, after questioning the traditional practice of racial classification, Cavalli-Sforza casually refers to "Caucasoid," "Mongoloid," and "African" races.[122] He says: "North Africa is populated with Caucasoid people like Europeans"; "We find significant areas of admixture between Whites (Caucasoids) and Blacks in Africa"; "The Berber populations nearer the Mediterranean coast were probably Caucasoids"; and "The Uralic people of Asia are generally Mongoloid."[123] These claims, however, are at odds with his point about the "near total genetic continuity between all regions." Even if there were evident clusters of gene frequencies among populations that roughly corresponded to the broad categories of "Caucasoids," "Mongoloids," and "Africans," this would not provide sufficient grounds to regard these groups as races, and the best available evidence indicates that these categories poorly represent humanity's genetic similarity and diversity. In the end, Cavalli-Sforza's talk of Caucasoids, Mongoloids, and Africans reveals the degree to which racialist notions continue to shape scientific and popular understandings of human diversity.

## *"Race" and Society*

Montagu was on the right track when he said, "Race is the phlogiston of our time."[124] But his analogy between "phlogiston" and "race" as flawed scientific concepts is not quite accurate. The history of the "race" concept, as we have seen, involved an intermingling of science and politics (or power) in a manner that has no direct parallel in the science of phlogiston. The "race" concept has been a key component of scientific efforts (by ethnologists, anthropologists, and biologists) to understand human diversity for about three hundred years; but, in contrast to phlogiston, race has also been integrally bound up with social and political practices of enslavement, colonialism, genocide, civic exclusion and subordination, and more subtle forms of intergroup discrimination.[125] Moreover, until the middle of the twentieth century the scientific study of race was dominated by a priori assumptions of racial difference and inequality. As a social and political construct, then, "race" may have more in common with the seventeenth-century New England Puritans' concept of "witch"—another mythical category that served to rationalize oppression—than with "phlogiston." But because "race" is at once a scientific concept and a social and political one, we need to keep in mind simultaneously what it shares with both "witch" and "phlogiston."

My analysis so far immediately suggests two further questions about the "race" concept. First is whether anything further can be said in support of the existence of biological races. Some anti-racist thinkers have challenged the idea that "race is merely a social construct."[126] Yet they fail to provide compelling grounds to conclude that human races exist in the biological sense.

For instance, sociologist Troy Duster suggests that developments within molecular biology "subvert the idea that we can easily separate scientific from racial thinking."[127] Focusing on the U.S. population, Duster notes that certain diseases, such as sickle-cell anemia, cystic fibrosis, and Tay-Sachs disease, occur disproportionately in certain conventionally defined racial groups—sickle-cell anemia chiefly in persons of West African descent; cystic fibrosis primarily in persons of northern European descent; and Tay-Sachs mainly among Jews of Eastern European descent. He acknowledges that in medicine such categories are rarely discrete, so that "there are African-Americans with cystic fibrosis" and whites "with sickle-cell anemia."[128] Still, he says that race becomes a factor when we consider the genetic tests that have been developed to "detect whether a person is a carrier of the genes for one of these diseases." While "Americans of northern European descent are more likely than other Americans" to carry a particular genetic mutation linked to cystic fibrosis, Zuni Indians are put at risk for this disease by a different mutation. At this point, race becomes a factor in two ways. The genetic test that has been developed for cystic fibrosis detects only the mutation (known as DF508) that is associated with persons of northern European descent, not the mutation that endangers the Zunis. In addition, "the DF508 test is not equally sensitive in the different groups we associate with the social categories of white, Asian, and black." Duster also cites recent "pharmacogenomic" research suggesting "that different races responded differently to different drugs," along with the fact that "the rate of prostate cancer is approximately twice as high among African-American males aged 50 to 70 as it is among white males of comparable age." He concludes, therefore, that it is "both naive and futile to try to abolish the concept of race" as a mere social construction. "We can and should refer to race when we consider it as part of a complex interaction of social forces and biological feedback loops."[129]

Most of Duster's analysis is important and unproblematic. The problem is that there is no evidence that "race" in the biological sense is at issue, and to suggest that (biological) race is a factor obscures our ability to grasp the actual causal factors. Consider sickle-cell anemia. It is especially common among people of African, Arabic, and Asian Indian origin but also among some Greeks, Italians, and Turks.[130] It appears to have developed in regions where malaria has been common, as the "heterozygous" (or recessive) form of the sickle-cell gene mutation (a combination of sickle-cell and normal red-blood-cell genes) uniquely enabled people to survive malarial conditions.[131] There is nothing *racial* about this, however, just as there is nothing racial about the incidence of Tay-Sachs disease among some Ashkenazi Jews or cystic fibrosis among some Zunis and some persons of northern European descent. As Naomi Zack says, "None of the scientists using populations as units for genetic research on disease suggest that all members of the populations in question . . . or that no members of other populations may have a particular population-based disease. This means that population membership is neither a sufficient or a necessary condition for the presence of the diseases associated with specific populations."[132] Moreover, "breeding" populations are not equivalent to "races." Accordingly, it is misleading to use the concept of race in such cases: it wrongly implies that something *racial* is a causal factor in these diseases (or in social or political outcomes) when what is involved is the presence or absence of certain genes in certain populations.

Duster's point about the disproportionately high incidence of prostate cancer among African American men compared with white men is related to race as a social phenomenon but not as a biological one. The social fact Duster reports does not support the thesis that there are biological races; instead, it is a consequence of how racial categories and racism have been used historically to establish social and political practices of exclusion and inequality, including racialized slavery, Jim Crow segregation, labor market and housing market discrimination, and unequal medical care.[133] As Feldman, Lewontin, and King note, "The conventional, social definition of race is useful in the medical context as it provides information about the social circumstances and lifestyles of patients. But this is a consequence of social history, so any variation is (at least in principle) transitory."[134] Duster clearly has something like this in mind when he refers to "a complex interaction of social forces and biological feedback loops." Nevertheless, any suggestion that biological race is a factor here is unsubstantiated. "Race" is a factor here *only* with respect to how dominant social and political groups have attached racial meanings to certain phenotypic differences between groups of people as a basis for producing and perpetuating racialized social divisions and inequalities.[135]

Philosopher Philip Kitcher offers another attempt to sustain a biological concept of race. Kitcher claims that "the concept of race may have biological significance" and that while some "talk of race is overtly racist," there are other "cases in which the concept of race fulfills a function in raising important social problems."[136] These are actually two distinct claims because, as I have just noted, there are ways to talk about race as a consequence of social history while insisting that race has no biological significance. In advancing his biological claim, Kitcher explicitly endorses two basic points made by those who insist that race has "no biological significance":[137] "First, the phenotypic characters used to demarcate races ... neither have any intrinsic significance nor have been shown to correlate with characteristics of intrinsic significance. Second, although genetic and phenotypic studies have shown that certain alleles, dispositions to disease, and phenotypes occur at different frequencies in different racial groups, intraracial diversity is far more pronounced than interracial diversity."[138] (Keep in mind that if there are no biological human races, we can speak meaningfully only about intrapopulation and interpopulation genetic variation.) Kitcher, then, offers a "minimalist" notion of race that entails only that the concept does have some biological significance.[139]

He basically defines "pure races" as "completely inbred lineages," and the overall effect of his theory is to redefine "race" in terms of relatively isolated reproductive populations. The reproductive isolation at issue may be due either to geographical barriers (consistent with the Coon and Garn notion of "geographical races") or to social mechanisms, such as racism and racial segregation.[140] In Kitcher's view, "[T]he core of any biological notion of race should be that phenotypic differences have been fashioned and sustained through the transmission of genes through lineages initiated by founding populations that were geographically separated." He adds, "There surely were geographically separated populations that would serve as founder populations for making such racial divisions."[141]

Kitcher's last point about the development of geographically separated populations of human beings is unproblematic. There is now a wealth of evidence indicating that *Homo sapiens* migrated from Africa to different geographic regions, where they developed different phenotypic traits (through genetic mutations, natural selection in different environments, and genetic drift).[142] Kitcher acknowledges that none of this would be "of the slightest biological [i.e., racial] significance" unless "the members of the pure races thus characterized have some distinctive phenotypic or genetic properties."[143] Here's the rub. Given the clinal (or continuous) character of human genetic and phenotypic diversity—the fact that most genetic diversity among human beings (by far) is found *within* rather than *between* populations—and the superficial and atypical character of the phenotypic traits that have been used historically to assign "race" categories, there is no good reason to regard *any* of the phenotypic or genetic properties that vary across human populations as *racially* significant. In the end, Kitcher's effort to articulate a more biologically defensible definition of "race" in terms of reproductively isolated breeding populations fails in the way that Dobzhansky's earlier (and related) effort failed: it calls for a substantial modification of prevailing understandings of race while referring to phenomena that can be described more readily in terms of populations and gene frequencies. In addition, as Joshua Glasgow says, "[s]uch a position bears the burden of explaining how it would be practically possible to revise so significantly entrenched racial discourse."[144] This burden is compounded when we remember two facts about the history of racial thought: the erroneous meanings conveyed by the "race" concept and the role of social and political forces in determining how certain phenotypic traits came to be regarded as racially significant in various racial divisions of the world's populations.

Still, Kitcher's further claim, that there are times when "talk of race" can serve to raise "important social problems," relates directly to my second question about the race concept: What are the implications of abandoning the notion that race is biologically meaningful for other forms of "race talk"? I will address this question more fully in the final chapter, but it is important to emphasize that the nonexistence of human races in the biological sense does not entail that we should drop any reference to race as a social and political phenomenon. In fact, the nonexistence of human races in the biological sense indicates that *everything significant about "race" is social and political*. As Montagu says, "Classifications of races exist; races do not."[145] Classifications of races have been and continue to be social and political, and they have had and continue to have profound social and political consequences. This attests to the need to analyze carefully the beliefs and exclusionary social practices that have been anchored in "race" ideas —that is, racism and racialized social and political practices, identities, and inequalities—despite the falsehood of biological race. At the same time, understanding the falsehood of biological race establishes some significant parameters for this task.

# 7

## "Where Caucasian Means Black"
### *"Race," Nation, and the Chechen Wars[1]*

> Every manufacturer lives in his factory like the colonial and the sub-version of Lyons is a sort of insurrection of San Domingo. . . . The barbarians who menace society are neither in the Caucasus nor in the Steppes of Tartary; they are in the suburbs of our industrial cities.　　　　　　　　　　—Saint-Marc Girardin (1831)[2]

As we have seen, the history of the Caucasus region is both intertwined with and distinct from the history of the "Caucasian race" myth. As I discussed in chapter 2, German philosopher Christoph Meiners and German physician and anthropologist Johann Blumenbach coined the "Caucasian race" idea was with reference to the Caucasus region and mountains. Blumenbach in particular aligned scientific authority behind myths about the Caucasian origins of humanity and tales of the unique beauty of the Caucasian peoples, especially Circassians and Georgians.

Yet, while Blumenbach famously cast Georgians as prototypical members of a Caucasian race in an eighteenth-century context that encouraged such an expansive view of Europeans' racial affinities, Caucasian peoples have been racially identified in various ways, and not always as "white" and "European." Nineteenth-century raciologists such as Robert Gordon Latham, William Ripley, and Joseph Deniker rejected the notion of a widespread Caucasian race that encompassed northern and western Europeans as well as Georgians, Chechens, Dagestanis, and Armenians and peoples from North Africa, India, and the Middle East. At the same time, they considered the Caucasian peoples to be racially distinct from various "races of Europe." The revival of Georges Cuvier's old three-race theory (of "Caucasian," "Negro," and "Mongolian" races) between 1935 and the 1950s repositioned the Caucasian peoples within the "Caucasian race" category.

In Russia, however, popular racial discourse has gone in a different direction. In recent decades, Russians have taken to referring to the peoples of the Caucasus as "black" (*chernyi*), especially during the recent Russian-Chechen wars.

Such shifting racial classifications in the sciences of race, as we have seen, have been impelled by social and political developments more than by autonomous advances in science. Changing ideas about the "racial" identity of peoples of the Caucasus have expressed myths of human and European origins, changing ideas about Europe's boundaries, and Russia's debates and anxieties concerning its "Europeanness"—and racial "whiteness"—compared to "Asiatic" Caucasians. The Russians' labeling of Caucasians as "blacks," then, follows a typical pattern of race-making, or racialization. It recalls how Europe itself was given racial meaning in the eighteenth century, and how this is happening again today;[3] how medieval ethnic divisions within "Christendom" were given racial meanings in the nineteenth century, and how, as Étienne Balibar says, "the discourses of race and nation are never very far apart."[4]

So far, I have examined processes of race-making largely through the history of race science. This chapter, by exploring the emergence of Russia's racial discourse of "black" Caucasians, highlights another facet of the history the "Caucasian race" idea: how people once regarded as exemplary "whites" could, in another time and place, be regarded racially as "blacks." This racialization process has its roots in four sets of historical events: the long-running confrontation of Christianity and Islam on the Eurasian landmass; more than two centuries of struggles by Caucasian peoples against Russian (and Soviet) imperial domination; political struggles concerning the place of Russia and Caucasia within Europe and Asia; and conflicts within post-Soviet Russia concerning global status, economic well-being, and Russian identity. This case of race-making also sheds light on the various ways in which notions of racial "whiteness" and "blackness" still serve political projects of racialized domination and exclusion. It clarifies how notions of a "white race," or racial whiteness, have a broader reach than the history of the "Caucasian race" category, which has been a specific permutation of the history of racial whiteness. Whiteness, as Vron Ware says, "is not reducible to skin color but refers to ways of thinking and behaving 'steeped' in histories of raciology."[5]

## Russia and Caucasia

Basic to this story is the character of the Caucasus region as a crossroads for Muslim, Orthodox Christian, and Persian peoples and cultures and the history of Russian imperialism in the region. Caucasia, the region that encompasses the great Caucasus Mountains, comprises northern Caucasia (or Ciscaucasia), which includes Chechnya and Dagestan, and Transcaucasia (or southern Caucasia), south of the mountains. Transcaucasia now comprises the independent states of "Georgia in the northwest, Azerbaijan in the east, and Armenia, situated largely on the high mountainous plateau south of Georgia and west of Azerbaijan" (see figure 13).[6] Between antiquity and the fourteenth century CE, Caucasia experienced invasions by Scythians, Alani, Huns, Khazars, Arabs, Seljuq Turks, and Mongols. Its later history began with prolonged rivalry between Ottoman Turkey and Persia (now Iran) and has been marked by Russian power and "culture, which penetrated farther and farther into Caucasia from the sixteenth century onward."[7]

The region contains enormous ethnic and linguistic diversity. More than fifty different peoples inhabit Transcaucasia alone, with several language families. The Georgian language, which is part of a larger Kartvelian (or South Caucasian) language group, is the most widely spoken Caucasian language, and it is represented by a literary tradition that dates back to the fifth century.[8] In light of Europe's emergence from the earlier religious and geographical idea of Christendom, it is significant that Christianity reached Armenia in 314 and Georgia in 330, before it came to most of Europe.[9] Persian influences came to the region in the fifth and sixth centuries, and Islam followed in the seventh century.[10] The Ottomans cut Georgia off from western Christendom when they conquered Constantinople in 1453, and during the next three centuries the region became a site of Turkish and Persian domination and competition.[11] While Orthodox Christianity, with affinities to Russian Orthodoxy, has remained the dominant religion in Georgia and Armenia (in Transcaucasia), Christianity lost ground in the western and central North Caucasus in the seventeenth and eighteenth centuries, and Islam became the dominant religion there.[12] The Chechens converted to (Sunni) Islam, which Dagestanis had brought to the North Caucasus in 1650.[13] Moreover, as I will explain shortly, the Muslim faith of the Chechens and Dagestanis has been central to their resistance to Russian expansion.

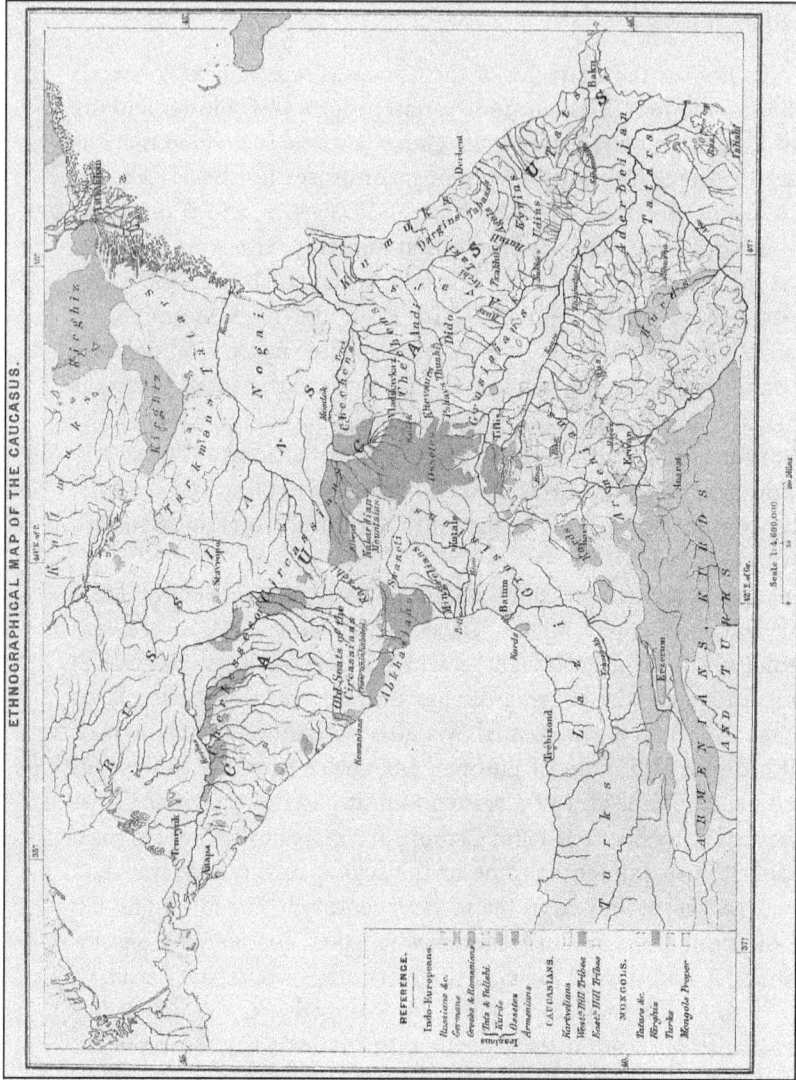

Figure 13: "Ethnological Map of the Caucasus" (1876). Reprinted from Élisée Reclus, *The Universal Geography: The Earth and Its Inhabitants*, ed. A. H. Keane (London: J. S. Virtue, 1876), p. 46.

Russian imperial expansion into the Caucasus, which began with Cossack incursions into the region in the sixteenth century, has been a central part of subsequent Caucasian history. Russia's empire differed from the empires of the great Western imperial powers. Russia colonized contiguous borderlands rather than distant colonies, "and its enduring *ancien régime* social order and its 'emperor of all Russian (*rossiiskoe*) lands' pose a series of contrasts to the European experience."[14] The Russian Empire created a distinction between those people who were within Russia's imperial orbit (*rossiiskii*) and those who ethnically Russian (*russkii*).[15]

Russia's first systematic advance into the region occurred during 1783–1824. In 1783, Georgia's king entered into an alliance with Catherine II of Russia for protection against Islamic expansion with the Treaty of Georgievsk, in which Russia guaranteed Georgia's independence and territorial integrity.[16] Yet Georgia was overrun by Persian forces in 1795, and in 1801, Russian czar Alexander I incorporated the Georgian kingdom of Kartli-Kakheti into the Russian Empire. Russia annexed the western Georgian kingdom of Imereti in 1810, followed by Guria, Mingrelia, Svaneti, and Abkhazia between 1829 and 1864.[17] Georgia retained a distinct national identity and experienced a national revival—economically and culturally—in the nineteenth century. After the Russian Revolution of 1917, the Bolsheviks established a short-lived Transcaucasian federation, encompassing Georgia, Armenia, and Azerbaijan. Georgians briefly set up an independent Georgian state in 1918, but in February 1921, Stalin installed a Soviet regime in Georgia's capital, Tbilisi.[18]

During the Stalinist era (1928–53), Georgia suffered forced collectivization of peasant agriculture, repression of all expressions of nationalism, and political purges. It was transformed from an agrarian country to a largely urban, industrial one. With Soviet leader Mikhail Gorbachev's reforms in the late 1980s, Georgians began to organize for independence, and Georgia gained independence on April 9, 1991. Conflicts soon emerged with "breakaway elements" in South Ossetia and Abkazia that remain unresolved; and after eleven years of rule by Eduard Shevardnadze, the former Soviet politician, Georgia had what one observer has called "the second birth of Georgian independence": a peaceful "revolution of roses" in November 2003 that brought Mikheil Saakashvili to power.[19]

Georgia's relationship to Russia has always been different from that of the North Caucasians. As Austin Jersild says, "Eastern Orthodoxy obviously created some natural affinities between Russia and Georgia, but the cooperation extended beyond matters of faith and the church."[20] Georgians also shared many other ideas and assumptions with Russians. In the late nineteenth century, educated "Georgians viewed Russia as their bridge to Europe, and themselves as the chief representative of the 'West' on the 'Eastern' frontier of the Caucasus." Although they tended to regard the mountain peoples of the north as "the savage 'other,'" they thought of Georgia's mountain people as providing "a glimpse into the past of a hardy and enduring Georgian identity."[21]

Russia's encounter with the North Caucasus has been substantially different. Russia conquered Transcaucasia first, while in the North Caucasus "the vast mountain range shielded its inhabitants from Russian rule."[22] The region was linguistically and socially disunited when Russia pushed into it in the 1780s, but most of the North Caucasus from 1785 to 1791, including Chechnya and Dagestan, united behind Sheikh Mansur Ushurma, a Chechen Muslim sheikh of the Naqshbandiya Sufi order, in a "holy war against the Russians."[23] The Russians were able to defeat the North Caucasians by 1791, but the *jihad* "left the memory that resistance as well as unity around Islam were possible."[24]

Between 1824 and 1922, North Caucasus experienced recurring holy wars. The feudal system was replaced by an economic order of clans and free peasant societies, "and the *tariqat* (the Sufi orders) provided a new ideology and became deeply implanted among the population."[25] Unity developed in the region around Islamic *shariat* law, and "Arabic language and culture spread from Daghestan to the Adyghe [Circassian] territories."[26] Between 1834 and 1859, the Chechens and other North Caucasians fought an aggressive but ultimately unsuccessful guerrilla war against the Russians behind the leadership of Imam Shamil. In 1865, "the Russians deported 39,000 Chechens to Ottoman Turkish territory," and North Caucasians rose up again against the Russians in 1877–78 and 1921–22.[27] After 1922, North Caucasians revolted sporadically, and the USSR added to earlier Russian efforts to pacify the North Caucasians—which had included settlement of Russian peasants, assimilation, co-optation of Caucasian elites, and efforts to uproot Islam—by attempting "genocide through the deportation of entire North Caucasian nations."[28]

With the end of the Soviet Union, much of the Caucasus entered a period of turmoil. While most of the autonomous republics of the North Caucasus remained part of the new Russian Federation, Chechnya quickly moved toward independence. The first Chechen war broke out in 1994 when Russia invaded Chechnya, allying itself with Chechen opponents of the government of General Djokar Dudayev, who took control of the

Chechen government in 1991 and proclaimed Chechen independence.[29] Russian leaders have been motivated by a long-standing Russian aim to dominate the region between the Black Sea and the Caspian Sea. They have sought to secure Russian trade routes and southern borderlands, as well as to control trade to central Asia. The stakes of this imperial project have been raised recently by the development of oil and gas fields around the Caspian Sea.[30] These energy resources have also attracted the interest of the world's leading industrial powers, particularly the United States, which has extended economic and military aid to Georgia and established a military presence there.[31]

## Russian Images of Caucasians

This history plays a complex role in the present. Christian Caryl explains, "Islam remains a source of identity and even militancy for many Caucasians; yet this fails . . . to explain why so many Muslim Caucasians, in contrast to the Chechens, seem to have made their peace with the modern Russian state, and why so many Christian Caucasians, most notably the Georgians, have since become intensely anti-Russian."[32] Still, the history of Russian-Caucasian relations, including historical Russian images of Caucasian peoples, has informed contemporary Russian beliefs and prejudices about Caucasians.

During the nineteenth century, Russian writers tended to refer to Caucasians, especially North Caucasian mountaineers, as "savages" (*dikie*).[33] Russian civil servant Platon Zubov wrote in 1834 that the Chechens "stand out among all other mountain tribes by their particular propensity for robbery and predatoriness, their avidity for pillage and murder, their perfidy, bellicose spirit, audacity pigheadedness, savageness, fearlessness and unbridled insolence."[34] Zubov expressed similar views of the Lezgins in Dagestan and the Abkhazians, and he called the population of Transcaucasia "excessively lazy" and "Intellectually limited." He contended that Russian conquest of the Caucasus would serve "the greater benefit of the Empire and of the Caucasians."[35] General A. P. Yermolov (1777–1861) declared, "There is not under the sun a people more vile, perfidious and criminal than [the Chechens]."[36]

Yet Russia's Orthodox Christian heritage has led Russians to regard Muslim and Christian Caucasians in different ways. Russians have tended to regard Muslim adversaries as "stupid, primitive, sly, treacherous," and to treat them "as 'rebels' and 'bandits.'"[37] In contrast, they often considered the peoples of the Christian Transcaucasian nations, Georgia and Armenia, as culturally and morally superior to the Muslims "in the Russian hierarchy of ethnic prejudices."[38] Zubov, for instance, said that the Armenians, who dominated regional trade, "in many respects deserve esteem and attention." The Georgians "always distinguished themselves by a spirit of bravery, courage and martial prowess," although they "have not taken an interest in the sciences, in commerce and other peaceful occupations."[39]

Russian anti-Muslim prejudices have been reinforced by recent wars with Muslims in Tadjikistan and Chechnya. Among the ethnic non-Russians that make up the population of contemporary Russia, about 18 to 20 million are Sunni Muslims. Most of them are concentrated in the North Caucasus and the Volga-Ural region (conquered by Russia in the sixteenth century). Some Russian nationalists present Russian "as a noble 'crusader' in [this] contact zone between Christianity and Islam in the border area between Europe and Asia."[40] In addition, Russians' awareness of the Chechen Mafia operating in Russia has fueled Russian popular images of Chechen criminality, even though Caucasians in general and Chechens in particular are responsible for only a small proportion of the crime in Russia.[41]

## Nineteenth-Century European Images of Caucasus and Russia

The historical Russian images of Caucasians were closely related to nineteenth-century European racialized discourses about Caucasians and Russians. Consider a couple representative examples of this tradition. An article on the Caucasus in the 1853 *Encyclopaedia Britannica* (Edinburgh), which was published at the start of the Crimean War and in the wake of several decades of Russian advances into the North Caucasus, reiterated old European assessments of the distinctive beauty of some of the Caucasian peoples: "Several of the tribes [of the Caucasus], particularly the Circassians, Georgians, and Imeretians, are accounted the handsomest people in the world, the men being tall and powerful, the women slender and graceful, and both having regular features and expressive eyes."[42] The remark about "regular features" repeats earlier Eurocentric notions of beauty among these "exotic" Asiatic peoples. In this account, the "Abasians and Ossetes are described as the rudest of the mountain tribes. With dark complexions and irregular features, the former have generally a very repulsive expression of countenance, emblematic of their moral and social inferiority."[43] The article also included a harsh judgment of Russia's actions in the region:

> With that indomitable spirit of independence which most of the Caucasian tribes have displayed, it is scarce to be expected that they will ever cultivate the arts of peace under the domination of the Russians. . . . Many of the inhabitants are inclined to commercial pursuits; and if they were not disturbed by the alarms of hostile invaders, commerce would do more to advance the general cultivation of the people than its conquest by a nation which is itself only half civilized.[44]

This survey of the Caucasus was published at a time when European commentators melded together ideas of "race" and "nation." Accordingly, it ended with population estimates for the "various principal races" in the region: "tribes of the race of Kartvel" (i.e., Georgians), Armenians, Turkish and Persian tribes, Lesghians, Abasians, and Circassians.[45]

French geographer Élisée Reclus (1830–1905) offered another characteristic European account of Caucasia in his multivolume work *The Universal Geography* (1876): "The Caucasian mountain system is often regarded as belonging to Europe." Noting the Promethean myth of the ancient Greeks, he said:

> A sort of superstition . . . formerly induced savants to apply the term Caucasian to all the fair European and Asiatic races, thus testifying to the instinctive reverence with which the nations have ever regarded these mountains forming the barrier between the two worlds. This border-land was supposed to be still inhabited by the purest representatives of the race, whose beauty, symmetry, and graceful carriage were spoken of as physical advantages peculiar to all white peoples. Nor has this term Caucasian yet quite disappeared from ordinary language as the synonym of the White, Aryan, or Indo-European stock.[46]

For Reclus, there was no longer any question "that the Caucasus belongs to Asia." Concerning the Caucasian peoples, he added:

> Historically, also, the inhabitants of the Caucasus belong to the Asiatic world. Before the intervention of Russia the Georgians, Mingrelians, Armenians, Kurds, Tatars, and other Transcaucasian peoples maintained re-

lations . . . chiefly with the inhabitants of Anatolia and Persia. The south-ern slopes facing the sun are also much more densely peopled than those turned towards the arid steppes of Europe. Hence, even after their an-nexation to Russia, the centre of gravity of these Asiatic lands was natu-rally found at the southern foot of the Caucasus, where is concentrated the aggressive force of the empire against the other regions of Western Asia.[47]

Reclus's geographical view of the Caucasus and Caucasians basically corre-sponded to the racial classification of Caucasians that Deniker and Ripley put forward in their "races of Europe" schemes (see chapter 4).[48]

## *"Black" Caucasians*

Like these European images of Russia and the Caucasus, Russians' ideas about themselves and Caucasians have also been influenced by the history of racial thought. Between about 1930 and 1950, as European and U.S. sci-entists recovered the notion of a "Caucasian race," Victor Bunak and other Soviet anthropologists posited a separate "Caucasian race in Georgia and the central Terek region of the northern Caucasus."[49] Given the long-stand-ing disputes about the European or Asian pedigree of Russians and Cau-casians, it is also significant that Soviet anthropologists carried forward certain "races of Europe" notions at least through the 1970s. Writing on the "Races of Man" in the *Great Soviet Encyclopedia* for 1978, Soviet anthropol-ogist N. N. Cheboksarov named three "basic racial groups: the Negroid, Europeoid, and Mongoloid race."[50] (Note that Cheboksarov used "Eu-ropeoid" rather than "Caucasian" or "Caucasoid.") Anthropologists, Cheboksarov said, distinguished various "local" or "second order races" among the Europeoids, including three "short-headed (brachycephalic) southern Europeoids": the Adriatic (or Dinaric) race, the Armenoid race, and the Pamiro-Ferganian race.[51] These categories, which went back to Deniker and Ripley at the turn of the twentieth century, placed Caucasian peoples in the "Armenoid race." Russians, by contrast, were either "Alpine" and "Middle European" or members of a "Baltic" (or "White Sea-Baltic") race.[52]

Russian popular racial discourse moved in a different but related direc-tion. Russians have used the term *chernyi* (black) since the nineteenth cen-tury to refer to people with dark complexion or dark eyes and hair.[53] But in recent years they have taken to referring more pointedly to people from the Caucasus as "blacks." Against the backdrop of the ongoing Russian-Chechen wars (1994–96 and 1999– ), Russians have aimed this epithet especially at Chechens. In 1994, after more than two hundred former paratroopers in Moscow beat up several dark-skinned Caucasian bystanders at the annual August pogrom on Russia's airborne forces day, a traffic police officer said, "When these blacks rape your daughters, you'll be complaining. Let these guys sort them out." Reflecting on the rising tensions in Russia between Slavic and non-Slavic citizens due to the first Russian-Chechen war, Abdul-Vakhed Niyazov, head of the Islamic Cultural Center of Russia in Moscow, commented, "It's natural that a country going through difficult times finds itself with various movements and parties who try to exploit the dark image of ethnic and religious minorities."[54] Five years later, in 1999, after two Moscow apartment buildings were leveled by explosions, thousands of dark-skinned natives of Dagestan, Chechnya, Ingushetia, and other areas in the Caucasus found themselves "suspects—and potential scapegoats—in Russia's reaction to the suspected bombings." They faced calls for Caucasians to be deported from Russia and graffiti urging Russians to "Kill the Blacks."[55]

The label "blacks," Alf Grannes explains, has been based on the fact that many Caucasian peoples "have a somewhat darker complexion than the typical Slavs" of Russia.[56] But the Caucasians' darker complexions alone do not explain why Russians call them blacks. Rather, the use of "black" (*chernyi*) enables Russians to assert a deep "racial" difference between themselves and Caucasians. In a manner reminiscent of how Caribbean and South Asian immigrants to England were named "blacks" in the 1980s, Russians have taken up old and widely traveled aesthetic and moral connotations of racial "blackness" and projected them onto Caucasians.[57] Simultaneously, they have implicitly claimed for themselves old aesthetic and moral connotations of "whiteness." Grannes notes that while in recent years a cultural racism has become prominent in the West, emphasizing "insurmountable *cultural* differences" rather than *biological* differences, "Russian racism has more in common with the biological racism of the 1920s and 1930s."[58] Notions of "racial hygiene" still circulate in Russia beyond the ranks of avowed racists, along with concerns that "real Russians" are disappearing due to the misfortune of the Russian people having been "so 'miscegenated' by non-Russians (Jews, Tatars, Finno-Ugric peoples, etc.)." In the pseudoscientific remarks on race of many contemporary Russians, *geny* (genes) is a key word, along with the nation's *genfond* "gene pool" or *genbank* "gene bank." . . . Since genes, and not primarily social environment, are seen as the prime clues to human behavior, one must be aware of "bad genes"! Thus the important [but popularly overestimated] role played by Caucasians in organized crime in Russia is often explained as a genetic phenomenon: *"èto u nikh v genakh sidit!"* "it sits in their genes!"

In sum, Russians exhibit a widespread tendency to explain the behavior of Caucasian peoples, particularly Chechens, Azerbaijanis, Georgians, and sometimes Armenians, in terms of "inherent features."[59]

## How Caucasians Became "Blacks"

It is not surprising that, as Niyazov says, "a country going through difficult times" would find "itself with various movements and parties who try to exploit the dark image of ethnic and religious minorities." Yet two aspects of this situation are far from "natural" (Niyazov's term): accumulated Russian anti-Caucasian prejudices that have fed the Caucasians' "dark image," and the way in which this image has been put to use in a process of distinctly *racial* "othering," or racialization. This situation demands further analysis, but this much can be said with confidence: the Caucasians became "blacks" as Russians refashioned well-established negative stereotypes of "dark-skinned" Caucasians in light of modern race ideas. As I noted earlier, Soviet raciologists from the 1930 through (at least) the 1970s considered Caucasians racially distinct from Slavic Russians, but without any necessary connotations of racial superiority and inferiority.[60] The demeaning Russian popular characterization of "black" Caucasians, however, is decidedly different from the Soviet raciologists' views, incorporating widely traveled connotations of abject racial "blackness" into older anti-Caucasian prejudices.

This development needs to be understood in relation to Russia's domestic political and economic struggles in the post-Soviet era. Ronald Grigor Suny observed in 1996, "Almost five years after the end of the Soviet Union, Russia has not consolidated its own identity, has not settled on what kind of state it will become or what form the nation [or nations] within it will take."[61] This remains true today. "Since 1992," Catherine Danks observes, the Russian Federation has been described as being "in transition" from Soviet socialism to a liberal-democratic market economy. This has been a disorienting time which has led to the pauperization of the majority of the population. Little wonder then that the Russians describe themselves as "humiliated and degraded" and that there is widespread belief that outside forces have both promoted and are taking advantage of Russia's weakened condition.[62]

These struggles, which have been strongly felt by ordinary Russians, are just the sorts of social and political dynamics that often spur people to construct racial others or inferiors. Russia's difficulties have been compounded, moreover, by its loss of "superpower" status, its fragile (and internally contested) sense of "Europeanness"—exacerbated by the inclusion of former "Soviet Bloc" states in the European Union—and its "inferiority complex" in relation to the Europe and the West. Russians may find some compensation for these material and psychological burdens by casting themselves as racially superior to Caucasians, especially in the context of the ongoing Chechen wars.[63]

One aspect of this racialization process is curious, however. Russians call all Caucasians "blacks," including the largely Christian Georgians and Armenians as well as Muslim Chechens and Dagestanis.[64] Yet, as I said earlier, Russians also tend to hold Georgians and Armenians in somewhat higher regard. The history of racialization processes that I have traced throughout this book suggests this inconsistency in Russian ethno-racial thought may not hold up indefinitely. For now, the history of Russian colonialism and Russians' sense of all Caucasians as "Asiatic" seem to have overriding significance. Keep in mind that North Caucasians, including Chechens and Dagestanians, are geographically closer to Russia than the Transcaucasian states of Georgia and Armenia.[65] The latter, while largely Orthodox Christian, are located closer to Asia and the Middle East. Geographic proximity, however, has never been the sole (or even the most important) determinant of how dominant groups or peoples have mapped racialized affinities and differences, and religion and politics may soon trump geography. The Muslim Chechens remain at war with Russia, with Russians readily labeling Chechen fighters Islamic "terrorists." At the same time, the United States has begun to befriend Georgia and some Georgians are seeking links to Europe. These developments could lead to the end of "black Caucasians." Time will tell, but Russians (perhaps at the urging of the United States and western Europe) may soon learn to see Georgians as fellow "whites" while they continue to call the Chechens "blacks"; and all these designations may change.

## Conclusion

In the meantime, a recent scientific discovery has given further impetus to voices of Georgian exceptionalism. In the summer of 1999, scientists found two fossil human skulls, estimated to be 1.7 million years old, near Dmanisi, "on a slope of the Caucasus Mountains 55 miles southwest of Tbilisi, the Georgian capital."[66] The skulls are thought to be the oldest human fossils found outside Africa. Scientists who have studied them have concluded (in an article published in *Science* in 2000) that *Homo sapiens* appears to have migrated out of Africa earlier than previously thought. The site, they said, indicates "a rapid dispersal from Africa into the Caucasus via the Levantine corridor, apparently followed by a much later colonization of adjacent European areas."[67]

This theory is unlikely to be the final word on the migration of *Homo sapiens* out of Africa. Nevertheless, it is noteworthy in the present context for a couple reasons. First, it provides a curious secular and evolutionary parallel to the story of Noah's ark, which informed the beliefs of Blumenbach, Meiners, and many other scholars from the Middle Ages through the eighteenth century that humankind originated in the Caucasus region (see chapter 2). Where the biblical story tells of the ark landing in the mountains of Ararat, from where Noah's three sons dispersed to Europe, Asia, and Africa, the new scientific theory suggests that some human beings left Africa and migrated through the region now known as Georgia before dispersing into Asia, Europe, and the Americas. While some orthodox Jews and Christians might find special solace in this parallel, it seems to me to be either an interesting coincidence or confirmation that myths and folktales are sometimes valuable sources of knowledge.

Second, and perhaps more instructive, is the way that Georgian archeologist David Lordkipanidze has appropriated the Dmanisi discovery for political purposes. Neal Ascherson reports Lordkipanidze's proposition that the Dmanisi might be considered "the cradle of Europe," which fits nicely with the aims of those Georgians (such as President Saakashvili) who wish to "Westernize Georgia and set it on a track which leads towards the European Union."[68] "Dmanisi," Lordkipanidze says, "has given Europe a chance to claim a part in human beginnings: before, they were set only in Africa. And this is also a big chance for Georgia, a stroke of luck."[69] Other Georgians strongly dispute this vision of "Georgia in Europe," however. Georgian novelist Dato Turashvili says, "What I dread is Georgia signing up to an American-ruled West whose creed is anti-Islamic and built on the idea of inevitable culture-clash. This would be utterly wrong for Georgia. Our identity is intimate with the Muslim world, and especially with Iran and Persian civilization."[70]

None of this is necessarily "racial." In fact, as I suggested in chapter 2, it indicates the advantages of eighteenth-century German philosopher Johann Gottfried Herder's physical-geographical approach to human diversity—a missed path that Herder put forward when Meiners and Blumenbach invented the Caucasian race. Herder explicitly challenged the "race" concept and said that "each people is a people: it has its national culture and its language; the zone in which each of them is placed has sometimes put its stamp, sometimes only a thin veil, on each of them." Human diversity "belongs less to the systematic history of nature than to the physical-geographical history of humanity."[71] Herder's views were not unproblematic. He overstated the cultural distinctiveness of nations and peoples, imagining that each nation, due to geography, has an "original ancestral core."[72] Still, his emphasis on nation over race is compelling. From Herder's perspective, the ideas of a "Caucasian race" and "black" Caucasians are deeply muddled. We can speak meaningfully of Russian nationality and nationalism and of Caucasian nations, such as Georgians, Armenians, Circassians, and Chechens (which is not to say that these notions are uncontentious). While we should avoid Herder's mistake of thinking that each nation has an "ancestral core," his emphasis on *nations* enables us to address appropriately the historical nationalist struggles in the Caucasus.

There are no "races" at war in the Caucasus. That said, it is clear that many Russians (and probably others) have brought race thinking into these conflicts—that is, have interpreted them, at least in part, in racial terms.[73] Not only was the Caucasus region the site of the invention of the idea of a "Caucasian race," but the Caucasus today is marked by a new processes of racialization: the making of "black" Caucasians. Moreover, this is another chapter in the history of how Europe—as both idea and actuality—has been bound up with racism and racialization projects for more than 350 years. It also shows how the histories of racism and racial whiteness and blackness have diverged from the more specific history of the idea of a Caucasian race.

# Conclusion

## Deconstructing "Caucasia," Dismantling Racism

[T]he word is the medium in which power works. Don't clutch onto the word, but do clutch onto certain ideas about it.
—Stuart Hall (1998)[1]

Race does not exist. But it does kill people. It also continues to be the backbone of some ferocious systems of domination.
—Colette Guillaumin[2]

The idea of a Caucasian race has had a prominent place in the history of race science. Yet, while there are numerous Caucasian peoples—Georgians, Armenians, Chechens, Circassians, Dagestanians, and Ingushetians among them—there is no *Caucasian race*. Even so, the *idea* of the Caucasian race has been highly consequential, politically and socially, and its history has profound implications for the politics of race and the politics of knowledge.

My overarching aim has been to contribute to a critical theory of social identities, with special reference to "racial" identities. Social identities—class, religious, ethnic, racial, national, gender, and sexual—are sources of meaning and affiliation but are also bound up with social relations of power and domination. Because different social identities connect to relations of power and domination in various ways, some benign and some oppressive, a critical theory of social identity must be selective in how it addresses different manifestations of social identities. Specifically, it will insist that certain kinds of social identities—such as caste or class identities—should be overturned rather than celebrated, and it will support public recognition for expressions of social identity only insofar as they "can be coherently combined with the social politics of equality."[3]

"Racial," or rather *racialized,* identities cry out for such a critical accounting. They provide people with a way to interpret their relationships to others and their place in contemporary societies, and with a basis for anti-racist politics; but they are based on the falsehood of "race" and have been used to produce and justify oppression and social stratification. The history of the "Caucasian race" category indicates that the "race" concept and racial categories have always been integral to, and even generative of, social practices of exploitation, exclusion, and oppression. The "race" concept, from its introduction in the seventeenth century, has been fundamentally bound up with constructing and rationalizing inegalitarian social relations. This raises the question of what kind of public recognition, if any, is due to "racial" identities.

With respect to this last point, it is important to keep in mind that "race" is a peculiar kind of *social* identity category because it has been understood historically as an element of *natural history.* That is, "race" has been understood (and is still sometimes understood) as a "natural kind," such that human beings (*Homo sapiens*) are *naturally* divisible into three or five or nine or twenty-nine distinct human *races.* On this view, identifying human races is not just a convenient way to differentiate human populations but is also a way to represent the natural order of things. Moreover, throughout the history of race science and racial thought more generally, it has generally been assumed that race is more than "skin deep." The usual assumption has been, as Ashley Montagu says, that "[t]here is something called 'race' that is responsible for the physical characteristics, the behavioral traits, and the cultural achievements of different peoples."[4]

### *"Looking Black," "Looking Jewish," and Being* Racialized

The history of the "Caucasian race" category illuminates the falsehood of the "race" concept and the actuality of processes of *racialization.* Consider this example. A few years ago, teaching a course on U.S. politics, I was explaining to my class how the nineteenth-century French political theorist Alexis de Tocqueville's notion of "individualism" related to the contemporary notion of the "American dream." I discussed how my Jewish maternal grandfather, Meyer Bloomfield, came to the United States from Romania in the early twentieth century. My grandfather, I said, settled in New York City, worked at various jobs, and eventually moved to Stamford, Connecticut, where he co-owned a delicatessen. His story was not quite "rags to riches," but he escaped the confines of Romanian peasant life and found in the United States (along with his brothers and sisters) the freedom and independence that came with working for himself, raising a family (with my late grandmother Frieda), home owning, and practicing his religion as he wished. After class, one of my students, Sele, came up to me and told me that she also had a Jewish grandfather on her mother's side who immigrated to New York City in 1931; got married; started a pharmacy in Greenwich Village; moved to Crown Heights, Brooklyn, and then, in 1963, to Stamford. Her grandparents moved to a neighborhood near where my parents moved in 1964, from another part of Stamford.

The parallel paths of our Jewish immigrant grandparents, through New York to Stamford, struck me as more than just an interesting coincidence because of my own racialized preconceptions concerning Sele. Although Sele's skin tone is only a shade more brown than mine, I had assumed that she was African American, and so I was surprised to find that she had Jewish grandparents who, like mine, moved from Europe through New York to Stamford. And I was not exactly wrong about Sele's racialized background. Sele's father was African American and his parents were both African American, although his mother's father was Native American (Choctaw) and his mother's mother was African American. Sele considers herself to be "Black and white." And, like me (both of my parents are Jewish), she has always thought of herself as ethnically Jewish, having learned a lot about Jewish traditions from her grandmother Florence.

Now, if "race" is not a biologically meaningful category but merely a social (or political) construction, then what can it mean to say that Sele *looks* African American, and for her actually to *be*, at least in part, African American or Black? Is this necessarily a case of thinking in classically *racial* terms, or can and should it be differently understood? What does it mean for how we should understand race and ethnicity? Consider also that several times in my life people who did not know me have asked me if I was Jewish. Typically, I answered yes to indicate that I consider myself ethnically Jewish even though I am not really religiously Jewish. So, what can it mean that people have said that I *look* Jewish, and for me to actually *be* ethnically Jewish? Is this necessarily a case of thinking in classically *racial* terms, or can and should it be differently understood? And what does it mean for how we should understand race and ethnicity? (I have also been asked whether I was "mixed"—i.e., "Black and white"—due to my tightly curled dark brown hair and brown eyes.)

Now consider a related example. In applying for university teaching positions in the United States, I have often been asked to fill out affirmative action applicant survey forms. I have always indicated "White" (or "Caucasian") for "ethnicity" or "race," and I contend that I have been right to do so. I have been right to do so, however, *not* because I belong to an actually existing white or Caucasian race, or because being white is a meaningful *ethnic* category in the United States. Instead, the rightness of my self-designation as white (or Caucasian) is due to the fact that the United States is a racialized society, where I have been *racialized* as "white" (for which the term *Caucasian* is sometimes used in these surveys), and racialized identity is what is really at issue in such cases.[5] My "white" identity has conferred upon me some significant social and economic advantages that have nothing to do with "race" in the biological sense and everything to do with a history of divisive, exclusionary social and political practices built around race ideas. For Sele, in contrast, I contend that it would be equally legitimate for her to indicate her "race" as either "Black/African American" or "White" (or "Mixed-Race," if that were an option).[6] If Sele had been born in the United States in 1910 or 1920, when the "one-drop rule" was still around (according to which anyone with any African ancestry was considered "Negro" or "Black"), she would almost certainly have been counted as "Negro" or "Black," unless she was able and willing to "pass" for "white."[7] Today, she will still sometimes be seen as Black, and she ought to have a voice in defining her own racialized identity.[8]

Since such ethnic or racialized identifications of persons as Jewish or Black rely on physical characteristics (e.g., skin color, hair color and texture, facial features), this might seem to suggest that we are identifying people by *race*, which would take us back to the idea that there is a "Jewish race" as well as a "Black" or "Negroid race." As Jonathan Marks notes, "both Jews and non-Jews alike can identify people who 'look Jewish.'"[9] Yet this does not mean that there is a Jewish race or any other human races. Instead, it "simply reflects the fact that a significant proportion of Jews (particularly in America) have ancestry from southeastern Europe, and consequently tend to look more like one another than like people from Norway or Pakistan." At the same time, "many Jews do not 'look Jewish,' and many non-Jews do."[10] The same can be said of the racialized category "Black," or "African American." Certain phenotypic traits, such as brown skin (of various shades) and tightly curled black hair, are common among African Americans, most of whom have ancestors from Central–West

Africa. (This has changed recently, with new immigrants from such East African countries as Ethiopia and Somalia.)[11] These particular traits are also common among people from other parts of Africa. Yet not all persons with African ancestry can be reliably recognized by such traits.

The fact that human populations can be grouped together artificially according to such superficial physical traits, which are associated with regions of geographic origin, does not mean that we should regard such groupings as *human races*. As Marks says, "racial" categories such as "European," "African," and "Asian" (or "Caucasoid," "Negroid," and "Mongoloid") "divide by nomenclature people who cannot be easily divided from one another biologically in the Old World, except at the extremes." Such categories

> do not represent fundamental biological divisions in our species—they represent, rather, only biological patterns perturbed by social and historical forces [such as human migrations]. Those biological patterns are principally geographical gradients, upon which we have tended to impose discrete cultural boundaries. People from the same part of the world tend to look more like each other than they look like people from a very different part of the world; but there are no natural borders between them.[12]

In short, there are no "fundamental biological divisions in our species" such as our talk of human races implies.

To address such difficulties, Montagu called for abandoning the "race" concept and proposed the use of *ethnic group* in place of *race*. Whereas the term *race* fundamentally obscures the actual character of human diversity, "'ethnic group' meets the realities of the situation head on."[13] An ethnic group, he said, "may be defined as one of a number of breeding populations, which . . . together comprise *Homo sapiens,* and which individually maintain their differences, physical or genetic and cultural, by means of isolating mechanisms such as geographic and social barriers."[14] Montagu's approach overemphasizes the role of physical differences in the making of ethnic groups insofar as ethnic group identity, or ethnicity, is a matter of historically contingent symbolic and cultural affiliation that may or may not underwrite social stratification.[15] Despite this, his call to replace *race* with *ethnic group* captures something important. The latter refers to something real and tangible in a way that the former does not. There are meaningful *ethnic* differences between human populations—differences of customs, traditions, and languages, for instance—that are sometimes highly significant. In contrast, to talk of "race differences" implies that there are basic, innate differences between different geographically based populations where there are really only ethnic differences and superficial phenotypic (or morphological) differences that misleadingly have been *called* "racial."

Yet Montagu's proposal also sidesteps the manifest "racialization of the world"—the way in which racial categories and identities have been ascribed to different groups of people and have served as the basis for brutally real practices of racist oppression, exclusion, discrimination, and social stratification.[16] It has been evident, for instance, in the use of the "race" concept and racial classifications in various countries to justify modern slavery, colonialism, lynchings, immigration restrictions, genocide, labor and housing market discrimination, and unequal citizenship status, education, and health care. If the racialization of the world had not happened, then it would be appropriate to say that *any* talk of race distorts our understanding of human diversity and social stratification. But since the world has been (and continues to be) racialized, it is deeply misleading to redescribe *racialized* social divisions and inequalities as merely *ethnic group* differences. It overlooks the various ways in which ethnic group differences *have been racialized*—that is, have been given distinctly "racial" meanings in social and political processes. Consequently, Montagu's proposal would do little or nothing to redress the inequities that have been produced and perpetuated by historical (and current) forms of racism and racialized exclusion. Of course, it is quite possible, as Montagu says, "to feel 'ethnic group prejudice' as it is to feel 'race prejudice.'"[17] Still, ethnic group differences refer to real differences, and these need not be—and indeed are not always and everywhere—subject to intergroup conflict and ethnocentrism.

The limitations of the "ethnic" alternative become clearer if we consider the ethnic categories that Orlando Patterson recommends in his book on "America's 'Racial' Crisis." He confronts the difficulties inherent in the "race" concept as follows:

> Afro-Americans are not a "race" in any meaningful sense, but an aggregate of 33 million people that is better described as an ethnic group if one must speak of the entire collectivity. I therefore use the term *ethnic* instead of racial and refer to an *ethnic group* instead of a *race*.
>
> I think that the time has come to abandon the terms black and white in reference to Americans. They are linguistically loaded terms and empha-

size the physical, which is precisely what we want to get away from in inter-ethnic relations. The term *Afro-American* will be used to refer to persons of African ancestry who identify themselves with this ethnic group. . . . If we abandon the term black, however—whether in favor of *African American* or *Afro-American*—it makes no sense to continue to use the term white. I therefore use the term *Euro-Americans* to describe the people elsewhere known as *whites*.[18]

Patterson is right to say that these groups are not *racial* groups in the biological sense. Still, his "ethnic group" alternative introduces other problems. First, his groupings are not coherent ethnic groups in that each category encompasses numerous ethnic groups (e.g., Irish Americans and Italian American in his "Euro-American" ethnic group). African Americans in the United States (Patterson's "Afro-Americans") originally came from various African ethnic groups, tribes, or peoples.[19] Many, if not most, now share an identification as "Black" (or "African American") that has notable *ethnic* dimensions in that it is defined in part by a shared history, heritage, and traditions, but this does not make being Black (or African American) *merely* an ethnic group identity. The shared experience *relates to having been racialized in the same basic way.* As Adrian Piper says, "[I]t is the shared experience of being visually or cognitively *identified* as black by a white racist society, and the punitive and damaging effects of the identification."[20]

Second, Patterson's categories of "Afro-Americans" and "Euro-Americans" designate two groupings that historically have been *racially defined*, or given racial meaning, and have been central categories in U.S. (and other) racialized and racist social divisions (with whites being dominant and most advantaged and African Americans deeply subordinated). In other words, these groups of people have been made into "blacks" and "whites," and this was a social and political process. Racial identity, as Lawrence Blum says, is "bound up with a group's place in (historic and current) systems of racial dominance and subordination, justice and injustice, advantage and disadvantage. Part of the experience of one's racial identity . . . is precisely that one's [racialized] group occupies some general location in these hierarchical systems."[21]

This is just as true for Patterson's Euro-American ethnic group as it is for African Americans, although with different ramifications. While there is no "white race" (or "Caucasian race") in the biological sense, there is a white *racialized* group. Moreover, it is crucial for social justice purposes to confront the way in which this collectivity has been socially and politically constructed, mobilized, and perpetuated. In modern times, one thing that has sometimes (but not always) joined various European peoples together has been their categorization as part of a white or Caucasian race.

In the U.S. case, what joined European immigrants together, other than their becoming Americans, was their becoming identified (and treated by law and custom) as racially white. Moreover, while there may be some benign cultural phenomena that can be considered distinctly "white," these are notoriously difficult to identify. The most obvious cultural expressions of racialized "whiteness" (i.e., the cultural practices that historically joined together European immigrants to the United States as racially white) have been far from benign. They have been basic to the history of U.S. racism and to the social-political processes through which various ethnic groups in the United States have been *racialized*: seventeenth-century distinctions, enacted by "whites," between "black" persons who could "rightfully" be kept as perpetual slaves and "white" persons who could not; the requirement of being a "free white person" in the first U.S. citizenship and nationalization of 1790; the residential restrictive covenants, or "Caucasian codes," that proliferated in the northern United States between the 1910s and 1940s; the entire Jim Crow system that defined the southern United States from the 1890s through the 1960s; and White Citizen Councils in the South that worked to sustain Jim Crow segregation and white supremacism.[22]

Patterson says that it is time that we "abandon the terms black and white in reference to Americans" because they undermine our collective capacity to effectively deal with "inter-ethnic relations." The problem is that we are not dealing simply with *interethnic relations*; we are dealing with a history of racism and *racialized* relations.[23] Therefore, while there are no white and black *races* in the biological sense, there have been (and still are) white and black racialized groups, and these racialized group identities have had and continue to have enormous social, cultural, and material consequences.[24]

## "Race" and Racialized Identity

The conclusion that I have been working toward is a version of what is sometimes called "eliminativism" or "quasi-racialism" concerning the "race" concept.[25] This view has been most persistently developed by K.

Anthony Appiah, who says that "while there aren't any 'races,' there are 'racial identities.' They don't have any biological significance, but they are significant socially."[26] Race eliminativists such as Appiah tend to place "race" in quotation marks to indicate its peculiar epistemic character— that is, it has no biological reality but still has major social and political consequences or effects due to erroneous beliefs about the reality of race and social practices built upon such beliefs. Paul Taylor says that quasi-racialists similarly maintain that "races aren't real," but they maintain that "ideas about race still shape social life . . . and that this is reason enough to keep talking about race."[27] On this account, Appiah can be considered a quasi-racialist, since he holds that racial identities are socially significant.

Taylor offers a counterpoint to the "no race" view, but his view introduces some further confusion. He agrees with eliminativists that while "race" is not biologically meaningful, it *is* socially and political significant; yet he maintains that modern practices of race thinking and racialization have *made* races real. "[O]ur Western races are social constructs. They are things we humans create in the transactions that define social life." They were initially created through modern societies by racist practices that involved racially defining and dividing people, "and the on-going political developments in these societies continued to re-create them."[28] Races, then, are "institutional facts." They were not just "out there" in the human world waiting to be named but are reliant "on a network of conventions, agreements, institutions, and practices" through which people have made them. "Race-talk" is useful because it enables us to make sense of "the ways in which people are already, and really, implicated in schemes of social interaction." This means that "we should be willing to say that a person who is properly implicated in social relations [i.e., involved in them in a particular way] really is, say, a white person."[29]

Much of Taylor's analysis is on target. He rightly emphasizes how different types of bodies (or certain phenotypic traits of bodies) have been assigned racial meaning through racializing social processes, and he highlights how these populations become similarly situated in racialized processes of social stratification. He also usefully distinguishes between race and ethnicity: "Ethnicity is principally about shared culture, and derivatively about 'blood ties.'" Ethnic differences can become racialized if they are transformed into racialized differences and conflicts; but "ethnic groups needn't be racialized, and members of racial[ized] populations needn't have ethnic ties to each other."[30] Taylor confuses matters, though, when he says that "we can speak of . . . the populations [that these processes] create as races."[31] His retention of the term *race* perpetuates errors that his analysis aims to overcome. Using "race" without quotation marks or some other explicit qualifier reinforces "the deep implicit meanings this term possesses for the majority of its users."[32] Moreover, we can convey the same information about the social consequences of "race" by speaking of racialized identities, or "social races."[33]

The term *racialized identity* runs against the grain of ordinary language usage. Yet it has notable advantages. First, it unsettles and challenges those dubious "deep implicit meanings" embedded in the "race" concept. Second, it is descriptively accurate. It indicates that "races" are not biologically real but are social and political constructions, products of social and political processes. Robert Miles and Rodolfo Torres explain, "[P]eople do not see 'race': rather, they observe certain combinations of real and sometimes imagined somatic and cultural characteristics, to which they attribute meaning with the idea of 'race.'"[34] To speak of racialized identities, then, indicates that we do not encounter actual human *races*, but confront the effects of social and political processes of racialization. Racism, racialized identities, and racialized inequalities are quite real, but they do not refer back to any actual races in the biological sense.

Furthermore, this analysis indicates that if "races" (and racialized identities) have been socially and politically produced—if they are "social constructions"—then they can be unmade. Theoretically, we *could* then have a world in which *race* has no currency and there would only be *ethnic groups*. Yet this world is far from where are now, and it will take vigorous political efforts to overcome all traces of systemic racism and racialized inequality. In the United States, for example, institutionalized racism and ongoing "racial" beliefs and racialized inequalities perpetuate social, political, and cultural dynamics whereby African Americans, European Americans, Asian Americans, Native Americans, and Latina/os, while not *races*, are not yet merely ethnic groups. Because of how they are implicated in racialized social relations in the United States, they are *racialized* groups, although they may *also* manifest certain characteristics of ethnic groups.

## "Race," Power, and Knowledge

The modern practice of naming and classifying human "races," then, was never merely a matter scientific knowledge. It was ultimately a matter of intergroup domination, or, rather, "of knowledge-as-domination."[35] When

Europeans in the seventeenth century introduced modern race thinking, it originally served, like Aristotle's musings about citizens and slaves in ancient Greece, as a way to assert that "[s]ome men are by nature rational and deserve to rule, while others are natural slaves."[36] While race thinking has not been restricted to justifying slavery, it has been integrally bound up with practices of domination and subordination, marginalization and social stratification, based on ideas about grades of relative "fitness" or "humanity" of different populations implicit in "race." What emerges from examining the history of the "Caucasian race" category is that "race" is, among other things, a modality of power: a means by which some groups of people act upon the possible actions of others.[37] This aspect of "race" can be difficult to grasp or track because it operates through language or discourse. That is, one of the ways in which people exercise power over others is through their control of language. This is the meaning of Stuart Hall's remark that "the word is the medium in which power works."[38]

Concerning how power is exercised with respect to race, racial discourse "organizes, regulates, and gives meaning to social practices through the distribution of symbolic and material resources between different groups and the establishment of racial hierarchy." Those who authoritatively employ racial discourse, who establish racial categories and meanings, exercise power as they "produce, mark, and fix the infinite differences and diversities of human beings through a rigid binary coding."[39] Racial discourse establishes ideas about who counts as fully human and who counts as less than fully human (sometimes with several gradations), who should be a fully participating member of society and who "does not belong."[40] Racial discourses also constitute different human populations as different kinds of political subjects: some as naturally suited for self-governing citizenship, others inclined to be wards of the state; some as naturally fit for "higher education" and high-status careers, others as predisposed to be subordinates or "guestworkers."[41] In this way, powerful groups have used racial discourse to justify enslavement, colonialism, racially exclusionary citizenship and immigration laws, and racialized discrimination in educational institutions, labor markets, and housing markets. Processes of racialized and class stratification have often been closely intertwined in the ways that modern elites and states have managed the material inequalities and the labor market instabilities generated by capitalism. Consequently, the construction and use of racial categories has been integrally related to the development of modern nation-states and nationalism.[42]

Moreover, the history of the "Caucasian race" idea reveals that racialized power is exercised not only where dominant racialized groups expressly subordinate other racialized groups or act to perpetuate existing racialized inequalities; it has also been manifest in the scientific study of "race." The "sciences of race" were never merely a neutral way to describe the world. They have always been a form of "knowledge-as-power," if not always "knowledge-as-domination." By inventing the "race" concept and human races, European elites developed a new way to understand and govern different groups of human beings. Scientists in the fields of natural history, ethnology, anthropology, and biology then took up and refined the "race" concept as an object of study *as scientists,* but their guiding assumptions were deeply informed by prevailing social, political, and cultural forces.[43] Moreover, not only was their scientific work deeply shaped by broader social and political power relationships, but their claims of truth concerning "race," in turn, have had significant social and political consequences.

This indicates that, as Michel Foucault has argued, there is a "politics of truth." In other words, the scientific pursuit of truth is deeply enmeshed with and shaped by the larger world of social and political power relationships.[44] At the same time, the history of the "Caucasian race" idea—its rise and fall, and rise and fall within science—suggests that we should not regard scientific inquiry as intrinsically corrupted by relations of power and bias. Instead, this history supports what Naomi Zack calls a "minimalist" scientific realism. Against the view that all claims about reality are equally arbitrary, Zack maintains there is a real "world that exists independent of thought, sensation, perception, language, and other symbolic representation" against which we can assess "false social constructions."[45] For instance, there really are human beings, and these human beings really do have different skin colors and blood types, cultures and religions, and—due to the way that the world has been racialized—different *racialized* identities. But there are *not* biologically distinct human *races.* Concerning the limitations of historical forms of science, Susan Haack explains, "It is true that both the internal organization of science and its external environment can affect how well or how poorly scientific work gets done." It is also true that in "scientific inquiry and in inquiry of every kind, what we take to be legitimate questions sometimes turn out to be flawed."[46] Yet neither of these observations discredits the practice of science and the pursuit of truth per se. "Although what is true is not relative to perspective, what is accepted as true is." The fact that powerful groups can sometimes get bogus and even pernicious beliefs "accepted as true" does not mean "that the concepts of truth, fact and evidence are ideological humbug."[47]

The upshot of all this is that we can acknowledge Foucault's insight that power relationships always shape prevailing forms of knowledge without abandoning the practice of science or the concept of truth. As I said in this book's introduction, all other things being equal, forms of power that are inclusive, democratic, and egalitarian are more likely to generate true knowledge about such things as "race" than forms of power that are undemocratic, exclusionary, and asymmetrical. This means that scientific inquiry is most likely to be both successful and ethically responsible when it is supported by democratic social contexts and marked by relatively democratic, nonhierarchical, and inclusive relations of cooperation, as opposed to social contexts characterized by authoritarianism and social exclusivity.[48] This ideal of a democratic science finds support, moreover, in how great democratizing social and political movements of the twentieth century (extensions of political democracy, anti-racism, decolonization, the U.S. Civil Rights movement, and feminism) spurred the development of an anti-racist (and eventually anti-racial) science of "race." By calling into question dubious but widely accepted assumptions about the world, these democratizing social and political movements have revealed limitations of existing theories about the world and generated advances in human knowledge. For the development of a more valid science of "race," the crucial change was, not surprisingly, a shift away from a priori racialist and racist assumptions among a critical mass of scientists who studied human biological diversity. Historically, it was not science per se but science guided by flawed assumptions that had generated flawed conclusions.

"Race" remains a challenging and important subject for scientific inquiry because of how it has crossed the boundaries between the natural sciences and the social sciences and humanities. For generations, "race" was understood erroneously as a "natural kind" and, thus, as something to be addressed largely by the *natural* sciences, particularly natural history, ethnology, physical anthropology, and biology. Despite (and in some ways because of) the dubious character of this scientific research, "race" ideas and racialized social practices and institutions have profoundly shaped our social world. Therefore, we need ongoing social-scientific and humanistic inquiries into the social and political effects of racialized identities and inequalities, even though biological race is a false social construction.[49]

## Racialized "Whiteness" and the "Caucasian Race"

One important social and political consequence of modern processes of racialization is that some old racial categories, such as "Caucasian race," "white," and "black," remain highly salient to the politics of racialized inequality, particularly in the United States. In this regard, we need to understand the history of the "Caucasian race" idea as part of the larger history of white supremacism, racism, and white racialized identity.[50] The "Caucasian race" category has been integrally linked with what Ruth Frankenberg calls "the co-constitution of whiteness and racial domination"—that is, the way in which the history of modern racist domination has been bound up with the history of how European peoples defined themselves (and sometimes some other peoples) as members of a superior "white race."[51] As I discussed in chapter 1, the idea of a white race preceded the development of the idea of a Caucasian race by about 140 years.

Racial classifications, as we have seen, were first developed by European scientists and philosophers such as Bernier, Linnaeus, Kant, and Blumenbach, who called themselves "white" people and (with some exceptions, like Blumenbach) described whites as the superior "race." For most of the period from the early nineteenth century through the twentieth century (with the exception of the "races of Europe" period), the notion of a Caucasian race gave the popular notion of a white race and practices of white supremacism auras of scientific solidity. Thus, when the "Caucasian race" idea entered into popular discourse in the United States in the early to mid–twentieth century, to "become 'Caucasian' . . . was not simply to be 'white' . . . ; it was to be conclusively, certifiably, scientifically white."[52]

When the "sciences of race" initially developed, European ethnologists were imbued with notions of European "racial" and civilizational superiority. In this context, the "Caucasian race" idea placed the authority of science behind a hierarchical racial ranking of "white" and "nonwhite" peoples — Blumenbach's "Mongolians," "Ethiopians," "Americans," and "Malays"—that rationalized global white supremacism. European "racial" unity was internally shattered in the 1840s and after by European nationalism and European migrations, which turned European peoples against each other. Consequently, the reign of the "Caucasian race" idea in race science was disrupted between 1840 and 1935 by the proliferation of "races of Europe" theories among European raciologists. At that time, given Europe's ongoing global dominance, European political and imperialist elites continued to emphasize "racial" differences between so-called white and nonwhite "races," and European raciologists continued to affirm this distinction. After World War II, the idea of a pan-European Caucasian race was reaffirmed by scientists while the white supremacist global racial order persisted. But since the partial break of the white supremacist racial order during the 1950s and 1960s, scientists increasingly have rejected the "race" concept along with the "Caucasian race" idea.

Still, it is crucial to remember that the postwar break with the history of white supremacism, while profound, has been incomplete. "Race" remains one of the most important axes of social power and inequality in the contemporary world, and a white racialized identity remains a significant source of social and economic advantages. As Howard Winant says, on every social indicator of well-being we look at "the results will be the same: the worldwide correlation of wealth and well-being with white skin and European descent, and of poverty and immiseration with dark skin and 'otherness.'"[53] More than ever in our globalized capitalist world, these points are true in a probabilistic way. There are poor and marginalized "white" people, even in the world's affluent North, and there are some wealthy people "of color" as well.[54] The world's distribution of wealth and power is structured by class and gender as well as by racialized identity. Consequently, racial whiteness does not *guarantee* anyone an advantaged social position, and it never has; but it remains a source of material advantage and social capital.

Sorting out these issues—particularly the continuing power of "race" along with class as a source of socially structured inequality—is surely one of the great political challenges of the twenty-first century. Given the role of white supremacism and racialized whiteness in this history, those of us who have been taught to see ourselves as "white" face a distinctive challenge—one that must be specified in different national contexts and internationally. In the United States, we need to recognize that in a world still structured by racialized inequality, it is disingenuous for us to celebrate "color-blindness" and insist that "race" and our "whiteness" no longer matter. Such a posture will only perpetuate the existing racialized inequalities because "whiteness continues to structure life chances and opportunities in every domain of social existence."[55]

Therefore, with or without the idea of a Caucasian race we must not, as James Baldwin has warned, "take refuge in [our] whiteness."[56] Baldwin's chief concern was with the politically distorting and disabling role of white racialized identity and allegiance with respect to how racialized and class stratification reinforce and sustain each other in the United States. Economic insecurities and hardships that many "white" people experience in the United States are due to broad economic conditions and the class structure, which hurt and make vulnerable millions of poor, working-class, and middle-class white people along with millions of poor, working-class, and middle-class Blacks, Asian Americans, Latino/as, and Native Americans. Despite this, many whites in the United States have been "tak[ing] refuge in their whiteness" for quite some time. For example, the 1964 presidential election was the last one in which a Democratic presidential candidate won the support of a majority of white voters. Subsequently, a majority of whites adopted a form of "white" identity politics that has led them to regard the Democratic Party as the party of "minority" interests and the "undeserving poor," and the Republican Party as the party of "ordinary," hard-working white citizens.[57]

By 1967, Martin Luther King Jr. noted a "white backlash" against nascent efforts of the time to achieve social justice with respect to the U.S. history of racism. "The white backlash," King said, "is an expression of the same vacillations, the same search for rationalizations, the same lack of commitment that have always characterized white America on the question of race."[58] White citizens, rather than addressing as political actors (e.g., in voting) how their economic hardships and vulnerabilities are rooted in the U.S. class structure and broad political-economic patterns, such as deindustrialization, "outsourcing," and insufficient government funding for health care and education, too often mobilize *as whites* behind racial and cultural explanations. This proprietary identification with racialized whiteness by white Americans "fuels a discourse that demonizes people of color for being victimized by these changes, while hiding the privileges of whiteness by attributing the economic advantages enjoyed by whites to their family values, faith in fatherhood, and foresight."[59]

The "white backlash" that King noted in 1967, which has been continued in recurrent white working-class conservatism since then, has been a manifestation of this. It has been the response of many whites to perceived threats to the institutionalized advantages, rooted in the history of white supremacy, that have become part of their settled expectations as white persons concerning such goods as social status, income, opportunity, security, and power.[60] Moreover, while this proprietary interest in whiteness confers on whites certain advantages, it also involves certain costs for them as well as for nonwhites. It serves in part to obscure class divisions among whites, so that it also works to sustain a political-economic order that hurts many whites as well as many nonwhites.[61] None of this concerns being "white" in a biological or racial sense; instead, it is a matter of being *counted* as white and of *identifying* oneself as white.[62]

### "Race" and Planetary Humanism

Finally, the history of the Caucasian race illuminates one of the deepest injustices of race thinking and racism: the denial of basic human dignity to all those persons counted (and treated) as members of "lesser races." Race thinking established—implicitly and explicitly—a scale of "humanness" whereby only the "superior races" were regarded (or regarded themselves) as fully human. To overcome this history of dehumanization, Paul Gilroy calls for a "radically nonracial . . . planetary humanism."[63] Other notable critics of "race" and racism also recommend humanism. "The basic question concerning human beings," Montagu says, "is not whether they belong to some classificatory group or 'race' or not . . . but whether they are human beings."[64] Zack suggests that in confronting the legacy of racism, the "core of good politics is a commitment to the life and dignity of all human beings."[65] Such humanism cannot provide a complete framework for politics and ethics insofar as it leaves open the question of our ethical responsibilities to nonhuman animals and our environment.[66] Nonetheless, Zack is right to insist that it should be a core principle of an antiracist politics of social justice. The crucial question today concerns what kinds of political action and public policy are needed to achieve planetary humanism in light of the histories of racism and raciology in our racialized world.

Gilroy advocates "the deliberate and self-conscious renunciation of 'race' as a means to categorize and divide humankind."[67] He contends that even anti-racists who say that we need to retain a notion of race as a critical concept because race still matters socially and politically become complicit "in the reification of racial difference."[68] Accordingly, he rejects the now common anti-racist strategy of placing "race" in quotes to signify its constructed character while insisting on its continuing sociological and political significance:

> [O]ur perilous predicament, in the midst of a political and technological
> sea-change, which somehow strengthens ethnic absolutism and primor-

dialism, demands a radical and dramatic response. This must be one that steps away from the pious ritual in which we always agree that "race" is invented but are then required to defer to its embeddedness in the world and to accept that the demand for justice nevertheless requires us to enter the political arenas that it helps to mark out.[69]

There *are* risks involved in using racial categories in efforts to overcome racism—most important, this practice may perpetuate racialist thinking despite the most vigilant efforts to critique "race." Yet Gilroy's call to renounce any use of race as a critical concept is itself a problematic route to planetary humanism in a world with enduring racialized social and political inequalities. An effective planetary humanism must confront directly the reality of racialized groups and racialized inequalities. For instance, while groups such as "whites," "blacks," "Asians," and "Native Americans" in the United States are not *races*, "they are racialized groups." Racialized groups have been treated "as if there were inherent and immutable differences between them; *as if* certain somatic characteristics marked the presence of significant characteristics of mind, emotion, and character; *as if* some were of greater worth than others."[70]

Racialization and racialized groups are *social structural* phenomena that are closely related to but analytically distinct from class stratification. As capitalism developed during the last three centuries, processes of racialization—the making of racialized groups and hierarchies—have served a significant political-economic role. Capitalism creates a class division between wage earners and employers (capitalists), along with hierarchies among workers. Marxist theory has emphasized the basic *class* division in capitalist societies between workers and employers of labor, as well as the hierarchy of workers under capitalism, but it does not explain why certain groups of persons tend to fill certain places in the economy.[71] Racialization is one of the social processes (along with the construction of gender distinctions) through which societies determine who fills the "empty places," or structural class locations, in capitalist economies. That is, in racialized societies such as the United States, racialized group identities—being racialized as white, black, Asian, Latino/a, or Native American—structure differential life chances and opportunities. Racialized identity shapes access to education, training, employment, wealth, and social capital, which, in turn, shapes who fits where in the class structure and who is likely to fall outside the mainstream class structure, as a kind of "underclass." In the United States, this has produced a class structure that is deeply marked by racialized inequality, so that whites are *relatively* insulated from poverty (though many whites are nonetheless poor) and relatively overrepresented in higher class positions in the economy, and Latinos, African Americans, and Native Americans disproportionately experience poverty and are underrepresented in higher class positions in the economy.

The U.S. case is distinctive mainly with respect to specific groups that have been racialized there, *how* they have been racialized historically, and the particular effects of this racialization. But racialization processes remain a pervasive feature of the modern world. Consequently, achieving planetary humanism requires vigorous and vigilant efforts to end all racialized inequality as part of a broader politics of equality. Ultimately, it will also require that we end definitively the myth of "the Caucasian race" along with what Baldwin called the "delusion of whiteness."[72] We cannot do this, however, by simply denying or ignoring how whiteness still operates as a source of racialized advantage. In many cases, and certainly in the United States, achieving planetary humanism will require not the renunciation of all race talk and racial categorization but a more subtle approach of "taking race into account" through policies such as affirmative action to get us beyond the nefarious effects of racism and racialism.[73] This approach would sometimes use existing racialized categories in a deliberate and self-critical way *as a means to dismantle enduring racialized inequalities.* The relevant categories for such purposes will not necessarily coincide with the racial categories of raciologists like Blumenbach, Cuvier, or the UNESCO scientists of 1950. Instead, they should correspond to the significant and relatively enduring racialized divisions of particular societies, distinguishing historically advantaged and subordinated racialized identity groups. In the U.S. context, for instance, there are good reasons to refer to "white," "black," "Asian," "Latino/a" (or "Hispanic"), and "Native Americans" racialized groups, with Blacks, Latino/as, and Native Americans recognized as historically oppressed groups.[74]

In the same breath, anti-racism (or "racial justice") requires that people who have benefited from being racialized as white *avow* their whiteness even as they seek to put an end to it. That is, we need to recognize how our whiteness is complicit in continuing racialized inequalities. One way for white people to do this is to support affirmative action and other policies to overcome racialized injustice as part of a larger politics that aims to affirm fully the dignity of all human beings. Because the task here is for white people to work with others to overcome racialized inequalities, and even racialized group identities as such, such action is radically opposed to whites "taking refuge in their whiteness." The prospect that concerns Gilroy, that any use of racial categories will be complicit "in the reification of racial difference," can be prevented if we keep in mind that what is at issue is not biological *race* but the reality of *racialized* groups and *racialized* inequality.[75]

# Notes

NOTES TO THE INTRODUCTION

1. Thomas Hobbes, *Leviathan,* ed. C. B. Macpherson (Harmondsworth: Penguin Books, 1985), pp. 116–17, Hobbes's emphasis.

2. Max Horkheimer, "Traditional and Critical Theory," in *Critical Theory: Selected Essays,* trans. Matthew J. O'Connell et al., introduction by Stanley Aronowitz (New York: Herder and Herder, 1972), pp. 199–200.

3. Georgia Warnke, "Social Identity as Interpretation," in *Gadamer's Century: Essays in Honor of Hans-Georg Gadamer,* ed. Jeff Malpas, Ulrich Arnswald, and Jens Kertscher (Cambridge, MA: MIT Press, 2002), p. 307.

4. David Brion Davis, "Slavery—White, Black, Muslim, Christian," *New York Review of Books* 48, July 5, 2001, p. 51.

5. The Moors were a Muslim people of Berber and Arab lineage who inhabited northwestern Africa. They conquered the Iberian peninsula in the eighth century and controlled parts of Spain until the fifteenth century.

6. Davis, "Slavery," p. 52.

7. Ibid.

8. Neil Kottler, "The Statue of Liberty as Idea, Symbol, and Historical Presence," in *Making a Universal Symbol: The Statue of Liberty Revisited,* ed. Wilton S. Dillon and Neil Kottler (Washington, DC: Smithsonian Institution Press, 1994), pp. 4–5, quoted in Linda Zerilli, "Democracy and National Fantasy: Reflection on the Statute of Liberty," in *Cultural Studies and Political Theory,* ed. Jodi Dean (Ithaca: Cornell University Press, 2000), p. 167.

9. Zerilli, "Democracy," p. 169.

10. Nicholas Kristoff, "Chinese Students, in About Face, Will Continue to Occupy Square," *New York Times,* May 30, 1989, pp. A1, A10, at A10. The phrase "Goddess with Caucasian Face" is the heading of the fourth section of Kristoff's article.

11. David Theo Goldberg, *Racial Subjects: Writing on Race in America* (New York and London: Routledge, 1997), p. 54.

12. Naturalization laws between 1790 and 1870 reserved the right of naturalization to "free white persons." The 1870 law extended naturalization rights to

"aliens of African nativity and persons of African descent." See Ian F. Haney López, *White by Law: The Legal Construction of Race* (New York: New York University Press, 1996), p. 2.

13. Ibid.

14. *United States v. Bhagat Sigh Thind*, 261 U.S. 204 [1923], in López, *White by Law*, pp. 223–24. I discuss Keane's work in chapter 4.

15. Goldberg, *Racial Subjects*, pp. 54–55.

16. Royce Rensberger's article in the *Washington Post* (April 15, 1997) was titled "Skeletons Suggest Caucasoid Early American." See David Hurst Thomas, *Skull Wars: Kennewick Man, Archeology, and the Battle for Native American Identity* (New York: Basic Books, 2000), p. 114.

17. Thomas, *Skull Wars*, p. xx. While Chatters named the skeleton "Kennewick Man," the Umatilla tribe, which claimed the skeleton as its own, called it "The Ancient One" (p. xxxix).

18. Douglas Preston, "The Lost Man," *New Yorker*, July 16, 1997, p. 72; Thomas, *Skull Wars*, p. xix.

19. Alan Goodman, "Racializing Kennewick Man," *Anthropology Newsletter*, October 1997, pp. 3, 5; Thomas, *Skull Wars*, chap. 11.

20. Iver B. Neumann, *Uses of the Other: "The East" in European Identity Formation* (Minneapolis: University of Minnesota Press, 1999).

21. Michael R. Gordon, "Caught in a Backlash to Moscow's Bombings," *New York Times*, September 15, 1999, p. A1.

22. Blumenbach is usually credited with coining the term *Caucasian race*, but as I explain in chapter 2 this is not strictly true.

23. Johann Friedrich Blumenbach, *On the Natural Variety of Mankind (De Generis Humani Varietate Nativa)*, 3d ed. (1795), in *The Anthropological Treatises of Johann Friedrich Blumenbach*, ed. Thomas Bendyshe (London: Longman, Roberts, and Green, 1865), p. 269.

24. *Racialism*, Kwame Anthony Appiah explains, concerns the belief "that there are heritable characteristics, possessed by members of our species, which allow us to divide them" in a biologically meaningful way "into a small set of races." Arguably, racialism is a precondition for *racism*, which generally starts from (but is not limited to) the supposition that there are superior and inferior human *races*. Yet, even though racialism marks an important step on the way toward racism, it is possible, in principle, to believe that racialism is true and also to oppose racism. See Kwame Anthony Appiah, *In My Father's House: Africa in the Philosophy of Culture* (New York: Oxford University Press, 1993), pp. 13–14.

25. On the race ideas of U.S. white supremacists, see Abby L. Ferber, "Constructing Whiteness," in *Racism*, ed. Martin Bulmer and John Solomos (Oxford: Oxford University Press, 1999), pp. 213–23.

26. See Jacques Barzun, *Race: A Study in Modern Superstition* (New York: Harper and Row, [1937] 1965); Leon Poliakov, *The Aryan Myth: A History of*

*Racist and Nationalist Ideas in Europe* (London: Chatto Heinemann for Sussex University Press, 1974); Peter van der Veer, *Imperial Encounters: Religion and Modernity in India* (Princeton: Princeton University Press, 2001). While the origin of the Caucasian race is commonly noted among scholars, the subsequent history of the category has not yet been explored in a sustained way.

27. In North America it is still used widely and uncritically as a biologically as well as socially meaningful notion. For instance, a recent newspaper article in *The Province* (Vancouver) reported the results of a scholarly study on representation of visible minorities on Canadian television dramas. The article runs under a subtitle that reads "Caucasians dominate Canadian TV screen, says [Simon Fraser University] report," and begins: "Mainstream TV drama in Canada still looks overwhelmingly Caucasian." See Emily Yearwood-Lee, "Few Lead Roles for Minorities," *The Province*, August 26, 2002, p. B5.

28. As I will explain shortly, this is not to say that there has been no progress over the past three centuries in our collective knowledge about race.

29. Stephen Jay Gould, *The Mismeasure of Man,* rev. and exp. ed. (New York: W. W. Norton & Co., [1981] 1996), p. 20.

30. Warnke, "Social Identity," p. 307.

31. George Fredrickson, *Racism: A Short History* (Princeton: Princeton University Press, 2001), p. 11.

32. Immanuel Wallerstein, *Historical Capitalism* (London: Verso, 1983), pp. 77–79.

33. Nancy Fraser, *Justice Interruptus: Critical Reflections on the "Postsocialist" Condition* (New York: Routledge, 1997), p. 12.

34. Fredrickson, *Racism,* pp. 10–11. See also Thomas F. Gossett, *Race: The History of an Idea in America,* new ed. (Oxford: Oxford University Press, [1965] 1997), chap. 1.

35. Robert Miles, *Racism* (London: Routledge, 1989).

36. Gossett, *Race,* pp. 3–8. Fredrickson makes a similar claim while insisting on the distinctive character of "Western racism." See Fredrickson, *Racism,* pp. 5–24.

37. Ashley Montagu, *Man Observed* (New York: G. P. Putnam's Sons, 1968), p. 195.

38. For example, George Fredrickson, the renowned historian of racism, resists the social constructionist view: "It is a useful postmodern insight that race and color are, to a considerable extent, 'social constructions.' But surely the difference between very light and very dark skin was a physical fact that had an independent effect on the evaluations being made." See George M. Fredrickson, "The Skeleton in the Closet," *New York Review of Books* 47, November 2, 2000, p. 66. Similarly, Alexander Saxton warns against "a failure to distinguish between *race* as an objectively visible fact and *racism* as an ideological construct." See Alexander Saxton, *The Rise and Fall of the White Republic: Class Politics and Mass Culture in Nine-*

*teenth-Century America* (London and New York: Verso, 1990), p. 20n.31, emphasis in original.

39. To say this is the "commonsense" understanding of race in our time is not to say that it is a discerning view in the way that common sense is often "good sense." Rather, as Antonio Gramsci says, it is simply the understanding that has *become* the commonsense one as "a product of history and a part of the historical process." See Antonio Gramsci, *Selections from the Prison Notebooks,* ed. and trans. Quintin Hoare and Geoffrey Nowell Smith (New York: International Publishers, 1971), pp. 325–26, 326n.

40. Miles, *Racism,* p. 74. This is not strictly true with respect to contemporary forms of "neoracism" that posit virtually intractable *cultural* differences. These differences are typically associated with distinct ethno-cultural groups rather than with biology per se. See Étienne Balibar, "Is There a 'Neo-Racism'?" in Étienne Balibar and Immanuel Wallerstein, *Race, Nation, Class: Ambiguous Identities,* trans. of Balibar by Chris Turner (London and New York: Verso, 1991).

41. George M. Fredrickson, "Reflections on the Comparative History and Sociology of Racism," in *Racism,* ed. Leonard Harris (Amherst, NY: Humanities Press, 1999), p. 333; Miles, *Racism,* chaps. 3–4. This formulation actually begs important questions about what constitutes an *ethnic* group. The term *ethnic* carries historical connotations of "not Christian or Jewish; Gentile, heathen, pagan" and "peculiar to a race or nation" (*Oxford English Dictionary* entry, reprinted in *Theories of Ethnicity: A Classical Reader,* ed. Werner Sollors [New York: New York University Press, 1996], pp. 2–3). For present purposes, the following definitions by John Rex and Roger Sanjek will suffice. Rex says that while "racial differentiation . . . is in terms of physical differences thought to be biologically inherited, ethnic differentiation is in terms of cultural differences which have to be learned." Sanjek defines ethnicity as "expressive processes of cultural identification" and racial identity in terms of "repressive processes of social exclusion." See John Rex, "Ethnicity," in *The Blackwell Dictionary of Twentieth-Century Social Thought* (Oxford: Blackwell, 1993), p. 205; Roger Sanjek, "Race," in *Encyclopedia of Social and Cultural Anthropology* (London and New York: Routledge, 1996), p. 164.

42. Matthew Frye Jacobson, *Whiteness of a Different Color: European Immigrants and the Alchemy of Race* (Cambridge: Harvard University Press, 1998), p. 105; Robert Miles and Rodolfo D. Torres, "Does 'Race' Matter? Transatlantic Perspectives on Racism after 'Race Relations,'" in *Race, Identity, and Citizenship: A Reader,* ed. Rodolfo D. Torres, Louis F. Mirón, and Jonathan Xavier Inda (Malden, MA, and Oxford: Blackwell, 1999), pp. 21–27.

43. Lawrence Blum, "Multiculturalism, Racial Justice, and Community: Reflections on Charles Taylor's 'The Politics of Recognition,'" in *Defending Diversity: Contemporary Philosophical Perspectives on Pluralism and Diversity,* ed. L. Foster and P. Herzog (Amherst: University of Massachusetts Press, 1994), p. 188.

44. Miles, *Racism,* pp. 77–84; Fredrickson, "Reflections," pp. 335–40.

45. George Samuel Morton advocated such a view in the early nineteenth century (see chapter 3). For recent expressions of this view, see Richard Hernnstein and Charles Murray, *The Bell Curve: Intelligence and Class Structure in American Life* (New York: Free Press, 1994); J. Philippe Rushton, *Race, Evolution, and Behavior: A Life History Perspective* (New Brunswick: Transaction Books, 1995).

46. Paul Gilroy, "Race Ends Here," *Ethnic and Racial Studies* 21 (September 1998), pp. 838–39, 840, 842.

47. Michael Omi and Howard Winant, "On the Theoretical Concept of Race," in *Race, Identity and Representation in Education,* ed. Warren Crichlow and Cameron McCarthy (New York: Routledge, 1993), p. 5; Thomas C. Holt, *The Problem of Race in the Twenty-first Century* (Cambridge: Harvard University Press, 2000).

48. Michel Foucault, *The History of Sexuality,* vol. 1: *An Introduction,* trans. Robert Hurley (New York: Vintage Books, 1978), p. 60.

49. Michel Foucault, *"Society Must Be Defended": Lectures at the Collège de France, 1975–76,* ed. Mauro Bertani and Alessandro Fontana, trans. David Macy (New York: Picador, 2003); Anne Laura Stoler, *Race and the Education of Desire: Foucault's History of Sexuality and the Colonial Order of Discourse* (Durham: Duke University Press, 1995).

50. The racialized status of race scientists did not strictly determine the results of their researches. Yet race scientists who possessed a similarly dominant racialized status and worked in roughly the same historical period have tended to approach "race" and "racial classification" in similar ways, through shared paradigms of scientific inquiry in Thomas Kuhn's sense (see Thomas S. Kuhn, *The Structure of Scientific Revolutions,* 2d ed. [Chicago: University of Chicago Press, 1970]). In addition, the gender norms that governed entry into scientific professions ensured that most of the influential figures in this history were men, especially prior to the twentieth century.

51. This tendency was manifest in particularly telling ways in Europe between the middle of the nineteenth century and the early twentieth century. For instance, French thinkers celebrated the distinctive talents of the so-called Celtic or Gaulic race; Germans theorized Teutonic or Nordic or Aryan superiority; Italians championed a Mediterranean race; and myths of Teutonic and Anglo-Saxon origins were prominent among "whites" of German and English origins in the United States (see chapters 3 and 4).

52. Kwame Anthony Appiah, "Race, Culture, Identity: Misunderstood Connections," in Kwame Anthony Appiah and Amy Gutmann, *Color Conscious: The Political Morality of Race* (Princeton: Princeton University Press, 1996), p. 41.

53. Kuhn, *Structure.*

54. For critical studies, see Frederick Douglass, "The Claims of the Negro Ethnologically Considered" (1854), in *The Life and Writings of Frederick Douglass,* ed. P. S. Foner (New York: International Publishers, 1953); Ashley Montagu, *Man's*

*Most Dangerous Myth: The Fallacy of Race* (New York, 1942); William Stanton, *The Leopard's Spots: Scientific Attitudes toward Race in America, 1815–59* (Chicago: University of Chicago Press, 1960); George W. Stocking Jr., *Race, Culture, and Evolution: Essays in the History of Anthropology,* with a new preface (Chicago: University of Chicago Press, 1982); Gould, *Mismeasure of Man;* Nancy Leys Stepan, *The Idea of Race in Science: Great Britain, 1800–1950* (London: Macmillan, 1982); Elazar Barkan, *The Retreat of Scientific Racism: Changing Concepts of Race in Britain and the United States between the World Wars* (Cambridge: Cambridge University Press, 1992).

55. Gould, *Mismeasure of Man;* pp. 405–6; Audrey Smedley, *Race in North America: Origin and Evolution of a Worldview,* 2d ed. (Boulder: Westview Press, 1998), pp. 3–5.

56. Adam Lively, *Masks: Blackness, Race and the Imagination* (Oxford and New York: Oxford University Press, 2000), p. 49.

57. Bob Carter, *Realism and Racism: Concepts of Race in Sociological Research* (London and New York: Routledge, 2000), pp. 32, 30.

58. Ibid., p. 97.

59. My account of conceptual and cultural change is based on Margaret Archer's "morphogenetic" version of critical realist social theory. See Margaret S. Archer, *Culture and Agency: The Place of Culture in Social Theory,* rev. ed. (Cambridge: Cambridge University Press, 1996); Carter, *Realism,* chaps. 3 and 5.

60. The basic idea here derives from Karl Marx's observation that human beings make our own history, but not "under circumstances chosen by [ourselves], but under circumstances directly encountered, given and transmitted from the past" (*The Eighteenth Brumaire of Louis Bonaparte* [New York: International Publishers, [1852] 1963], p. 15). Archer refines Marx's insight through the notion of analytical dualism, which concerns the interplay of human agency and social structures across time. People shape their social structures and cultural systems in relation to the inherited ideas and material resources made available to them by the social structures and cultural systems of their time and place. See Margaret S. Archer, *Realist Social Theory: The Morphogenetic Approach* (Cambridge: Cambridge University Press, 1995); Carter, *Realism,* pp. 99, 103–4.

61. James Farr elucidates why "conceptual histories are never finished": "The explanatory project embedded in telling a concept's story—what problems its invocation attempted to solve, what contradictions when criticized paved the way for its metamorphosis—must allow for the tentative and promissory character of conceptual histories." See James Farr, "Understanding Conceptual Change Politically," in *Political Innovation and Conceptual Change,* ed. Terence Ball, James Farr, and Russell Hanson (Cambridge: Cambridge University Press, 1989), p. 39.

62. Miles, *Racism,* p. 11.

63. Tom Nairn, "Waiting to Be Special," *London Review of Books,* March 21, 1998, p. 10.

64. Carter, *Realism,* p. 86, emphasis in the original.

65. That is, while the claim that there are *no races* (in the biological sense) is a claim about what human beings really are *by nature,* the claim that there are *racialized identities* is a social and political fact. To speak of racialized identities is to refer to how different groups of people have been socially and politically defined, classified, and treated *as if* they belonged to different human "races." It also refers to the social hierarchies and inequalities that have been produced and sustained by this political construction.

66. See Sandra Harding, "Introduction: Eurocentric Scientific Illiteracy—A Challenge for the World Community," in *The "Racial" Economy of Science: Toward a Democratic Future,* ed. Sandra Harding (Bloomington and Indianapolis: Indiana University Press, 1993), p. 18. Foucault may have had something like this in mind when he called for "a new politics of truth." This would not seek to "emancipat[e] truth from every system of power," something impossible, but would detach "the power of truth from the forms of hegemony, social, economic and cultural, within which it operates at the present time." See Michel Foucault, "Truth and Power," in *Power/Knowledge: Selected Interviews and Other Writings, 1972–1977,* ed. Colin Gordon (New York: Pantheon, 1980), p. 133; Joseph Rouse, "Foucault and the Natural Sciences," in *Foucault and the Critique of Institutions,* ed. John Caputo and Mark Yount (University Park: Pennsylvania State University Press, 1993).

67. Political theorists have explored these last two questions in different ways. Cf. Eric Voegelin, "The Growth of the Race Idea," *Review of Politics* 2 (July 1940), pp. 283–317; Hannah Arendt, *The Origins of Totalitarianism,* new ed. (San Diego: Harvest/Harcourt Brace, [1951] 1973); Ivan Hannaford, *Race: The History of an Idea in the West,* foreword by Bernard Crick (Baltimore: Johns Hopkins University Press, 1996); Charles W. Mills, *The Racial Contract* (Ithaca and London: Cornell University Press, 1997).

68. Rogers M. Smith, *Civic Ideals: Conflicting Visions of Citizenship in U.S. History* (New Haven: Yale University Press, 1997), p. 1.

69. Michael Goldfield, *The Color of Politics: Race and the Mainsprings of American Politics* (New York: New Press, 1997), p. 9; Anthony W. Marx, *Making Race and Nation: A Comparison of South Africa, the United States, and Brazil* (Cambridge: Cambridge University Press, 1998), p. 4.

70. Joel Olson, *The Abolition of White Democracy* (Minneapolis: University of Minnesota Press, 2004), p. xii.

71. Mills, *Racial Contract,* p. 3, Mills's emphasis; Olson, *Abolition,* p. xviii; Jacqueline Stevens, *Reproducing the State* (Princeton: Princeton University Press, 1999), p. 173.

72. I am indebted to Joel Olson for helping me clarify this point.

73. On "whiteness," see David R. Roediger, *The Wages of Whiteness: Race and the American Working Class,* rev. ed. (London and New York: Verso, [1991] 1999); Cheryl Harris, "Whiteness as Property," *Harvard Law Review* 106 (June 1993),

1709–91; Noel Ignatiev, *How the Irish Became White* (New York: Routledge, 1995); Karen Brodkin Sacks, *How Jews Become White Folks and What That Says about Race in America* (New Brunswick: Rutgers University Press, 1998); Jacobson, *Whiteness.*

74. Ruth Frankenberg, "Introduction: Local Whitenesses, Localizing Whiteness," in *Displacing Whiteness: Essays in Social and Cultural Criticism*, ed. Ruth Frankenberg (Durham: Duke University Press, 1997), p. 4.

75. Jacobson, *Whiteness*, p. 94.

76. Paul Gilroy, *Against Race: Imagining Political Culture Beyond the Color Line* (Cambridge: Belknap Press/Harvard University Press, 2000), p. 17.

77. Paul Gilroy, "Race Ends Here," *Ethnic and Racial Studies* 21 (September 1998), pp. 838–39.

78. Richard Lewontin, "Of Genes and Genitals," *Transition*, new series, no. 69 (1996), p. 193.

79. The question was from political theorist Bonnie Honnig.

80. Blumenbach, *On the Natural Variety of Mankind*, 3d ed., pp. 264–65.

81. Étienne Balibar, "Racism and Nationalism," in Balibar and Wallerstein, *Race, Nation, Class*, p. 37.

NOTES TO CHAPTER 1

1. Ian Hacking, "Inaugural Lecture: Chair of Philosophy and History of Scientific Concepts at the Collège de France, 16 January 2001," *Economy and Society* 31 (February 2002), p. 8.

2. Norman Davies, *Europe: A History* (New York: Harper Perennial, 1996), p. 217.

3. Peter J. Geary, *The Myth of Nations: The Medieval Origins of Europe* (Princeton: Princeton University Press, 2002), p. 10; Davies, *Europe*, pp. 215–38.

4. Cedric J. Robinson, *Black Marxism: The Making of the Black Radical Tradition*, foreword by Robin D. G. Kelley, with a new preface (Chapel Hill: University of North Carolina Press, [1983] 2000), p. 67. Robinson frames the development of European racialism somewhat differently, suggesting that medieval European society was already marked by "racial ordering" and "racial beliefs."

5. Kenan Malik, *The Meaning of Race: Race, History and Culture in Western Society* (London: Macmillan, 1996), p. 43.

6. On these concepts of difference, see Geary, *Myth of Nations*, pp. 43–57.

7. The ancient Greeks and Romans also distinguished themselves from "barbarians." See Anthony Pagden, *Peoples and Empires: A Short History of European Migration, Exploration, and Conquest from Greece to the Present* (New York: Modern Library, 2001), pp. 12–13, 29–30; Davies, *Europe*, pp. 213–17.

8. Malik, *Meaning of Race*, p. 45; James Muldoon, "Race or Culture: Medieval

Notions of Difference," in *Race and Racism in Theory and Practice* (Lanham, MD: Rowman and Littlefield, 2000).

9. "Latin Christendom," the historical precursor to modern Europe, refers to the geographical and cultural space inhabited by Christian churches that worshiped in Latin in a manner approved by the papacy. See Robert Bartlett, *The Making of Europe: Conquest, Colonization and Cultural Change, 950–1250* (Princeton: Princeton University Press, 1993), p. 18.

10. Bartlett has in mind the relations between such peoples as Germans and Slavs. Likewise, Thomas Hahn contends that the "earliest accounts of the Norman Conquest of England make striking use of race as a trope of difference." See Bartlett, *Making of Europe,* p. 197; Thomas Hahn, "The Difference the Middle Ages Makes: Color and Race before the Modern World," *Journal of Medieval and Early Modern Studies* 31 (Winter 2001), p. 7; Robert Bartlett, "Medieval and Modern Concepts of Race and Ethnicity," *Journal of Medieval and Early Modern Studies* 31 (Winter 2001), pp. 39–56.

11. Regino of Prüm, *Epistula ad Hathonem archiepiscopum missa,* ed. Friedrich Kurze, *Reginonis . . . chronicon* (SRG, Hanover, 1890), pp. xix–xx, quoted in Bartlett, *Making of Europe,* p. 197.

12. Bartlett, *Making of Europe,* p. 197.

13. Thus, in a recent article on race in the medieval period Bartlett explicitly treats the terms *racial* and *ethnic* as synonyms. See Bartlett, "Medieval and Modern Concepts," pp. 41–42. Despite these conceptual confusions, his account of cleavages within and beyond Latin Christendom in the Middle Ages provides important clues to why some of these same divisions were *later* racialized. See Bartlett, *Making of Europe,* pp. 8–23, 197–242.

14. Susan Reynolds comments, "Medieval *gentes* were not 'races' in any sense in which the word can be used without misunderstanding in the late nineteenth century." The tendency among some scholars to translate the Latin word *gens* as "race" derives from now-discredited nineteenth-century usage. See Susan Reynolds, *Kingdoms and Communities in Western Europe 900–1300,* 2d ed. (Oxford: Clarendon Press, 1997) pp. 255, 254; Geary, *Myth of Nations,* chap. 1.

15. John V. Tolan, *Saracens: Islam in the Medieval European Imagination* (New York: Columbia University Press, 2002), pp. xix, 127–28, 287n.25; Ann Thomson, "Ottoman Empire," in *Encyclopedia of the Enlightenment,* vol. 3 (Oxford: Oxford University Press, 2003), p. 220; Cemal Kafadar, "The Ottomans and Europe," in *Handbook of European History, 1400–1600: Late Middle Ages, Renaissance and Reformation,* vol. 1: *Structures and Assertions,* ed. Thomas A. Brady, Heiko A. Oberman, and James D. Tracy (Leiden, New York, and Klön: E. J. Brill 1994), pp. 619–20; "Ethnic," in *Oxford English Dictionary,* quoted in *Theories of Ethnicity: A Classical Reader,* ed. Werner Sollors (New York: New York University Press, 1996), p. 2.

16. Fernand Braudel, *A History of Civilizations,* trans. Richard Mayne (Lon-

don: Allen Lane/Penguin Press, 1994; originally published in France in 1963), p. 304.

17. Bartlett, *Making of Europe,* p. 1. The idea of Europe goes back to the ancient Greek myth of "Europa," which was mentioned in passing by the Greek poet Homer and then discussed more fully in *Europa and the Bull,* attributed to Moschus of Syracuse, and in the Roman poet Ovid's *Metamorphoses.* See Davies, *Europe,* pp. xvii, xix; Anthony Pagden, "Prologue: Europe and the World Around," in *Early Modern Europe: An Oxford History,* ed. Euan Cameron (Oxford: Oxford University Press, 1999), pp. 1–4; J. G. A. Pocock, "What Do We Mean by Europe?" *Wilson Quarterly* 21 (Winter 1997), pp. 12–29.

18. Bartlett, *Making of Europe,* p. 1.

19. Benedict Anderson, *Imagined Communities: Reflections on the Origin and Spread of Nationalism,* 2d ed. (London: Verso, 1991), p. 7. Anderson calls *nations* "imagined communities."

20. For instance, the Russian Slavophile Nikolay Danilevskiy (1822–85) argued that "Russia possessed a distinctive Slavic civilization of its own, midway between Europe and Asia." See Davies, *Europe,* p. 11.

21. Pagden, "Prologue," p. 14.

22. Davies, *Europe,* p. 266.

23. Davies, *Europe,* pp. 266, 254–58, 641, 1259; Stanford Jay Shaw, "The Ottoman Empire," in *The New Encyclopaedia Britannica,* vol. 28 (Chicago: Encyclopaedia Britannica, Inc., 1997), pp. 948–57.

24. David Brion Davis, "Slavery—White, Black, Muslim, Christian," *New York Review of Books* 48, July 5, 2001, p. 52.

25. Ibid., p. 52; David Brion Davis, "A Big Business," *New York Review of Books* 45, June 11, 1998, pp. 50–53.

26. Ronald Grigory Suny, *The Making of the Georgian Nation,* 2d ed. (Bloomington and Indianapolis: Indiana University Press, 1994), pp. 24–27. Like the Celts in Ireland, the Armenian and Georgian churches developed distinctive forms of Christianity. See Davies, *Europe,* pp. 263, 265.

27. Suny, *Georgian Nation,* pp. 49–59.

28. Richard Hakluyt, *Voyages and Discoveries: The Principal Navigations, Voyages, Traffiques and Discoveries of the English Nation,* ed. Jack Beeching (London: Penguin Books, 1972), pp. 80, 123, 245. Hakluyt's collection of travelers' reports was first published in 1589–90.

29. Pagden, "Prologue," pp. 12–13.

30. Pagden, *Peoples and Empires,* pp. 50–52.

31. William E. Burns, "Race," in *The Scientific Revolution: An Encyclopedia* (Santa Barbara: ABC-CLIO, 2001), p. 267; Jan Nederveen Pieterse, "Unpacking the West: How European Is Europe?" in *Racism, Modernity and Identity: On the Western Front,* ed. Ali Rattansi and Sallie Westwood (Cambridge: Polity Press, 1994).

32. Pagden, "Prologue," pp. 7–16; Robert Miles, *Racism* (London: Routledge,

1989), pp. 17–30; Pieterse, "Unpacking the West"; Donald F. Lach and Edwin J. Van Kley, "Asia in the Eyes of Europe: The Seventeenth Century," in *Facing Each Other: The World's Perception of Europe and Europe's Perception of the World,* part 1, ed. Anthony Pagden (Aldershot, Burlington, Singapore, and Sidney: Ashgate, 2000).

33. Miles, *Racism,* pp. 17–18.

34. Benjamin Braude, "The Sons of Noah and the Construction of Ethnic and Geographical Identities in the Medieval and Early Modern Periods," *William and Mary Quarterly* 54 (January 1997), pp. 103–42.

35. Pagden, "Prologue," pp. 2–3.

36. Giambattista Vico, *The First New Science* (1725), ed. and trans. Leon Pompa (Cambridge: Cambridge University Press, 2002), pp. 11, 40, 46, 70–72, 142, 208.

37. For example, the German disciple of Grotius, Georgius Hornius, propounded a quasi-racial account of Noah's descendants in *Arca Noae, sive historia imperiorum et regnorum . . .* (1666). In his scheme "the Japhethites became Whites, the Semites became the Yellow Races, and the Hamites became Negroes." See Léon Poliakov, *The Aryan Myth: A History of Racist and Nationalist Ideas in Europe,* trans. Edmund Howard (New York: Basic Books, 1974), pp. 142–43.

38. Bartlett, *Making of Europe,* p. 23. The Ruthenians were from a region on the southern slopes of the Carpathian Mountains, now a region of western Ukraine.

39. Ibid.

40. Hahn, "Difference the Middle Ages Makes," p. 8.

41. Ibid.

42. Robert Bonfil, "Aliens Within: Jews and Antijudaism," in *Handbook of European History, 1400–1600,* pp. 267–68.

43. Ibid., p. 272; George M. Fredrickson, *Racism: A Short History* (Princeton: Princeton University Press, 2001), p. 32.

44. Fredrickson, *Racism,* p. 32.

45. Assaults on Moorish culture provoked a rebellion in 1568 that was brutally suppressed. Then, between 1609 and 1614, the entire *Morisco* population was forced out of Spain. See Fredrickson, *Racism,* pp. 34–35; Poliakov, *Aryan Myth,* pp. 12–13.

46. Poliakov, *Aryan Myth,* p. 12.

47. The expulsion of Jews from western Europe culminated with their expulsion from England in 1290 and from areas subject to French rule in 1394. This process was partly reversed with the reintegration through ghettoization of Jews that began in the late sixteenth century. See Davies, *Europe,* p. 412; Bonfil, "Aliens Within," pp. 267, 291–96.

48. Bonfil, "Aliens Within," p. 270; Hannah Arendt, *The Origins of Totalitarianism,* new ed. (San Diego: Harcourt Brace, [1951] 1979), part 1, chap. 2.

49. Bonfil, "Aliens Within," pp. 270–73, quoting Bernardino of Feltre from Léon Poliakov, *Les banchieri juifs et le Saint-Siège du XIIIe au XVIIe siècle* (Paris–The Hague, 1965), pp. 205–6, at p. 272.

50. Bonfil, "Aliens Within," pp. 272–73.

51. Davies, *Europe*, pp. 454–55; Pagden, *Peoples and Empires*, pp. 52–53.

52. Fredrickson, *Racism*, p. 36; Tzvetan Todorov, *The Conquest of America*, trans. Richard Howard (New York: Harper Torchbooks, 1984), pp. 150–61.

53. Las Casas, quoted in Todorov, *Conquest of America*, p. 162.

54. Todorov, *Conquest of America*, pp. 161–64. This position was endorsed by Paul III's papal bull of 1537.

55. Pagden, *Peoples and Empires*, pp. 71–72

56. Geary, *Myth of Nations*, p. 145.

57. Edward Gibbon, *Decline and Fall of the Roman Empire*, chap. 42, quoted in Davies, *Europe*, p. 225.

58. Richard Hellie, "Slaves," *Encyclopedia of European Social History: From 1350–2000*, vol. 3 (New York: Charles Scribner's Sons, 2001), p. 165.

59. This ethnic association of "slave" and "Slav" in modern European languages was generated "in the early Middle Ages when captives from the Balkan region were often transported overland to Muslim Spain." See Davis, "Big Business," p. 52n.12; Charles Verlinden, *The Beginnings of Modern Colonialism*, trans. Yvonne Freccero (Ithaca: Cornell University Press, 1970), p. 35.

60. Hellie, "Slaves," pp. 166–68.

61. Ibid., p. 168.

62. Ibid.; Davies, *Europe*, p. 655.

63. Bartlett, *Making of Europe*, p. 238.

64. On color consciousness in ancient and medieval China, see Frank Dikötter, *The Discourse of Race in Modern China* (Stanford: Stanford University Press, 1992), chap. 1. Dikötter counts the skin-color consciousness of some premodern Chinese writers as a form of *race* consciousness, or racialism. His claim, however, is based on a questionable rendering of the relevant Chinese concepts. See Arif Dirlik, "Review Article: The Discourse of Race in Modern China," *China Information* 7 (Spring 1993), pp. 68–71; Alastair Bonnett, "Who Was White? The Disappearance of Non-European White Identities and the Formation of European Racial Whiteness," *Ethnic and Racial Studies* 21 (November 1998), pp. 1031–36.

65. C. Loring Brace, "The Race Concept," in *History of Physical Anthropology: An Encyclopedia*, vol. 2 (New York and London: Garland Publishing, 1997), p. 861.

66. Frank Snowden, *Before Color Prejudice: The Ancient View of Blacks* (Cambridge: Harvard University Press, 1983), excerpted in *Racism*, ed. Martin Bulmer and John Solomos (Oxford: Oxford University Press, 1999), pp. 24, 28, Snowden's emphasis.

67. Snowden, *Before Color Prejudice*, p. 30.

68. Hahn, "Difference the Middle Ages Makes," pp. 10, 31n.33, 11.

69. Winthrop Jordan, *White over Black: American Attitudes toward the Negro, 1550–1812* (Baltimore: Penguin, 1969), pp. 17–18; Braude, "Sons of Noah."

70. Paul Freedman, *Images of the Medieval Peasant* (Stanford: Stanford University Press, 1999), chap. 4.

71. Ibid., p. 89; Bernard Lewis, *Race and Slavery in the Middle East: An Historical Inquiry* (New York: Oxford University Press, 1990), pp. 44–45, 55, 125.

72. Fredrickson, *Racism*, p. 29.

73. Bonnett, "Who Was White?" pp. 1034–35; David M. Goldenberg, "The Development of the Idea of Race: Classical Paradigms and Medieval Elaborations," *International Journal of the Classical Tradition* 5 (Spring 1999), pp. 561–70.

74. Ibn Khaldun, *Muqaddima*, ed. E. Quatremere (Paris, 1858), vol. 1, p. 269, quoted in Goldenberg, "Development of the Idea of Race," p. 567.

75. Fredrickson, *Racism*, p. 29.

76. Geary, *Myth of Nations*, p. 137; Davies, *Europe*, p. 286.

77. Davies, *Europe*, p. 222.

78. Geary, *Myth of Nations*, pp. 137–38, 136.

79. Ibid., p. 140; Poliakov, *Aryan Myth*, p. 18; Davies, *Europe*, p. 318.

80. Poliakov, *Aryan Myth*, p. 20.

81. Ibid., pp. 73, 17, 21.

82. Ibid., p. 31; Arendt, *Origins of Totalitarianism*, pp. 161–65; Robert Miles, "The Civilization and Racialization of the Interior," in *Racism after "Race Relations"* (London and New York: Routledge, 1993), pp. 88–94.

83. Poliakov suggests that the distinction referred to "a superiority both of race and class, because the two notions of upper and lower classes and of superior and inferior races . . . were not so easy to disentangle when it was a question of contrasting conquering peoples with those they conquered" (*Aryan Myth*, p. 17). It would be more accurate, however, to say that it referred to both *ethnic* and class (or social status) superiority insofar as it was not initially a *racial* distinction.

84. François de Belleforest, *Les grandes annales et histoires générales de France, de la venue des Francs en Gauls*, 1579, vol. 1, fol. 364, quoted in Poliakov, *Aryan Myth*, p. 21; Davies, *Europe*, p. 317.

85. Loyseau is quoted from Roland Mousnier, *Fureurs paysannes* . . . (Paris, 1967), p. 32, in Polikov, *Aryan Myth*, p. 22.

86. Polikov, *Aryan Myth*, p. 26.

87. Abbé Sièyes, *Qu'est-ce que le Tiers État?* quoted in Poliakov, *Aryan Myth*, p. 28.

88. La Tour d'Auvergne-Corret, quoted in Poliakov, *Aryan Myth*, p. 29.

89. Poliakov, *Aryan Myth*, p. 30.

90. Augustin Thierry, *Sur l'antipathie de race qui divise la nation française* (1820), pp. 261–62, 258, quoted in Poliakov, *Aryan Myth*, p. 30.

91. Poliakov, *Aryan Myth*, pp. 37–38, 45; Davies, *Europe*, pp. 231–32, 339; Geary, *Myth of Nations*, pp. 141–42.

92. Poliakov, *Aryan Myth,* p. 45.

93. Ibid., pp. 46–47.

94. Ibid., p. 50; Thomas Gossett, *Race: The History of an Idea in America,* new ed. (Oxford: Oxford University Press, [1965] 1997), chap. 5; Reginald Horsman, *Race and Manifest Destiny: The Origins of American Racial Anglo-Saxonism* (Cambridge: Harvard University Press, 1981), chap. 4; and chapter 4, below.

95. Davies, *Europe,* appendix 3, p. 1236.

96. Bartlett, *Making of Europe,* p. 21.

97. Ibid., pp. 22–23.

98. *Laudabiliter* (Papal Bull, 1155), *Irish Historical Documents 1172–1922,* ed. Edmund Curtis and R. B. McDowell (New York, [1943] 1968), pp. 17–18, quoted in Muldoon, "Race or Culture," p. 85.

99. Muldoon, "Race or Culture," p. 85.

100. Ibid., pp. 86–87.

101. Davies, *Europe,* p. 490; Robinson, *Black Marxism,* p. 37; Theodore W. Allen, *The Invention of the White Race,* vol. 1: *Racial Oppression and Social Control* (London and New York: Verso, 1994), p. 57.

102. Allen, *Invention of the White Race,* vol. 1, pp. 48–51, 65–69; Philip Yale Nicholson, *Who Do We Think We Are? Race and Racism in the Modern World* (Armonk, NY: M. E. Sharpe, 1999), p. 74.

103. In the most "successful" plantation, established in Ulster in 1609, the plantation system involved the immigration of Protestant Scots and the establishment of a system of Protestant privilege for these Scottish immigrants and their descendents. See Allen, *Invention of the White Race,* vol. 1, pp. 58–60, 115–24.

104. Nicholson, *Who Do We Think We Are?* p. 75.

105. Theodore Allen claims that it was a form of "religio-racial oppression." See Allen, *Invention of the White Race,* vol. 1, pp. 47–51, 66–69; Nicholson, *Who Do We Think We Are?* pp. 74–75. Allen is right to insist that racial oppression does not rely always or necessarily rely on differences in skin color (p. 22), but that is not a decisive point.

106. See Muldoon, "Race or Culture"; Henry Louis Taylor Jr., review of Allen, *Invention of the White Race,* vol. 1, *Labor History* 37 (Winter 1995–96), pp. 111–12; Dale T. Knobel, review of Allen, *Invention of the White Race,* vol. 1, *American Historical Review* 101 (February 1996), p. 151; Alden T. Vaughan, review of Allen, *Invention of the White Race,* vols. 1 and 2, *William and Mary Quarterly* 56 (October 1999), p. 83. Religious and cultural differences were probably not the primary cause of English colonialism in Ireland and the subsequent conflicts. Religion was employed in the service of political and economic interests. See Allen, *Invention of the White Race,* vol. 1; Fintan O'Toole, "Lesser Evils," *New Republic* 227, August 19 and 26, 2002, pp. 41–45.

107. For example, under the rules of the Ulster plantation (1572–73) English colonists declared that "no Irishman, born of Irish race, shall purchase land, bear

office, be chosen of any jury or admitted witness in any real personal action, nor be bound apprentice to any science or art that may endamage the Queen's Majesty's subjects." See Historical Manuscript Commission, *De l'Isle and Dudley, MSS,* II, pp. 12–15, quoted in David Beers Quinn, *The Elizabethans and the Irish* (Ithaca: Cornell University Press, 1966), p. 108.

108. As Dale Knobel notes with reference to white racism against African Americans, "Few African Americans could 'become' white, and they certainly were not encouraged to 'pass.'" See Knobel, review of Allen, p. 151.

109. Horsman, *Race and Manifest Destiny*; Dale T. Knobel, *Paddy and the Republic: Ethnicity and Nationality in Antebellum America* (Middletown, CT: Wesleyan University Press, 1986); David R. Roediger, *The Wages of Whiteness: Race and the Making of the American Working Class,* rev. ed. (London: Verso, 1999), chap. 7.

110. Matthew Frye Jacobson, *Whiteness of a Different Color: European Immigrants and the Alchemy of Race* (Cambridge: Harvard University Press, 1998), p. 33.

111. I will use italics to indicate the word *race* and double quotation marks to denote the concept. Compare Jacqueline Stevens, *Reproducing the State* (Princeton: Princeton University Press, 1999), preface, n. 1. Any effort to isolate the "origins" of race and racism, including this one, is bound to be somewhat arbitrary. See Anne Laura Stoler, "Racial Histories and Their Regimes of Truth," *Political Power and Social Theory* 11 (1997), pp. 183–206.

112. Alan Ryan, "Property," in *Political Innovation and Conceptual Change,* ed. Terence Ball, James Farr, and Russell Hanson (Cambridge: Cambridge University Press, 1989), p. 309.

113. This is so even though the concept of race, when it was used by German Nazis in a form of exterminationist racism against Jews, was indeed linked to a genocidal effort to make a *so-called* race of people cease to exist.

114. Historically, racialists have put forward varying views on this matter, particularly before and after the impact of Darwin's theory of evolution. Currently, the notion of "raciation" is used by Lucius Outlaw, who propounds an idiosyncratic anti-racist form of racialism. Outlaw views "race" mostly as a "social formation" but maintains that it is also partially determined by biology "in complex interplay with environmental, cultural, and social factors." See Lucius Outlaw, "Toward a Critical Theory of 'Race,'" in *Anatomy of Racism,* ed. David Theo Goldberg (Minneapolis: University of Minnesota Press, 1990), p. 68. The idea or concept of raciation—of race-making *as a matter of natural history*—is basic to racialist thought by definition.

115. Bob Carter, *Realism and Racism: Concepts of Race in Sociological Research* (London and New York: Routledge, 2000), chap. 1.

116. James Farr, "Understanding Conceptual Change Politically," in *Political Innovation and Conceptual Change,* ed. Ball, Farr, and Hunson, p. 27, n. 2. See also Arnold I. Davidson, *The Empire of Sexuality: Historical Epistemology and the Formation of Concepts* (Cambridge: Harvard University Press, 2001), chap. 7.

117. At the same time, it is clear that there was racism—exclusionary practices based on ideas about race—before the emergence of the term in the 1930s. See Fredrickson, *Racism*, pp. 7–10, 151–70.

118. Eric Voegelin, *History of the Race Idea: From Ray to Carus,* trans. Ruth Hein, ed. Klaus Vondung, in *The Collected Works of Eric Voegelin* (Baton Rouge: Louisiana State University Press, [1933] 1968), pp. 80–81; Audrey Smedley, *Race in North America: Origin and Evolution of a Worldview,* 2d ed. (Boulder: Westview Press, 1998), pp. 37–41. The word *race* seems to have first appeared in English at the beginning of the sixteenth century. William Dunbar wrote, in 1508, of "Bakbyttaris of sindry racis." See *The Oxford English Dictionary,* 2d ed. (Oxford: Clarendon Press, 1989), vol. 13, p. 69: "race," 8a.

119. Voegelin, *History of the Race Idea,* pp. 82–83.

120. *Oxford English Dictionary,* 2d ed., vol. 13, p. 69: "race," 1a, 2b.

121. Ibid. Later T. H. Huxley, writing about crayfish in 1880, spoke of how "a variety, or race, is generated within the species" (Ibid., p. 69: "race," 3a). Against this use of *race* in zoology, see Stephen Jay Gould, "Why We Should Not Name Human Races—A Biological View," in *Ever since Darwin: Reflections in Natural History* (New York: W. W. Norton, 1979).

122. *Oxford English Dictionary,* 2d ed., vol. 13, p. 69: "race," 1c. Two other interesting early usages in English denoted differences of sex and class. For example, Edmund Spenser, in the *Faerie Queene* (1590), wrote, "In gentle Ladies breste and bounteous race Of woman kind." And Charles Lamb, in *Essays of Elia* (1822), spoke of "*The Two Races of Men,* The men who borrow, and the men who lend" (Ibid., p. 69: "race," 8b, 8a, emphasis in the original).

123. Margaret T. Hodgen, *Early Anthropology in the Sixteenth and Seventeenth Centuries* (Philadelphia: University of Pennsylvania Press, 1964), p. 214.

124. See Gossett, *Race,* chap. 3; Miles, *Racism,* pp. 20–30; Smedley, *Race in North America;* Ivan Hannaford, *Race: The History of an Idea in the West* (Baltimore: Johns Hopkins University Press, 1996); Burns, "Race," p. 267.

125. Smedley, *Race in North America,* pp. 39, 40–41.

126. Fredrickson, *Racism,* p. 52

127. Robinson, *Black Marxism,* p. 82. See also Kwame Anthony Appiah, *In My Father's House: Africa in the Philosophy of Culture* (New York: Oxford University Press, 1993), pp. 20–27, 62.

128. Jordan, *White over Black,* p. 56.

129. Davis, "Slavery—White, Black, Muslim, Christian," pp. 51–55; Robinson, *Black Marxism,* pp. 88, 95.

130. Verlinden, *Beginnings of Modern Colonialism,* p. 39; Jordan, *White over Black,* p. 57.

131. It was mostly restricted to "frontier regions" as the Crown sought to incorporate Indians into Christian society. With increasing European knowledge about indigenous Americans, Europeans (particularly Spanish thinkers) also pro-

posed possible links between native Americans and the sons of Noah. See Verlinden, *Beginnings of Modern Colonialism,* pp. 40–42, 43; Poliakov, *Aryan Myth,* pp. 137–39; Braude, "Sons of Noah, p. 140.

132. Jordan, *White over Black,* pp. 61, 52–56. On how contact with native Americans in the sixteenth and seventeenth centuries contributed to English "race" thinking, see Karen Ordahl Kupperman, "Presentment of Civility: English Reading of American Self-Presentation in the Early Years of Colonization," *William and Mary Quarterly* 54 (January 1997), pp. 193–228; Joyce E. Chaplin, "Natural Philosophy and an Early Racial Idiom in North America: Comparing English and Indian Bodies," *William and Mary Quarterly* 54 (January 1997), pp. 229–52.

133. Jordan, *White over Black,* p. 61. This linguistic development marked the onset of a historically new equation of "Negro" and "slave." See Jordan, *White over Black,* pp. 56–98; Robinson, *Black Marxism,* p. 82.

134. Nicholson, *Who Do We Think We Are?* p. 64.

135. Verlinden, *Beginnings of Modern Colonialism,* p. 34.

136. Daniel A. Segal, "'The European': Allegories of Purity," *Anthropology Today* 7 (October 1991), p. 7; Jordan, *White over Black,* pp. 48–52; Edmund S. Morgan, "Slavery and Freedom: The American Paradox," *Journal of American History* 59 (June 1972), pp. 13–21.

137. Jonathan Dewald, "The Early Modern Period," in *Encyclopedia of European Social History: From 1350–2000,* vol. 1 (New York: Charles Scribner's Sons, 2001), p. 172.

138. Morgan, "Slavery and Freedom," p. 14.

139. Jordan, *White over Black,* p. 47.

140. Richard Jobson, *Golden Trade* (1623), p. 112, quoted in Jordan, *Black over White,* p. 61. Sixteenth-century English travelers who first encountered sub-Saharan Africans met them not as slaves but as peoples strikingly different from themselves in appearance, ways of life, and religion whom they sometimes called "black Moors" or "Blackamoores." See Jordan, *White over Black,* pp. 6, 5, 96.

141. Jordan, *White over Black,* pp. 52, 47.

142. Ibid., pp. 47, 55.

143. George M. Fredrickson, *White Supremacy: A Comparative Study in American and South African History* (Oxford: Oxford University Press, 1981), pp. 70, 73.

144. Ibid., p. 73.

145. Morgan, "Slavery and Freedom," p. 17.

146. Ibid.

147. Kenneth Morgan, *Slavery and Servitude in North America, 1607–1800* (Edinburgh: Edinburgh University Press, 2000), p. 35.

148. Morgan, "Slavery and Freedom," pp. 20, 7–12.

149. Ibid., pp. 20–21.

150. Ibid., p. 22; Theodore W. Allen, *The Invention of the White Race,* vol. 2:

*The Origins of Racial Oppression in Anglo-America* (London and New York: Verso, 1997), pp. 210–15.

151. Allen, *Invention of the White Race,* vol. 2, p. 215

152. Morgan, "Slavery and Freedom," pp. 25, 24.

153. Morgan, *Slavery and Servitude in North America,* p. 37.

154. Large-scale enslavement of Indians in North America was never successful. See Morgan, *Slavery and Servitude in North America,* pp. 27–28.

155. Jordan, *White over Black,* p. 92.

156. Allen, *Invention of the White Race,* vol. 2, p. 250, Allen's emphasis. For a documentation of this point, see pp. 239–53; Jordan, *White over Black,* pp. 94–95.

157. Quoted in Jordan, *White over Black,* pp. 79–80.

158. Jordan, *White over Black,* p. 96.

159. Ibid., pp. 87–88, quoting William Waller Hening, ed., *The Statutes at Large Being a Collection of All the Laws of Virginia,* 13 vols. (Richmond, NY, and Philadelphia, 1809–23), II, pp. 289–90, 464–65.

160. Jordan, *White over Black,* pp. 63, 88–90, 54.

161. Segal, "'The European,'" p. 7.

162. The term had occasionally been used earlier, as in an 1652 Rhode Island law that officially prohibited enslavement and in some statutes of the 1660s. See Jordan, *White over Black,* pp. 70, 95, 96n.123.

163. Morgan, "Slavery and Freedom," p. 28.

164. Segal, "'The European,'" p. 8. Class, racialized, and gendered distinctions intersect in such a way that women who possessed a privileged class position or racialized status benefited in tangible ways from the class and racialized hierarchies (e.g., they enjoyed wealth and status) but also suffered from gendered constraints on their social status and opportunities.

165. Allen, *Invention of the White Race,* vol. 2, p. 243.

166. See George M. Fredrickson, "Reflections on the Comparative History and Sociology of Racism," in *Racism,* ed. Leonard Harris (Amherst, NY: Humanities Press, 1999), p. 335.

167. C. R. Boxer, *Four Centuries of Portuguese Expansion, 1415–1825: A Succinct Survey* (Johannesburg: Witwatersrand University Press, 1961), pp. 42–44; C. R. Boxer, *The Dutch Seaborne Empire, 1600–1800* (New York: Alfred A. Knopf, 1965), chap. 8; Fredrickson, *White Supremacy,* pp. 81–85.

168. David Brion Davis, "The Culmination of Racial Polarities and Prejudice," *William and Mary Quarterly* 54 (January 1997), p. 762; Jordan, *White over Black,* p. 80.

169. Michel Foucault, *The Order of Things: An Archaeology of the Human Sciences* (New York: Vintage, 1973), p. 133.

170. Ibid., p. 128.

171. Siep Stuurman, "François Bernier and the Invention of Racial Classification," *History Workshop Journal,* no. 50 (Autumn 2000), p. 13.

172. Ibid.; Hodgen, *Early Anthropology,* pp. 418, 424; Edward Tyson, *Orang-Outang, sive Homo silvestris; or, the anatomy of a pygmie* (London, 1699), quoted in *Readings in Early Anthropology,* ed. J. S. Slotkin (Chicago: Aldine Publishing Company, 1965), p. 94.

173. Andreas Vesalius, *De humani corporis* (1543), p. 23, quoted in *Readings in Early Anthropology,* ed. Slotkin, p. 40.

174. Marquis of Lansdowne, "Introduction," *The Petty Papers: Some Unpublished Writings of Sir William Petty,* ed. Marquis of Lansdowne, 2 vols. (New York: Augustus M. Kelley, [1927] 1967), vol. 1, p. xiii; vol. 2, p. 19.

175. Allen, *Invention of the White Race,* vol. 1, pp. 68–69, 72, 75; Lansdowne, "Introduction," p. xxxi.

176. William Petty, "The Scale of Creatures" (A Letter to Sir Robert Southwell, 1677), in *The Petty Papers,* vol. 2, p. 23. Although Petty never published his "Scale of Creatures," he seems to have delivered a version of it to the Royal College of Physicians in Dublin. See Lansdowne, "Introduction," vol. 2, p. 19.

177. Slotkin, ed., *Readings in Early Anthropology,* p. 87.

178. Petty, "Scale of Creatures," vol. 2, p. 23.

179. William Petty, "The Scale of Animals (a fragment)," in *Petty Papers,* vol. 2, p. 26.

180. Ibid., pp. 30–31.

181. Ibid., p. 31.

182. Robert Bernasconi and Thomas L. Lott, "Introduction," in *The Idea of Race,* ed. Robert Bernasconi and Thomas L. Lott (Indianapolis: Hackett, 2000), p. viii.

183. Frank Spencer, "Bernier, François (1620–1688)," in *History of Physical Anthropology: An Encyclopedia,* vol. 1 (New York and London: Garland Publishing, 1997), p. 169; Stuurman, "François Bernier," p. 1.

184. Bernasconi and Lott, "Introduction," p. viii.

185. François Bernier, "A New Division of the Earth," trans. T. Bendyshe, in *Memoirs Read before the Anthropological Society of London,* vol. 1 (1863–64), pp. 360–64, reprinted in *Idea of Race,* ed. Bernasconi and Lott, pp. 1–2.

186. Spencer, "Bernier, François," p. 170; Stuurman, "François Bernier," pp. 3, 12. I address the debate between monogenists and polygenists—who contend that the different "races" of human beings were different "species" with distinct geographical origins—in the next two chapters.

187. Bernier, "New Division," p. 2.

188. Ibid.

189. See Henry Louis Gates Jr., "Editor's Introduction: Writing 'Race' and the Difference It Makes," *Critical Inquiry* 12 (Autumn 1985), pp. 4–5; Miles, *Racism,* pp. 9–10, 121–31.

190. Freedman, *Images of the Medieval Peasant,* p. 139.

191. Bernier, "New Division," p. 2.

192. Ibid., pp. 2–3.

193. Ibid., p. 3.

194. Ibid., p. 2.

195. He said that the Lapps were "wretched animals" and that the "blacks of the Cape of Good Hope are small, thin, ugly"; they drink "seawater when they can get no other, and [speak] a language altogether strange" (Bernier, "New Division," p. 3).

196. His hesitancy to include native Americans in this "race" (in contrast to Persians, Egyptians, and Indians) was probably related to the then-common European view that they were "savages." Stuurman, "François Bernier," pp. 4–5.

197. Stuurman, "François Bernier," p. 4.

198. Bernier, "New Division," p. 3.

199. Ibid., p. 4.

200. Ibid.

201. Brace, "Race Concept," p. 861.

202. Ibid., p. 862.

203. Pierre H. Boulle, "Race," in *Encyclopedia of the Enlightenment*, vol. 3 (Oxford: Oxford University Press, 2002), p. 384.

NOTES TO CHAPTER 2

1. Carolus Linnaeus, "Tal" (1759), p. 92, quoted in Lisbet Koerner, *Linnaeus: Nature and Nation* (Cambridge: Harvard University Press, 1999), p. 94.

2. Johann Friedrich Blumenbach, *Contributions to Natural History* (1806), 2d ed., part 1, in *The Anthropological Treatises of Johann Friedrich Blumenbach*, ed. Thomas Bendyshe (Boston: Milford House, 1973; reprint of the 1865 edition, London: Longman, Green, Longman, Roberts, and Green), p. 298. Hereafter I will cite this text in parentheses as CNH.

3. Johann Friedrich Blumenbach, *On the Natural Variety of Mankind* (De Generis Humani Varietate Nativa), 3d ed. (1795), in *Anthropological Treatises of Johann Friedrich Blumenbach*, ed. Bendyshe. Hereafter this work will be cited in parentheses as ONVM, followed by the year of its edition. Blumenbach later called these five "races."

4. John Locke, *Second Treatise of Government*, ed. C. B. Macpherson (Indianapolis: Hackett, 1980), p. 9. Evidence indicates that Locke began to write his *Two Treatises* in 1679, before Bernier's "New Division," but published it only after the Glorious Revolution of 1688; See Macpherson, "Editor's Introduction," p. ix.

5. See Max Horkheimer and Theodore W. Adorno, *The Dialectic of Enlightenment*, trans. John Cumming (New York: Seabury Press, 1973); Michel Foucault, "What Is Enlightenment?" in *The Foucault Reader*, ed. Paul Rabinow (New York: Pantheon, 1984). George Fredrickson explains that the Enlightenment's "simultaneous challenge to hierarchies based on faith, superstition, and prejudice [was

joined with] the temptation it presented to create new ones based on reason, science, and history." See George M. Fredrickson, *Racism: A Short History* (Princeton: Princeton University Press, 2002), p. 63.

6. Karl Marx, *Capital,* vol. 3, ed. Frederick Engels (New York: International Publishers, [1894] 1967), p. 820.

7. On racialism, racism, and the Enlightenment, see *Race and the Enlightenment: A Reader,* ed. Emmanuel Chukwudi Eze (Oxford: Blackwell, 1997).

8. Siep Stuurman, "François Bernier and the Invention of Racial Classification," *History Workshop Journal,* no. 50 (Autumn 2000), pp. 10–13 (quoting Bernier, *Abrégé de la Philosophie de Gassendi,* 3d ed. [Paris: Fayard, 1992; orig. 1684], vol. 1, p. 39).

9. John Locke, *Two Treatises of Government (First Treatise),* ed. Peter Laslett (Cambridge: Cambridge University Press, 1988), p. 141.

10. *The Works of John Locke* (London: Thomas Tegg, 1823), vol. 10, p. 196, quoted in James Farr, "'So Vile and Miserable an Estate': The Problem of Slavery in Locke's Political Thought," *Political Theory* 14 (May 1986), pp. 263–89, at 265–66.

11. Anthony Pagden, *Peoples and Empires* (New York: Modern Library, 2001), p. 108. Bernier appears to have influenced the development of Locke's philosophical anthropology. See Stuurman, "François Bernier," pp. 1 and 17n.5. On the relationship between Locke's ideas about slavery and his philosophy, see Farr, "'So Vile and Miserable an Estate'"; Naomi Zack, *Bachelors of Science: Seventeenth-Century Identity, Then and Now* (Philadelphia: Temple University Press, 1996), pp. 171–78.

12. Zack, *Bachelors of Science,* pp. 172–81; Farr, "'So Vile and Miserable an Estate,'" pp. 277–81; Winthrop Jordan, *White over Black: American Attitudes toward the Negro, 1550–1812* (Baltimore: Penguin, 1969), pp. 3–98; and chapter 1, above.

13. Jordan, *White over Black,* p. xiii.

14. Fredrickson, *Racism,* pp. 11–12.

15. Ibid., p. 11.

16. Kenan Malik, *The Meaning of Race: Race, History and Culture in Western Society* (Houndsmills, Basingstoke: Macmillan, 1996), p. 40.

17. E. J. Hobsbawm, *The Age of Revolution, 1789–1848* (New York: New American Library, 1962), pp. 38, 81.

18. Malik, *Meaning of Race,* p. 39.

19. Jonathan Dewald, "The Early Modern Period," in *Encyclopedia of European Social History: From 1350–2000,* vol. 1 (New York: Charles Scribner's Sons, 2001), p. 172.

20. Ibid., p. 173.

21. In his *Notes on the State of Virginia* (1785), Jefferson said, "It is not against experience to suppose that different species of the same genus, or varieties of the same species, may possess different qualifications." See Thomas Jefferson, *Notes on the State of Virginia,* excerpt in *Documents of American Prejudice: An Anthology of*

*Writings on Race from Thomas Jefferson to David Duke,* ed. S. T. Joshi (New York: Basic Books, 1999), p. 11.

22. Eric Voegelin, *The History of the Race Idea: From Ray to Carus,* trans. Ruth Hein, ed. Klaus Vondung, in *The Collected Works of Eric Voegelin* (Baton Rouge: Louisiana State University Press, [1933] 1998), p. 54.

23. *The Works of Voltaire: A Contemporary Version with Notes by Tobias Smollett,* rev. and modernized by William F. Fleming (New York, 1901), vol. 39, pp. 240–41, quoted in Thomas F. Gossett, *Race: The History of an Idea in America,* new ed. (Oxford: Oxford University Press, [1963] 1997), p. 45; Fredrickson, *Racism,* p. 62.

24. Lord Kames, *Sketches of the History of Man Considerably Enlarged by the Last Addition and Corrections of the Author* (Edinburgh, [1774] 1788), vol. 1, pp. 12–13, quoted in Gossett, *Race,* p. 45.

25. Gossett, *Race,* pp. 46–47, 50.

26. The great Scottish philosopher David Hume also affirmed this view in a notorious footnote to his essay "Of National Character" (1748), which he added between 1753 and 1754: "I am apt to suspect the Negroes and in general all other species of men (for there are four or five different kinds) to be naturally inferior to the whites. There was never a civilized nation of any other complexion than white, nor even any individual eminent in action or speculation." See David Hume, "Of National Character," in *Essays: Moral, Political, and Literary,* ed. T. H. Green and T. H. Grose, 2 vols. (London, 1875), vol. 1, p. 252, quoted in Jordan, *White over Black,* p. 253.

27. Frank Spencer, *Ecce Homo: An Annotated Bibliographic History of Physical Anthropology* (New York: Greenwood Press, 1986), p. 101.

28. Reginald Horsman, *Race and Manifest Destiny* (Cambridge: Harvard University Press, 1981), pp. 59–50; Léon Poliakov, *The Aryan Myth: A History of Racist and Nationalist Ideas in Europe,* trans. Edmund Howard (New York: Basic Books, 1974), p. 178.

29. Edward Long, *The History of Jamaica,* 3 vols. (London: Lownes, 1774), pp. 351–75, quoted in Spencer, *Ecce Homo,* p. 101.

30. The idea that humankind may have had multiple origins was considered by, among others, the tenth-century historian al-Masudi, the fourteenth-century Spanish monk Tomas Scotus, and Paracelsus and Giordano Bruno in the sixteenth century. In 1655, French Protestant Isaac de la Peyrère asserted that there were two separate creations in the book of Genesis and that there was a race of men before Adam ("Pre-Adamites"). See Poliakov, *Aryan Myth,* pp. 132–33; Gossett, *Race,* p. 15.

31. Gottfried W. von Leibniz, *Otium Hanoveranum sive Miscellanes ex ore . . .* (Leipzig, 1718), p. 37, quoted in Gossett, *Race,* pp. 34–35.

32. Carl von Linné (Carolus Linnaeus), "The God-given Order of Nature," excerpt from *The System of Nature,* vol. 1 (London: Lackington, Allen and Co., 1806), in *Race and the Enlightenment,* ed. Eze, p. 12.

33. Koerner, *Linnaeus,* p. 16.

34. Linné, "God-given Order of Nature," pp. 12–13.

35. Koerner, *Linnaeus,* pp. 26–30; Linnaeus, *Deliciae Naturae* (1772), p. 108, quoted in Koerner, *Linnaeus,* p. 25.

36. Koerner, *Linnaeus,* pp. 31, 15–16.

37. Phillip Sloan, "The Gaze of Natural History," in *Inventing Human Science: Eighteenth Century Domains,* ed. Christopher Fox, Roy Porter, and Robert Wokler (Berkeley: University of California Press, 1995); E. C. Spary, "Linnaeus, Carolus," in *Encyclopedia of the Enlightenment,* vol. 2 (Oxford: Oxford University Press, 2002), pp. 410–13.

38. Sloan, "Gaze of Natural History," p. 122.

39. Carolus Linnaeus, *Systema Naturea,* 10th ed. (Stockholm, 1758–59), pp. 20–22, quoted in *Readings in Early Anthropology,* ed. J. S. Slotkin (Chicago: Aldine, 1965), pp. 177–78. The partial translation for the "Monstrous" category is taken from Walter Scheidt, "The Race Concept in Anthropology and the Divisions into Human Races from Linnaeus to Deniker" (1924–25), in *This Is Race: An Anthology Selected from International Literature on the Races of Man,* ed. Earl W. Count (New York: Henry Schuman, 1950), p. 357.

40. Linnaeus distinguished four *genera* in the order Primates: *Homo, Simia, Lemur,* and *Vespertilio* (bats). See Gunnar Brøberg, "Linnaeus' Anthropology," *History of Physical Anthropology: An Encyclopedia,* vol. 1 (New York: Garland Publishing, 1997), p. 617.

41. Sloan, "Gaze of Natural History," p. 122; Brøberg, "Linnaeus' Anthropology," pp. 616–18.

42. Voegelin, *History of the Race Idea,* p. 41; C. Loring Brace, "Chain of Being," in *History of Physical Anthropology,* vol. 1, p. 260.

43. Sloan, "Gaze of Natural History," p. 123.

44. This claim generated intense criticism from Blumenbach, among others, since it seemed to blur the boundary between human beings and the rest of the natural world. Yet Linnaeus's view of an affinity between humans and apes was borne out by Darwin's later evolutionary thesis. Cf. Brøberg, "Linnaeus' Anthropology," p. 617; Sloan, "Gaze of Natural History," p. 123; Koerner, *Linnaeus,* p. 87.

45. C. Linnaeus, *Fauna Suecia,* trans. T. Bendyshe (London, 1863–64), quoted in Slotkin, ed., *Readings,* p. 179.

46. Ibid. Blumenbach would later make more of this human capacity.

47. Sloan, "Gaze of Natural History," pp. 123–26.

48. Ibid.; Voegelin, *History of the Race Idea,* p. 53.

49. Johann Friedrich Blumenbach, *On the Natural Variety of Mankind,* 1st ed. (1775), in *Anthropological Treatises of Johann Friedrich Blumenbach,* ed. Bendyshe, p. 99.

50. Koerner, *Linnaeus,* p. 61.

51. Ibid., pp. 59–76.

52. See Linnaeus, *Fauna Suecia,* quoted in Slotkin, ed., *Readings,* p. 178; Brøberg, "Linnaeus' Anthropology," p. 617; Koerner, *Linnaeus,* p. 57.

53. Johannes Schefferus published an early anthropological monograph, *Lapponia* (1673), but without ever visiting Lapland. Harald Vallerius considered Laplanders in a 1705 essay on the origin and physical appearance of human races. Vallerius, who probably influenced Linnaeus, identified four major divisions of human beings: Ethiopians; Lapps and Samojeds; Italians, Spaniards, and French; and "Leuko-Ethiopians," or "white negroes." See Slotkin, ed., *Readings,* p. 96; Koerner, *Linnaeus,* p. 57; Per Holck, "Sweden," in *History of Physical Anthropology: An Encyclopedia,* vol. 2, p. 1005.

54. Phillip R. Sloan, "Buffon, Georges-Louis Leclerce de," in *Encyclopedia of the Enlightenment,* vol. 1 (Oxford: Oxford University Press, 2003), p. 177.

55. Comte de Buffon, "Premier discours," in *Histoire naturelle générale et particulière,* vol. 1 (Paris, 1749), quoted in Sloan, "Gaze of Natural History," p. 130.

56. Jonathan Marks, "Buffon's Natural History," in *History of Physical Anthropology,* vol. 1, p. 233; Voegelin, *History of the Race Idea,* pp. 54–56.

57. Comte de Buffon, *Histoire naturelle, générale et particulière,* vol. 4, p. 172, quoted in Voegelin, *History of the Race Idea,* p. 46n.3

58. Marks, "Buffon's Natural History," p. 233.

59. Comte de Buffon, "L'Asne," in *Histoire naturelle générale et particulière,* vol. 4 (Paris, 1753), quoted in Sloan, "Gaze of Natural History," p. 132.

60. Sloan, "Gaze of Natural History," pp. 132–33.

61. Comte de Buffon, *A Natural History, General and Particular* (1749 [1860]), in *This Is Race,* ed. Count, 15.

62. Ibid., p. 3.

63. Buffon, *Histoire naturelle, générale et particulière,* 4th ed. (Paris, 1752), vol. 6, p. 58, quoted in Voegelin, *History of the Race Idea,* p. 58n.2.

64. Buffon, *Natural History,* in *This Is Race,* ed. Count, pp. 3–14.

65. Ibid., p. 15.

66. Marks, "Buffon's Natural History," p. 232; Sloan, "Gaze of Natural History," pp. 135–36.

67. Buffon, *Natural History,* in *This Is Race,* ed. Count, pp. 15, 14.

68. Ibid., p. 15.

69. Ibid., p. 14.

70. Voegelin, *History of the Race Idea,* p. 64; Tzvetan Todorov, *On Human Diversity: Nationalism, Racism, and Exoticism in French Thought,* trans. Catherine Porter (Cambridge: Harvard University Press, 1993), pp. 96–106.

71. Comte de Buffon, *Natural History* (1817), p. 398, quoted in Todorov, *On Human Diversity,* p. 97.

72. Spencer, *Ecce Homo,* p. 87.

73. Buffon extended the figure to 2,993,280 years in some unpublished manuscripts. See Sloan, "Buffon," p. 178.

74. Robert Bernasconi and Tommy Lott, "Introduction," in *The Idea of Race,* ed. Robert Bernasconi and Tommy Lott (Indianapolis: Hackett, 2000), p. viii.

75. John H. Zammito, "Kant, Immanuel," in *Encyclopedia of the Enlightenment,* vol. 2 (Oxford: Oxford University Press, 2003).

76. Robert Bernasconi, "Will the Real Kant Please Stand Up: The Challenge of Enlightenment Racism to the Study of Philosophy," *Radical Philosophy,* no. 117 (January/February 2003), pp. 13–22.

77. Immanuel Kant, *Observations on the Feeling of the Beautiful and Sublime* (1764), excerpt in *The Portable Enlightenment Reader,* ed. Isaac Kramnick (New York and London: Penguin Books, 1995), pp. 637–38.

78. Bernasconi and Lott, "Introduction," p. viii. He returned again to the issue in 1785 and 1788, during his crucial "critical" period, when he published his *Critique of Pure Reason, Critique of Practical Reason,* and *Critique of Judgment.* See David Bindman, *Ape to Apollo: Aesthetics and the Idea of Race in the Eighteenth Century* (London: Reaktion Books, 2002), pp. 181–89; Nicholas Jardine, *The Scenes of Inquiry: On the Reality of Questions in Science,* 2d ed. (Oxford: Clarendon Press, 2000), pp. 28–33.

79. Immanuel Kant, "Different Human Races," in *Idea of Race,* ed. Bernasconi and Lott p. 9.

80. Ibid.

81. Ibid., pp. 9–10.

82. Ibid., pp. 10–11. "Natural history," he explained, "would teach us about how changes in the earth's form, including changing that the earth's creatures (plants and animals) have sustained as a result of migrations, and about the deviations from the prototypes of the lineal root genus that have originated as a consequence of migrations. Natural history would presumably lead us back from the great number of seemingly different species to races of the same genus" (p. 13n.1).

83. Voegelin, *History of the Race Idea,* p. 6.

84. Kant, "Different Human Races," p. 9; Peter McLaughlin, "Blumenbach, Johann Friedrich (1752–1840)," in *Encyclopedia of the Enlightenment,* vol. 1, p. 156. Kant more clearly anticipates what George Stocking calls "neo-polygenism," an approach to race differences that developed after Darwin's work effectively ended polygenism proper. See George W. Stocking Jr., *Race, Culture and Evolution: Essays in the History of Anthropology* (New York: Free Press, 1968), chap. 3; and chapter 4, below.

85. Voegelin, *History of the Race Idea,* p. 76.

86. He supported this claim by appealing to David Hume's authority: "Mr. Hume challenges anyone to cite a single example in which a Negro has shown talents, and asserts that among the hundreds of thousands of blacks who are transported elsewhere from their countries, although many of them have been set free, still not a single one was ever found who presented anything great in art or science or any other praiseworthy quality, even though among the whites some continually rise aloft from the rabble." See Kant, *Observations,* p. 638.

87. Kant, "Different Human Races," pp. 11–12.

88. Ibid., p. 11.

89. Bernasconi and Lott, ed., *Idea of Race,* p. 5. Norman Davies writes, typically, "The notion that all the peoples of Europe belonged to one white race which originated in the Caucasus can be traced to a learned professor at Göttingen, Johann Friedrich Blumenbach." See his *Europe: A History* (New York: HarperPerennial, 1998), p. 734.

90. His other publications ranged from his *Handbook of Natural History,* which went through ten editions (1779–1830), to articles "On the Love of Animals" (1781) and "On the Natural History of Serpents" (1788), to his *Introduction to the Literary History of Medicine* (1786). See K. F. H. Marx, "Life of Blumenbach" (1840), in *Anthropological Treatises of Johann Friedrich Blumenbach,* ed. Bendyshe, pp. 3–45; McLaughlin, "Blumenbach," p. 156; Jardine, *Scenes of Inquiry,* pp. 22–28.

91. Johann Friedrich Blumenbach, "Introductory Letter to Joseph Banks" (ONVM, 1795, 150); Jordan, *White over Black,* pp. 221–22.

92. Polygenism, he thought, "found particular favour with those who made it their business to throw doubt on the accuracy of Scripture" (ONVM, 1775, 98). This point is particularly apt with respect to Voltaire's polygenism. See Fredrickson, *Racism,* p. 63.

93. Londa Schiebinger, "The Anatomy of Difference: Race and Sex in Eighteenth Century Science," *Eighteenth-Century Studies* 23, no. 4 (Summer 1990), p. 396; Bindman, *Ape to Apollo,* p. 220.

94. Johann Friedrich Blumenbach, *On the Natural Variety of Mankind,* 2d ed. (1781), in *Anthropological Treatises of Johann Friedrich Blumenbach,* ed. Bendyshe, p. 99n.4. The editor of the English edition of Blumenbach's *Anthropological Treatises* included excerpts from the 1781 edition of *On the Natural Variety of Mankind* in footnotes to the first edition.

95. Eric Voegelin, "The Growth of the Race Idea," *Review of Politics* 2 (July 1940), p. 297. Blumenbach, however, never quite accepted Kant's idea that the "races" were irreversible, natural subdivisions of human beings. See McLaughlin, "Blumenbach," p. 156.

96. See also Johann Friedrich Blumenbach, *Abbildungen naturhistorischer Gegenstände* (Göttingen: Bey Heinrich Dieterich, 1810).

97. Martin Bernal, *Black Athena Writes Back: Martin Bernal Responds to His Critics,* ed. David Chioni Moore (Durham: Duke University Press, 2001), pp. 182–83; Bindman, *Ape to Apollo,* pp. 190–201.

98. In *Contributions to Natural History* (1806), Blumenbach said that "all the differences in mankind, however surprising they may be at first glance, seem, upon a nearer inspection, to run into one another by unnoticed passages and shapes; no other very definite boundaries can be drawn between these varieties, especially if, as is but fair, respect is had not only to one or the other, but also to

the peculiarities of a natural system, dependent upon all bodily indications alike" (CNH, 303).

99. Voegelin, "Growth of the Race Idea," p. 297; Stephen Jay Gould, "The Geometer of Race," *Discover* 15, November 1994, pp. 65–69, at 69.

100. Gould, "Geometer of Race," p. 68.

101. Fredrickson notes, "The neoclassical conceptions of beauty that prevailed in eighteenth-century Europe and America were based primarily on Greek and Roman statuary. The milky whiteness of marble and the facial features and bodily form of the Apollos and Venuses that were coming to light during the seventeenth and eighteenth centuries created a standard from which Africans were bound to deviate." See Fredrickson, *Racism*, pp. 59–60; Bindman, *Ape to Apollo*, pp. 81–92

102. He maintained that his collection of skulls had been useful "for the determination of the really most beautiful form of skull, which my beautiful typical head of a young Georgian female always of itself attracts every eye, however little observant" (CNH, 300). He also indicated his indebtedness to the neoclassical norm of beauty along with his reluctance to make hard and fast generalizations about the relative beauty or ugliness of the different races. In discussing the Negro, he wrote, "As to the physiognomy of the negro, the difference no doubt is astonishing if you put an ugly negro (and there are ugly negroes as well as ugly Europeans) exactly opposite the Greek ideal. . . . If, on the contrary, one investigates the transitional forms in this case also, the striking contrast . . . vanishes away" (CNH, 306).

103. Schiebinger, "Anatomy of Difference," p. 396. European men were the standard of comparison for European women and non-European men. Non-European women were typically left out of such comparisons.

104. This view stood in contrast to Kant's view that four contemporary human "races" all descended from one earlier "lineal root genus" of white and brownish or "brunette" inhabitants from the temperate zone of the "old world." See Kant, "Different Human Races," p. 19.

105. Daniel Pick, *Faces of Degeneration: A European Disorder, c. 1848–c. 1918* (Cambridge: Cambridge University Press, 1989).

106. Gould, "Geometer of Race," p. 68.

107. Ibid., pp. 66–68.

108. Alan Frost, "The Pacific Ocean: The Eighteenth Century's 'New World,'" in *Facing Each Other: The World's Perception of Europe and Europe's Perception of the World*, part 1, ed. Anthony Pagden (Aldershot: Ashgate, 2000), pp. 625–26; Bindman, *Ape to Apollo*, p. 201. In the third edition of his book (1795), Blumenbach named his fifth variety "Malay" "because the majority of men in this variety . . . use the Malay idiom" (ONVM, 1795, 275).

109. Likewise, he distinguished "the Chinese and Japanese from the Mongolian; the Hottentots from the Ethiopian; so also the North American Indians from those in the southern half of the new world; and the black Papuans in New Hol-

land, &c. from the brown Otaheitans and other islanders of the Pacific Ocean" (CNH, 304).

110. Martin Bernal, *Black Athena: The Afroasiatic Roots of Classical Civilization*, vol. 1: *The Fabrication of Ancient Greece, 1785–1985* (New Brunswick: Rutgers University Press, 1987), p. 219.

111. "Asia," in *The New Encyclopaedia Britannica*, vol. 14 (Chicago: Encyclopaedia Britannica, Inc., 1997), p. 170; Ivor H. Evans, *Brewer's Dictionary of Phrase and Fable*, rev. ed. (London: Cassell, 1981), pp. 896, 491–92.

112. Bernal, *Black Athena*, p. 219. The Bible is vague about the resting place of Noah's ark, identifying "the mountains of Ararat" in Genesis 8:4, and commentators from the early Christian period to the late Middle Ages located its resting place variously: for instance, on Mount Taurus or Mount Lubar. Many early translations of the Bible rendered "Ararat" as "Armenia," which is in the southern Caucasus. The idea that the ark landed on a specific "Mount Ararat" was part of a later tradition of interpretation. See Don Cameron Allen, *The Legend of Noah: Renaissance Rationalism in Art, Science, and Letters* (Urbana: University of Illinois Press, 1963), p. 73.

113. John Chardin, *Travels of Sir John Chardin into Persia and the East Indies, through the Black-Sea and the Country of Colchis* (London: Moses Pitt, 1686), p. 189.

114. Ibid., p. 253, emphasis in the original.

115. Janet Browne, *The Secular Ark: Studies in the History of Biogeography* (New Haven: Yale University Press, 1983), p. 26. The belief that the human species originated in western Asia, near the Caucasus Mountains, was reiterated in geography texts up through the middle of the nineteenth century. See J. M. Blaut, *The Colonizer's Model of the World: Geographical Diffusionism and Eurocentric History* (New York and London: Guilford Press, 1993), p. 43n.2.

116. Scheidt, "Race Concept in Anthropology," p. 367; Spencer, *Ecce Homo*, p. 107.

117. Bindman, *Ape to Apollo*, p. 25.

118. Oliver Goldsmith, *History of the Earth, and Animated Nature* (London: J. Nourse, 1774), vol. 2, pp. 230–31.

119. He included southern Europeans, as well as Abyssinians, Turks, Samoeides, and Laplanders, in a "light brown race" and "almost all the remaining Europeans," along with Georgians and Mingrelians, and possibly Pacific islanders, in a "white race." See John Hunter, *Inaugural Disputation on the Varieties of Man*, in *Anthropological Treatises of Johann Friedrich Blumenbach*, ed. Bendyshe, pp. 367, 363.

120. The English version of Chardin's text reads: "The Complexion of *Georgian* is the most beautiful in all the East; and I can fairly say, That I never saw an ill-favour'd Countenance in all that Country, either of the one or the other Sex." See Chardin, *Travels*, p. 190, emphasis in the original.

121. Chardin, *Travels,* pp. 190–91.

122. John H. Zammito, *Kant, Herder, and the Birth of Anthropology* (Chicago: University of Chicago Press, 2002), pp. 9–10, 183, 246, 302–7, 344–45. Kant pursued related anthropological concerns in his writings on race in the 1770s. Johann Gottfried Herder, a student and rival of Kant, was the outstanding intellectual figure to emerge from these developments. I discuss some of his ideas at the end of this chapter.

123. [Christoph Meiners], *Revision der Philosophie* (Göttingen and Gotha: Dietrich, 1772), p. 139, quoted in Zammito, *Kant, Herder,* p. 249. Meiners published this book anonymously.

124. Christoph Meiners, *Grundriss der Geschichte der Menschheit* (Lemgo, 1785), Borrede (foreword), paragraph 11. All translations from the first edition of Meiners's book are by Anna Karlen.

125. Ibid., p. 6. In the 1793 edition of the *Grundriss,* he added that there "are no lands more fertile in Asia, and even in the whole world, as the Caucasian: in particular Mingrelia, Georgia, Circassia, and the neighboring regions." See Christoph Meiners, *Grundriss der Geschichte der Menschheit,* 2d ed. (Lemgo, 1793), p. 49. All translations from the 1793 edition of Meiners's book are by Taiwo Adetunji Osinubi.

126. Meiners, *Grundriss* (1785), p. 6. Meiners reiterates this claim in the 1793 edition of his book: the Mongolians are "so different from the inhabitants of the Caucasus region and their descendants in physiognomy, intellectual capabilities and temperament, that one could consider this branch the result or remnant of an altogether different genesis." See Meiners, *Grundriss* (1793), p. 47.

127. Meiners, *Grundriss* (1785), pp. 30–31. Meiners repeated this claim almost verbatim in the 1793 edition of his book. See Meiners, *Grundriss* (1793) pp. 74–75. *Tartar* refers to "a member of a group of Turkic peoples inhabiting parts of European and Asiatic Russia, especially parts of Siberia, the Crimea, the Caucasus, and districts along the Volga." See *The Canadian Oxford Dictionary* (Oxford: Oxford University Press, 1998), p. 1485.

128. Meiners, *Grundriss* (1785), pp. 26–27.

129. Spencer, *Ecce Homo,* p. 340; Horsman, *Race,* p. 33.

130. William Jones, *Works of William Jones: Anniversary Discourses* (1784–1789), ed. A. M. Jones (London, 1807), pp. 340–41, quoted in Spencer, *Ecce Homo,* pp. 111–12.

131. Poliakov, *Aryan Myth,* pp. 189–90.

132. Meiners, *Grundriss* (1793), pp. 4–6.

133. Ibid., pp. 5, 74.

134. Ibid., pp. 109, 115–16, 123. At the same time, he claimed that among the whites "the Slavs and eastern peoples have a stronger predilection for sensual lust than the Celtic nations," and that among the latter "the southerners are more sensual then the northerners" (p. 123).

135. Ibid., pp. 75, 7.

136. Ibid., p. 75.

137. Ibid., p. 122.

138. Meiners, in *Göttingisches Historisches Magazin,* 8 (1790), pp. 119ff., quoted in Bindman, *Ape to Apollo,* p. 219.

139. Bindman, *Ape to Apollo,* p. 220.

140. The 1865 English translation of Blumenbach's Latin has him speaking of "the Jewish race" here, but this is likely a mistranslation. David Bindman notes that Blumenbach generally spoke in such cases of the "nation face" or "national" physiognomy, but "in the nineteenth-century translation [this] becomes, inevitably, 'racial face'" (Bindman, *Ape to Apollo,* p. 201). In the 3d ed., Blumenbach reiterated that all Jews could be identified by the same "fundamental configuration of the face," which displayed "a racial character almost universal" (ONVM, 1795, 234).

141. "Meiners," Blumenbach wrote, "refers all nations to two stocks: (1) handsome, (2) ugly; the first white, the latter dark. He includes in the handsome stock the Celts, Sarmatians, and oriental nations. The ugly stock embraces the rest of mankind" (ONVM, 1795, 268).

142. Bindman, *Ape to Apollo,* pp. 154, 219, 244n.14.

143. Ibid., p. 201.

144. Gould, "Geometer of Race," p. 67; Bindman, *Ape to Apollo,* p. 201.

145. See also Bindman, *Ape to Apollo,* p. 197 (regarding a similar illustration in *Contributions to Natural History,* 2d ed.); Schiebinger, "Anatomy of Difference," p. 398.

146. In *Abbildungen naturhistorischer Gegenstände,* Blumenbach repeated his view that over time the "Caucasian race . . . changed into two extremes, namely on one hand the Mongolian race with the flat face, and on the other hand the Ethiopian with the prominent jaw." See Blumenbach, *Abbildungen,* "I-5. Characterisische Musterköpfe von Mänern aus den 5 Hauptrassen im Menschengeshlechte," paragraph 6.

147. Isidore Geoffroy Saint-Hilaire, *Classification Anthropologique,* Mém. de la Soc. d'Anthrop. de Paris, vol. 1, p. 129, sq., quoted in Thomas Bendyshe, "Editor's Preface," in *Anthropological Treatises of Johann Friedrich Blumenbach,* p. xi.

148. Bindman, *Ape to Apollo,* pp. 203–9; Nancy Stepan, *The Idea of Race in Science: Great Britain 1800–1960* (London: Macmillan, 1982), pp. 8–9.

149. See Anne Laura Stoler, "Racial Histories and their Regimes of Truth," *Political Power and Social Theory* 11 (1997), p. 190; Schiebinger, "Anatomy of Difference."

150. Benjamin Franklin, *Observations concerning the Increase of Mankind* (1751), in Leonard W. Larabee et al., eds., *The Papers of Benjamin Franklin* (New Haven: Yale University Press, 1959– ), vol. 4, p. 234, quoted in Jordan, *Black over White,* p. 254. Similarly, the English writer John Pinkerton argued in his *Disserta-*

*tion on the Origin of the Scythians or Goths* (1787) that the Celts were an inferior people "who had been driven out of much of Europe by the Goths—a term which included Greeks and Romans as well as Germans and Scandinavians." See Horsman, *Race*, p. 31.

151. Johann Gottfried Herder, *Ideas on the Philosophy of the History of Humankind* (1784), 3d ed. (1828), trans. Thomas Nenon (1999), in *Idea of Race*, ed. Bernasconi and Lott, p. 25, Herder's emphasis.

152. Ibid., p. 26, Herder's emphasis.

153. Herder provocatively said that "the negro has as much right to term his savage robbers albinos and white devils . . . as we have to deem him the emblem of evil, and a descendent of Ham." He also spoke, however, of "the negro race" and "the negro form" and said that the "finer intellect" of the European was "incompatible" with the physical "structure" given to the "negro." See Johann Gottfried Herder, "Organization of the Peoples of Africa," excerpt from *Ideas on the Philosophy of the History of Humankind,* in *Race and the Enlightenment,* ed. Eze, pp. 71, 73, 77. See also Fredrickson, *Racism*, p. 70.

NOTES TO CHAPTER 3

1. [William B. Carpenter], "Ethnology, or the Science of Races," *Edinburgh Review* 88 (October 1848), pp. 429–87, at 434.

2. Johann Friedrich Blumenbach, *On the Natural Variety of Mankind*, 3rd ed. (1795), in *The Anthropological Treatises of Johann Friedrich Blumenbach,* ed. Thomas Bendyshe (London: Longman, Green, Longman, Roberts, and Green, 1865), pp. 264–65, emphasis in the original.

3. George W. Stocking Jr., *Race, Culture, and Evolution: Essays in the History of Anthropology* (New York: Free Press, 1968), p. 28.

4. Alexander von Humboldt, *Cosmos: A Sketch of a Physical Description of the Universe,* trans. E. C. Otté (London, 1848), quoted in Léon Poliakov, *The Aryan Myth: A History of Racist and Nationalist Ideas in Europe,* trans. Edmund Howard (New York: Basic Books, 1974), pp. 174–75.

5. Marvin Harris, *The Rise of Anthropological Theory: A History of Theories of Culture,* updated ed., introduction by Maxine L. Margolis (Walnut Creek: AltaMira Press, 2001), p. 81.

6. Stocking, *Race, Culture, and Evolution,* pp. 35–36.

7. Norman Davies, *Europe: A History* (New York: HarperPerennial, 1998), p. 677; E. J. Hobsbawm, *The Age of Revolution, 1789–1848* (New York: New American Library, 1962), chap. 3.

8. George M. Fredrickson, *Racism: A Short History* (Princeton: Princeton University Press, 2002), p. 69.

9. Frank E. Manuel, "From Equality to Organicism," *Journal of the History of Ideas* 17 (January 1956), p. 54; Poliakov, *Aryan Myth*, p. 205.

10. David Bindman, *Ape to Apollo: Aesthetics and the Idea of Race in the Eighteenth Century* (London: Reaktion Books, 2002), p. 221.

11. Winthrop D. Jordan, *White over Black: American Attitudes toward the Negro, 1550–1812* (Baltimore: Penguin, 1969), p. 498; Thomas F. Gossett, *Race: The History of an Idea in America*, new ed. (Oxford: Oxford University Press, [1963] 1997), p. 50.

12. Gossett, *Race*, pp. 47–48.

13. Charles White, *An Account of the Regular Gradation in Man* . . . (London, 1799), p. 34, quoted in Gossett, *Race*, p. 49.

14. Charles White, *An Account of the Regular Gradation in Man, and in Different Animals and Vegetables* . . . (London, 1799), pp. 134–35, quoted in Poliakov, *Aryan Myth*, pp. 158–59.

15. Jean-Joseph Virey, *Histoire naturelle du genre humain* (1800–1801), pp. 145–46, quoted in Poliakov, *Aryan Myth*, p. 180. Meiners also joined the reactionary movement, writing a defense of slavery during the second year of the French Revolution. See Bindman, *Ape to Apollo*, p. 221.

16. Manuel, "Equality to Organicism," p. 65; Hobsbawm, *Age of Revolution*, p. 285.

17. *Lettres d'un habitant de Genève, Oeuvres de Claude-Henri de Saint-Simon* (Paris, 1966), vol. 1, p. 46, quoted in Poliakov, *Aryan Myth*, p. 217; Fredrickson, *Racism*, p. 67.

18. Poliakov, *Aryan Myth*, pp. 99–101.

19. Friedrich Schlegel, quoted in Poliakov, *Aryan Myth*, pp. 191–92.

20. Poliakov, *Aryan Myth*, pp. 190–93; George W. Stocking Jr., *Victorian Anthropology* (New York: Free Press, 1987), p. 23.

21. Hobsbawm, *Age of Revolution*, p. 164.

22. Ibid., pp. 52, 351–52.

23. Ibid., pp. 59–60; Leslie Page Moch, "Migration," in *Encyclopedia of European Social History: From 1350–2000*, vol. 2 (New York: Charles Scribner's Sons, 2001), p. 134.

24. George Fredrickson, "Social Origins of American Racism," in *Racism*, ed. Martin Bulmer and John Solomos (Oxford: Oxford University Press, 1999), p. 81; Audrey Smedley, *Race in North America*, 2d ed. (Boulder: Westview Press, 1998), pp. 226–27.

25. Smedley, *Race in North America*, p. 232.

26. Davies, *Europe*, pp. 637, 831; Hobsbawm, *Age of Revolution*, pp. 136, 355; Thomas Macaulay, quoted in Anthony Pagden, *Peoples and Empires: A Short History of European Migration Exploration and Conquest from Greece to the Present* (New York: Modern Library, 2001), p. 152.

27. Michel Foucault, *The Order of Things: An Archaeology of the Human Sciences* (New York: Vintage, 1973), p. 270.

28. Nancy Stepan, *The Idea of Race in Science: Great Britain 1800–1960* (London: Macmillan, 1982), p. 40.

29. Ibid., p. 21.

30. Ibid., pp. 22, 26.

31. Ibid., pp. 40–45.

32. Stocking, *Victorian Anthropology,* pp. 49–52.

33. Ibid., pp. 49–52, 244.

34. Carpenter, "Ethnology." The 1875 edition of *Chambers's Information for the People* reported, "Ethnology as the science of races is only a branch of the great science [anthropology] that investigates all the phenomena presented by man as an inhabitant of the globe." See "Anthropology," *Chambers's Information for the People,* 5th ed., vol. 2 (London and Edinburgh: W. & R. Chambers, 1875), p. 53.

35. Stocking, *Victorian Anthropology,* p. 247.

36. Gossett, *Race,* chaps. 1–4; Ivan Hannaford, *Race: The History of an Idea in the West,* foreword by Bernard Crick (Baltimore: Johns Hopkins University Press, 1996).

37. American polygenists tended to speak of "types of mankind." See William Stanton, *The Leopard's Spots: Scientific Attitudes toward Race in America, 1815–59* (Chicago: University of Chicago Press, 1960).

38. Chevalier de Lamarck, *Zoological Philosophy* (1809), in *This Is Race: An Anthology Selected from International Literature on the Races of Man,* ed. Earl W. Count (New York: Henry Schuman, 1950), p. 40.

39. *Lettres de Georges Cuvier à C. M. Pfaff sur l'histoire naturelle, la politique et la littérature, 1788–1792,* trans. Louis Marchant (Paris, 1858), p. 201, letter of December 31, 1790, quoted in Stocking, *Race, Culture, and Evolution,* p. 35.

40. Peter J. Bowler, "Cuvier, Georges Léopold Chrétien Fréderic Dagobert (Baron) (1769–1832)," in *History of Physical Anthropology: An Encyclopedia,* vol. 1 (New York: Garland Publishing, 1997), p. 305.

41. Georges Cuvier, *The Animal Kingdom* (1817), trans. H. McMurtrie (New York, 1831), in *This Is Race,* ed. Count, p. 44.

42. Count, ed., *This Is Race,* p. 706; Jack Carrick Trevor, "Race," in *Chambers's Encyclopaedia,* new ed. (London: George Newnes Ltd., 1950), p. 430. For instance, in 1850, John Bachman, a U.S. minister, naturalist, critic of polygenism, *and* supporter of slavery, regarded Shem, blessed by Noah, as the "parent of the Caucasian race," the Mongolians as descended from Japheth, and Negroes as the "accursed" descendants of Ham (Bachman, quoted in Gossett, *Race,* p. 63).

43. Strictly speaking, Cuvier's scheme was not quite a tripartite one because he was unable to find a place within it for Malays, Papuans, and native Americans. Cuvier, *Animal Kingdom,* p. 46; Count, ed., *This Is Race,* p. 706.

44. Cuvier, *Animal Kingdom,* p. 44.

45. Ibid., emphasis in the original.

46. Michael Banton, "The Classification of Races in Europe and North America: 1700–1850," *International Social Science Journal,* no. 111 (February 1987), p. 53; Michael Banton, *Racial Theories* (Cambridge: Cambridge University Press, 1987), pp. 28–29.

47. Cuvier, *Animal Kingdom,* p. 44.

48. Ibid., p. 45.

49. Ibid.

50. William Lawrence, *Lectures on Physiology, Zoology, and the Natural History of Man,* 3rd ed. (London: James Smith, [1819] 1823), pp. 473–75.

51. Ibid., p. 408.

52. Ibid., pp. 411, 410.

53. Ibid., p. 415.

54. Ibid., pp. 474–75. See also Gossett, *Race,* p. 57.

55. Ibid., p. 475.

56. Ibid., p. 476.

57. Jacques Barzun, *Race: A Study in Modern Superstition,* rev. 2d ed. (New York: Harper and Row, [1937] 1965), chaps. 6–7; and chapter 4, below.

58. Gossett, *Race,* p. 57.

59. Lawrence, *Lectures,* pp. 302–3.

60. Barzun, *Race,* p. 116; Stocking, *Race, Culture, and Evolution,* pp. 56–59.

61. A. H. Keane, *Ethnology* (Cambridge: Cambridge University Press, [1896] 1909), p. 164; Trevor, "Race," p. 430.

62. Stanton, *Leopard's Spots,* pp. 30–31, 204n.10.

63. Samuel George Morton, *Crania Americana; or A Comparative View of the Skulls of Various Aboriginal Nations of North and South America; to which is prefixed an Essay on the Varieties of the Human Species* (Philadelphia: J. Dobson, 1839), p. 3.

64. Ibid., p. 5n., emphasis in the original.

65. Banton, "Classification of Races," p. 54.

66. Morton, *Crania Americana,* pp. 4–5.

67. Ibid., p. 5.

68. Ibid., pp. 5–7.

69. Ibid., p. 5.

70. Ibid., pp. 7, 8.

71. Ibid., p. 17, Morton's emphasis.

72. Ibid., pp. 16, 17.

73. Stanton, *Leopard's Spots,* p. 33; George W. Stocking Jr., "From Chronology to Ethnology: James Cowles Prichard and British Anthropology, 1800–1850," in James Cowles Prichard, *Researches into the Physical History of Man* (1813), ed. George W. Stocking Jr. (Chicago: University of Chicago Press, 1973).

74. Stephen Jay Gould, *The Mismeasure of Man,* rev. ed. (New York: W. W. Norton & Co., [1981] 1996), chap. 2.

75. Morton, *Crania Americana*, p. 260n.; Stanton, *Leopard's Spots*, pp. 32–41.

76. Samuel George Morton, [Some observations on a mode of ascertaining the internal capacity of the human cranium]; [Results of the measurements of forty-five adult negro cranium], *Proceedings*, Academy of Natural Sciences of Philadelphia, vol. 1 (1841), p. 135, *Brief Remarks*, pp. 14–15, 21–22, quoted in Stanton, *Leopard's Spots*, p. 41.

77. Morton, *Crania Americana*, p. 25.

78. Ibid., p. 29.

79. Cuvier, quoted in Morton, *Crania Americana*, p. 31.

80. Josiah Nott, *Two Lectures on the Natural History of the Caucasian and Negro Races* (Mobile: n.p., 1844), p. 8, Nott's emphasis, quoted in Robert J. C. Young, *Colonial Desire: Hybridity in Theory, Culture and Race* (London and New York: Routledge, 1995), p. 127. In *Types of Mankind*, Nott and Glidden leaned on Morton's work, but they more emphatically supported polygenist theory and its racist implications. By 1860 their book had gone through eight editions.

81. Morton also published this work as "Observations on Egyptian Ethnography, Derived from Anatomy, History, and the Monuments," in *Transactions of the Philosophical Society, Held at Philadelphia, for Promoting Useful Knowledge*, vol. 9 (1846), 93–159.

82. Morton, "Observations," quoted in James Cowles Prichard, *The Natural History of Man*, 2d enlarged ed. (London: Hippolyte Bailliere, 1845), p. 574. Morton acquired the crania from Gliddon, and he admitted that he had "no clue" as to the "the epoch to which these remains belonged" (p. 572).

83. Morton, "Observations," quoted in Prichard, *Natural History*, pp. 574–75, emphasis in the original.

84. Morton, "Observations," pp. 157–58, quoted in Young, *Colonial Desire*, pp. 128–29.

85. Stanton, *Leopard's Spots*, pp. 39–53; Young, *Colonial Desire*, chap. 5.

86. Young, *Colonial Desire*, p. 129.

87. Prichard, *Researches*, pp. 1–2.

88. Ibid., p. 2. On Prichard's status in the development of anthropology, see Stocking, "Chronology to Ethnology."

89. Prichard, *Researches*, pp. 208–32; Frank Spencer, "Prichard, James Cowles (1786–1848)," in *History of Physical Anthropology: An Encyclopedia*, vol. 2 (New York: Garland, 1997), p. 841.

90. Prichard, *Researches*, p. 233.

91. Ibid., pp. 75, 85–86.

92. Stocking, "Chronology to Ethnology," pp. ixx–lxxxiii.

93. Prichard, *Natural History*, p. 546.

94. Ibid., p. 133.

95. Ibid., pp. 133–34.

96. Ibid., p. 134.

97. Ibid., pp. 135, 136.

98. Ibid., pp. 136–38, Prichard's emphasis.

99. Ibid., pp. 139–40.

100. Stocking, "Chronology to Ethnology," pp. lxxx–lxxxiv, lxxvi.

101. Prichard, *Natural History*, p. 183.

102. Ibid., p. 253.

103. Ibid., p. 179.

104. Ibid., pp. 154, 161, 577–78.

105. Stocking, *Victorian Anthropology*, p. 53.

106. Stocking, "Chronology to Ethnology," p. ciii; Stocking, *Victorian Anthropology*, pp. 62–69; Young, *Colonial Desire*, p. 122.

107. Banton, "Classification of Races," p. 55. Smith divided his Caucasians into two groups: the "typical Caucasians," including European nations along with the Circassians and Georgians of the Caucasus, and the "Semitic Caucasians" ("Arabs; Hebrews; Babylonians, Chaldees, and Assyrians; Gaurs and Persians"). He said that the first group embraced those with "the greatest cerebral development in width and depth, combined with the highest form of beauty, strength, and powers of endurance." See Charles Hamilton Smith, *The Natural History of the Human Species* (Boston: Gould and Lincoln, 1851; orig. published in London, 1848), pp. 358–419, 383.

108. Robert Gordon Latham, *The Natural History of the Varieties of Man* (London: John van Voorst, 1850), p. 564, Latham's emphasis.

109. Ibid., Latham's emphasis.

110. Ibid., p. 14.

111. Ibid., p. 107, Latham's emphasis.

112. Ibid., Latham's emphasis.

113. Elsewhere he explained that he took the term *Dioscurian* from "the town *Dioscurias*, wherein [Roman statesman and scholar] Pliny says that 130 interpreters were wanted; so numerous were the dialects of the Caucasus." See Robert Gordon Latham, "Ethnology," in *The Encyclopaedia Britannica*, 8th ed., vol. 9 (Edinburgh: Adam and Charles Black, 1853), p. 346.

114. Latham, *Natural History*, p. 111.

115. Ibid., pp. 108–9, Latham's emphasis. He later wrote, "In the western Caucasus the physiognomy is Persian rather than Mongolian; in the eastern part it approaches the Mongolian." See Latham, "Ethnology," p. 346.

116. Ibid., pp. 511–26.

117. Ibid., pp. 471, 529–31.

118. "Physical History of Man—Ethnology," in *Chambers's Information for the People*, new ed., vol. 2 (London and Edinburgh: W. & R. Chambers, 1850), and "Anthropology," in *Chambers's Information for the People*, 5th ed., vol. 2 (London and Edinburgh: W. & R. Chambers, 1875), p. 4.

119. "Anthropology," in *Chambers's*, p. 3.

120. Carpenter, "Ethnology," p. 434. Even Latham had difficulty avoiding Blumenbach's terminology. In the *Encyclopaedia Britannica,* he wrote: "The European physiognomy is generally considered to be Caucasian as opposed to Mongolian, i.e., Caucasian in the wide, Blumenbachian, and inconvenient sense of the term." See Latham, "Ethnology," p. 350.

121. Daniel Webster, *The Works of Daniel Webster,* vol. 2 (Boston: Little, Brown and Co, 1853), pp. 212–14.

122. Benjamin Disraeli, *Coningsby, or the New Generation* (Harmondsworth: Penguin, [1844] 1983), p. 271, quoted in John M. Efron, *Defenders of the Race: Jewish Doctors and Race Science in Fin-de-Siècle Europe* (New Haven: Yale University Press, 1994), pp. 48–49.

123. John Stuart Mill, *Principles of Political Economy,* books 4 and 5, along with book 2 as an appendix, ed. Donald Winch (New York: Penguin Books, [1848] 1985), p. 113n.1.

124. Max Stirner, *The Ego and His Own* (London, 1912), trans. S. T. Byington, p. 67, quoted in Poliakov, *Aryan Myth,* p. 244, emphasis in the original.

125. Robert Gordon Latham, *Opuscula: Essays, Chiefly Philological and Ethnological* (Edinburgh: William and Norgate, [1853] 1860), p. 140, Latham's emphasis.

126. Robert Gordon Latham, *The Ethnology of Europe* (London: John van Voorst, 1852), p. 126. In the *Encyclopaedia Britannica,* Latham offered a tentative defense of the "race" concept, drawing his answer from Prichard: "Suppose an inquirer into the natural history of mankind is doubtful whether a certain division constitute[s] a *species* or a [permanent] *variety.* . . . In such a case *race* is a useful word, being one which can be used when there are doubts as to whether we are dealing with a separate species or a variety of some species already recognised." See Latham, "Ethnology," p. 341, emphasis in the original.

127. William Smellie, *The Philosophy of Natural History* (1835), quoted in Stepan, *Idea of Race,* p. 8.

128. Louis L. Snyder, *The Idea of Racialism: Its Meaning and History* (New York and Cincinnati: Van Nostrand Reinhold, 1962), p. 12.

129. Paul Broca, "On the Phenomena of Hybridity in the Genus Homo" (1855), in *This Is Race,* ed. Count, p. 69. On Broca, see Barzun, *Race,* chap. 7.

130. Charles Darwin, *The Descent of Man,* 2d ed. (1874), in *This Is Race,* ed. Count, p. 134.

131. Prichard even dedicated the second and third editions of his *Researches* to Blumenbach. See Stepan, *Idea of Race,* p. 31.

NOTES TO CHAPTER 4

1. Karl Marx to Sigfrid Meyer and August Vogt, 9 April 1870, in Karl Marx and Friedrich Engels, *Ireland and the Irish Question* (New York: International Publish-

ers, 1972), quoted in Cedric J. Robinson, *Black Marxism: The Making of the Black Radical Tradition*, foreword by Robin D. G. Kelley, with a new preface (Chapel Hill: University of North Carolina Press, [1993] 2000), p. 329n.72.

2. G. Vacher de Lapouge, *L'Aryen, son rôle social* (Paris, 1899), p. vii, quoted in Léon Poliakov, *The Aryan Myth: A History of Racist and Nationalist Ideas in Europe*, trans. Edmund Howard (New York: Basic Books, 1974), p. 270, emphasis in the original.

3. Robert Miles, *Racism after "Race Relations"* (London: Routledge, 1993), pp. 10, 60; E. J. Hobsbawm, *Nations and Nationalism since 1780*, 2d ed. (Cambridge: Cambridge University Press, 1990), p. 9. Recent scholarship has also illuminated the politically constructed character of nations. See Benedict Anderson, *Imagined Communities: Reflections of the Origins and Spread of Nationalism*, rev. ed. (London: Verso, 1991); Peter J. Geary, *The Myth of Nations: The Medieval Origins of Europe* (Princeton: Princeton University Press, 2002).

4. John Higham, *Strangers in the Land: Patterns of American Nativism 1860–1925* (New York: Antheum, 1967), p. 134. Indicative of this shift in "racial" thought, it became common for late-nineteenth-century European thinkers to speak of the "English race," "French race," and "German race."

5. Robinson, *Black Marxism*, pp. 37–38; Higham, *Strangers in the Land*, chap. 3; Gwendolyn Mink, *Old Labor and New Immigrants: Union, Party, and State, 1875–1920* (Ithaca: Cornell University Press, 1986); Robert Miles, *Racism* (London: Routledge, 1989), pp. 111–13; Lisa Lowe, *Immigrant Acts: On Asian American Cultural Politics* (Durham: Duke University Press, 1996), chap. 1.

6. Jacques Barzun, *Race: A Study in Modern Superstition* (New York, [1937] 1965), p. 134; Paul Gordon Lauren, *Power and Prejudice: The Politics and Diplomacy of Racial Discrimination* (Boulder and London: Westview, 1988), pp. 51–55.

7. Higham, *Strangers in the Land*, chap. 6; Matthew Frye Jacobson, *Whiteness of a Different Color: European Immigrants and the Alchemy of Race* (Cambridge: Harvard University Press, 1998); Barzun, *Race*.

8. On imperialism, see Norman Davies, *Europe: A History* (New York: Harper-Perennial, 1998), pp. 848–54.

9. Rudyard Kipling, "The White Man's Burden," *McClure's Magazine* 122 (February 1899), pp. 290–91.

10. Geoffrey Barraclough, *An Introduction to Contemporary History* (Harmondsworth: Penguin Books, 1967), pp. 63, 81.

11. Hilaire Belloc, "The Three Races," in *Cautionary Verses* (London: Duckworth, 1939), p. 127.

12. Cathy A. Frierson, "Peasants and Rural Laborers," in *Encyclopedia of European Social History*, vol. 3 (New York: Charles Scribner's Sons, 2001), pp. 154, 157.

13. Eric J. Hobsbawm, *The Age of Revolution, 1789–1848* (New York: New American Library, 1962), p. 361.

14. George W. Stocking Jr., *Victorian Anthropology* (New York: Free Press,

1987), p. 63; John M. Efron, *Defenders of the Race: Jewish Doctors and Race Science in Fin-de-Siècle Europe* (New Haven: Yale University Press, 1994), p. 45.

15. Hobsbawm, *Age of Revolution,* p. 169.

16. Eugene MacLaughlin, "Irish and Colonization," in *Dictionary of Race and Ethnic Relations,* ed. Ellis Cashmore, 4th ed. (London: Routledge, 1996), p. 181; Leslie Page Moch, "The European Perspective: Changing Conditions and Multiple Migrations, 1750–1914," in *European Migrations: Global and Local Perspectives,* ed. Dirk Hoerder and Leslie Page Moch (Boston: Northwestern University Press, 1996), p. 126.

17. Dirk Hoerder, *Cultures in Conflict: World Migrations in the Second Millennium* (Durham: Duke University Press, 2002), pp. 342, 345.

18. Ibid., pp. 334.

19. Ibid., p. 336; Higham, *Strangers in the Land,* p. 15.

20. Hoerder, *Cultures,* pp. 339–42; Davies, *Europe,* pp. 842–3; E. J. Hobsbawm, *The Age of Capital, 1848–1875* (New York: New American Library, 1975), p. 215.

21. Saskia Sassen, *Guests and Aliens* (New York: New Press, 1999), p. xvi.

22. Dale T. Knobel, *Paddy and the Republic: Ethnicity and Nationality in Antebellum America* (Middletown: Wesleyan University Press, 1986), p. 88.

23. Ibid., p. 73.

24. Ibid., p. 98; Reginald Horsman, *Race and Manifest Destiny* (Cambridge: Harvard University Press, 1981).

25. Knobel, *Paddy,* p. 88.

26. Ibid., p. 90.

27. Robert Miles, *Racism and Migrant Labour* (London: Routledge & Kegan Paul, 1982), pp. 128, 133, 129.

28. Ibid., pp. 135–38, 140.

29. David R. Roediger, *The Wages of Whiteness: Race and the Making of the American Working Class,* 2d ed. (New York and London: Verso, [1991] 1999), p. 150; Knobel, *Paddy,* pp. 178–79; Jacobson, *Whiteness.*

30. Davies, *Europe,* p. 847.

31. Ibid.; Hannah Arendt, *The Origins of Totalitarianism,* new ed. (San Diego: Harcourt Brace, [1951] 1979), p. 89; George L. Mosse, *Toward the Final Solution: A History of European Racism* (New York: Howard Fertig, 1978), pp. 117–18.

32. Mosse, *Final Solution,* p. 151.

33. Ibid., pp. 151–52.

34. Ibid., pp. 151, 155, quoting Drumont on p. 151.

35. Ibid., p. 162.

36. Ibid., p. 163.

37. Ibid., pp. 164–66.

38. Jennifer Guglielmo, "Introduction: White Lies, Dark Truths," in *Are Italians White? How Race Is Made in America,* ed. Jennifer Guglielmo and Salvatore Salerno (New York: Routledge, 2003), p. 8; Sassen, *Guests,* p. 69.

39. Sassen, *Guests*, pp. 69–73.

40. Guglielmo, "Introduction," pp. 8–9; Giuseppe Sergi, *The Mediterranean Race* (1901), in *This Is Race: An Anthology Selected from International Literature on the Races of Man*, ed. Earl W. Count (New York: Henry Schuman, 1950), pp. 227–28.

41. Davies, *Europe*, pp. 869–71; David Gilmour, "Little War, Big Mess," *New York Review of Books* 48, April 12, 2001, pp. 76–78.

42. Barzun, *Race*, chaps. 5–6; Ivan Hannaford, *Race: The History of an Idea in the West*, foreword by Bernard Crick (Baltimore: Johns Hopkins University Press, 1996), p. 287.

43. Alfred C. Haddon, *History of Anthropology* (London: Watts and Co., 1934), p. 27; Hannaford, *Race*, p. 288. On the "Teutonic race" and "Anglo-Saxons," see Thomas Gossett, *Race: The History of an Idea in America*, new ed. (Oxford: Oxford University Press, [1963] 1997), pp. 84–87.

44. Andrew Zimmerman, *Anthropology and Antihumanism in Imperial Germany* (Chicago: University of Chicago Press, 2001), p. 135.

45. Jacobson, *Whiteness*, pp. 22, 227.

46. Justice Henry Brown, in *Plessy v. Ferguson: A Brief History with Documents*, ed. Brook Thomas (Boston: Bedford Books, 1997), p. 42.

47. Jacobson, *Whiteness*, p. 227; Ian F. Haney López, *White by Law: The Legal Construction of Race* (New York: New York University Press, 1996), pp. 5–6.

48. Bernard Bailyn, Robert Dallek, David Brion Davis, Donald Herbert Donald, John L. Thomas, and Gordon S. Wood, *The Great Republic: A History of the American People*, vol. 1 (Lexington, MA: DC Heath & Co. 1992), p. 682; Mink, *Old Labor*, chap. 3.

49. Jacobson, *Whiteness*, pp. 78–90. Canada's immigration history was similar. It included a "head tax" to curb Chinese immigration, followed by the 1923 Chinese Immigration Act, which stopped Chinese immigration; restrictions on immigration from Japan and India in 1907; and laws restricting European immigration in 1906, 1910, and 1919. See Howard Palmer and Leo Driedger, "Prejudice and Discrimination," in *The Canadian Encyclopedia, Year 2000 Edition* (Toronto: McClelland and Stewart, 1999), p. 1889.

50. *Hitler's Second Book: The Unpublished Sequel to "Mein Kampf,"* trans. forthcoming from Enigma Books, quoted in the *New York Times*, Sunday, June 22, 2003, sec. 4, p. 3.

51. Hodgkin, quoted in Stocking, *Victorian Anthropology*, p. 63.

52. Gossett, *Race*, p. 88; Stocking, *Victorian Anthropology*, p. 62.

53. John Knox, *The Races of Man: A Fragment* (1850), p. 10, quoted in Efron, *Defenders*, p. 47.

54. John Knox, *The Races of Man* (1850), pp. 57–58, quoted in Knobel, *Paddy*, p. 109.

55. Arthur de Gobineau, *The Inequality of the Human Races*, trans. Adrian

Collins, introduction by Oscar Levy (New York: Howard Fertig, [1854] 1967), p. 179.

56. Ibid., p. 146.

57. Ibid., pp. 212, 152.

58. Barzun, *Race*, p. 100; Gossett, *Race*, p. 126.

59. Ernest Renan, *Histoire générale et système comparé des langues sémitiques* (1847–1855), in *Oeuvres*, vol. 8, p. 586, quoted in Poliakov, *Aryan Myth*, p. 207.

60. Stocking, *Victorian Anthropology*, p. 63.

61. Poliakov, *Aryan Myth*, pp. 257–58, 213–14. Müller declared in 1872, "Aryan and Semitic languages exist, but it is unscientific . . . to speak of an Aryan race" (quoted in Poliakov, *Aryan Myth*, p. 214).

62. Barzun, *Race*, p. 134.

63. Ibid., pp. 314–18.

64. Houston Stewart Chamberlain, *Foundations of the Nineteenth Century,* trans. John Lees, vol. 1 (London, 1912), excerpted in Louis L. Snyder, *The Idea of Racialism: Its Meaning and History* (New York: Van Nostrand Reinhold, 1962), p. 133.

65. George Stocking Jr., *Race, Culture, and Evolution: Essays in the History of Anthropology* (New York: Free Press, 1968), p. 56.

66. Ibid.

67. Michael Bérubé, *Life as We Know It: A Father, a Family and an Exceptional Child* (New York: Vintage, 1998), p. 25.

68. Francis Galton, *Hereditary Genius* (Cleveland: Meridian Books, [1869] 1962); Daniel J. Kevles, *In the Name of Eugenics: Genetics and the Uses of Human Heredity* (Berkeley: University of California Press, 1985), p. 3.

69. Nicholas Lemann, "The IQ Meritocracy," *Time* 153, March 29, 1999, p. 83; Leon J. Kamin, "The Pioneers of IQ Testing," in *The Bell Curve Debate*, ed. Russell Jacoby and Naomi Glauberman (New York: Times Books, 1995).

70. Lemann, "IQ Meritocracy," p. 83; Kamin, "Pioneers," pp. 487–506.

71. Kenan Malik, *The Meaning of Race: Race, History and Culture in Western Society* (Houndsmills, Basingstoke: Macmillan, 1996); Mark Mazower, *Dark Continent: Europe's Twentieth Century* (New York: Vintage Books, 1998), chap. 1.

72. Malik, *Meaning of Race*, p. 109.

73. Gossett, *Race*, pp. 75–76.

74. Per Holck, "Sweden," in *History of Physical Anthropology: An Encyclopedia*, vol. 2 (New York: Garland Publishing, 1997), p. 1005.

75. Stocking, *Race, Culture, and Evolution*, chap. 3; Barzun, *Race*, chap. 7. In the next century several measures of race difference were used to supplement or replace the cephalic index: hair types; measurements of jaws and other body parts; a "nasal index"; and, more recently, blood types and gene frequencies. See L. H. Dudley Buxton, "Races of Mankind," in *The Encyclopaedia Britannica*, 13th ed., vol. 11 (London, 1926), p. 272; and chapter 6, below.

76. Holck, "Sweden," p. 1005.

77. Hugh Seton-Watson, *Nations and States: An Enquiry into the Origins of Nations and the Politics of Nationalism* (Boulder: Westview Press, 1977), pp. 68, 71.

78. Ibid., p. 71.

79. Ibid.

80. Ibid.; Davies, *Europe*, p. 818.

81. Anders Retzius, "A Glance at the Present State of Ethnology, with Reference to the Form of Skull" (1856), in *This Is Race*, ed. Count, pp. 75–77.

82. Ibid., pp. 78–79.

83. Thomas Henry Huxley, "On the Method and Results of Ethnology" (1865), in *This Is Race*, ed. Count, p. 120.

84. Ibid., pp. 113–14.

85. Ibid., p. 114.

86. Ibid.

87. Snyder, *Idea of Racialism*, p. 12.

88. Huxley, "Method and Results of Ethnology," p. 119.

89. Thomas Henry Huxley, "Emancipation—Black and White" (1865), in *Collected Essays*, vol. 3 (New York: Greenwood Press, [1898] 1968), pp. 66–67.

90. Thomas H. Huxley, "On Some Fixed Points in British Ethnology" (1871), in *Man's Place in Nature and Other Anthropological Essays, Collected Essays*, vol. 7 (London: Macmillan, 1900), pp. 260, 262; T. H. Huxley, "British Race-Types of To-day," Letter to the Editor, *The Times*, Wednesday, October 12, 1887, p. 8.

91. Huxley, "Some Fixed Points," pp. 264–68; Huxley, "British Race-Types," p. 8.

92. Stocking, *Victorian Anthropology*, pp. 299–300

93. Edward Burnett Tylor, "Anthropology," in *The Encyclopaedia Britannica*, 9th ed., vol. 2 (Edinburgh, 1875), p. 111.

94. Ibid., p. 113.

95. Ibid.

96. Edward B. Tylor, *Anthropology: An Introduction to the Study of Man and Civilization* (New York: D. Appleton & Co., [1881] 1898), pp. 105–6.

97. Ibid., pp. 106–7.

98. Ibid., pp. 110–11.

99. In *In re Najour*, 174 735 (N.D. Ga. 1909), District Judge Newman cited Keane's book, *The World's People*; and Justice Southerland of the U.S. Supreme Court cited Keane in *United States v. Bhagat Sigh Thind*, 261 U.S. 204 (1923) (quoted in López, *White by Law*, pp. 212–13, 221–25). In *The World's People*, Keane popularized his more scholarly arguments from *Ethnology* (1895) and *Man: Past and Present* (1899).

100. *United States v. Bhagat Sigh Thind*, 261 U.S. 204 (1923), quoted in López, *White by Law*, pp. 223–24. See also Jacobson, *Whiteness*, p. 236.

101. A. H. Keane, *Ethnology* (Cambridge: Cambridge University Press, [1895] 1901), p. vii.

102. Ibid., pp. 2, 5.

103. Ibid., p. 171.

104. Ibid., p. 191. He also emphasized the significance of the number of cerebral convolutions of the brain, which he claimed were "smaller and more complex in the higher races" (pp. 193–94).

105. Ibid., p. 221.

106. Ibid., p. 223.

107. Ibid., p. 226.

108. Ibid., pp. 222–23.

109. Ibid., p. 223. See also A. H. Keane, "Negro," in *The Encyclopaedia Britannica,* 9th ed., vol. 17 (Edinburgh: Adam and Charles Black, 1875), p. 317.

110. Ibid., p. 223.

111. Ibid., p. 225.

112. Ibid., pp. 226–27.

113. Ibid., p. 227.

114. Ibid., p. 375.

115. Ibid., pp. 376–77.

116. Ibid., pp. 379–91.

117. Ibid., p. 382, 385.

118. Ibid., p. 380.

119. A. H. Keane, *Man: Past and Present,* rev., and largely rewritten by A. Hingston Quiggin and A. C. Haddon (Cambridge: Cambridge University Press, 1920). Due to the revisions of Quiggin and Haddon, the precise authorship of phrases and categories is obscure. Therefore, I refer to "the authors'" and "the book's" claims.

120. Lauren, *Power,* pp. 52–55; and see below.

121. Keane, *Man,* pp. 443–44.

122. Ibid., pp. 451–52.

123. Ibid., pp. 452–53, 438–40.

124. Ibid., p. 443ff.

125. Ibid., p. 439.

126. Ibid., p. 440.

127. Ibid., p. 441.

128. Ibid., p. 442.

129. Ibid., p. 443.

130. Ibid.

131. Carleton Stevens Coon, *The Races of Europe* (New York: Macmillan, [1939] 1954).

132. Stocking, *Victorian Anthropology,* pp. 66–67, quoting Beddoe on p. 66; Efron, *Defenders,* pp. 55–56.

133. John Beddoe, *The Anthropological History of Europe* (1892–93 [1912]), in *This Is Race,* ed. Count, p. 163.

134. Ibid.

135. Ibid., p. 167.

136. Ibid.

137. Ibid., p. 168.

138. Ibid.

139. Ibid., p. 170.

140. Higham, *Strangers in the Land,* p. 137. One notable exception was anthropologist Daniel Brinton, who maintained, "The leading race in all history has been the White Race." Brinton called it "Eurafrican," rejecting the designations "Caucasian," "Japetic" and "European race" because "the race never originated in the Caucasus" and its first great historical domain was "not in Europe, nor yet in Asia, but in Africa." He identified two branches and several "types" within this race. See Daniel G. Brinton, *Races and Peoples: Lectures on the Science of Ethnology* (New York: N. D. C. Hodges, 1890), pp. 103–8.

141. Higham, *Strangers in the Land,* pp. 153–54.

142. Ibid., pp. 54, 140.

143. Ibid., pp. 147–48, 153.

144. William Z. Ripley, *The Races of Europe* (New York: D. Appleton & Co., 1899), p. 34; Higham, *Strangers in the Land,* p. 154; Stocking, *Race, Culture, and Evolution,* p. 61.

145. Ripley, *Races,* p. 35.

146. Ibid., p. 36.

147. Ibid., p. 1.

148. Ibid., p. 32, Ripley's emphasis.

149. Ibid., p. 103.

150. Ibid., pp. 103–4.

151. Ibid., p. 105, Ripley's emphasis.

152. Ibid., pp. 107, 111.

153. Ibid., p. 112. George Stocking notes the Platonic character of this mode of racial reasoning: true "racial" types were akin to Platonic forms that were knowable to the scientist, even if there were no individuals who were identical to these types. See Stocking, *Race, Culture, and Evolution,* p. 57; Ripley, *Races,* p. 112.

154. Ripley, *Races,* pp. 121–22.

155. Ibid., pp. 123–24.

156. Ibid., p. 128.

157. Ibid., p. 130, citing Sergi.

158. Ibid., pp. 129, 123.

159. Ibid., p. 130.

160. Ibid., pp. 513–36.

161. Ibid., p. 549.

162. Ibid., p. 557.

163. Ibid., p. 436.

164. Ibid., p. 437.

165. Ibid., p. 441.

166. Ibid., p. 448.

167. Ibid., pp. 400, 391.

168. Ibid., pp. 371–72.

169. Ibid., pp. 372–73.

170. Ibid., pp. 373, 383.

171. William Z. Ripley, "Races in the United States," *Atlantic Monthly* 102, December 1908, p. 746.

172. Ibid., pp. 746–47.

173. In his book he regarded the Slavs as part of the Alpine race. See Ripley, *Races,* pp. 355–58.

174. Ripley, "Races," p. 747.

175. Ibid., p. 759.

176. Ibid., p. 751.

177. Ibid., p. 759.

178. Jacobson, *Whiteness,* pp. 80–96.

179. Madison Grant, *The Passing of the Great Race, or the Racial Basis of European History,* 4th rev. ed. (New York: Charles Scribner's Sons, [1916] 1921), pp. 20–32.

180. Ibid., pp. 65–66.

181. Joseph Deniker, *The Races of Man: An Outline of Anthropology and Ethnology* (London: Walter Scott, 1900), pp. vii, 1.

182. Ibid., p. 7.

183. Ibid., p. 8.

184. Ibid., pp. 8–9, emphasis in the original.

185. Ibid., p. 280.

186. Ibid., pp. 280–81.

187. Ibid., p. 287.

188. Ibid., pp. 284–90.

189. Hobsbawm, *Nations and Nationalism,* p. 108n.13; Ripley, *Races,* p. 128.

190. Deniker, *Races of Man,* pp. 295–96.

191. Ibid., pp. 353–58, 355.

192. Efron, *Defenders,* pp. 4–5; Nancy Leys Stepan and Sander L. Gilman, "Appropriating the Idioms of Science: The Rejection of Scientific Racism," in *The "Racial" Economy of Science,* ed. Sandra Harding (Bloomington: Indiana University Press, 1993); Mia Bay, *The White Image in the Black Mind: African-American Ideas about White People, 1830–1925* (Oxford: Oxford University Press, 2000), p. 39. Du Bois eventually moved close to a political constructivist view of "race" (see below), and later subaltern intellectuals such as Franz Fanon were in the forefront of the movement to refute thoroughly the "race" concept (see chapter 6).

193. Martin R. Delany, *The Condition, Elevation, Emigration, and Destiny of the*

*Colored People of the United States* (Philadelphia: by the author, 1852; reprint, New York: Arno Press and the New York Times, 1968), p. 36, quoted in Bay, *White Image*, p. 65.

194. Martin R. Delany, *The Origin of Races and Color* (Baltimore: Black Classics Press, 1991; reprint of *Principia of Ethnology: The Origin of Races and Color, with an Archeological Compendium of Ethiopian and Egyptian Civilization* [Philadelphia: Harper and Brother, 1879]), pp. 10–27.

195. Ibid., pp. 19, 25.

196. Ibid., pp. 37–86.

197. Ibid., p. 94.

198. On the development of Du Bois's thinking about race, see Joel Olson, "W. E. B. Du Bois and the Race Concept," in *Racially Writing the Republic: Racists, Race Rebels, and Transformations of American Identity,* ed. Bruce Baum and Duchess Harris (Durham: Duke University Press, forthcoming).

199. W. E. B. Du Bois, "The Conservation of Races," in *On Sociology and the Black Community,* ed. Dan S. Green and Edwin D. Driver (Chicago: University of Chicago Press, 1980), p. 240.

200. Ibid., pp. 239–40, 241.

201. Ibid., pp. 241–42.

202. Efron, *Defenders,* p. 121.

203. Robert Gordon Latham, *The Natural History of the Varieties of Man* (London: John van Voorst, 1850), p. 107.

204. John Beddoe, "On the Physical Characteristics of the Jews," *Transactions of the Ethnological Society of London* 1 (1861), p. 236, quoted in Efron, *Defenders,* p. 56.

205. Zimmerman, *Anthropology and Antihumanism,* pp. 137–45.

206. Mosse, *Final Solution,* p. 120.

207. Ibid., p. 123.

208. Ibid., pp. 75, 122–23. The idea of a Jewish race was also affirmed by Jewish anthropologist Joseph Jacobs in *The Jewish Encyclopedia*: "Anthropologically considered, the Jews are a race of markedly uniform type, due either to unity of race or similarity of environment." See Joseph Jacobs, "Anthropology," in *The Jewish Encyclopedia* (New York: Funk and Wagnalls, 1901), p. 601.

209. Efron, *Defenders,* p. 92.

210. Samuel Weissenberg, "Der jüdische Typus," *Globus* 97, no. 20 (1910), p. 309, quoted in Efron, *Defenders,* p. 94.

211. Samuel Weissenberg, "Die südrussischen Juden: Eine anthropomentrische Studie," AA 23 (1895), pp. 568–73, quoted in Efron, *Defenders,* p. 199n.33.

212. Weissenberg, "Die südrussischen Juden," p. 562–64, quoted in Efron, *Defenders,* pp. 103–4.

213. Weissenberg, "Die südrussischen Juden," p. 575, quoted in Efron, *Defenders,* p. 105.

214. Weissenberg, "Die südrussischen Juden," pp. 578–79, quoted in Efron, *Defenders*, p. 107.

215. Efron, *Defenders*, p. 107.

216. Mosse, *Final Solution*, p. 172.

217. Ibid., pp. 178–80.

218. Robert Proctor, *Racial Hygiene: Medicine under the Nazis* (Cambridge: Harvard University Press, 1988), chap. 1.

219. Ibid., p. 27; Mosse, *Final Solution*, p. 189.

220. Hans Günther, *The Racial Elements of European History*, trans. C. G. Wheeler (Port Washington, NY: Kennikat Press, [1927] 1970), pp. 3–4.

221. Ibid., p. 267.

222. Ibid., pp. 74–75.

223. Ibid., p. 78.

224. Ibid., p. 74.

225. Ibid., p. 257n.1.

226. Mosse, *Final Solution*, pp. 204–5.

227. Edward Burnett Tylor, "Anthropology," in *Encyclopaedia Britannica*, 11th ed., vol. 2 (Cambridge: Cambridge University Press, 1910), p. 113.

228. "Ethnology and Ethnography," in *Encyclopaedia Britannica*, 11th ed., vol. 9, p. 850.

229. John Bealby, "Caucasia," in *Encyclopaedia Britannica*, 11th ed., vol. 5, p. 548.

230. Grafton Elliot Smith, "Anthropology," in *Encyclopaedia Britannica*, 12th ed. (London: Encyclopaedia Britannica, 1922), p. 147.

231. Rudolf Virchow, *Race Formation and Heredity* (1896), in *What Is Race*, ed. Count, pp. 180–81.

232. Ibid., pp. 191, 188.

233. Ibid., p. 190.

234. Franz Boas, "Review of William Z. Ripley, 'The Races of Europe'" (1899), in *Race, Language and Culture* (New York: Macmillan, 1940), p. 157.

235. Ibid., pp. 158–59.

236. Franz Boas, "Changes in Bodily Form of Descendants of Immigrants," in *This Is Race*, ed. Count, p. 120. See Claudia Roth Pierpont, "The Measure of America," *New Yorker*, March 24, 2004, pp. 55–57, 63.

237. George M. Fredrickson, *Racism: A Short History* (Princeton: Princeton University Press, 2002), p. 158.

238. Ibid., p. 159.

239. Frank H. Hankins, *The Racial Basis of Civilization: A Critique of the Nordic Doctrine* (New York, 1926), p. ix, quoted in Fredrickson, *Racism*, p. 160.

240. Deniker, *Races of Man*, pp. 2–3, Deniker's emphasis.

241. Deniker's use of *ethnical* complicates matters because it can imply certain physical characteristics. Still, as I explain in the concluding chapter, *ethnic* can be

used fruitfully to indicate to linguistic, social, and cultural affinities within and distinctions between groups without reference to physical traits.

242. Deniker, *Races of Man*, p. 8.

243. Ibid., p. 121.

244. Gustav Spiller, *Papers on Inter-Racial Problems Communicated to the First Universal Races Congress Held at the University of London, July 26–29, 1911* (London: P. S. King and Son, 1911), p. v, quoted in Julia E. Liss, "Diasporic Identities: The Science and Politics of Race in the Work of Franz Boas and W. E. B. Du Bois, 1894–1919," *Cultural Anthropology* 13 (May 1998), pp. 138–39.

245. W. E. B. Du Bois, "The First Universal Races Congress" (1911), in *The Oxford W. E. B. Du Bois Reader*, ed. Eric J. Sundquist (New York: Oxford University Press, 1996), p. 55.

246. Gustav Spiller, quoted in Du Bois, "First Universal Races Congress," p. 58.

247. Jean Finot, quoted in Du Bois, "First Universal Races Congress," p. 59.

248. Franz Boas, "An Anthropologist's View of War," *International Conciliation* (March 1912), p. 10, quoted in Liss, "Diasporic Identities," p. 142.

249. Franz Boas, "Race," in *Encyclopaedia of the Social Sciences*, vol. 13 (New York: Macmillan, 1934), p. 34; Gossett, *Race*, pp. 418–29.

250. W. E. B. Du Bois, "The Negro's Fatherland," *The Survey* 39 (November 10, 1917), p. 141, quoted in Liss, "Diasporic Identities," p. 148.

251. W. E. B. Du Bois, "On Being Ashamed of Oneself: An Essay on Race Pride," in *Oxford W. E. B. Du Bois Reader*, pp. 74–75.

252. Du Bois, "First Universal Races Congress," p. 58.

NOTES TO CHAPTER 5

1. Julian S. Huxley and A. C. Haddon, *We European: A Survey of "Racial" Problems*, with a chapter on "Europe Overseas," by A. M. Carr-Saunders (London: Jonathan Cape, 1935), p. 287.

2. "Appendix: Text of the Statement of 1950," in UNESCO, *The Concept of Race: The Race Question in Modern Science* (Paris: UNESCO, 1951), p. 90.

3. Norman Davies, *Europe: A History* (New York: HarperPerennial, 1996), pp. 1016–21; George L. Mosse, *Toward the Final Solution: A History of European Racism* (New York: Howard Fertig, 1978), chap. 13; United States Holocaust Memorial Museum, at http://www.ushmm.org/wlc/en/index.php?lang=en&ModuleId=10005143.

4. Elazar Barkan, *The Retreat of Scientific Racism: Changing Concepts of Race in Britain and the United States between the World Wars* (Cambridge: Cambridge University Press).

5. Nancy Stepan, *The Idea of Race in Science: Great Britain 1800–1960* (London: Macmillan, 1982); Barkan, *Retreat*. For a related account of the "Caucasian

race" revival, see Matthew Frye Jacobson, *Whiteness of a Different Color: European Immigrants and the Alchemy of Race* (Cambridge: Harvard University Press, 1998).

6. Davies, *Europe*, p. 848.

7. Geoffrey Barraclough, *An Introduction to Contemporary History* (Harmondsworth: Penguin, 1967), p. 66.

8. W. E. B. Du Bois, "To the Nations of the World," in *The Oxford W. E. B. Du Bois Reader*, ed. Eric J. Sundquist (Oxford: Oxford University Press, 1996), p. 625.

9. Kenan Malik, *The Meaning of Race: Race, History and Culture in Western Society* (Houndsmills, Basingstoke: Macmillan, 1996), p. 117.

10. Frank Füredi, *The Silent War: Imperialism and Changing Perception of Race* (London: Pluto Press, 1998), p. 27.

11. Ibid.

12. Davies, *Europe*, p. 851; Barraclough, *Contemporary History*, pp. 68–75.

13. Robert Miles, *Racism* (London: Routledge, 1989), pp. 91–93; Malik, *Meaning of Race*, p. 118.

14. Anne McClintock and Rob Nixon, "No Names Apart: The Separation of Word and History in Derrida's 'Le Dernier Mot du Racisme,'" *Critical Inquiry* 13 (Autumn 1986), p. 149.

15. Barraclough, *Contemporary History*, chap. 3; Füredi, *Silent War*, chap. 1. Immanuel Wallerstein usefully defines the pan-European world as the prosperous "white"-dominated political-economic zone that encompasses "Western Europe plus North America and Australasia, but not east-central Europe." See Immanuel Wallerstein, "The Albatross of Racism," *London Review of Books*, May 11, 2000, p. 11.

16. Bronislaw Malinowski, "A Plea for an Effective Colour Bar," *The Spectator*, June 27, 1931, quoted in Füredi, *Silent War*, p. 94.

17. *The Spectator*, September 12, 1931, quoted in Füredi, *Silent War*, pp. 94–95.

18. Mark Mazower, *Dark Continent: Europe's Twentieth Century* (New York: Vintage Books, 1998), pp. 72–73.

19. Füredi, *Silent War*, p. 114.

20. Quoted in Füredi, *Silent War*, p. 114.

21. Sir John Simon, "Frontiers," *International Affairs* 12 (November 1933), quoted in Füredi, *Silent War*, p. 120.

22. R. S. Baker, *Woodrow Wilson and the World Settlement*, vol. 2 (New York, 1922), p. 234, quoted in Füredi, *Silent War*, p. 122.

23. W. O. Brown, "The Nature of Race Consciousness," *Social Forces* 10, no. 1 (1931), p. 97, quoted in Füredi, *Silent War*, p. 123.

24. Brown, "Race Consciousness," p. 96, quoted in Füredi, *Silent War*, pp. 122–23.

25. Füredi, *Silent War*, p. 123.

26. Barraclough, *Contemporary History*, p. 76.

27. Ibid., p. 77.

28. Ibid., pp. 78–79.

29. Ibid., p. 79.

30. Ibid., pp. 98–99.

31. Füredi, *Silent War*, p. 68.

32. Robert E. Park and Ernest Burgess, *Introduction to the Science of Sociology* (Chicago, 1926), p. 636, quoted in Füredi, *Silent War*, p. 68.

33. Barraclough, *Contemporary History*, p. 81.

34. The influx of Japanese immigrants was small compared to the 30 million European immigrants to the United States between the Civil War and 1924: approximately 275,000, with 245,000 entering the country during 1901–24. See Roger Daniels, *The Politics of Prejudice: The Anti-Japanese Movement in California and the Struggles for Japanese Exclusion* (New York: Atheneum, 1972), p. 1.

35. Woodrow Wilson, quoted in Daniels, *Politics of Prejudice*, p. 55. Wilson's statement, published in the San Francisco *Daily News*, was drafted by James Duval Phelan, a leading Democratic anti-Japanese activist. See pp. 55, 134n.47.

36. Barraclough, *Contemporary History*, p. 156.

37. Ibid., pp. 155, 161, 180.

38. Ibid., pp. 172–74.

39. Füredi, *Silent War*, p. 42; Mazower, *Dark Continent*, p. 64.

40. Quoted in Füredi, *Silent War*, p. 42.

41. Füredi, *Silent War*, p. 43.

42. Quoted in Mazower, *Dark Continent*, p. 64.

43. Harold Nicholson, *Peacemaking 1919* (London, 1933), p. 145, quoted in Füredi, *Silent War*, p. 43.

44. Füredi, *Silent War*, p. 44.

45. Quoted in Füredi, *Silent War*, p. 44.

46. Barraclough, *Contemporary History*, pp. 157–59.

47. Davies, *Europe*, p. 899.

48. Quoted in Robert W. D. Boyce, *British Capitalism at the Crossroads, 1919–1932: A Study in Politics, Economics, and International Relations* (Cambridge: Cambridge University Press, 1987), p. 114.

49. Quoted in Boyce, *British Capitalism*, p. 108.

50. Quoted in Mazower, *Dark Continent*, p. 109.

51. Mazower, *Dark Continent*, pp. 110–15.

52. Madison Grant, *The Passing of the Great Race, or the Racial Basis of European History*, 4th rev. ed. (New York: Charles Scribner's Sons, [1916] 1921), pp. 65–66.

53. Jacobson, *Whiteness*, p. 96.

54. Lothrop Stoddard, quoted in Jacobson, *Whiteness*, pp. 96–97.

55. Lothrop Stoddard, *Reforging America* (1927), quoted in Jacobson, *Whiteness*, p. 98.

56. Jacobson, *Whiteness*, p. 21. Brazil also adopted a version of the color line in

its 1940 census. Census takers classified Brazilians as "white, black, or yellow," which was a departure from prior Brazilian notions of race. See Melissa Nobles, "Racial Categorization and Censuses," in *Census and Identity: The Politics of Race, Ethnicity, and Language in National Censuses,* ed. David I. Kertzer and Dominique Arel (Cambridge: Cambridge University Press, 2002), p. 62.

57. Clement E. Vose, *Caucasians Only: The Supreme Court, the NAACP, and the Restrictive Covenant Cases* (Berkeley: University of California Press, 1967), p. 9.

58. Along with the people of African, Chinese, and Japanese descent, the most common targets of restrictive covenants, covenants also prohibited Jews from buying homes in certain areas. Yet, while Jews faced anti-Semitism in this era, they were also in the process of becoming accepted as "Caucasian" in the United States. See Vose, *Caucasians,* pp. 2, 6–13; Jacobson, *Whiteness,* pp. 91–128; Bruce Lambert, "At fifty, Levittown Contends with Its Legacy of Bliss," *New York Times,* Metro Section, December 28, 1997, p. 26.

59. Vose, *Caucasians,* pp. vii–viii, 9.

60. Oswald Spengler, *Man and Technics* (New York, 1932), pp. 101–2, quoted in Mazower, *Dark Continent,* p. 110.

61. Malik, *Meaning of Race,* p. 117. Universal and equal white male suffrage was widely established in pan-European countries between 1874 and 1918. Women's suffrage generally lagged, and restrictions on the suffrage of nonwhites persisted in Canada (through the 1930s) and Australia (until 1962), as well as in the United States (until 1965), where white male suffrage had been established in the early nineteenth century. See Samuel Bowles and Herbert Gintis, *Democracy and Capitalism* (New York: Basic Books, 1987), p. 217n.32.

62. Mazower, *Dark Continent,* p. 4.

63. Malik, *Meaning of Race,* chap. 4; Mazower, *Dark Continent,* chap. 1.

64. Eugenicists established the Russian Eugenics Office, the Eugenics Record Office in the United States, the German Society for Race and Social Biology, and the British Eugenics Education Society, among other organizations, between 1928 and 1936. Eugenically inspired voluntary sterilization laws were passed in Switzerland, Denmark, Germany, Sweden, Norway, Finland, and Estonia, and sterilization laws were passed even earlier by some state governments in the United States. See Mazower, *Dark Continent,* pp. 92, 97; Daniel J. Kevles, *In the Name of Eugenics* (Berkeley: University of California Press, 1986), p. 47.

65. Füredi, *Silent War,* p. 163.

66. Quoted in Paul Gordon Lauren, *Power and Prejudice: The Politics and Diplomacy of Racial Discrimination* (Boulder: Westview, 1988), p. 137.

67. Ibid.

68. Ibid.

69. Gunnar Myrdal, *An American Dilemma: The Negro Problem and Modern Democracy* (New York: Harper and Row, [1944] 1962), p. 1004.

70. Füredi, *Silent War,* pp. 18, 164–65.

71. Lauren, *Power,* chap. 5; Füredi, *Silent War,* chap. 6.

72. Quoted in Lauren, *Power,* p. 138.

73. Quoted in Lauren, *Power,* pp. 143–44.

74. Lauren, *Power,* pp. 144–45.

75. Penny M. von Eschen, *Race against Empire: Black Americans and Anticolonialism, 1937–57* (Ithaca: Cornell University Press, 1997), pp. 45–52.

76. Füredi, *Silent War,* p. 181.

77. France, unique among the European states, supported prohibitions against racial discrimination, and the Soviet Union, which had opposed human rights at the more exclusive 1944 Dumbartton Oaks Conference, also supported anti-discrimination proposals. See Lauren, *Power,* pp. 152–55.

78. Füredi, *Silent War,* p. 201; Lauren, *Power,* pp. 152, 156, 171.

79. Wallerstein, "Albatross of Racism," p. 12.

80. George Bell, *The Church and Humanity* (London, 1946), quoted in Davies, *Europe,* p. 923.

81. Anne Deighton, "The Remaking of Europe," in *The Oxford History of the Twentieth Century,* ed. Michael Howard and Wm. Roger Louis (Oxford: Oxford University Press, 1998), pp. 192–95.

82. Mazower, *Dark Continent,* pp. 292–93.

83. Füredi, *Silent War,* p. 194.

84. Lauren, *Power,* pp. 202–4; Barraclough, *Contemporary History,* chap. 6.

85. George M. Fredrickson, *White Supremacy: A Comparative Study in American and South African History* (Oxford: Oxford University Press, 1982), p. 240.

86. Michael Banton, "1960: A Turning Point in the Study of Race Relations," *Daedalus* 103 (Spring 1974), p. 32.

87. Robert E. Park, "The Nature of Race Relations" (1939), quoted in Jacobson, *Whiteness,* p. 104.

88. Jacobson, *Whiteness,* p. 104.

89. Banton, "Turning Point," pp. 34–35.

90. George M. Fredrickson, *Racism: A Short History* (Princeton: Princeton University Press, 2002) pp. 162, 163.

91. Barkan, *Retreat,* pp. 3–4.

92. Lancelot Hogben, *Genetic Principles in Medicine and Social Science* (London: Williams and Norgate, 1931), p. 122.

93. Elazar Barkan, "The Politics of the Science of Race: Ashley Montagu and UNESCO's Anti-Racist Declarations," in *Race and Other Misadventures: Essays in Honor of Ashley Montagu in His Nineteenth Year,* ed. Larry T. Reynolds and Leonard Lieberman (Dix Hills, NY: General Hall, 1996), pp. 96–97.

94. Barkan, *Retreat,* p. 5; Stepan, *Idea of Race* , pp. 141–43.

95. Stepan, *Idea of Race,* p. 141.

96. Barkan, *Retreat,* p. 346.

97. Ibid., p. 344.

98. Stepan, *Idea of Race,* p. 143.

99. Barkan, *Retreat,* p. 343.

100. Ibid., 228.

101. Ibid., p. 231.

102. Ibid., p. 127.

103. Ibid., p. 133.

104. Julian Huxley, "Eugenics and Society" (1936), in *Man Stands Alone* (Freeport, NY: Books for Libraries Press, 1970; reprint of 1941 edition); Barkan, *Retreat,* pp. 243–44.

105. Quoted in Barkan, *Retreat,* p. 238.

106. Julian Huxley, *African View* (London: Chatto & Windus, 1932), p. 388.

107. Ibid., pp. 388–89. A. H. Keane had expressed a similar evolutionist view.

108. Huxley, "Eugenics," p. 53.

109. Ibid.

110. Julian Huxley, "Colonies and Freedom," *New Republic,* January 24, 1944, quoted in Füredi, *Silent War,* p. 108.

111. Huxley and Haddon, *We Europeans.* For details of this collaboration, which also included other contributors, see Barkan, *Retreat,* pp. 302–6. The more conservative Haddon was a reluctant coauthor who had previously counted several European races. See A. C. Haddon, *The Races of Man,* rev. ed. (Cambridge: Cambridge University Press, 1929).

112. Barkan, *Retreat,* pp. 281–85, 310–15.

113. Ibid., p. 286.

114. Ibid., pp. 287–88. One racist committee member, Reginald Ruggles Gates, contended, "If the same criteria of species [used to classify plants and animals] were applied to mankind as to other animals, it appears that the White, Black, and Yellow types of man at least would be regarded as belonging to separate species" (quoted at p. 291).

115. Huxley and Haddon, *We Europeans,* p. 7.

116. Ibid. p. 27.

117. Ibid., p. 105, emphasis in the original.

118. Ibid., pp. 105–6.

119. Ibid., pp. 106–7, emphasis in the original. Recall that for similar reasons Blumenbach initially preferred speaking of human *varieties* instead of human *races.*

120. Ibid., p. 107.

121. Ibid., p. 128.

122. Ibid., pp. 108, 136.

123. Ibid., pp. 111, 113.

124. Ibid., p. 135.

125. Ibid., p. 136.

126. Ibid., p. 92.

127. Barkan, *Retreat*, pp. 280–81.

128. Boas initiated and supported this publication. See Barkan, *Retreat*, p. 333.

129. Violet Edwards, "Note on *The Races of Mankind*," in Ruth Benedict, *Race: Science and Politics*, rev. ed. with "The Races of Mankind," by Ruth Benedict and Gene Weltfish (New York: Viking Press, [1940] 1947), pp. 167–68; Jacobson, *Whiteness*, pp. 106–9.

130. Benedict and Weltfish, "Races of Mankind," pp. 171–72.

131. Ibid., pp. 180–86.

132. M. F. Ashley Montagu, *Man's Most Dangerous Myth: The Fallacy of Race*, with a foreword by Aldous Huxley (New York: Columbia University Press, 1942), p. 3.

133. Ibid., pp. 43, 34–42.

134. Ibid., pp. 32–33.

135. Ibid., p. 44.

136. Ibid., p. 4.

137. Ibid., p. 44.

138. Barkan, *Retreat*, pp. 280–81. Montagu played a leading role in composing the 1950 statement.

139. UNESCO, "Statement of 1950," in *Concept of Race*, pp. 90, 92.

140. Barkan, *Retreat*, p. 341.

141. UNESCO, *Concept of Race*, p. 9; Barkan, "Politics of the Science of Race," pp. 96–105. Montagu played a lesser role in the second statement, while Julian Huxley contributed to its final wording.

142. UNESCO, *Concept of Race*, p. 12.

143. Ibid., pp. 13–16.

144. Among anthropologists, A. H. Keane's work kept the "Caucasian race" category in circulation from the 1880s through 1920 (see chapter 4).

145. A. L. Kroeber, *Anthropology* (New York: Harcourt, Brace, and Company, 1923), p. 36.

146. Ibid.

147. Ibid., p. 40.

148. Ibid., pp. 37–38. Recall that Boas found that the cephalic index was affected by environment, but he did not refute the idea that skull shape was to some extent a heritable trait (see chapter 4).

149. Ibid., p. 38.

150. Ibid., pp. 38–40.

151. Ibid., pp. 38–39.

152. Ibid., p. 42.

153. Ibid.

154. Kroeber listed Keane's *Ethnology* and Ripley's *Races of Europe* in his bibliography but did not cite them directly.

155. Kroeber, *Anthropology*, p. 42.

156. Ibid., pp. 43–44.

157. Ibid., pp. 52–53.

158. Michael L. Blakey, "Skull Doctors Revisited: Intrinsic Social and Political Bias in the History of American Physical Anthropology. With Special Reference to the Work of Aleš Hrdlička," in *Race and Other Misadventures*, ed. Reynolds and Lieberman, pp. 64–93

159. Aleš Hrdlička, "Human Races," in *Human Biology and Racial Welfare*, ed. Edmund V. Cowdry (London: H. K. Lewis, 1930), pp. 165–66, emphasis in the original.

160. Ibid., p. 166–67.

161. Ibid., p. 172. Hrdlička also identified "additional strains in this large stem" that were best understood as "*sub-races* . . . rather than races": Dinaric, Baltic, Armenoid, Turcic, etc. (ibid.).

162. Ibid., pp. 179–80.

163. Ralph Linton, *The Study of Man: An Introduction*, student's ed. (New York: D. Appleton-Century Co., 1936), pp. 40–41.

164. Franz Boas, "Race," in *General Anthropology*, ed. Franz Boas (Boston: D. C. Heath, 1938), p. 104.

165. Ibid., p. 115.

166. Hogben, *Genetic Principles*, p. 124.

167. Ibid.

168. Ibid., pp. 124–27.

169. Huxley and Haddon, *We Europeans*, pp. 135–36, 115. Discussing the "broad and convenient classification of skin color," they introduced the term *Leucoderm* to designate "white skinned (Caucasian) peoples" (p. 115). There they used *Xanthoderms* for "yellow-skinned peoples" and *Melanoderms* for "black-skinned peoples." "The term Caucasian in ethnology," they said, "must not be linked with the geographical region which it suggests" (p. 115n.1).

170. Ibid., p. 137, emphasis in the original.

171. Montagu, *Man's Most Dangerous Myth*, p. 7.

172. Ruth Benedict, *Race*, in *Theories of Race and Racism*, ed. Les Back and John Solomos (London: Routledge, 2000), pp. 113, 115.

173. Ibid., p. 113.

174. Benedict and Weltfish, "Races of Man," p. 177.

175. UNESCO, "Statement of 1950," p. 90. The second UNESCO statement challenged the first statement's view of race difference, but it did not challenge the racial classification recommended in 1950.

176. In the 1965 edition of *World Book Encyclopedia*, for instance, Wilton Krugman asserted, "Most of the peoples of Europe belong to the Caucasoid group. Some of the best known Caucasoid races are the Nordic, the East Baltic, the

Alpine, the Dinaric [southern European], and the Mediterranean." See Wilton Marion Krugman, "Races of Man," in *World Book Encyclopedia,* vol. 16 (Chicago: Field Enterprises Educational Services, 1965), p. 50.

177. Quoted in Jacobson, *Whiteness,* p. 92.

178. Laura Z. Hobson, *Gentleman's Agreement* (New York, 1947), p. 196, quoted in Jacobson, *Whiteness,* p. 127.

179. Jacobson, *Whiteness,* pp. 127–31.

180. Ibid., p. 129. See also Karen Brodkin Sacks, "How Did the Jews Become White Folks?" in *Race,* ed. Steven Gregory and Roger Sanjek (New Brunswick: Rutgers University Press, 1994).

181. While the ninety-six prominent scientists who signed the second UNESCO statement of 1951 rejected the strong claim of the 1950 statement about equivalent cognitive abilities in the three major races, they acknowledged that scientific research had provided no evidence of heritable racial inequality. To be clear, there were rare race egalitarians throughout the history of race science, but they were decidedly in the minority prior to the present period.

182. Montagu, *Man's Most Dangerous Myth,* p. 43.

183. Ibid., p. 44.

184. Benedict, *Race,* p. 113.

NOTES TO CHAPTER 6

1. Richard Wright, *The Color Curtain,* foreword by Gunnar Myrdal, afterword by Amritjit Singh (Jackson: University of Mississippi/Banner Books, [1956] 1994), pp. 11–12, emphasis in the original.

2. Henry Louis Gates Jr., "Editor's Introduction: Writing 'Race' and the Difference It Makes," *Critical Inquiry* 15 (Autumn 1985), p. 5.

3. John Solomos and Les Back, "Introduction: Theorising Race and Racism," in *Theories of Race and Racism* (London: Routledge, 2000), p. 6.

4. Nancy Stepan, *The Idea of Race in Science: Great Britain 1800–1960* (London: Macmillan, 1982), pp. 173–77.

5. Howard Winant, *The World Is a Ghetto: Race and Democracy since World War II* (New York: Basic Books, 2001), p. 2.

6. Leonard Lieberman and Larry T. Reynolds, "Race: The Deconstruction of a Scientific Concept," in *Race and Other Misadventures: Essays in Honor of Ashley Montagu in His Ninetieth Year,* ed. Leonard Lieberman and Larry T. Reynolds (Dixon Hills, NY: General Hall, 1996), p. 152, emphasis in original.

7. Alice Littlefield, Leonard Lieberman, and Larry T. Reynolds, "Redefining Race: The Potential Demise of a Concept in Physical Anthropology," *Current Anthropology* 23 (December 1982), p. 644. Lawrence Blum usefully refines this point: "Races are not socially constructed; they simply do not exist. Racialized groups, however, are socially constructed, by the historical processes of racialization." See

Lawrence Blum, *"I'm Not a Racist, but . . .": The Moral Quandary of Race* (Ithaca: Cornell University Press, 2002), p. 163. I discuss the notion of *racialized groups* in the concluding chapter.

8. Some prominent social scientists in North America, notably Charles Murray and Richard Herrnstein in the United States and J. Philippe Rushton in Canada, have continued to employ racist assumptions of the old science of race. See Richard Hernnstein and Charles Murray, *The Bell Curve: Intelligence and Class Structure in American Life* (New York: Free Press, 1994); J. Philippe Rushton, *Race, Evolution, and Behavior: A Life History Perspective* (New Brunswick: Transaction Books, 1995).

9. Winant, *World Is a Ghetto,* p. 205.

10. Ibid., p. 134.

11. Wm. Roger Louis, "The European Colonial Empires," in *The Oxford History of the Twentieth Century,* ed. Michael Howard and Wm. Roger Louis (Oxford: Oxford University Press, 1998), pp. 95–100.

12. Quoted in Michael Banton, *The International Politics of Race* (Cambridge: Polity Press, 2002), p. 1.

13. Geoffrey Barraclough, *An Introduction to Contemporary History* (Harmondsworth: Penguin, 1967), pp. 153, 194.

14. Wright, *Color Curtain,* pp. 113–54; Penny Von Eschen, *Race against Empire: Black Americans and Anticolonialism, 1937–57* (Ithaca: Cornell University Press, 1997), pp. 168–73.

15. James Baldwin, *Nobody Knows My Name* (New York: Dell, 1961), pp. 24–54; Von Eschen, *Race against Empire,* pp. 174–75.

16. Eric Foner and Randall Kennedy, "*Brown* at 50," *The Nation* 278, May 3, 2004, pp. 15–17; David J. Garrow, "Why *Brown* Still Matters," *The Nation* 278, May 3, 2004, pp. 45–50.

17. Ronald Takaki, "Reflections of Racial Patterns in America," in *From Different Shores: Perspectives on Race and Ethnicity in America,* 2d ed., ed. Ronald Takaki (New York: Oxford University Press, 1994), p. 223; David M. Reimers, "Immigration," in *Encyclopedia of American Social History,* vol. 1 (New York: Charles Scribner's Sons, 1993), p. 588.

18. Victoria Hattam, "Ethnicity: An American Genealogy," in *Not Just Black and White: Historical and Contemporary Perspectives on Immigration, Race, and Ethnicity in the United States,* ed. Nancy Foner and George M. Fredrickson (New York: Russell Sage, 2004), p. 53, Hattam's emphasis.

19. Matthew Frye Jacobson, *Whiteness of a Different Color: European Immigrants and the Alchemy of Race* (Cambridge: Harvard University Press, 1998), pp. 274–80.

20. *Report of the National Advisory Commission on Civil Disorders,* with a special introduction by Tom Wicker (New York: Bantam Books, 1968), p. 1.

21. Michael K. Brown, Martin Carnoy, Elliott Currie, Troy Duster, David B.

Oppenheimer, Marjorie M. Schultz, and David Wellman, *Whitewashing Race: The Myth of a Color-Blind Society* (Berkeley: University of California Press, 2003).

22. Frantz Fanon, *Black Skins, White Masks,* trans. Charles Lam Markmann (New York: Grove Press, [1952] 1968), p. 110.

23. James Baldwin, *The Fire Next Time* (New York: Dell, 1963), pp. 139–40.

24. Anne Deighton, "The Remaking of Europe," in *Oxford History of the Twentieth Century,* ed. Howard and Lewis, p. 195.

25. The United Kingdom, Ireland, and Denmark joined in 1973, followed by Greece (1981); Spain and Portugal (1986); the former East Germany after German unification (1990); and Sweden, Finland, and Austria (1995). In May 2004, Estonia, Latvia, Lithuania, Poland, the Czech Republic, Slovakia, Hungary, Slovenia, Malta, and Cyprus were admitted. See Patrick E. Tyler, "Old Doubts Hang over Celebrations of a New Europe," *New York Times,* Sunday, May 2, 2004, p. A8.

26. Deighton, "Remaking of Europe," p. 194.

27. Étienne Balibar, *Politics and the Other Scene* (London: Verso, 2002), pp. 110–13.

28. Deighton, "Remaking of Europe," p. 190; Mark Mazower, *Dark Continent: Europe's Twentieth Century* (New York: Vintage Books, 1998), chap. 9.

29. Karen Brodkin Sacks, "How Did the Jews Become White Folks?" in *Race,* ed. Steven Gregory and Roger Sanjek (New Brunswick: Rutgers University Press, 1994); Winant, *World Is a Ghetto.*

30. Leslie Page Moch, "Migration," in *Encyclopedia of European Social History: From 1350–2000,* vol. 2 (New York: Charles Scribner's Sons, 2001), p. 140.

31. Ibid. p. 141.

32. Ibid.; Michael Dummett, *On Immigration and Refugees* (London: Routledge, 2001), pp. 93–96.

33. Moch, "Migration," p. 141.

34. Ibid., p. 142.

35. Ibid., p. 141; Mazower, *Dark Continent,* pp. 323–26.

36. Gisela Kaplan, "Racism," in *Encyclopedia of European Social History: From 1350–2000,* vol. 1 (New York: Charles Scribner's Sons, 2001), p. 550.

37. George M. Fredrickson, *Racism: A Short History* (Princeton: Princeton University Press, 2002), p. 141.

38. Étienne Balibar, "Is There a 'Neo-Racism'?" in Étienne Balibar and Immanuel Wallerstein, *Race, Nation, Class: Ambiguous Identities,* translation of Balibar by Chris Turner (London: Verso, 1990), p. 21.

39. Banton, *International Politics,* pp. 31–32.

40. Ibid., p. 35; Robert Miles, *Racism* (London: Routledge, 1989), p. 46.

41. Banton, *International Politics,* pp. 36–37; Michael Banton, "Racism Today: A Perspective from International Politics," *Ethnic and Racial Studies* 22 (May 1999), p. 607; Nicole Davis, "Race to Durban," *ColorLines* 4 (Fall 2001), pp. 10–13.

42. Makani Thmba-Nixon, "Race in the 'Post–Third World,'" *ColorLines* 4 (Fall 2001), p. 14.

43. Martin Bulmer and John Solomos, "Introduction," in *Racism,* ed. Martin Bulmer and John Solomos (Oxford: Oxford University Press, 1999), p. 14.

44. Stepan, *Idea of Race,* pp. 170–71.

45. Ibid., p. 176.

46. This was the title of a 1962 article by Frank Livingstone (see below).

47. Stepan, *Idea of Race,* p. 176.

48. Stanley M. Garn and Carleton S. Coon, "On the Number of Races of Mankind," *American Anthropologist* 57 (October 1955), p. 996.

49. Ibid.

50. Ibid., pp. 996–97.

51. Ibid., pp. 997–98.

52. See Stepan, *Idea of Race,* p. 177.

53. Garn and Coon, "Number of Races," pp. 999–1000. They spoke of "micro-geographical races" where boundaries between local "race-populations" were "not neatly defined" (pp. 997–98).

54. Ibid., p. 999.

55. William C. Boyd, "Genetics and the Human Race," *Science* 140, June 1963, p. 1057.

56. Ibid., p. 1060.

57. Ibid., pp. 1063–64.

58. Jean Hiernaux, "The Concept of Race in the Taxonomy of Mankind," in *The Concept of Race,* ed. Ashley Montagu (London: Collier Books, [1964] 1970), p. 38.

59. Stanley M. Garn, "Races of Man," in *World Book Encyclopedia,* vol. 16 (Chicago: Field Enterprises Educational Corp., 1974), p. 51, emphasis in the original.

60. Ibid., p. 52.

61. Stanley M. Garn, "Caucasoid," in *Encyclopaedia Britannica,* 14th ed., vol. 5 (Chicago: Encyclopaedia Britannica, Inc., 1970), p. 96.

62. Carleton S. Coon, "Evolution, Human: Races of Homo Sapiens," in *New Encyclopaedia Britannica,* vol. 18: *Macopaedia* (Chicago: Encyclopaedia Britannica, Inc., 1989), p. 970, emphasis added. Garn contributed other parts of the entry.

63. Ibid., pp. 973–78.

64. Stanley M. Garn, "Evolution, Human: Modern Human Populations," in *New Encyclopaedia Britannica,* vol. 18: *Macopaedia* (Chicago: Encyclopaedia Britannica, Inc., 1998), p. 844.

65. Ibid., p. 850.

66. Garn and Coon, "Number of Races," p. 1000.

67. Carleton S. Coon, *The Origin of Races* (New York, 1962), p. 116, quoted in Ashley Montagu, "On Coon's *The Origin of Races,*" in *Concept of Race,* ed. Montagu, p. 237. Coon argued that five geographic races of *Homo erectus* each evolved independently into *Homo sapiens* (Montagu, "On Coon's *Origin,*" p. 229). Garn has called this theory "both exciting and debatable" and, to his credit, disputed claims linking race and intelligence. See Garn, "Modern Human Populations," pp. 846–47, 849–50.

68. Michael Banton, "1960: A Turning Point in the Study of Race Relations," *Daedalus* 103 (Spring 1974), p. 38.

69. Ashley Montagu, "Introduction," in *Concept of Race,* ed. Montagu, p. xii.

70. Ibid., p. xv.

71. Ashley Montagu, "The Concept of Race," in *Concept of Race,* ed. Montagu, p. 14.

72. Ibid., pp. 20–21.

73. Hiernaux, "Concept of Race," p. 43.

74. Ibid., p. 30.

75. Ibid., p. 32.

76. Ibid., p. 33

77. Ibid., pp. 39–40.

78. Ibid., p. 36.

79. Ibid., p. 37.

80. Frank B. Livingstone, "On the Nonexistence of Human Races," in *Concept of Race,* ed. Montagu, p. 47.

81. Ibid., pp. 46–47.

82. Ashley Montagu, "Glossary," in *Concept of Race,* ed. Montagu, pp. 261–62; Livingstone, "Nonexistence," pp. 52–54.

83. Livingstone, "Nonexistence," p. 54.

84. Theodosius Dobzhansky, "Comment," *Current Anthropology* 3 (June 1962), pp. 279–80. Dobzhansky introduced this notion of geographical races in 1937. See Marcus W. Feldman, Richard C. Lewontin, and Mary-Claire King, "Race: A Genetic Melting Pot," *Nature* 424, July 24, 2003, p. 374.

85. Ibid., p. 280.

86. Livingstone, "Nonexistence," p. 57.

87. Ibid.

88. Ibid., pp. 56–57.

89. Montagu, "Concept of Race," pp. 19–20.

90. Ibid., pp. 19–20, 26.

91. Solomos and Back, "Introduction," p. 6; Miles, *Racism.*

92. Richard C. Lewontin, "The Apportionment of Human Diversity," *Evolutionary Biology* 6 (1972), p. 8.

93. Ibid., p. 7, emphasis added.

94. Masatoshi Nei and Arun K. Roychoudhury, "Gene Differences between

Caucasian, Negro, and Japanese Populations," *Science* 177, August 4, 1972, p. 26. Their data for "Caucasians" and "Negroes" were mostly "from the American Caucasians . . . and American Negroes"; a sample of Japanese represented the "Mongoloids" (pp. 26–27).

95. Ibid., pp. 26–27.

96. Masatoshi Nei and Arun K. Roychoudhury, "Genetic Relationship and Evolution of Human Races," *Evolutionary Biology* 14 (1982), pp. 2, 10–11.

97. Lewontin, "Apportionment," pp. 12–22.

98. Ibid., p. 22.

99. Ibid., p. 23.

100. Ibid.

101. Ibid., p. 12.

102. According to the *Los Angeles Times*, this was the largest study yet of human genetic variation. See Robert Lee Hotz, "People Are Same, but Different; Humans Can Be Sorted into Five Groups Based on Ancestry, Major Genetic Study Finds," *Los Angeles Times*, December 20, 2002, p. A41.

103. They used genotypes at 377 autosomal microsatellite loci. See Noah A. Rosenberg, Jonathan K. Pritchard, James L. Weber, Howard M. Cann, Kenneth K. Kidd, Lev A. Zhivotovsky, and Marcus W. Feldman, "Genetic Structure of Human Populations," *Science* 298, December 20, 2002, pp. 2381–85.

104. Ibid., p. 2381.

105. Ibid., pp. 2381–82.

106. Ibid., p. 2384.

107. Ibid., p. 2382.

108. Ibid., pp. 2382–83.

109. Ibid., p. 2384.

110. Nicholas Wade, "Gene Study Identifies Five Main Human Populations, Linking Them to Geography," *New York Times*, December 20, 2002, Late City Edition, Section A, p. 37.

111. Ibid.

112. Ibid. Wade ended his article by noting that many sociologists and anthropologists insist "that race is a cultural idea, not a social one," but he effectively discounted this view.

113. Hotz, "People Are Same," p. A41, emphasis added.

114. Personal communication from Noah Rosenberg, June 21, 2004. The five major geographical regions of the world that the *Science* authors identified correspond to popular notions of race, but in the context of the overall findings and conclusions, this fact in no way lends support to popular notions of race.

115. Feldman, Lewontin, and King, "Race," p. 374.

116. Ibid.

117. Luigi Luca Cavalli-Sforza, *Genes, Peoples, and Languages* (Berkeley: University of California Press, 2000), pp. 9–10.

118. Ibid., pp. 12–13.

119. Ibid., pp. 28–29. He estimates that with regard to any particular genetic marker that we might select, "the variation between two random individuals within any one population is 85 percent as large as that between two individuals randomly selected from the world's population" (p. 29).

120. Ibid., pp. 29–30.

121. Ibid., pp. 30–31.

122. Ibid. p. 145.

123. Ibid., pp. 52, 121, 122.

124. Montagu, "Introduction," p. xii.

125. Montagu certainly understood this. One key reason to abandon "this chimerical concept," he said, was that "the fallacies . . . inherent in the concept of 'race' . . . constitute myths which have been and continue to be extremely destructive." See Ashley Montagu, "'Race' and Humanity," in *Man Observed* (New York: Tower Books, 1971), p. 148.

126. Troy Duster, "Buried Alive: The Concept of Race in Science," *Chronicle of Higher Education*, September 14, 2001, p. B11.

127. Ibid.

128. Ibid.

129. Ibid., p. B12.

130. Cavalli-Sforza, *Genes*, p. 48; Frank B. Livingstone, "Reply," *Current Anthropology* 3 (June 1962), p. 280.

131. Naomi Zack explains that "people homozygous for sickle cell anemia would succumb to that, and people with normal red blood cells could succumb to malaria, so that those heterozygous for sickle cell anemia had the best chances of surviving and reproducing." See Naomi Zack, *Philosophy of Science and Race* (New York: Routledge, 2002), p. 54.

132. Ibid., p. 101.

133. See Paul C. Taylor, *Race: A Philosophical Introduction* (Cambridge: Polity Press, 2004), pp. 80–84.

134. Feldman, Lewontin, and King, "Race," p. 374.

135. Elsewhere, Duster addresses more directly what I call processes of racialization. See Troy Duster, "The 'Morphing' Properties of Whiteness," in *The Making and Unmaking of Whiteness*, ed. Birgit Brander Rasmussen, Eric Klineberg, Irene J. Nexica, and Matt Wray (Durham: Duke University Press, 2001), pp. 113–37.

136. Philip Kitcher, "Race, Ethnicity, Biology, Culture," in *Racism*, ed. Leonard Harris (Amherst, NY: Humanities Books, 1999), pp. 107, 91,

137. Kitcher renders this as "the thesis that races have no biological significance" (ibid., p. 87). This is misleading since it implies that there *are* races but that they "have no biological significance." Those theorists such as K. Anthony Appiah and Naomi Zack who argue that there are *no races* are arguing just that. In Appiah's words, "The truth is that there are no races: there is nothing in the world

that can do all we ask 'race' to do for us." See Anthony Appiah, "The Uncompleted Argument: Du Bois and the Illusion of Race," *Critical Inquiry* 12 (Autumn 1985), p. 35.

138. Kitcher, "Race," p. 87.

139. Ibid., p. 92.

140. Ibid., pp. 93–107.

141. Ibid., p. 97.

142. See Cavalli-Sforza, *Genes*, pp. 57–72; Zack, *Philosophy*, chap. 2; Christopher Stringer and Robin McKie, *African Exodus: The Origins of Modern Humanity* (New York: Henry Holt, 1996).

143. Kitcher, "Race," p. 94.

144. Joshua M. Glasgow, "On the New Biology of Race," *Journal of Philosophy* 100 (September 2003), p. 473.

145. Montagu, "'Race' and Humanity," p. 148.

NOTES TO CHAPTER 7

1. My chapter title is taken from a 1994 article about the first Russian-Chechen war (1994–96) in *The Guardian* (London). See James Meek, "Where Caucasian Means Black," *The Guardian*, December 3, 1994, p. 15.

2. Saint-Marc Girardin, in *Journal des Débats*, December 1831, quoted in E. J. Hobsbawm, *The Age of Revolution, 1789–1848* (New York: New American Library, 1962), p. 238.

3. Étienne Balibar, *Politics and the Other Scene*, trans. Christine Jones, James Swenson, and Chris Turner (London: Verso, 2002), chap. 5.

4. Étienne Balibar, "Racism and Nationalism," in Étienne Balibar and Immanuel Wallerstein, *Race, Nation, Class: Ambiguous Identities*, translation of Balibar by Chris Turner (London and New York: Verso, 1991), p. 37.

5. Vron Ware, "Perfidious Albion: Whiteness and the International Imagination," in *The Making and Unmaking of Whiteness*, ed. Birgit Brander Rasmussen, Eric Klineberg, Irene J. Nexica, and Matt Wray (Durham: Duke University Press, 2001), p. 205.

6. "Transcaucasia," in *New Encyclopaedia Britannica*, vol. 28 (Chicago: Encyclopaedia Britannica, Inc., 1998), p. 751.

7. Ibid., p. 755.

8. Ibid.

9. Norman Davies, *Europe: A History* (New York: HarperPerennial, 1998), pp. 265, 275–84.

10. Ronald Grigor Suny, *The Making of the Georgian Nation*, 2d ed. (Bloomington and Indianapolis: Indiana University Press, 1994), pp. 24–27.

11. Ibid., pp. 49–59.

12. Marie Bennigsen Broxup, "Introduction: Russia and the North Caucasus,"

in *The North Caucasus Barrier: The Russian Advance towards the Muslim World,* ed. Marie Bennigsen Broxup (London: Hurst and Co., 1992), p. 3.

13. James Minahan, *Encyclopedia of the Stateless Nations: Ethnic Groups and National Groups around the World* (Westport, CT: Greenwood Press, 2002), p. 438.

14. Austin Jersild, *Orientalism and Empire: North Caucasus Mountain Peoples and the Georgian Frontier, 1845–1917* (Montreal and Kingston: McGill-Queen's University Press, 2002), pp. 6–7.

15. Ibid., p. 7; Catherine J. Danks, "Russia in Search of Itself," in *Globalization and National Interests: Crisis or Opportunity?* ed. Paul Kennedy and Catherine J. Danks (New York: Palgrave, 2001), p. 37.

16. "Transcaucasia," pp. 756, 772.

17. Ibid., p. 772; Suny, *Georgian Nation,* p. 59.

18. "Transcaucasia," p. 772.

19. Neal Ascherson, "After the Revolution," *London Review of Books* 26, March 4, 2004, pp. 5, 3.

20. Jersild, *Orientalism and Empire,* p. 8.

21. Ibid.

22. Ibid., p. 4

23. Broxup, "Introduction," p. 3.

24. Ibid.

25. Ibid., p. 4.

26. Ibid.

27. Minahan, *Encyclopedia,* p. 438; Broxup, "Introduction," p. 4.

28. Broxup, "Introduction," pp. 4–11. The Chechens and Ingush managed to survive a massive World War II "deportation during which half of their population died" (p. 10). Minahan says that between "1940 and 1945 the Chechen population is estimated to have declined by at least 25%." See Minahan, *Encyclopedia,* p. 440.

29. The lead-up to the first Chechen war included a move by the Ingush in 1992, with support from Russia, to separate themselves from Chechnya; increasing internal opposition to Dudayev's government in 1993 and 1994; and widespread mobilization against Russia behind Dudayev in 1994, after Russia expelled hundreds of Chechens from Moscow in 1993. See Minahan, *Encyclopedia,* pp. 440–41; Robert Cottrell, "Chechnya: How Russia Lost," *New York Review of Books* 45, September 24, 1998, p. 45.

30. Cottrell, "Chechnya," p. 44.

31. Christian Caryl, "Mysteries of the Caucasus," *New York Review of Books* 51, March 11, 2004, p. 30.

32. Ibid., p. 31. In contrast, Broxup, writing in 1992, suggested that this apparent acquiescence was "not the sign of a lack of desire for independence or political maturity, but . . . points to the fact that the North Caucasians remain faithful to a certain ideal of a 'mountain confederation' where the uniting factor was always

Islam. You cannot have a 'national front' in Daghestan where there are some twenty different nations." See Broxup, "Introduction," p. 12.

33. Alf Grannes, "'Persons of Caucasian Nationality'—Russian Negative Stereotypes," in *Contrasts and Solutions in the Caucasus,* ed. Ole Høiris and Sefa Martin Yürükel (Aarhus, Denmark: Aarhus University Press, 1998), p. 22.

34. P. Zubov, *Kartina kavkazskago kraja* . . . (A Picture of the Caucasian Region and Neighboring Lands Belonging to Russia) (St. Petersburg, 1834), p. 173, quoted in Grannes, "'Caucasian Nationality,'" p. 22; Broxup, "Introduction," p. 9.

35. Grannes, "'Caucasian Nationality,'" p. 23; Zubov quoted in Broxup, "Introduction," p. 9.

36. Quoted in Grannes, "'Caucasian Nationality,'" p. 22.

37. Broxup, "Introduction, " p. 13.

38. Ibid., pp. 29, 24.

39. Zubov, quoted in Grannes, "'Caucasian Nationality,'" p. 24.

40. Grannes, "'Caucasian Nationality,'" pp. 28–29.

41. Ibid., pp. 26–27.

42. "Caucasus," in *Encyclopaedia Britannica* (Edinburgh: Adam and Charles Black, 1853), p. 340.

43. Ibid., p. 342.

44. Ibid., p. 343.

45. Ibid.

46. Élisée Reclus, *The Universal Geography: The Earth and Its Inhabitants,* ed. A. H. Keane (London: J. S. Virtue, 1876), p. 33.

47. Ibid., pp. 33–34.

48. Reclus's view is closer to Ripley's, however, since both place the Caucasians outside Europe, while Deniker counts them among the "races and peoples of Europe." See chapter 4.

49. Jack Carrick Trevor, "Race," in *Chamber's Encyclopedia,* new ed., vol. 11 (London: George Newnes, 1950), p. 433. Trevor cites an 1932 article by Bunak on this issue (p. 437).

50. N. N. Cheboksarov, "Races of Man," in *Great Soviet Encyclopedia,* translation of the 3d ed., vol. 21 (New York: Macmillan, 1978), p. 377.

51. Ibid.

52. Ripley himself distinguished the Caucasians from the "Armenoid type," represented primarily by Armenians. The Caucasians were also racially distinct from the Russian Slavs in the north and the Iranian peoples of the south. He also noted that Deniker's "Adriatic" or "Dinaric race" encompassed Serbians, Croatians, and Albanians. See William Z. Ripley, *The Races of Europe* (New York: D. Appleton & Co., 1899), pp. 412, 440–41, 444. Cheboksarov's "Pamiro-Ferganian" refers to peoples of the Pamir Mountain region of central Asia, encompassing Tajikistan, Kyrgyzstan, Afghanistan, and Pakistan.

53. Alaina Lemon, "Slurs, Socialism, and 'Civilization,'" *Transition* 2 (January 12, 1996), p. 26.

54. Meek, "Where Caucasian Means Black," p. 15.

55. Michael R. Gordon, "Caught in a Backlash to Moscow's Bombings," *New York Times,* September 15, 1999, sec. A, p. 1.

56. Grannes, "'Caucasian Nationality,'" p. 20.

57. On England's "blacks," see Paul Gilroy, *"There Ain't No Black in the Union Jack": The Cultural Politics of Race and Nation,* foreword by Houston A. Baker Jr. (Chicago: University of Chicago Press, [1987] 1991).

58. Grannes, "'Caucasian Nationality,'" p. 21. Grannes rightly adds that this is not to say that the more traditional sort of racism has disappeared in the West.

59. Ibid., pp. 21–22, 19.

60. Frank Füredi notes that officially, at least, the USSR "preached a universalistic creed which was hostile to any manifestation of discrimination." See Frank Füredi, *The Silent War: Imperialism and Changing Perceptions of Race* (London: Pluto Press, 1998), p. 213; and N. N. Cheboksarov, "Racism," in *Great Soviet Encyclopedia,* vol. 21, p. 381.

61. Ronald Grigor Suny, "The State of Nations: The Ex–Soviet Union and Its Peoples," *Dissent* 43 (Summer 1996), p. 96.

62. Danks, "Russia in Search of Itself," p. 44.

63. Ibid., pp. 39–45; Grannes, "'Caucasian Nationality,'" p. 30.

64. Grannes, "'Caucasian Nationality,'" p. 24.

65. The North Caucasian nations also currently remain within the Russian-recognized boundaries of the Russian Federation. See Cottrell, "Chechnya"; Caryl, "Mysteries of the Caucasus."

66. John Noble Wilford, "Skulls in the Caucasus Linked to Early Humans in Africa," *New York Times,* Friday, May 12, 2000, p. A28.

67. Quoted in ibid.

68. Ascherson, "After the Revolution," pp. 6, 5.

69. Ibid., p. 6

70. Ibid.

71. Johann Gottfried Herder, *Ideas on the Philosophy of the History of Humankind* (1784), 3d ed. (1828), trans. Thomas Nenon (1999), in *The Idea of Race,* ed. Robert Bernasconi and Tommy Lott (Indianapolis: Hackett, 2000), p. 26.

72. Ibid.

73. Grannes notes that stereotypes are "no less prevalent among Caucasians than among Russians." He does not discuss race thinking among Caucasians, however. See Grannes, "'Caucasian Nationality,'" p. 20.

NOTES TO THE CONCLUSION

1. Stuart Hall, "Subjects in History: Making Diasporic Identities," in *The House That Race Built,* ed. Wahneema Lubiano (New York: Vintage Books, 1998), p. 299.

2. Colette Guillaumin, "'I Know It's Not Nice, but . . .': The Changing Face of Race," in *Race, Identity, and Citizenship: A Reader,* ed. Rodolfo D. Torres, Louis F. Mirón, and Jonathan Xavier Inda (Malden, MA, and Oxford: Blackwell, 1999), p. 46.

3. Nancy Fraser, *Justice Interruptus: Critical Reflections on the "Postsocialist" Condition* (New York: Routledge, 1997), p. 12.

4. Ashley Montagu, "'Race' and Humanity," in *Man Observed* (New York: Tower Publications, 1971), p. 149.

5. I still have a copy of the University of California, Davis's "Confidential Applicant Survey" from 1997, form D4483–3 (11/97) Cal Code 71461–188. This form asks applicants to identify themselves, for affirmative action purposes, in terms of "sex" and "ethnicity." Its ethnicity categories are: American Indian, Asian/Pacific Islander, Black (i.e., "Black/African American [not of Hispanic origin]"), Hispanic ("including Black individuals whose origins are Hispanic"), and White (i.e., "White/Caucasian [including the Middle East]").

6. Keep in mind, though, that I am also arguing that no one is really of a "mixed-race" background in the biological sense.

7. Adrian Piper, "Passing for White, Passing for Black," in *Passing and Fictions of Identity,* ed. Elaine K. Ginsberg (Durham: Duke University Press, 1996).

8. If I had been born in the United States in 1910 or 1920 rather than in 1960, I would not have been unequivocally "white" due to my Jewish Eastern European *ethnic* background. That is, Jews of Eastern European origin then had a more marginalized and racially ambiguous status in the United States, but that has changed. See Matthew Frye Jacobson, *Whiteness of a Different Color: European Immigrants and the Alchemy of Race* (Cambridge: Harvard University Press, 1998).

9. Jonathan Marks, *Human Biodiversity: Genes, Race, and History* (New York: Aldine de Gruyter, 1995), p. 162.

10. Ibid., p. 163.

11. This leads Orlando Patterson to distinguish between "Afro-Americans" (persons who identify themselves as having African ancestry but who are more "American" than "African") and "African Americans" (referring to more recent African immigrants to the United States). See Orlando Patterson, *The Ordeal of Integration: Progress and Resentment in America's "Racial" Crisis* (Washington, DC: Civitas, 1998), p. xi.

12. Marks, *Human Biodiversity,* p. 162.

13. Ashley Montagu, "The Concept of Race," in *The Concept of Race,* ed. Ashley Montagu (London: Collier Books, [1964] 1970), p. 17.

14. Ibid., p. 25.

15. Werner Sollors, "Foreword: Theories of Ethnicity," in *Theories of Ethnicity: A Classical Reader*, ed. Werner Sollors (New York: New York University Press, 1996).

16. Howard Winant, *The World Is a Ghetto: Race and Democracy since World War II* (New York: Basic Books, 2001), p. 292.

17. Montagu, "Concept of Race," p. 25.

18. Patterson, *Ordeal*, p. xi.

19. On African ethnic diversity, see K. Anthony Appiah, *In My Father's House: Africa in the Philosophy of Culture* (Oxford: Oxford University Press, 1993), chap. 4.

20. Piper, "Passing," p. 267, emphasis in the original.

21. Lawrence Blum, "Multiculturalism, Racial Justice, and Community: Reflections on Charles Taylor's 'The Politics of Recognition,'" in *Defending Diversity: Contemporary Philosophical Perspectives on Pluralism and Diversity*, ed. L. Foster and P. Herzog (Amherst: University of Massachusetts Press, 1994), p. 188.

22. See Grace Elizabeth Hale, *Making Whiteness: The Culture of Segregation in the South, 1890–1940* (New York: Vintage, 1998).

23. Jacobson, *Whiteness*, p. 105; Robert Miles and Rodolfo D. Torres, "Does 'Race' Matter? Transatlantic Perspectives on Racism after 'Race Relations,'" in *Race, Identity, and Citizenship*, ed. Torres, Mirón, and Inda, pp. 21–27. There is more to be said about the genealogy of "ethnicity" and the relationship between "ethnicity" and "race." See Victoria Hattam, "Ethnicity: An American Genealogy," in *Not Just Black and White: Historical and Contemporary Perspectives on Immigration, Race, and Ethnicity in the United States*, ed. Nancy Foner and George M. Fredrickson (New York: Russell Sage, 2004); Sollors, "Theories of Ethnicity."

24. Paul Taylor summarizes just how racialized identities continue to matter in the United States:

> [F]or the year 2000, 7 percent of whites fell below the poverty line, compared to 11 percent of Asians and over 20 percent of Latinos, African Americans, and Native Americans. . . . [F]rom 1998 to 2000, the median income for white households was more than $45,000, while the figure was a bit lower for Asian households, around $41,000, and much lower for Latinos, African Americans, and Native Americans, none of whom rose above $32,000 (with Native Americans on reservations or in native villages coming in at about $18,000). . . . [N]on-whites are much more likely to be unemployed, to commit and become victims of violent crime, to receive substandard medical care, to live in inadequate housing, or to lack health insurance.

Paul C. Taylor, *Race: A Philosophical Introduction* (Cambridge: Polity, 2004), p. 81. The wealth gap between U.S. racialized groups is even larger than the income gap. See Melvin Oliver and Thomas Shapiro, *Black Wealth/White Wealth: A New Perspective on Racial Inequality* (New York: Routledge, 1995).

25. See Taylor, *Race,* pp. 87–95.

26. Kwame Anthony Appiah, "Dialogue between Kwame Anthony Appiah and Robert S. Boyton," *Daedalus* 132 (Summer 2003), p. 108. See also K. Anthony Appiah, "Race, Culture, Identity: Misunderstood Connections," in K. Anthony Appiah and Amy Gutmann, *Color Conscious: The Political Morality of Race* (Princeton: Princeton University Press, 1996).

27. Taylor, *Race,* p. 95.

28. Ibid., p. 86.

29. Ibid., pp. 108–9.

30. Ibid., pp. 56–57.

31. Ibid., p. 117.

32. Montagu, "Concept of Race," p. 26.

33. On "social races," see Naomi Zack, *Philosophy of Science and Race* (New York: Routledge, 2002).

34. Miles and Torres, "Does 'Race' Matter?" p. 32.

35. John Rodman, "The Dolphin Papers," *North American Review* 259 (Spring 1974), p. 16.

36. Ibid.

37. Michel Foucault, "The Subject and Power," in Hubert L. Dreyfus and Paul Rabinow, *Michel Foucault: Beyond Structuralism and Hermeneutics,* 2d ed. (Chicago: University of Chicago Press, 1983), p. 220.

38. Hall, "Subjects in History," p. 299.

39. Ibid., p. 290.

40. Ibid., p. 298. People also exercise power in related ways through discourses of nation, civilization, gender, sexuality, intelligence, and able-bodiedness/disability.

41. See Foucault, "Subject and Power," p. 212; Donald S. Moore, Anand Pandian, and Jake Kosek, "Introduction. The Cultural Politics of Race and Nature: Terrains of Power and Practice," in *Race, Nature, and the Politics of Difference,* ed. Donald S. Moore, Jake Kosek, and Anand Pandian (Durham: Duke University Press, 2003), p. 43.

42. Étienne Balibar, "Racism and Nationalism," in Étienne Balibar and Immanuel Wallerstein, *Race, Nation, Class: Ambiguous Identities,* translation of Balibar by Chris Turner (London and New York: Verso, 1991).

43. Stephen Jay Gould, "The Geometer of Race," *Discover* 15, November 1994, p. 67.

44. Michel Foucault, "Truth and Power," in *Power/Knowledge: Selected Interviews and Other Writings, 1972–1977,* ed. Colin Gordon (New York: Pantheon, 1980); Anne Fausto-Sterling, "Is Science Objective?" *Women's Review of Books* 21 (April 2004), pp. 7–8.

45. Zack, *Philosophy,* p. 5.

46. Susan Haack, "Staying for the Answer," *Times Literary Supplement,* July 9, 1999, p. 13.

47. Ibid. One necessary caveat to Haack's view is that with respect to social reality, what is true is in some ways relative to perspective, or social convention. For instance, when I raise my hand in a certain context, it means that am voting yes (or no) to a certain proposition, but this holds true only in certain contexts, in relation to certain conventions. That said, the rest of her argument holds true. In the social sciences and humanities as well as in the natural sciences, claims of truth are important, and we need to distinguish between what is true and what is merely accepted as true.

48. Sandra Harding says, "[T]he systematic activation of democracy-increasing interests and values—especially in representing diverse interests in the sciences when socially contentious issues are the object of concern—in general contributes to the objectivity of science." See Sandra Harding, "Introduction: Eurocentric Scientific Illiteracy—A Challenge for the World Community," in *The "Racial" Economy of Science*, ed. Sandra Harding (Bloomington and Indianapolis: Indiana University Press, 1993), p. 18. See also Linda Martín Alcoff, "Immanent Truth," *Science in Context* 10 (Spring 1997), pp. 97–112.

49. Zack, *Philosophy*, pp. 4–5.

50. This book, then, is closely related to critical studies of racialized whiteness. See David Roediger, *Colored White: Transcending the Racial Past* (Berkeley: University of California Press, 2002), chap. 1.

51. Ruth Frankenberg, "Introduction: Local Whitenesses, Localizing Whiteness," in *Displacing Whiteness: Essays in Social and Cultural Criticism*, ed. Ruth Frankenberg (Durham: Duke University Press, 1997), p. 4.

52. Jacobson, *Whiteness*, pp. 94–95.

53. Winant, *World Is a Ghetto*, p. 305.

54. Ibid.

55. Lawrence Blum, *"I'm Not a Racist, but . . .": The Moral Quandary of Race* (Ithaca: Cornell University Press, 2002), p. 149.

56. James Baldwin, "An Open Letter to My Sister, Angela Davis," in Angela Y. Davis and other political prisoners, *If They Come in the Morning*, foreword by Julian Bond (New York: Signet, 1971), p. 22.

57. Clayborne Carson, "Parting the Country," *Dissent* 45 (Summer 1998), p. 111; Micaela di Leonardo, "White Ethnicities, Identity Politics, and Baby Bear's Chair," *Social Text* 41 (Winter 1994), pp. 165–91; Eric Foner, "Response to Eric Arnesen," *International Labor and Working-Class History* 60 (Fall 2001), pp. 57–60.

58. Martin Luther King Jr., *Where Do We Go from Here: Chaos or Community?* (New York: Harper and Row, 1967), p. 68.

59. George Lipsitz, *The Possessive Investment in Whiteness* (Philadelphia: Temple University Press, 1998), pp. 18, 16–19.

60. Cheryl Harris, "Whiteness as Property," *Harvard Law Review* 106 (June 1993), p. 1777.

61. Ibid., p. 1741.

62. Ibid., p. 1742.

63. Paul Gilroy, *Against Race: Imagining Political Culture beyond the Color Line* (Cambridge: Harvard University Press, 2000), pp. 15, 18, 356.

64. Montagu, "'Race' and Humanity," p. 154.

65. Zack, *Philosophy,* p. 112.

66. See Rodman, "Dolphin Papers."

67. Gilroy, *Against Race,* p. 17

68. Paul Gilroy, "Race Ends Here," *Ethnic and Racial Studies* 21 (September 1998), pp. 838–39, 840, 842; Gilroy, *Against Race,* pp. 50–51.

69. Gilroy, "Race Ends Here," p. 842. Gilroy acknowledges that "to renounce race for analytical purposes is not to judge all appeals to it in the profane world of political cultures as formally equivalent" (p. 842).

70. Blum, *"Not a Racist,"* pp. 158, 147, emphasis in the original.

71. Heidi Hartmann, "The Unhappy Marriage of Marxism and Feminism," in *Dogmas and Dreams: A Reader in Modern Political Ideologies,* 2d ed., ed. Nancy Love (Chatham, NJ: Chatham House Publishers, 1998), p. 510.

72. James Baldwin, *No Name in the Street* (New York: Dial Press, 1972), p. 190.

73. Michael Eric Dyson, "The Labor of Whiteness, the Whiteness of Labor, and the Perils of Whitewashing," in *Audacious Democracy: Labor, Intellectuals, and the Social Reconstruction of America,* ed. Steven Fraser and Joshua B. Freeman (Boston: Houghton Mifflin, 1997), p. 171.

74. Blum, *"Not a Racist,"* pp. 149–55; Melissa Nobles, "Racial Categorization and Censuses," in *Census and Identity: The Politics of Race, Ethnicity, and Language in National Censuses,* ed. David I. Kertzer and Dominique Arel (Cambridge: Cambridge University Press, 2002), pp. 54–60. It is not always easy to decide who should (and should not) be included in each of these racialized categories, and the task is further complicated by ideas about "mixed-race" persons. These difficulties, however, do not invalidate the need to take account of racialized identities to overcome racialized inequality.

75. As Blum says, "The term 'racialized groups' is . . . a way of acknowledging that some groups have been *created* by being treated as if they were races, while also acknowledging that 'race' in its popular meaning is entirely false." See Blum, *"Not a Racist,"* p. 160.

# Index

Abolitionism, 99

Affirmative action, 19, 231, 252

Afghans, 104, 133

Africa: East, 238; North, 28–29, 53, 76, 83, 134, 141, 153, 168, 213, 219; Pan-African Congress, 168, 171; "scramble for," 121; southern, 199; West, 111, 113, 237–238

African Americans, 11, 13, 46, 152, 195–196, 215–216, 236–237, 239–240, 243, 252, 321n11; and hereditary servitude, 47; "Double V" campaign, 171; "great migration" of, 170; legal oppression of, 47

Africans: "black," 24, 28, 30, 34–36, 54, 63, 66, 84, 94, 164, 204; Congress of Negro-African Writers and Artists, 195; North, 104, 141–142, 152; and racial classification, 54, 69, 92, 104, 111–113, 153, 202, 215; sub-Saharan, 2, 28, 30, 36, 62, 271n140; West, 43, 204, 215

Algeria (also Algerians), 99, 195, 198; French colonialism in, 99, 121; independence from France, 195

Allen, Theodore, 268n105

Altai, Mount, 110

American race (also American Indian race), 78, 89–90, 106–107, 201–202, 209, 247; American variety, 76–77, 81, 89, 101, 103, 114

American Revolution, 46

Americans, 64–65, 69, 239; "Anglo-Teutonic," 144; Asian, 11, 243, 249, 251; Euro- (also European Americans), 120, 215, 240, 243. See also African Americans; Anglo-American; Latinos (also Hispanics); Native Americans (also American Indians, Indians); United States

Americas, 16, 62, 69, 75, 99, 124, 153, 164, 177, 210–211

Anatomy, 13, 91, 100–102, 105, 111, 202; comparative, 14, 50–51, 73, 77, 100, 129

Anderson, Benedict, 27. See also "Imagined community"

Anglo-American, 119–120, 124–125, 164–165, 171; "Anglo-American" branch, 114

Anglo-Saxons, 107, 124–125, 128, 132, 135, 144, 150, 153; supremacy of, 150

Anthropocentrism, 68–69

Anthropology: cultural, 135, 151, 174; genetical, 200; physical, 100, 107, 111, 117, 129, 144, 151, 154, 157, 173, 180–181, 200, 246; social, 174; in Soviet Union, 228, 230

"Anthropomorpha," 65

Anti-racism, 8, 14, 163, 168, 175–176, 178, 194, 199, 214, 235, 246, 250, 252

Anti-Semitism, 32, 96, 125–126, 154–155, 158

Apes, 66, 68, 91–92, 97

Appiah, Kwame Anthony, 13, 241–242, 256n24, 316n137

Arabs (Arabians), 23, 35, 43, 71, 73, 86, 103–104, 106, 108, 113, 133, 135, 152, 159, 167, 215, 221; Arabian branch, 87

Ararat, Mount, 82, 232, 282n112. *See also* Armenia (also Armenians); Noah; Noah's Ark

Aristotle, 244

Armenia (also Armenians), 2–3, 28, 58, 82, 93, 104, 147, 219, 221, 223, 226–227, 230–231, 233–234, 282n112; Armenian (or Syrian) branch, 103

Aryan race, 6–7, 21, 83, 87, 98, 111, 118, 120, 126, 128–129, 133, 136, 144–145, 154–157, 187, 227; Aryanism, 158; Aryan linguistic group, 137, 147, 152; supremacy of, 156, 160

Asians (Asiatics), 56, 66, 73, 88, 128, 132, 142, 172, 195–196, 198–199, 215, 252

"Atlantidae," 112–113

Atlas, Mount, 110

Australia, 16, 74, 111, 143, 164–168, 171–172, 191; Colored Races Restriction and Regulation Acts of, 164; "White Australia" policy, 165; Aboriginal Australians, 133, 135, 159, 183–184, 186; Euro-Australians, 120

Austria, 124–126, 150, 155, 170

Bacon, Francis, 51

Bacon's Rebellion, 46

Baldwin, James, 196, 248, 252

Balibar, Étienne, 21, 198, 220

Balkans, 23, 126; slavery in, 34; serfdom in, 34

Barkan, Elazar, 173–174, 180

Bartlett, Robert, 25, 263n10, 263n13

Barzun, Jacques, 173

Beddoe, John, 133, 135, 143–145, 154

Belgians (also Belgium), 99, 122–123, 158, 195, 197–198

Benedict, Ruth, 13, 178, 187, 190

Bernier, François, 24, 52–60, 64, 73–74, 81, 86, 247, 274n4

Biology, 9, 100, 153–154, 162–163, 173–178, 180, 192, 194, 198–200, 202, 204–208, 211, 213–218, 229, 237, 240–242, 245–246, 250, 253; molecular, 208, 214; "racial," 176

"Blackness," 109, 199, 220, 229–230, 233; as primeval, 109

Black people (also "Blacks"), 2, 164, 168, 171, 195–196, 204, 229, 235, 239–241, 247, 249, 251–252; physical superiority of, 152; political activism of, 171, 196; as slaves, 28, 204. *See also* African Americans; Africans; "Colored" peoples; Negroes

Blood: groups or types, 177, 186, 201–202, 242, 245; purity of, 31

Blum, Lawrence, 240, 310n7

Blumenbach, Johann Friedrich, 5–6, 13, 56–59, 73–92, 101–102, 106–107, 111–115, 119, 127, 130–131, 133–135, 137, 147, 154, 174, 177, 187, 201, 219, 232–233, 280n98; and "vertical scale," 77, 134. See also *On the Natural Variety of Mankind*

Boas, Franz, 157–160, 174–176, 178–179, 181, 186, 190, 308n128, 308n148

Boulainvilliers, Comte Henri de, 37–38

Boyd, William, 200–202

Brazil, 99, 172, 199, 304n56; slavery in, 121

British Isles, 38, 99, 133, 135

Broca, Paul, 101, 117, 129

Buffon, George Louis Leclerc, Comte de, 52, 57, 59, 63, 68–70, 80–81, 83, 109, 130

Burke, Edmund, 42, 97

Camper, Petrus, 91–92, 97, 119, 131

Canada, 164–165, 168, 171–172, 191, 257n27, 294n49; and Immigration Act of 1910, 165; immigration to, 294n49

Capitalism, 8, 9–10, 15, 23, 42, 61, 118, 126, 169, 204, 244, 247–248, 251; capitalist development, 119–120, 122

Caribbean, 99, 166, 198–199, 229

Carpenter, William, 95, 113

Caucasian, as race: beauty (handsomeness) of, 77, 102; branches of, 108; and "Caucasian-Jewish race," 115; as Caucasian or Tatar "branch," 85–86; as Caucasic division or type, 137, 141–143, 155, 162, 187; and Caucasic "family" of humankind, 106–107, 141, 143, 154; as Caucasic (or Caucasoid) "stock," 186, 188; as Caucasoid, 205, 208–209, 309n176; historical genealogy of, 12, 17, 30, 52–54, 58–59, 63, 73, 133, 233–234, 245; *Homo caucasicus*, 137, 141, 147; as misnomer, 147, 169; in popular discourse, 92, 95, 117, 247; in scientific discourse, 13, 92, 95; seven "families" of, 106–108; as "species," 105; supremacy of, 96, 107, 121, 143, 153; as "variety," 6, 76–77, 80–81, 88–89, 101, 103–104, 113–114. *See also* Blumenbach, Johann Friedrich; Meiners, Christoph

Caucasian peoples: as "Asiatic," 120, 220, 226–227, 231; beauty of, 56, 70, 83, 86, 102, 112, 219, 226–227; as "dark-skinned" or "black," 4–5, 21, 136, 141, 219–220, 229, 231, 233; as Europeans, 112, 120; European stereotypes of, 226–227; as independent, 227; as "lazy," 225; as "rebels" or "bandits," 226; Russian stereotypes of, 225–226; as "savages," 225; as Semitic or Arab, 152; as slaves, 2, 28, 34. *See also* Arme-

nia (also Armenians); Chechens (also Tschetshens); Circassians (also Adygei, Cherkess); Georgians (also Kartvelians)

Caucasus region (also Caucasia), 1, 20, 27–28, 58, 70, 73, 82–83, 85–86, 89, 102, 104, 106, 110, 133–134, 147–148, 151, 155, 157, 211, 219–229, 232–233, 282n115, 283n125, 283n127; Jews in, 155; Mount Caucasus, 5–6, 81–82, 110; North Caucasus (also Ciscaucasia), 221, 223–224, 226, 228; Russian conquest of, 224–225; Transcaucasia (also southern Caucasia), 221, 224–226, 231; Transcaucasian Federation, 223. *See also* Armenia (also Armenians); Chechens (also Tschetshens); Georgia; Russia

Cavalli-Svorza, Luigi Luca, 212–214

Celts (also Kelts), 22, 23, 36–38, 87–88, 103, 105–106, 119, 123–125, 128–129, 132, 134–135, 141, 144, 152, 189; Celtic language (also Gaelic), 135

Cephalic index, 21, 118, 129–132, 148–149, 158, 162, 182–183

Chamberlain, Houston Stewart, 7, 129, 157–158

Chechens (also Tschetschens), 4, 93–94, 148–149, 219, 221, 224–225, 229–234, 318n28; criminality of, 226; as "dark-skinned" or "black," 21, 199, 219, 221, 224, 229, 232; deportation of, 224; Russian-Chechen wars, 4, 21, 219–220, 224, 229, 231, 318n28

China, 25, 34, 55, 102, 166–168, 172, 177, 192; People's Republic of, 168, 173; and color consciousness, 266n64

Chinese people, 3, 64, 71, 86, 127, 133, 135, 169, 183, 187, 305n58

Christendom, 23–25, 27–28, 39, 58, 120, 172, 220–221; as Latin Christendom, 263n9, 263n13

Christianity (also Christians), 2, 23, 24, 27, 28, 30, 39, 61, 64, 76, 82, 172, 220–221, 225, 232; New Christians, 32–33; Orthodox, 221, 223, 225, 231–232; as slaves, 47

Circassians (also Adygei, Cherkess), 2, 28, 34, 56, 69–70, 81, 93, 104, 112, 120, 152, 154, 210–211, 219, 224, 227, 233–234; beauty of, 83–84, 102, 106, 112, 219, 226, 233

Civil Rights movement. *See* United States

Class conflict/stratification, 8, 120, 123, 144, 249, 251

Clines, 203, 205–206

Colonialism, 23, 38–39, 87, 94, 99, 126, 164–165, 167–168, 171–172, 192, 195–196, 203–204, 214, 231, 239, 244

Colonization, European, 10, 44, 57, 62, 94, 116, 143, 198, 204

"Color-blindness," 248

"Colored" peoples, 141, 165–166, 168–169, 171, 192, 195–196; "Charter for," 171; League of, 171. *See also* Black people (also "Blacks"); Negroes; People "of color"

"Color line," 162–165, 169, 172, 175–176, 181, 191

Columbus, Christopher, 32

Congo, 158, 195

Congress of Vienna, 97

Coon, Carleton, 143, 200, 202–204, 209, 217, 314n67

Crania: "cranial capacity," 105, 107–108, 137, 182; craniology, 14, 100, 109, 119, 131, 137, 143, 200; types of, 108, 130–134, 152, 158. *See also* Morton, Samuel George; Skulls

Crimean War, 126, 226

Critical realism, 16, 260n 51, 260n59, 260n60. *See also* Science, scientific realism

Critical theory, 8, 234

Crusades, 27

Cuvier, Georges, 20, 95–96, 100–104, 108–109, 111, 113, 153, 163, 181, 187, 190–191, 219, 252

Darwin, Charles (also Darwinian), 101, 117, 129–130, 133, 137, 151, 208, 269n114

Davis, David Brion, 2, 49, 266n59

Decolonization, 21, 167, 173, 193–195, 198, 203, 246

"Degeneration," racial, 69–70, 80–81, 87, 89, 108–109, 130

Delany, Martin R., 13, 152–153

De Lapouge, Georges Vacher, 118, 141, 144, 162

Democratization, 170, 305n61; democratizing movements, 17, 246

Deniker, Joseph, 13, 133, 143, 151, 156, 159, 183, 190, 219, 228, 319n48

Disraeli, Benjamin, 113–115

Dmanisi skulls, 232

Dobzhansky, Theodosius, 206–207, 217, 314n84

Down syndrome (also "mongolism"), 130

Du Bois, W. E. B., 13, 152–154, 159–160, 164, 168–169, 171, 181, 191, 299n192

Dudayev, General Djokar, 224, 318n29

Duster, Troy, 214–216, 316n135

Dutch, 46, 99, 132; colonies, 44–45, 49, 99

"Eastern Question," 126

Egalitarianism, 159, 174, 176, 178–180, 190, 193, 246. *See also* Equality

Egyptians, 53–54, 86, 103, 107–108, 110, 153; as Caucasians, 108, 111, 141; and Copts, 108

England, 36–38, 39, 44, 53, 57, 100, 111, 113, 118, 123, 125–126, 128, 132, 166, 199, 229; English people, 92, 107, 118–119, 132, 204; Glorious Revolution, 38; immigrants in, 199, 229; Tudor Dynasty of, 39–40

Enlightenment, 58, 61, 64, 71, 84, 89, 97, 274n5, 275n7

Equality, 8, 18, 59–61, 97–98, 118, 159, 166, 168, 171–172, 194–195, 234, 252

Ethiopia, 192, 238

Ethiopians: as a people, 35, 43, 64, 74, 86, 113, 153; as a race, 89–90, 102–103, 106–107, 116, 157, 247; as a "variety," 76–77, 80–81, 89, 101, 103, 114

Ethnic group, 24, 151, 159, 177, 180, 190, 196, 208, 238–240, 242–243; versus race, 6, 151, 177, 186, 258n41; racialized, 190, 239, 241

Ethnicity, 25, 119, 124, 198, 236–238, 240–242, 250, 301n241, 322n23; racialized, 242

Ethnocentrism, 9, 24, 60, 239

Ethnography, 151, 154, 157

Ethnology, 13, 14, 59, 96, 101, 107, 109–111, 113, 116–117, 133, 136–137, 143, 151, 154–157, 174, 287n34; "scientific," 133; subaltern, 152–155

Eugenics, 14, 130, 154, 156, 162, 175, 305n64

Eurasia, 9, 22–23, 25, 28, 58, 211, 220

Eurocentrism, 55, 57, 59, 67, 119

Europe, 9, 20, 22, 24–29, 32, 35, 82–83, 99, 116–117, 162, 166–168, 171, 198, 221, 224, 231–232; anti-immigrant movements in, 198; boundaries of, 197; European Coal and Steel Community, 172, 197; European Community, 172, 197–198; European Economic Community, 172, 197; "Europeanization," 172; European Union, 197, 231–232, 312n25; European unity, 193, 197–198; idea of, 25–27, 264n17; immigration to, 198; Locarno treaties, 169; Maastricht Treaty, 198; Marshall Plan, 172; pan-European

world, 165, 303n15, 305n61; "races of," 21, 22, 31, 117, 119–122, 128, 132–155, 156, 158, 163–164, 181–182, 219, 228; and race thinking, 6, 42, 53–54, 58–59, 61–62, 67, 69–70, 74–76, 87, 92, 97, 103, 120–157, 181, 183, 210–211, 220, 226–228, 281n103; revolutions in, 122–123, 128, 143, 155

Europeans, as race, 82–83, 91, 131, 186, 191, 202, 238; "European geographical race," 202; Europeoid race, 228; *Homo europaeus*, 59, 65, 67; and civilizational superiority, 247

Evolution, 101, 109, 133, 137, 141, 200, 208

Exclusionary practices, 9, 11, 17

Fascism, 165, 168

Fanon, Frantz, 196, 299n192

Farr, James, 41, 260n61

Feldman, Marcus, 211, 216

Feminism, 246

Fichte, Johann Gottlieb, 98

Finland: Russian control of, 132; Swedish colonialism in, 131

Finns, 67–69, 75–76, 87, 103–104, 117, 127, 130–133, 143, 152; Finno-Ugric peoples, 229

Forster, Johann Reinhold, 81

Foucault, Michel, 12, 14, 16–17, 245–246, 261n66

France, 36–38, 39, 53–54, 69, 99, 100, 124–126, 132–133, 135–136, 171–172, 195, 197–199; and anti-discrimination policy, 306n77; Dreyfus Affair, 125; Franco-Prussian War, 126, 128–129; French people, 46, 92, 104, 119, 152; French Revolution, 37–38, 95, 97–98, 102, 122, 286n15; Napoleon, 95, 97–98, 102. *See also* Gauls

Franklin, Benjamin, 92, 119

Franks, 22, 36–38, 57, 98, 119, 123, 132; "Frankish (Germanic) Europe," 30; Germanic-Frankish superiority, 38
Fredrickson, George, 43, 45, 61, 257n238, 274n5, 281n101
Füredi, Frank, 164–165

Galton, Francis, 130
Garn, Stanley, 200, 202–204, 217
Gauls, 22, 36–38, 57, 98, 119, 123, 132
Gender. *See* Race, and gender
Genetics, 10, 72, 174–176, 178, 181, 186, 189, 193–194, 200, 202, 204–206, 208–217, 229–230, 238; cluster analysis, 205, 210–211, 213; and pharmacogenomic research, 215. *See also* Clines
Genocide, 214, 224, 239
Genotypes, 204, 210
Gentiles, 156
Georgia, 28, 55, 58, 69–70, 82, 221, 223, 225–226, 228, 231–233; "revolution of roses" in, 223
Georgians (also Kartvelians), 2, 6, 28, 34, 55, 56, 81, 93–94, 104, 120, 136, 138, 152, 219, 223–227, 230–234, 282n119; beauty of, 6, 81–84, 102, 106, 112, 219, 226; character of, 84; Georgian exceptionalism, 232; language and literature, 152, 221; and skulls, 77–79, 112, 134, 232
Germans (Germanic peoples), 23, 38, 51, 53, 87–88, 92, 98, 104, 106, 119–120, 126, 128–129, 132–133, 135, 152, 154, 156; Pan-German, 126, 160; "true Germans," 127
Germany, 6, 53, 69, 96, 122, 124–126, 132, 145, 150, 154–156, 163, 170, 172, 178, 197–198; Nordic movement in, 156; Nuremberg Laws, 162; Sterilization Law in, 162. *See also* Nazism
Ghana, 171, 195

Gilroy, Paul, 19, 250–251. *See also* Humanism, planetary
Gobineau, Comte Joseph-Arthur de, 7, 128–129
Goldfield, Michael, 18
Gorbachev, Mikhail, 223
Gould, Stephen Jay, 8, 14, 80
Grant, Madison, 150–151, 169
Great Britain, 103, 123, 135, 143, 153, 163, 168, 171, 175, 195, 198; Commonwealth Immigrants Act, 198. *See also* British Isles; England; Ireland
"Great Chain of Being," 61, 64, 97
Great Depression, 169, 174–175, 190
Greece, 23, 99, 133–134, 143, 198, 244; Greeks, 28, 35, 50, 77, 82, 86, 88, 91–92, 108, 112, 128, 133–134, 150, 152, 154, 215, 227, 285n150
Günther, Hans, 156–157

Haack, Susan, 245, 324n47
Haddon, A. C., 141, 162, 176–178, 180, 186, 190, 208, 307n111. See also *We Europeans*
Hall, Stuart, 244
Ham, 29–30, 35, 54, 102, 110, 153. *See also* Noah; Old Testament
Hamites, 136, 141, 177
Harding, Sandra, 261n66, 324n48
Hawaii, 3, 136
Herder, Johann Gottfried, 82, 93, 96, 233, 285n153
Herodotus, 34, 56
Hiernaux, Jean, 204–205
Higham, John, 120
Hindus (also Hindoos), 54, 73, 81, 86–87, 104, 129, 133, 136, 141, 183; caste system of, 54, 86, 104, 136
Hirschfeld, Magnus, 173
Hitler, Adolph, 128, 156–157, 162–163, 169, 173; Third Reich, 7
Hobsbawm, Eric, 123

Hogben, Lancelot, 174–175, 177, 186, 193, 210

Holocaust, 163

Hominidae, 137, 140

*Homo sapiens*, 63, 65, 66, 70, 116, 190, 202, 217, 232, 235, 238

Hottentots, 58, 64, 111, 116

Hrdlicka, Ales, 183, 185

Humanism, 161, 250; egalitarian, 96; planetary, 19, 250–252

Human rights, 60, 172, 193–194

Hume, David, 71, 276n26, 279n86

Huxley, Julian, 162, 175–178, 180, 186, 190, 208. See also *We Europeans*

Huxley, Thomas Henry, 13, 133–137, 141, 175

Ibn Batutah, 34, 56

Ibn Khaldun, 36

"Imagined community," 27

Imam Shamil, 224

Imperialism, 120–121, 160, 164, 166, 175–176, 181, 203, 247; anti-imperialism, 168

Indentured servitude, in English colonies, 44–45, 47

India, 3, 9, 25, 29, 52, 136, 166–168, 170–172, 192, 198, 219; British colonial rule in, 87, 99, 121, 129; caste system in, 61, 136; independence of, 168, 173; "Indian Mutiny" of 1857, 129; Indian National Congress, 167

Indians, 53, 86, 98, 151, 166, 198, 215; Indian branch, 87; Indian-German-Pelasgic branch, 103

"Indians," American. See Native Americans (also American Indians, Indians)

Indo-European language group, 6, 86, 98, 137, 147. See also Sanskrit

Indo-Europeans, 98, 106, 110–111, 113, 128–129, 227

Indo-Germans, 98, 113, 145

Indonesia (also Indonesians), 99, 141–142, 168, 192; Bandung Conference, 195; independence of, 168, 173

Industrialization, 122, 167, 170; deindustrialization, 249

Intelligence testing (also IQ), 130

Ireland, 39, 106, 124; Catholic emancipation, 99; English colonialism in, 24, 39–40, 51, 118, 268n106, 268n107; famine in, 123; Penal Laws, 40; Protestant Ascendancy in, 39–40; Second Act of Union, 99

Irish people, 31, 39–40, 57, 132, 240; migration of, 123–125, 128; and racialization, 39–40; and racism, 40; as a race, 40, 125

Islam, 27–28, 34, 36, 43, 220–221, 223–225, 229, 231, 233; Pan-Islamism, 168. *See also* Muslims

Israel, 172

Italians, 92, 104, 119, 128, 130, 142–143, 187, 189, 198, 215, 240

Italy, 39, 99, 122, 124, 126, 132–133, 135, 143, 145, 165, 195, 197; invasion of Ethiopia, 165; Mussolini, 169; racial laws in, 165

Jacobson, Matthew Frye, 18, 189, 302n5

Japan, 3, 55, 102, 166–168, 171, 183, 192; Ainu, 183–184; Japanese people, 71, 86, 169, 304n34, 305n58; Russo-Japanese War, 121, 167

Japheth, 102, 110, 153

Jefferson, Thomas, 62, 275n21

Jews: Ashkenazim, 143, 154–155, 215; as Caucasians, 154; in the Caucasus, 155; as *conversos* (Spain), 31; as Europeans, 155; German, 154, 157, 162; "Jewish problem," 156; "Jewish question," 126; and *Protocols of the Elders of Zion*, 125; as race, 154, 157, 187, 189, 237, 284n140, 300n208; Russian, 125, 150,

Jews: Ashkenazim (*Continued*) 155; Sephardim, 143, 154–155; and Zionism, 156. *See also* Anti-Semitism

Johnson, Lyndon, 196

Jones, William, 86–88, 98

Jordan, Winthrop, 61

Kames, Lord (Henry Home), 63, 74

Kant, Immanuel, 52, 57, 59, 63, 68, 70–75, 93, 190, 247, 279n78; on race concept, 75, 119; and racial classification, 70–73, 81, 83, 119

Keane, A. H., 3, 133, 135–137, 140, 143, 147, 183, 222, 296n99, 308n144

Kennewick Man, 4–5

Kipling, Rudyard, 121

Kitcher, Philip, 216–218, 316n137

Knowledge, and power, 8, 12, 16–18, 243, 245–246, 261n65, 323n40

Knox, John, 128

Kroeber, A. L., 181–186, 190

Kuhn, Thomas, 259n50

Lamarck, Jean Baptiste, 101

Laplanders (Lapps), 52, 55, 63–64, 67–69, 75–76, 104, 117, 131, 143, 152, 274n195, 278n53

Las Casas, Bartolomé de, 32–33

Latham, Robert Gordon, 20, 87, 96, 109, 111–113, 116–117, 154, 219, 291n126

Latinos (also Hispanics), 8, 11, 99, 196, 243, 249, 251–252

Lawrence, William, 20, 95–96, 103–105

League of Nations, 168–169

Leibniz, Gottfried, 64

Lewontin, Richard, 19, 207–208, 201, 212, 216

Liberalism, 18, 60–62, 175

Linnaeus, Carolus, 13, 50, 52, 57–59, 61, 63, 64–70, 73–75, 81, 131, 137, 189, 201, 207, 247, 277n40, 277n44

Livingstone, Frank, 204–206

Locke, John, 60, 274n4

Long, Edward, 63–64

Macauley, Thomas, 99

Malay: race, 78, 89–90, 106–107, 187, 247; variety, 76, 81, 89, 101, 103–104, 114

Malinowski, Bronislaw, 165–166

Marks, Jonathan, 237–238

Marx, Anthony, 18

Marx, Karl, 60, 118–119, 260n60

Maryland, colonial, marriage and race, 47–48

Mediterranean race (or type), 121, 126, 141–142, 145–147, 150–151, 156–157, 169, 177, 183, 185–186, 189

Meiners, Christoph, 5, 59, 73, 83–85, 87–88, 98, 219, 232–233, 286n15

Melanochroi (also "dark whites"), 133, 135–136, 138, 152, 189. *See also* Huxley, Thomas Henry; Tylor, Edward Burnett

Mendel, Gregor, 72

Mexicans, 3, 127, 169. *See also* Latinos (also Hispanics)

Middle class, 167, 175, 249

Middle East, 25, 29, 219, 231

Migration, 16, 18, 21, 22, 44–46, 109, 111, 147, 155, 165, 196–198, 211, 229, 232, 236, 238; European, 119–120, 122, 125, 131, 151, 169, 247. *See also* United States, immigration to

Miles, Robert, 243

Mills, Charles, 18

Minorities, ethnic and religious, 166, 229–230

Mongolia (also Mongols), 33, 72, 109, 133, 151, 158, 177, 221

Mongolian race (also Mongolic), 5, 59, 86, 89, 90, 102–103, 106–107, 110, 116, 127, 141, 153–155, 157, 163, 166, 176–177, 182–183, 185, 186, 187, 189, 191, 193, 199, 209, 213–214, 219, 228,

238, 247; Mongolian branch, 85, 88; Mongolian variety, 76, 77, 80–81, 89,101,103, 114; "Mongolidae," 112–113; Mongoloid, 6, 155, 182, 205, 208–209; Mongoloid division, 162, 187; Mongoloid "stock," 186, 188

Monogenism (also Monogenesis), 53, 60, 63, 66, 68, 74, 76, 84–85, 101–103, 109, 117, 151

Montagu, Ashley, 10, 13, 175, 179, 187, 189, 190, 192–193, 200, 203–204, 207–208, 210, 212, 214, 218, 235, 238, 250, 316n125

Moors, 2, 28, 31–32, 35–36, 43, 69, 73, 255n5; "black Moors," 271n140; as *Moriscos*, 31, 265n45

Morgan, Edmund, 46, 271n136

Morton, Samuel George, 13, 20, 95–96, 105, 111, 259n45

Müller, Friedrich Max, 7, 129, 295n61

Multiculturalism, 11

Muslims, 2, 24–25, 27, 31, 34, 35, 57, 119, 221, 225–226, 231, 233; anti-Muslim prejudice, 226

Myrdal, Gunnar, 171, 173

Nationalism, 11, 99, 124–126, 128, 131, 143, 166–169, 203, 223, 244; Black, 152; economic, 168; European, 6, 18, 21, 120, 126, 131, 143, 155, 169, 247; and race science, 68, 259n51; Russian, 226, 233

Nationalist movements, 99, 132, 171; in the Caucasus, 233

"National Socialist" movements, 125–126

Native Americans (also American Indians, Indians), 11, 31–32, 99, 127, 236, 243, 249, 251–252, 272n154; and race thinking, 270n131, 271n132; racial classification of, 55–57, 63, 69, 71, 74–75, 104, 106–107, 111, 135, 159, 196, 202, 215, 274n196; Spanish

treatment of, 44; U.S. wars against, 121

Natural history, 24, 41, 49, 50–51, 58–59, 63–64, 67–68, 70–71, 73, 84, 91, 100, 103, 235, 245–246, 269n114, 279n82; versus "sacred history," 52, 56

Nazism, 6–7, 21, 87, 118, 120, 155–157, 162–163, 169–171, 175, 176, 178, 190. *See also* Hitler, Adolph

Negro, as race, 6, 43, 52, 91–92, 108, 110, 135, 137, 153–154, 163, 166, 176–177, 182–183, 185–186, 187, 189, 191, 193, 199, 219, 228, 237–238; Negroid, 6, 182, 205, 208–209; Negroid division, 162, 187; Negroid "stock," 186, 188

Negroes, 63–64, 69, 71–72, 76, 86, 97–98, 109–110, 113, 117, 125, 130, 133–134, 141, 151–152, 159–160, 169, 175–176, 182–183, 187, 196, 237, 269n113; in Ancient Egypt, 108; and racial inferiority, 101, 159; and slavery, 10, 43–44, 60, 95, 108, 121, 196. *See also* Black people (also "Blacks") Negro, as race

Nei, Masatoshi, 208–210

Netherlands, 123, 171, 195, 197–198. *See also* Dutch

New Zealand, 16, 75, 164–166, 171–172, 191

Nkrumah, Kwame, 171, 195

Noah, 29–30, 35, 82, 102, 110, 113, 153, 232, 265n37, 271n131, 287n42; Noah's Ark, 82, 232

Nordic race (also Nordics), 7, 18, 122, 142, 151–152, 156–159, 183, 185–186; Nordicism, 158, 169; Nordic type, 186; supremacy of, 7, 126, 156

Normans, 36–38, 57, 132; conquest of British Isles, 38, 123

North America, 71, 74, 99, 118, 120, 123, 143, 156, 167, 187, 198; slavery in, 43

North Atlantic Treaty Organization (NATO), 172

Old Testament, 23, 29, 35, 63, 153,
282n112; biblical chronology, 103
Olson, Joel, 18
*On the Natural Variety of Mankind*, 5, 59,
73–78, 80, 83, 88
Oppression, 8, 14, 40, 49, 160, 166, 172,
196, 199, 203, 214, 234–235, 239
Orangutans, 63, 66, 91–92
Orient, 29; Oriental people, 105, 150
"Otherness" (also "Othering"), 9, 29, 30,
39, 57, 230–231, 248
Ottoman Empire (also Ottoman Turkey),
2, 23, 25, 34, 126, 170, 221, 224; de-
cline of, 126, 170; slavery in, 34
Outlaw, Lucius, 269n114

Pacific islands (also Pacific Islanders), 62,
75, 81, 104, 111, 164, 171, 196, 202
Pakistan (also Pakistanis), 198, 210, 237;
Kalish people of, 210
Palestine, 124, 173
Park, Robert, 167, 173
Patterson, Orlando, 239–241
People "of color," 248–249
Persia (also Iran), 129, 134, 167, 221, 223;
Persians, 73, 82, 86–87, 89, 103, 106,
133, 141–142, 221, 227, 233
Petty, William, 50–51, 273n176
Phenotypes, 10–11, 179, 189, 204, 208,
212, 216, 218, 237, 239, 242
Philippines, 75, 99, 121, 172, 192
Philology, 98, 100, 107, 111
Phrenology, 100
Physiognomy, 11, 35, 56, 81, 88, 92
Poland, 33–34, 52, 53, 99, 124; Poles,
33–34, 128, 150; slavery in, 34; serf-
dom in, 34
Poliakov, Léon, 37, 265n37, 267n82
Polygenism (also Polygenesis), 63–64, 66,
72, 74, 83, 85, 96–97, 100–102,
110–111, 117, 129, 144, 151, 273n186,
276n30, 287n37, 287n42; "American

School" of, 105, 289n80; neo-poly-
genism, 130, 137, 202–203
Portugal, 124, 171, 195, 198; colonies of,
49, 99; Portuguese people, 2, 24, 28,
36, 43, 46
Power. *See* Knowledge, and power
Prichard, James Cowles, 13, 20, 87, 96,
100, 107, 109–111, 113, 117, 128
Primates, 63, 65–66, 129
Proletariat, 118, 145. *See also* Working
class
Prometheus, 84, 110, 227
Prussia, 126–127; Franco-Prussian War,
126, 128–129
Psychology, 14, 100, 130, 174, 178, 231

Race: and biology, 120; and caste, 86, 152;
and civilization, 96, 101–102, 109,
158; and class, 14, 19, 37, 46, 54, 98,
145, 248–249, 272n164; versus clines,
203; and color, 189, 196; as critical
concept, 250–251; versus ethnicity,
151, 236, 242, 267n82; and gender, 19,
48, 55–56, 97, 116, 175, 259n50,
272n164; and genetic diseases,
214–216; and inequality, 62; as "institutional fact," 242; and Medieval notions of difference, 22–25, 30–40, 42,
48, 263n10, 263n13, 263n14; and nation, 111, 227, 233; as "natural kind,"
235, 246; "no-race" view, 200,
241–242; origins of term, 42; political
theory of, 18; and popular discourse,
116, 187, 207, 211, 228; and population, 207, 211; and power, 8, 164, 244;
and privilege, 164, 170; "pure races,"
217; and scientific discourse 13, 15,
57, 96, 116, 160, 177, 214; social consequences of, 243; as a social/political
construct, 10, 153, 180–181, 194, 196,
214, 215, 236, 242–243, 246; "social
races," 243; and species, 63, 70–71,

101, 117, 180; as subjective term, 111; and subspecies, 63, 72, 178, 206; and type, 158; and "varieties," 63, 66, 72, 75, 89, 106, 112, 117, 135; word versus concept, 40–41, 270n118, 270n121, 270n122

Race concept, 9–10, 15–18, 23, 25, 40–49, 60–61, 68, 70, 72, 75, 91, 96, 100–101, 116, 119, 159, 163, 174–176, 178–179, 181, 186, 189–191, 193, 203–206, 210–218, 233, 235, 238–239, 241, 243, 245; and "families," 106; "geographical races," 200–202, 204, 217; "local races," 201–202. *See also* Buffon, George Louis Leclerc, Comte de; Kant, Immanuel; Montagu, Ashley; UN-ESCO, "Statements on Race"

Race consciousness, 34, 165–167

Race difference, 152, 159, 163, 165–166, 173–174, 176–179, 193, 196, 201–203, 206, 209, 212, 214, 229, 239, 247, 253

Race-making, 10, 220

Race relations, 11, 25, 174, 193, 203, 207

Race science, 6, 7, 14, 20, 68, 73, 96, 100–101, 118–121, 128, 131, 135, 144, 150, 152, 157, 163, 174–175, 189, 194, 197, 200, 202, 220, 235, 245; anti-racist science, 16, 193–194, 246. *See also* Anatomy; Anthropology; Biology; Crania, craniology; Ethnography; Ethnology; Genetics

"Race talk," 218, 239, 242, 252

Race thinking, 9, 16, 22, 24, 63, 94, 121, 123, 126, 163, 187, 191, 214, 233, 235–236, 242–244, 250–251

Racial categories, 11, 22, 193, 216, 239, 244, 247, 251–252. *See also* Aryan race; Caucasian, as race; Europeans, as race; Europe, "races of"; Jews, as race; Mediterranean race (or type); Mongolian race (also Mongolic); Negro, as race; Nordic race (also Nordics)

Racial classification: and aesthetic criteria, 55, 76–77, 80, 84, 88–89, 102, 141, 281n101; arbitrariness of, 202, 205; and genetic criteria, 201, 205; and geographic criteria, 213; and physical criteria, 76, 105, 135, 151, 175, 182–183, 190, 193, 237, 295n75; social or political nature of, 218; "three-race" scheme, 181, 183, 186–187, 189–191, 193, 200, 202, 205, 209, 219

Racial determinism, 100, 135, 137, 147, 175

Racial discrimination, 170–173, 199, 214, 239

Racial "fitness," 143, 244

Racial hierarchy, 121, 244

"Racial hygiene," 155–156, 229. *See also* Eugenics

Racial identity, 157, 196, 220, 234, 239–240, 242. *See also* Racialization

Racialism, 6, 31–40, 41, 62, 93, 96, 116, 159–160, 178, 194, 246, 251, 256n24; anti-racist, 160, 163; egalitarian, 163, 181, 185, 189, 194; quasi-, 241–242. *See also* Raciation; Science, scientific racialism

Racialization, 10–11, 124–125, 193, 220, 230–231, 233, 235–236, 239, 242, 247, 250–252, 310n7; of Africans, 43, 45; of Europeans, 43, 45, 248–249; of political relations, 120–121, 218, 242, 246, 251; racialized discourse, 226; racialized exclusion, 220, 239, 244; racialized identity, 11, 12, 17, 18, 235, 237, 241, 243, 245–248, 251, 253, 261n65, 272n164, 325n74, 325n75; racialized inequality, 6, 49, 195–196, 216, 218, 239, 243, 245–248, 251–253, 322n24; racialized linguistic ideas, 88; racialized nationalism, 118, 128; racialized power, 245; racialized slavery, 28, 36, 42–49, 99, 216; racialized stratification, 244, 248–249

Racial nativism, 144
Racial segregation, 173, 195, 217
Racial supremacism, 76, 161, 165, 180, 230
Racial variation, 68–69, 77, 109
Raciation, 41, 269n114
Raciology, 7, 52, 83, 101, 119, 121–122, 131, 144, 158, 181, 191, 219–220, 230, 247–248, 250, 252
Racism: cultural, 229; European, 7, 31, 45, 49; institutional, 243; "neo-racism," 198, 258n40; non-Western, 9; North American, 59, 144; in United States, 173; in Western societies, 8, 9
Radical right, 155
Reclus, Élisée, 227–228
Recognition, politics of, 8
Renaissance, 63
Renan, Ernst, 129
Retzius, Anders, 13, 129–134, 157
"Rights of Man," 59
Ripley, William, 133, 141, 143–145, 147–151, 156, 158, 183, 219, 228, 319n48, 319n52
Robinson, Cedric, 23
Roma, 162
Romania, 235–236
Romans, 77, 86, 88, 108, 112, 132, 134, 152, 154
Roosevelt, Franklin D., 170
Rosenberg, Noah, 211
Roychoudhury, Arun, 208–210
Russia: anti-Jewish pogroms in, 125; as European, 27; Bolsheviks in, 168–169; Catherine II (the Great), 27, 34, 223; and Congress of the Peoples of Asia, 168; imperialism of, 5, 21, 28, 126, 170, 220–221, 223, 231; Muscovy, 53, 55; Russian Federation, 94, 224, 231; Russian Revolution, 167, 223; Russo-Japanese War, 121, 167; serfdom in, 34; slavery in, 33–34; Treaty of

Georgievsk, 223. *See also* Caucasian peoples; Caucasus region (also Caucasia); Chechens (also Tschetschens); Crimean War; Russians; Soviet Union (also USSR)
Russians, 4, 13, 33–34, 92, 119, 130, 220, 223–231; "Europeanness" of, 220, 231; "real," 229; "whiteness" of, 5, 220

Saakashvili, Mikheil, 223, 232
Saint-Simon, Claude Henri, Comte de, 98
Sanskrit, 98
Saxons, 22, 36–38, 57, 92, 119, 123, 128
Scandinavia, 124, 145; Scandinavians, 38, 133, 135
Schlegel, Freidrich, 98
Science: democratic, 246, 324n48; history of, 13; and nationalism, 68; and politics, 6, 7–9, 174, 178, 194, 214, 245; scientific racialism, 50–57, 70, 88, 95, 161, 181; scientific racism, 95–96, 101–102, 129, 155–156, 158–159, 161, 163, 173–174, 176, 178, 180, 190–191, 193; scientific realism, 245; Scientific Revolution, 42, 50
Scottish people, 48, 112, 124, 132, 154
Semites (also Semitic peoples), 110, 113, 134, 141–142, 157, 177. *See also* Shem
Sepúlveda, Juan Ginés, 32–33
Sergi, Giuseppe, 126, 141, 145
Shem, 102, 153, 287n42; Shemite nations, 110. *See also* Noah; Old Testament
Shevardnadze, Eduard, 223
Sièyes, Abbé, 37
Simar, Théophile, 158
Skulls, 75–80, 91, 100, 105–108, 119, 130–132, 134, 157, 183, 232. *See also* Crania, "cranial capacity"; Dmanisi skulls
Slavery, 2, 23, 27–28, 30, 42, 46, 51, 60, 62–63, 94–95, 97–99, 101, 105, 107–108, 113, 160, 214, 239, 244;

Black slaves, 34, 35, 44, 49, 60, 94, 95; chattel, 43; English reluctance concerning, 44; "natural," 33; of Slavs, 33–34; white slaves, 34

Slavs (also Slavic peoples), 22, 23, 28, 30–31, 33–34, 35, 37, 57, 85, 87, 119, 123, 127, 129–130, 141, 143, 150, 152, 189, 229–230; Pan-Slavism, 160; and "slave," 34, 266n59. *See also* Poland, Poles; Russia; Ukraine

Smith, Charles Hamilton, 111

Smith, Grafton Elliot, 157

Smith, Rogers, 18

Social constructionism, 41

Social identity, 8, 234

Socialism, 98, 150, 175

Social stratification, 8, 49, 116, 235, 238–239, 242, 244

Sociology, 166–167, 173–174, 203, 214

Somatological units, 151

South Africa, 45, 164–165, 167, 170–173, 175, 191, 193–194, 199; apartheid in, 165, 173, 194, 199; Land Acts, 165; Nationalist Party, 173

South America, 123, 170–172

South Asians, 3–4,

Soviet Union (also USSR), 94, 172, 224, 229, 320n60; autonomous republics of, 224

Spain, 31–33, 39, 53, 69, 99, 124, 132–133, 145, 171, 198, 255n5, 265n45, 266n59; Iberian peninsula, 36, 38, 43, 141; imperial expansion of, 33; Spanish people (also Iberians, Spaniards), 46, 92, 119, 134, 142, 152, 198. *See also* Moors

Spengler, Oswald, 170

Stalin, Josef, 223

Statue of Liberty, 2–3

Stepan, Nancy Leys, 174, 200

Stevens, Jacqueline, 18, 269n111

Stocking, George, 129, 279n84, 298n153

Stoddard, Lothrop, 150, 169

Sweden, 53, 130–132; Peace of Noteborg, 131; Swedes, 67–68, 92, 119, 130–131, 135–136, 138–139; Swedish Reformation, 132; wars with Russia, 132

Switzerland (also Swiss), 69, 124, 132, 159, 198

Syria (also Syrians), 3, 104, 134, 150; Syro-Arabian nations, 110

Tahiti (also Tahitians), 75, 136

Taylor, Paul, 242

Teutons, 123, 125, 128, 135, 141, 143; supremacy of, 150, 158; Teutonism, 154, 158

Thierry, Augustin, 38, 98

Tiananmen Square, China, 2; Goddess of Democracy, 2–3, 5

Tocqueville, Alexis de, 235

Topinard, Paul, 129

Troglodytes, 65–66

Turashvili, Dato, 233

Turkey, 69, 167, 192, 198; Turkic peoples, 23, 73; Turks, 28, 46, 50, 103, 108, 132–133, 215, 221, 227

Tylor, Edward Burnett, 129, 133, 135–136, 138–139, 157

Tyson, Edward, 50, 68. *See also* Anatomy, comparative

Ukraine, 33, 69; slavery in, 33; Ukrainians, 33–34, 152, 154

UNESCO, 21, 190, 194–195, 199–200, 252; "Statements on Race," 162–163, 180–181, 187, 190, 199, 310n181

United Nations, 171–172, 193, 199; Atlantic Charter, 170; Declaration of, 171; and International Convention on the Elimination of All Forms of Racial Discrimination (ICERD), 199. *See also* UNESCO

United States, 6, 20, 100, 103, 108, 113, 114, 116, 127, 144, 152, 163, 165–173, 175–176, 181, 191, 193, 195–197, 214, 235–237, 247, 249; "American dream," 235; Anglo-Saxonism, 124, 170; annexation of Hawaii, 121; *v. Bhagat Sigh Thind*, 3, 136; *Brown v. Board of Education*, 195; "Caucasian codes" ("restrictive covenants") in, 170, 241; Caucasian unity in, 170; Census, 3, 125; Chinese Exclusion Act, 127; citizenship, 18, 241; Civil Rights Act, 195–196; Civil Rights movement, 21, 193, 195, 203, 246; Civil War, 127, 134; class structure in, 249; colonialism of, 121, 171; Congress of Racial Equality (CORE), 171; Democratic Party, 249; "Eight-hour" strikes, 144; and Georgia, 225, 231–232; global dominance of, 169; immigration to, 123–124, 126–127, 144, 150–151, 158, 169, 174, 196, 241, 304n34; Indian Removal Act, 99; *In re Ah Yup*, 127; "Jim Crow" segregation, 121, 127, 136, 152–153, 241; Johnson-Reed Immigration Act (1924), 128, 151, 167, 169; Kerner Commission, 196; "manifest destiny," 116, 120, 124; Marshall Plan, 172; naturalization laws, 3, 127, 255–256n. 12; "one-drop rule," 237; *Plessy v. Ferguson*, 127, 153; "poor whites" in, 118; Republican Party, 249; slavery in, 99, 101, 114, 121, 127; Thirteenth Amendment, 127; Voting Rights Act, 196; wars against native Americans, 121; White Citizen Councils, 241; "white ethnics," 196; "white" identity politics, 249. *See also* Americans; Maryland, colonial, marriage and race; Virginia, colonial
Urbanization, 121, 167

"Varieties," human, 63, 65, 67, 71, 73–76, 89, 95, 101, 110, 116–117, 135; versus species, 116. *See also* Linnaeus, Carolus
Vesalius, Andreas, 50–51, 119. *See also* Crania, craniology
Vico, Giambattista, 30
Vietnam, 195
Virchow, Rudolf, 127, 154, 157–158, 174, 181
Virginia, colonial, 45–48; Christians as slaves in, 47; fornication laws in, 47; free Negroes in, 46; perpetual hereditary slavery in, 46. *See also* Bacon's Rebellion
Voegelin, Eric, 62, 72, 75
*Volksgeist*, 93
Voltaire, 63, 74
von Humboldt, Alexander, 96

Wagner, Richard, 157
Waitz, Theodore, 129
Warnke, Georgia, 1, 8
Warsaw Pact, 172
*We Europeans*, 162, 176, 186
Weissenberg, Samuel, 13, 152, 154–155
West, 196, 224, 231, 233
White, Charles, 97
"White Man's Burden," 121, 127. *See also* Kipling, Rudyard
"Whiteness," 3, 5, 18, 35, 199, 220, 229, 233, 241, 247–248, 252–253, 261n73, 321n8, 324n50; and political rights, 48; and privilege, 249; and racial domination, 247; as normative, ideal type, 69–70; as primeval, 80, 83
White people (also "whites"), 3, 6, 11, 24, 59, 69, 87–89, 92, 125, 128, 134, 136, 154, 194, 204, 215, 227, 231, 236–237, 240–242, 247, 249–252; "Japetidae," 112–113; Leucoderm, 186; versus

nonwhite peoples, 20, 34, 57, 59, 71, 87, 94, 97–98, 104, 121, 127, 133, 151, 159, 163–164, 170–171, 177, 196, 247–248. *See also* Melanochroi (also "dark whites"); Xanthochroi (also "fair whites")

White supremacy, 6, 45, 59, 67, 97, 111, 119, 121, 134, 143, 150–151, 164, 169, 171, 194–195, 198, 203, 240–241, 247–249; and science, 57, 150

Wilson, Woodrow, 167–168

Winant, Howard, 194; and "postwar break" of white supremacy, 184–185, 248

Working class, 122–123, 125, 167, 170, 249. *See also* Proletariat

World War I, 126, 165, 168–170

World War II, 7, 168, 170, 181, 194, 199–200, 203; postwar economic boom, 196–197

Wright, Richard, 192

Xanthochroi (also "fair whites"), 133, 135–136, 138–139. *See also* Huxley, Thomas Henry; Tylor, Edward Burnett

Xenophobia, 174, 199

"Yellow Peril," 167

Zack, Naomi, 215, 245, 250, 275n11, 316n131

Zoology, 13, 42, 100–101, 103, 135, 137, 151, 159, 193

# About the Author

Bruce Baum is Assistant Professor of Political Science, University of British Columbia. He is the author of *Rereading Power and Freedom in J. S. Mill.*